EMPLOYMENT LAW STRATEGY

FROM INTAKE TO VICTORY

The Complete Guide to Employment Law in New York & California

NGOZI E. BOLIN, ESQ.

Book cover by Jim Olen.

Legal Disclaimer

Important Notice to Readers

THIS BOOK IS PROVIDED FOR INFORMATIONAL AND EDUCATIONAL PURPOSES ONLY AND IS NOT INTENDED TO CONSTITUTE LEGAL ADVICE.

No Attorney-Client Relationship

The information contained in this book does not create an attorney-client relationship between the author, publisher, and any reader or user of this material. Reading this book, accessing its content, or using any information contained herein does not establish any professional relationship or create any duties or obligations on the part of the author or publisher to any reader.

Not a Substitute for Professional Legal Counsel

The content of this book is general in nature and may not apply to your specific situation. Legal matters are highly fact-specific and jurisdiction-dependent. Laws, regulations, court decisions, and legal interpretations change frequently and vary significantly between jurisdictions. Nothing in this book should be used as a substitute for competent legal advice from a licensed attorney in your jurisdiction who is familiar with the specific facts of your case.

YOU SHOULD ALWAYS CONSULT WITH A QUALIFIED ATTORNEY BEFORE MAKING ANY LEGAL DECISIONS OR TAKING ANY ACTION BASED ON INFORMATION CONTAINED IN THIS BOOK.

Accuracy and Currency of Information

While every effort has been made to ensure the accuracy of the information contained in this book at the time of publication, the author and publisher make no representations or warranties regarding the completeness, accuracy, reliability, or currency of the information provided. Laws and legal precedents change constantly, and what may have been accurate at the time of writing may no longer be current or applicable.

The information in this book reflects the law as understood by the author as of the publication date. Legal developments occurring after the publication date are not reflected in this material.

Jurisdictional Limitations

Laws vary significantly among different countries, states, provinces, and localities. The information in this book may be based primarily on the laws of specific jurisdictions and may not be applicable in your location. Local laws should always be consulted, and local legal counsel should be retained for matters involving specific jurisdictions.

Limitation of Liability

TO THE FULLEST EXTENT PERMITTED BY LAW, THE AUTHOR, PUBLISHER, EDITORS, CONTRIBUTORS, AND DISTRIBUTORS OF THIS BOOK DISCLAIM ALL LIABILITY FOR ANY LOSS, DAMAGE, OR INJURY ARISING FROM THE USE OF OR RELIANCE ON THE INFORMATION CONTAINED HEREIN, WHETHER SUCH LIABILITY ARISES IN CONTRACT, TORT, STRICT LIABILITY, OR OTHERWISE.

This limitation applies to all damages or injuries, including but not limited to:

- Direct, indirect, incidental, and consequential damages
- Lost profits or business opportunities
- Legal fees and costs
- Punitive or exemplary damages
- Any other economic or non-economic losses

No Warranties

THIS BOOK IS PROVIDED "AS IS" WITHOUT WARRANTY OF ANY KIND, EXPRESS OR IMPLIED, INCLUDING BUT NOT LIMITED TO WARRANTIES OF MERCHANTABILITY, FITNESS FOR A PARTICULAR PURPOSE, OR NON-INFRINGEMENT.

Individual Circumstances

Every legal situation is unique. The examples, case studies, and scenarios presented in this book are for illustrative purposes only and may not reflect the full complexity of actual legal situations. The outcomes described may not be achievable in your circumstances, and past results do not guarantee future outcomes.

Updates and Revisions

The author and publisher are under no obligation to update or revise the content of this book to reflect changes in the law or legal practice. Readers are encouraged to verify all information with current legal sources and qualified legal professionals.

Third-Party Content and References

Any references to third-party materials, websites, organizations, or publications are provided for informational purposes only and do not constitute an endorsement of such materials or entities. The author and publisher are not responsible for the content, accuracy, or availability of third-party materials.

Compliance with Professional Rules

Readers who are legal professionals should ensure that their use of any information in this book complies with applicable professional conduct rules, ethical requirements, and licensing obligations in their jurisdiction.

Intellectual Property Notice

Severability

If any portion of this disclaimer is held to be invalid or unenforceable, the remaining portions shall remain in full force and effect.

BY READING AND USING THIS BOOK, YOU ACKNOWLEDGE THAT YOU HAVE READ, UNDERSTOOD, AND AGREE TO BE BOUND BY THE TERMS OF THIS DISCLAIMER.

IF YOU DO NOT AGREE WITH THESE TERMS, DO NOT USE THIS BOOK.

Contents

Introduction

Employment law sits at the intersection of human dignity and economic reality. Every day, millions of workers navigate complex relationships with their employers - relationships governed by an intricate web of federal statutes, state laws, and judicial interpretations that can mean the difference between justice and injustice, financial security and ruin.

For the employment lawyer, this complexity presents both opportunity and responsibility. Whether you represent the employee who suffered discrimination, the worker denied fair wages, or the employer seeking to understand compliance obligations, your role extends far beyond legal technicalities. You are an advocate for workplace fairness, a guardian of statutory rights, and often the last line of defense against abuse of power.

Why This Book Matters

The employment relationship - between employer and employee - is one of the most consequential legal and human interactions in society. It governs how people earn their livelihoods, how companies grow and protect their reputations, and how disputes are resolved when trust breaks down.

Yet the laws that govern this relationship are anything but simple. Particularly in New York and California, two states that often lead the nation in expanding employee protections, the legal landscape is dense, dynamic, and jurisdictionally unique. Understanding how to navigate these legal systems is no longer optional - it is mission-critical.

This book demystifies that complexity, offering not just legal information, but strategic guidance. It provides a comprehensive roadmap through the full lifecycle of an employment matter - from intake to investigation, litigation to resolution - focusing on both plaintiff and defense perspectives, and always grounded in the real-world pressures faced by modern workplaces.

Why New York and California Matter

This guide focuses on employment law practice in New York and California - two jurisdictions that together represent nearly one-quarter of the U.S. workforce and serve as bellwethers for employment law nationwide, and the author is admitted in both jurisdictions. These states have consistently led the charge in expanding worker protections, often going far beyond federal minimums:

- **California** pioneered comprehensive family leave policies, aggressive wage-and-hour protections, and the Private Attorneys General Act (PAGA), which empowers workers to enforce labor laws on behalf of the state.
- **New York**, particularly New York City, has enacted some of the most employee-friendly anti-discrimination laws in the country, with broader definitions of protected conduct and lower burdens of proof than federal statutes.

Understanding these jurisdictions is essential not only for practitioners within their borders, but for any employment lawyer whose work touches interstate commerce, remote work arrangements, or multi-state employers.

The Evolution of Employment Law

Employment law has undergone dramatic transformation over the past two decades. The #MeToo movement reshaped harassment law and confidentiality restrictions. The gig economy challenged traditional employee classifications. The COVID-19 pandemic accelerated remote work and highlighted workplace safety obligations. Recent legislative reforms in both New York and California have expanded worker protections while limiting employer defenses.

Today's employment practitioner must navigate not only traditional discrimination and wage claims, but also emerging issues around artificial intelligence in hiring, data privacy, social media policies, and the intersection of employment law with immigration, criminal justice, and public health concerns.

A Practical, Strategic Approach

This book is designed as a practical roadmap from initial client contact through case resolution and beyond. Rather than merely reciting statutory provisions, each chapter provides:

- **Strategic insights** drawn from real-world practice
- **Jurisdiction-specific guidance** highlighting differences between New York, California, and federal law
- **Ethical considerations** unique to employment litigation
- **Forms, checklists, and sample language** to streamline practice
- **Settlement and trial strategies** based on decades of courtroom experience

Who This Guide Serves

Attorneys - Whether you're building an employment law practice or seeking deeper expertise in New York and California labor codes, this guide offers detailed, strategic approaches that go far beyond case summaries. You'll find practical forms, litigation tips, ethical considerations, and jurisdiction-specific tactics for maximizing client outcomes.

HR Professionals & Executives - As the front line of compliance, you are often the first to receive employee complaints, manage investigations, and implement policies that reduce exposure. This book helps you understand the legal significance of your day-to-day decisions and provides the frameworks to do your job confidently and lawfully.

In-House Counsel - When employment disputes arise internally, your organization turns to you for clear legal guidance and risk assessment. This guide helps you speak both "legal" and "business," offering insight into how employment claims are evaluated by courts, regulators, and plaintiff's counsel alike.

Business Owners & Management Companies - If you're responsible for the culture, performance, and legal health of your workforce, this book equips you to understand the rules that govern employee relations - and how to avoid costly legal pitfalls before they occur.

Law Students & New Attorneys - Employment law is one of the most dynamic and emotionally charged areas of legal practice. This book bridges the gap between academic theory and courtroom reality, giving aspiring employment lawyers a blueprint for building successful, ethical, and effective practices.

This guide provides the depth and practical wisdom needed to represent clients effectively while building a sustainable practice.

The Human Element

Employment law is intensely personal. Behind every case is a human story: the single mother fighting for unpaid wages, the longtime employee facing age discrimination, the whistleblower who risked everything to expose wrongdoing. These stories remind us that employment law is not just about statutes and precedents - it's about dignity, fairness, and the fundamental right to earn a living free from discrimination and exploitation.

At the same time, employment law affects businesses of all sizes, from small startups to multinational corporations. Employers need clear guidance on compliance, practical strategies for managing workplace disputes, and representation when claims arise. The best employment lawyers understand both sides of this equation and approach each case with empathy, preparation, and strategic thinking.

How to Use This Guide

This book follows the chronological path of an employment case, beginning with client intake and concluding with post-resolution client care. Each chapter builds on the previous one, but practitioners can also use individual chapters as reference guides for specific issues.

Key features include:

- **Chapter summaries** for quick reference
- **Practice tips** highlighted throughout
- **Sample documents and forms** in appendices
- **Jurisdiction-specific procedures** clearly marked
- **Ethical reminders** integrated throughout
- **Current law updates** as of 2025

A Note on Evolving Law

Employment law continues to evolve rapidly. New statutes, regulations, and court decisions regularly reshape the landscape. While this guide reflects the law as of 2025, practitioners must stay current with developments in their jurisdictions. The analytical frameworks and strategic approaches outlined here will remain valuable even as specific legal standards change.

Commitment to Excellence

Representing employment law clients - whether employees or employers - demands the highest standards of legal competence, ethical conduct, and strategic thinking. This guide aims to elevate your practice by providing not just legal knowledge, but the practical wisdom that comes from decades of experience in courtrooms, settlement conferences, and client counseling sessions across New York and California.

Whether your goal is litigation, prevention, compliance, or cultural leadership, this book helps you see employment law not as a barrier - but as a blueprint for equity, accountability, and sustainability in the workplace.

The law is our tool, but justice is our goal. Let's begin the journey toward more effective, ethical, and successful employment law practice.

1

Employment Law Foundations

New York vs. California

Employment law governs the relationship between employers and employees, establishing the framework for rights, responsibilities, and remedies when workplace disputes arise. While federal statutes provide baseline protections for American workers, individual states possess broad authority to enact additional safeguards that often exceed federal minimums.

New York and California stand as the two most employee-protective jurisdictions in the United States, yet they achieve this protection through markedly different legal architectures, regulatory frameworks, and judicial philosophies. For employment law practitioners, understanding these distinctions is not merely academic - it directly impacts case strategy, venue selection, damages calculations, and ultimate client outcomes.

This foundational chapter provides practitioners with essential knowledge of both jurisdictions' employment law landscapes, examining key doctrines, statutory frameworks, and critical differences that shape employment litigation from initial client intake through final compensation awards.

1.1 At-Will Employment Doctrine and Its Exceptions

The Foundation: At-Will Employment Defined

At-will employment is the default legal relationship in both New York and California, meaning either party may terminate the employment relationship at any time, with or without cause, and with or without notice. This doctrine, originating from 19th-century common law, places few restrictions on an employer's termination decisions.

Legal Definition: At-will employment creates a rebuttable presumption that employment may be terminated by either party without liability, absent an express contract provision, statutory protection, or recognized common law exception.

Exceptions to At-Will Employment

Both states recognize three primary exceptions to at-will employment, though with varying degrees of acceptance and application:

1. Public Policy Exception

Definition: Prohibits termination when the firing violates clearly established public policy as articulated in constitutional provisions, statutes, or judicial decisions.

New York Application:

- Narrowly construed by courts.
- Requires clear statutory mandate or constitutional provision
- **Example**: Terminating an employee for filing a workers' compensation claim (protected under N.Y. Workers' Comp. Law § 120)
- **Example**: Firing an employee for jury service (protected under N.Y. Judiciary Law § 519)
- **Labor Law § 740.** In New York, employees generally cannot sue for wrongful termination based solely on public policy concerns, unless

a statute like Labor law § 740 or a contract provides such protection for employees. See also *Horn v. New York Times*, 100 N.Y.2d 85 (2003). Such statutory remedies may apply when, for example, a truck driver is fired for refusing to drive an overweight and unlawful vehicle.

California Application:

- More broadly interpreted than New York
- Courts willing to infer public policy from legislative schemes
- **Example**: Terminating an employee for refusing to violate environmental regulations
- **Example**: Firing an employee for refusing to participate in an illegal price-fixing scheme (*Tameny v. Atlantic Richfield Co.*, 27 Cal. 3d 167, 164 Cal. Rptr. 839, 610 P.2d 1330 (1980)

Key Difference: California courts demonstrate greater willingness to find implied public policies, while New York requires explicit statutory or constitutional foundations.

2. Implied Contract Exception

Definition: An employment contract may be created through employer handbooks, policies, oral statements, or conduct that creates reasonable employee expectations of job security.

California's Broad Approach:

- Leading jurisdiction in recognizing implied contracts
- Considers totality of circumstances including:
  - Employee handbook language
  - Employer's historical practices
  - Oral representations during hiring
  - Performance review processes
- **Landmark Case**: *Pugh v. See's Candies, Inc.*, 116 Cal. App. 3d 311, 171 Cal. Rptr. 917 (1981) - established multi-factor test for implied contracts
- **Example**: Handbook stating "employees will only be terminated for

cause" after completing probationary period

New York's Restrictive Approach:

- Requires clear, specific language creating contractual expectations
- General handbook disclaimers typically defeat implied contract claims
- Higher burden of proof for establishing contractual relationship
- **Example**: Vague handbook language about "progressive discipline" insufficient to create contract (*Lobosco v. New York Telephone Co.*, 96 N.Y.2d 312, 727 N.Y.S.2d 383, 751 N.E.2d 462 (2001)

Practical Tip: California practitioners should carefully review all employer communications and policies for potential implied contract theories, while New York practitioners must identify specific, unambiguous contractual language.

3. Covenant of Good Faith and Fair Dealing

Definition: An implied obligation that parties to a contract will act honestly and fairly toward each other, not undermining the contract's purpose or the other party's reasonable expectations.

Critical Jurisdictional Split:

California:

- **Recognizes** implied covenant in employment relationships
- **Leading case:** (*Cleary v. American Airlines*, 111 Cal. App. 3d 443, 168 Cal. Rptr. 722 (Cal. Ct. App. 1980) The court held that a long-term employee hired under an oral contract for an unspecified term can claim wrongful discharge based on an implied covenant of good faith and fair dealing and the employer's established policies.
- Prevents terminations designed to avoid paying earned benefits
- **Classic Example**: Firing a salesperson just before commission payment
- **Application**: Terminating employee to avoid pension vesting or bonus payments

New York:

- **Explicitly rejects** implied covenant in employment context
- Court reasoning: Would effectively eliminate at-will employment
- **Leading Case**: *Murphy v. American Home Products Corp.* 58 N.Y.2d 293, 461 N.Y.S.2d 232, 448 N.E.2d 86 (N.Y. Ct. App. 1983) - definitively rejected covenant theory
- **Alternative**: Employees must pursue specific statutory or contractual remedies

Strategic Implication: California practitioners have an additional theory of liability unavailable in New York, particularly valuable in cases involving commission sales, bonuses, or vesting benefits.

1.2 State Employment Law Frameworks

California's Comprehensive Approach

California has developed the most extensive employee protection regime in the United States through multiple, overlapping statutory schemes:

Fair Employment and Housing Act (FEHA) - California Government Code §§ 12900-12996

Scope: Employers with 5 or more employees (1+ for harassment claims)

Protected Classes: Race, religion, color, national origin, ancestry, physical disability, mental disability, medical condition, genetic information, marital status, sex, gender, gender identity, gender expression, age (40+), sexual orientation, and military/veteran status

Key Provisions:

- Broader disability accommodation requirements than ADA
- Pregnancy accommodation mandates beyond federal law
- Gender identity and expression protections
- **Unique Feature**: Individual liability for supervisors and co-workers

in harassment cases

Administrative Process:

- Department of Fair Employment and Housing (DFEH) investigation required
- Right-to-sue letter prerequisite for court filing
- One-year statute of limitations from right-to-sue issuance

California Labor Code - Wage and Hour Protections

Comprehensive Coverage: Over 2,000 sections governing virtually every aspect of employment

Key Provisions:

- **Meal Breaks**: 30-minute unpaid break for shifts over 5 hours (Labor Code § 512)
- **Rest Breaks**: 10-minute paid break per 4-hour work period (Wage Order regulations)
- **Overtime**: Daily overtime (8+ hours) and weekly overtime (40+ hours) - more generous than federal FLSA
- **Wage Theft**: Enhanced penalties including liquidated damages and attorney fees
- **Final Pay**: Immediate payment upon termination (within 72 hours if no notice given)

Example Calculation: An employee working 10 hours receives 8 hours regular pay + 2 hours overtime (1.5x rate), plus potential meal/rest break penalties if violations occurred.

Private Attorneys General Act (PAGA) - Labor Code §§ 2698-2699.5

Revolutionary Concept: Empowers employees to sue as "private attorneys general" on behalf of the state for Labor Code violations

Mechanism:

1. Employee notices employer of violations
2. 65-day cure period for most violations
3. If uncured, employee may file representative action
4. 75% of penalties go to state, 25% to aggrieved employees

Strategic Significance: Allows individual employees to pursue claims affecting entire workforce, creating substantial leverage in settlement negotiations

Example Case: Single employee's PAGA claim for meal break violations affects all 500 company employees, creating potential exposure of millions in penalties

New York's Multi-Layered System

New York employs a complex, multi-jurisdictional approach with overlapping federal, state, and local laws:

New York Human Rights Law (NYHRL) - Executive Law Article 15

Scope: Employers with 4 or more employees (1+ for harassment and certain other claims)

Protected Classes: Similar to California but includes additional protections for:

- Familial status
- Domestic violence victim status
- Prior arrest or conviction records (with limitations)
- Reproductive health decisions

Key Features:

- Individual liability for employees who aid, abet, incite, or coerce discriminatory acts
- Mandatory sexual harassment training requirements

- Enhanced remedies including punitive damages

New York Labor Law (NYLL) - Consolidated Laws Chapter 31

Wage and Hour Provisions:

- **Minimum Wage**: Varies by region and employer size
- **Overtime**: Follows federal FLSA standards (40+ hours weekly)
- **Wage Theft Prevention Act**: Detailed notice requirements and enhanced penalties
- **Pay Frequency**: Semi-monthly for most employees
- **Spread of Hours**: Additional pay for workdays spanning more than 10 hours

Safety Provisions:

- Construction industry safety standards (Labor Law §§ 240, 241)
- Elevator and scaffold safety requirements
- Workplace violence prevention programs

New York City Human Rights Law (NYCHRL) - Administrative Code Title 8

Unprecedented Breadth: Covers employers with as few as 1 employee for most provisions

Enhanced Protections:

- **Lower Burden of Proof**: Plaintiff need only show discriminatory treatment was “a motivating factor”
- **Broader Remedies**: Uncapped punitive damages, attorney fees, front and back pay
- **Unique Protected Classes**: Unemployment status, credit history, caregiver status

Comparative Advantage: Often provides stronger protections than state or federal law

Example: NYC employee can pursue discrimination claim against single-employee company under NYCHRL, while similar claim would fail under federal Title VII (15+ employee requirement) or NYHRL (4+ employee requirement)

1.3 Federal Employment Law Framework

Both states operate within the federal employment law framework, which provides baseline protections that states may exceed but not diminish:

Core Federal Statutes

Title VII of the Civil Rights Act of 1964 (42 U.S.C. § 2000e)

- **Coverage**: Employers with 15+ employees
- **Protected Classes**: Race, color, religion, sex, national origin
- **Administration**: Equal Employment Opportunity Commission (EEOC)
- **Key Remedies**: Back pay, front pay, compensatory damages (capped), punitive damages (capped)

Americans with Disabilities Act (42 U.S.C. § 12101)

- **Coverage**: Employers with 15+ employees
- **Requirements**: Reasonable accommodation, essential function analysis
- **Interactive Process**: Good faith dialogue regarding accommodations

Age Discrimination in Employment Act (29 U.S.C. § 621)

- **Coverage**: Employers with 20+ employees, protects workers 40+
- **Unique Features**: Allows jury trials, uncapped damages for willful violations

Fair Labor Standards Act (29 U.S.C. § 201)

- **Universal Application**: Covers virtually all employers
- **Core Requirements**: Federal minimum wage, 40-hour overtime threshold
- **Key Concept**: "Suffered or permitted to work" standard

Family and Medical Leave Act (29 U.S.C. § 2601)

- **Coverage**: Employers with 50+ employees
- **Entitlement**: 12 weeks unpaid leave for qualifying events
- **Job Protection**: Restoration to same or equivalent position

State Enhancement Principles

California's Approach: Systematically exceeds federal minimums

- Lower employer thresholds (5 vs. 15 employees for discrimination)
- Additional protected classes (gender identity, medical condition)
- Enhanced remedies (uncapped damages, attorney fees)
- Stricter standards (daily overtime vs. weekly only)

New York's Approach: Multi-layered enhancement

- State law improvements over federal baseline
- Local law (NYC) improvements over state law
- Sector-specific enhancements (construction, domestic workers)

1.4 Critical Jurisdictional Differences

Statutory Frameworks Comparison

The fundamental differences between California and New York employment law become apparent when examining key statutory provisions side by side. **Discrimination coverage** varies significantly between jurisdictions: California's Fair Employment and Housing Act applies to employers with 5 or more employees, while New York's Human Rights Law covers employers with 4 or more employees, and New York City's Human Rights Law extends protection to workplaces with as few as 1 employee. This creates a situation where New York City employees enjoy the broadest discrimination protection coverage in the nation.

Overtime regulations represent another critical distinction. California mandates both daily overtime (for work exceeding 8 hours in a single day) and weekly overtime (for work exceeding 40 hours in a week), providing dual protection for employees. New York follows the federal standard of weekly overtime only, requiring overtime pay solely for work exceeding 40 hours per week. This difference can result in substantially higher overtime obligations for California employers compared to their New York counterparts.

Meal break requirements illustrate California's more prescriptive approach to workplace regulation. California Labor Code Section 512 mandates a 30-minute unpaid meal break for shifts exceeding 5 hours, with specific timing and penalty provisions. New York has no comparable state-level meal break requirement, though some localities and collective bargaining agreements may impose such obligations.

At-will employment exceptions reveal philosophical differences between the jurisdictions. California recognizes all three major exceptions: public policy, implied contract, and the covenant of good faith and fair dealing. New York courts recognize public policy and implied contract exceptions but explicitly reject the covenant of good faith and fair dealing in employment relationships, viewing it as inconsistent with at-will employment principles.

Representative action mechanisms show California's innovation in employment enforcement. The Private Attorneys General Act (PAGA) creates a robust system allowing individual employees to pursue representative claims for Labor Code violations on behalf of all affected workers and the state. New York has no direct equivalent to PAGA, though it offers limited representative action options through traditional class action procedures and pattern-and-practice claims under human rights laws.

Individual liability standards apply differently across jurisdictions. California imposes individual liability on supervisors and co-workers specifically for harassment violations under FEHA, while New York's approach under the Human Rights Law extends individual liability more broadly to anyone who aids, abets, incites, compels, or coerces discriminatory acts across all protected categories, not just harassment.

Damages and Remedies Comparison

California Advantages:

- **Uncapped Damages**: No statutory caps on emotional distress damages under FEHA
- **Attorney Fees**: Routinely awarded to prevailing plaintiffs
- **PAGA Penalties**: Substantial civil penalties for Labor Code violations
- **Waiting Time Penalties**: Up to 30 days additional wages for final pay violations

New York Advantages:

- **NYC Law Benefits**: Uncapped punitive damages under NYCHRL
- **Individual Liability**: Personal liability for discriminatory actors
- **Construction Law**: Absolute liability standards under Labor Law §§ 240, 241
- **Liquidated Damages**: Double damages for certain wage violations

Procedural Differences

Administrative Exhaustion Requirements:

California:

- DFEH complaint required for FEHA claims
- 300-day filing deadline (1 year if age discrimination)
- Right-to-sue letter required before court filing
- DFEH investigation may take 6+ months

New York:

- DHR complaint required for NYHRL claims (with exceptions)
- 300-day filing deadline for DHR
- 1-year statute for NYCHRL (no administrative requirement)
- Dual filing with EEOC permitted

Class Action and Representative Proceedings:

California:

- PAGA representative actions for Labor Code violations
- Traditional class actions under Code of Civil Procedure
- Broad discovery rights in representative actions

New York:

- Traditional class actions under CPLR Article 9
- Limited representative action options
- Pattern and practice claims under human rights laws

1.5 Strategic Forum Selection Considerations

State vs. Federal Court Analysis

Advantages of State Court:

California State Court:

- Familiarity with FEHA and Labor Code
- No diversity jurisdiction requirements
- Potentially more employee-friendly juries
- Expedited trial calendars in some counties

New York State Court:

- Expertise in NYHRL and Labor Law

- Broad discovery rules
- No federal question complications
- Local jury pools in employee-favorable venues

Advantages of Federal Court:

Both Jurisdictions:

- Uniform federal procedural rules
- Potentially faster resolution
- Federal question jurisdiction for Title VII, ADA claims
- Appellate review by Circuit Courts of Appeals

Venue Selection Within States

California Strategic Venues:

- **San Francisco**: Historically employee-favorable juries
- **Los Angeles**: Large jury pools, experienced employment bar
- **Oakland/Alameda County**: Progressive jury demographics
- **Orange County**: More conservative, potentially employer-favorable

New York Strategic Venues:

- **Manhattan**: Sophisticated juries, high damages awards
- **Brooklyn**: Diverse demographics, employee-favorable
- **Bronx**: Historically high damages awards
- **Westchester**: Suburban venue, mixed jury demographics

Multi-State Employer Considerations

When representing employees of multi-state employers, practitioners must analyze:

1. **Choice of Law Provisions**: Contract clauses selecting governing law
2. **Most Favorable Law**: Comparative analysis of potential claims
3. **Practical Considerations**: Where witnesses and documents located
4. **Enforcement**: Which jurisdiction offers best collection prospects

Example Analysis: Employee working remotely for California company while residing in New York may have claims under both states' laws, requiring careful analysis of which provides better remedies for specific facts.

1.6 Statute of Limitations Quick Reference

California Limitations Periods:

- **FEHA Discrimination**: 300 days to DFEH, then 1 year from right-to-sue
- **Labor Code Violations**: 3 years (most provisions)
- **PAGA Claims**: 1 year from violation occurrence
- **Wrongful Termination**: 2 years (tort), 4 years (contract)
- **Wage Claims**: 3 years (Labor Code), 4 years (contract)

New York Limitations Periods:

- **NYHRL**: 300 days to DHR, then 1 year from complaint
- **NYCHRL**: 1 year (no administrative requirement)
- **Labor Law**: 6 years (wage claims), 3 years (discrimination)
- **Contract Claims**: 6 years
- **Tort Claims**: 3 years (general), 1 year (specific torts)

Critical Practice Tip: Always calculate limitations periods under federal, state, and local law, as they may differ significantly and provide different strategic options.

1.7 Emerging Trends and Recent Developments

California Innovations:

- **COVID-19 Workplace Safety**: Enhanced Cal/OSHA requirements
- **Gig Economy Regulation**: AB 5 (Dynamex test) for independent contractors
- **Pay Equity**: Enhanced reporting requirements for large employers
- **Arbitration Limitations**: Restrictions on mandatory arbitration agreements

New York Developments:

- **Salary History Bans**: Prohibited inquiries in hiring process
- **Sexual Harassment Reforms**: Mandatory training, expanded liability
- **Marijuana Legalization**: Employment implications for drug testing
- **Domestic Worker Rights**: Expanded protections under state and local laws

1.8 Practice Management Considerations

Client Intake Essentials

Documentation Checklist:

- Employment contract and handbook
- Performance reviews and disciplinary records
- Payroll records and time sheets
- Communications (emails, texts, witness statements)
- Medical records (if disability/medical leave involved)

Jurisdictional Analysis Questions:

1. Where did the employment relationship exist?
2. Where did the alleged violations occur?
3. What is the employer's business structure and locations?
4. Which laws provide the most favorable remedies?
5. What are the applicable limitations periods?

Fee Arrangements and Cost Considerations

California Factors:

- Attorney fee shifting under FEHA and Labor Code
- PAGA penalty sharing (25% to aggrieved employees)
- Contingency fee regulations and maximums
- Cost advancement requirements

New York Factors:

- Fee shifting under human rights laws
- Contingency fee limitations and court approval
- Security for costs in certain cases
- Municipal liability considerations (NYCHRL)

1.9 Conclusion and Strategic Takeaways

Understanding the distinct yet overlapping employment law frameworks in New York and California is essential for effective practice in these jurisdictions. Key strategic considerations include:

For Plaintiff's Counsel:

- California generally offers broader substantive protections and more generous remedies
- New York provides multiple layers of protection (federal/state/local) with varying standards

- Forum selection can significantly impact case value and success probability
- Administrative requirements must be carefully managed to preserve claims

For Defense Counsel:

- California's PAGA system creates substantial representative action exposure
- New York's individual liability provisions increase personal risk for supervisors
- Multi-jurisdictional employers need consistent policies meeting highest standards
- Early settlement consideration often advisable given potential damages exposure

For All Practitioners:

- Stay current with rapidly evolving state and local employment laws
- Develop systems for tracking multiple limitations periods
- Build relationships with experienced local counsel for referrals
- Invest in continuing education specific to employment law developments

The employment law landscape in both jurisdictions continues evolving rapidly, driven by legislative action, judicial decisions, and changing workplace dynamics. Successful practitioners must maintain current knowledge of these developments while mastering the fundamental frameworks outlined in this chapter.

In Chapter 2, we will examine the specific types of employment claims that arise in practice, providing detailed guidance on claim categorization, strategic prioritization, and early case development techniques that maximize client outcomes in both New York and California.

2

Understanding the Types of Employment Claims

Employment disputes can arise in a variety of contexts, from discriminatory terminations to unpaid wages. Identifying the type of claim at issue is the first and most critical step in formulating a legal strategy. This chapter provides an in-depth overview of the most common types of employment claims in New York and California, highlighting the statutory foundations, legal standards, strategic implications, and key differences between jurisdictions.

2.1 Wrongful Termination

Overview and Legal Foundation

Wrongful termination claims allege that an employee was discharged for an illegal reason, even in an at-will employment setting. At-will employment means that either the employer or employee can terminate the employment relationship at any time, for any reason, or for no reason at all - except when that reason violates the law.

The doctrine of wrongful termination creates exceptions to the at-will employment rule, protecting employees from discharge when such termination violates public policy, breaches an implied contract, or violates the implied covenant of good faith and fair dealing.

Common Grounds for Wrongful Termination Claims

Termination in Violation of Public Policy This occurs when an employee is fired for engaging in conduct that serves the public interest or for refusing to engage in conduct that would harm the public interest. Examples include:

- Reporting workplace safety violations to OSHA
- Filing a workers' compensation claim
- Serving jury duty
- Refusing to commit perjury or other illegal acts

Retaliation for Whistleblowing or Asserting Legal Rights Employees cannot be terminated for reporting illegal activities or asserting their legal rights. This protection extends to:

- Reporting violations of federal, state, or local laws
- Cooperating with government investigations
- Filing discrimination complaints
- Requesting reasonable accommodations

Breach of Implied Contract or Covenant of Good Faith This theory applies when an employer's conduct or policies create reasonable expectations of job security or fair treatment. Evidence may include:

- Employee handbooks with progressive discipline policies
- Verbal assurances of job security
- Established company practices
- Length of employment and consistent positive performance reviews

Key Jurisdictional Differences

California Approach California recognizes all three major wrongful termination theories and has developed robust protections for employees. Labor Code Section 1102.5 provides comprehensive whistleblower protections, covering employees who report suspected violations of local, state, or federal laws to government agencies or to their employers. California courts have also been more willing to find implied contracts based on employee handbooks and established company practices.

The implied covenant of good faith and fair dealing is particularly significant in California employment law. This covenant prevents employers from terminating employees in bad faith, such as firing a salesperson just before earning a large commission or terminating an employee to avoid paying vested benefits.

New York Approach New York takes a more restrictive approach to wrongful termination claims, primarily relying on specific statutory protections rather than broad common law theories. The state has limited recognition of implied contract theories and does not recognize the implied covenant of good faith and fair dealing in the employment context.

New York's primary wrongful termination protections come from statutes such as:

- New York Labor Law Section 740 (whistleblower protection)
- New York Human Rights Law (retaliation for discrimination complaints)
- Various industry-specific protections

Strategic Considerations

When evaluating wrongful termination claims, practitioners should consider the timing of the termination relative to protected activities, the employer's stated reasons for termination, any deviation from established company policies, and the availability of supporting documentation or witnesses.

2.2 Discrimination

Protected Characteristics and Legal Framework

Employment discrimination laws protect employees from adverse treatment based on specific characteristics deemed worthy of legal protection. These protections have evolved significantly over time, with state and local laws often providing broader coverage than federal statutes.

Federal Protected Characteristics Under federal law, the following characteristics are protected:

- Race and color (Title VII of the Civil Rights Act of 1964)
- National origin (Title VII)
- Sex, including pregnancy (Title VII and Pregnancy Discrimination Act)
- Religion (Title VII)
- Disability (Americans with Disabilities Act)
- Age (40 and older under the Age Discrimination in Employment Act)

State and Local Expansions Both California and New York have expanded protected categories beyond federal minimums:

- Sexual orientation and gender identity
- Marital and familial status
- Domestic violence victim status
- Criminal history (with limitations)
- Political activities or affiliations
- Military status

Key Statutory Frameworks

Federal Laws Title VII of the Civil Rights Act of 1964 is the cornerstone of federal employment discrimination law, applying to employers with 15 or more employees. The statute prohibits discrimination in hiring, firing, compensation, terms, conditions, and privileges of employment.

The Americans with Disabilities Act (ADA) requires employers to provide reasonable accommodations to qualified individuals with disabilities, unless doing so would cause undue hardship. A qualified individual is someone who can perform the essential functions of the job with or without reasonable accommodation.

The Age Discrimination in Employment Act (ADEA) protects individuals aged 40 and older from employment discrimination, applying to employers with 20 or more employees.

California: Fair Employment and Housing Act (FEHA) California's FEHA, codified in Government Code Section 12940 and following, provides broader protections than federal law. Key features include:

- Applies to employers with five or more employees (and one or more for harassment claims)
- Broader definition of disability, including any mental or physical condition that limits a major life activity
- Express protection for sexual orientation, gender identity, and gender expression
- Stronger pregnancy accommodation requirements
- Expanded coverage for domestic violence victims

New York: Human Rights Law (NYHRL) The New York Human Rights Law, found in Executive Law Section 290 and following, has undergone significant reforms in recent years. Major features include:

- Applies to all employers with one or more employees (as of 2020 reforms)
- Broader definition of sexual harassment
- Elimination of the "severe or pervasive" standard for harassment claims
- Express protections for domestic violence victims and military status
- Enhanced protections for reproductive health decisions

New York City Human Rights Law (NYCHRL) The NYCHRL provides even broader protections than state law and is interpreted independently of federal and state precedents. It covers additional protected classes and has lower thresholds for establishing discrimination claims. See *Williams v. New York City Housing Authority*, 61 A.D.3d 62, 872 N.Y.S.2d 27 (1st Dep't 2009).

Types of Discrimination Claims

Disparate Treatment This is the most common form of discrimination claim, alleging that an employee was treated differently because of their protected characteristic. Disparate treatment can be proven through direct evidence (such as discriminatory statements) or indirect evidence using the McDonnell Douglas burden-shifting framework.

Under McDonnell Douglas – *McDonnell Douglas Corp. v. Green*, 411 U.S. 792 (1973), a plaintiff must establish a prima facie case by showing:

1. They belong to a protected class
2. They were qualified for the position
3. They suffered an adverse employment action
4. The circumstances give rise to an inference of discrimination

If the prima facie case is established, the burden shifts to the employer to articulate a legitimate, non-discriminatory reason for the action. The plaintiff can then prove the stated reason is pretextual.

Disparate Impact This theory applies when a facially neutral employment practice has a disproportionate adverse impact on a protected group. Even without discriminatory intent, such practices may violate discrimination laws unless they are job-related and consistent with business necessity.

Common examples include:

- Height and weight requirements that disproportionately exclude women
- Written tests that disproportionately exclude racial minorities
- Criminal background check policies that have disparate racial impact

Jurisdictional Comparison: Burden of Proof and Standards

Federal Standard Federal discrimination law requires proof that the protected characteristic was a motivating factor in the employment decision. However, employers can limit damages by proving they would have made the same decision regardless of the discriminatory motive (the "same decision" defense).

California Standard California follows federal standards for most discrimination claims but has adopted more employee-friendly interpretations in some areas. For example, California courts have been more willing to find pretext and have expanded the definition of adverse employment actions.

New York Standard Recent reforms to the NYHRL have made it significantly more employee-friendly. The law now requires only that discrimination be "a motivating factor" rather than the sole or primary factor, and employers cannot assert the "same decision" defense to limit liability.

2.3 Harassment

Understanding Workplace Harassment

Workplace harassment is a form of discrimination that creates a hostile work environment or involves quid pro quo situations. Unlike other forms of discrimination that typically involve discrete employment actions, harassment often consists of ongoing patterns of conduct that make the workplace abusive or intolerable.

Types of Harassment Claims

Sexual Harassment Sexual harassment can take two primary forms:

Quid Pro Quo Sexual Harassment: This occurs when submission to or rejection of sexual conduct is used as the basis for employment decisions. Classic examples include:

- A supervisor demanding sexual favors in exchange for a promotion
- Threatening termination unless an employee submits to sexual advances
- Conditioning job benefits on sexual compliance

Quid pro quo harassment typically involves someone with authority over the victim and results in a tangible employment action. Employers are generally strictly liable for quid pro quo harassment by supervisors.

Hostile Work Environment Sexual Harassment: This involves unwelcome sexual conduct that is sufficiently severe or pervasive to alter the conditions of employment and create an abusive working environment. Examples include:

- Persistent unwelcome sexual advances or propositions
- Display of sexually explicit materials
- Sexual comments, jokes, or innuendo
- Unwanted touching or physical contact of a sexual nature

Non-Sexual Harassment Harassment based on other protected characteristics follows similar principles to sexual harassment. This can include:

- Racial slurs, jokes, or epithets
- Religious mockery or interference with religious practices
- Age-related taunts or stereotyping
- Disability-related mockery or exclusion
- National origin harassment, including accent discrimination

Evolution of Legal Standards

Traditional Federal Standard Under federal law, harassment must be "severe or pervasive" enough to alter the terms and conditions of employment. Courts consider factors such as:

- Frequency of the conduct
- Severity of the conduct
- Whether it was physically threatening or humiliating
- Whether it unreasonably interfered with work performance

Post-#MeToo Reforms in California and New York Both California and New York have moved away from the restrictive "severe or pervasive" standard:

California Approach: Following the #MeToo movement, California has clarified that harassment need not be severe or pervasive if it goes beyond petty slights or trivial inconveniences. The focus is on whether a reasonable person in the plaintiff's position would find the workplace hostile or abusive.

New York Approach: The 2019 amendments to the NYHRL eliminated the "severe or pervasive" requirement entirely. Harassment is now defined as subjecting an individual to inferior terms, conditions, or privileges of employment because of their protected status. This significantly lowers the bar for harassment claims in New York.

Employer Liability Standards

Supervisor Harassment When harassment is committed by someone with authority over the victim, employers face different liability standards:

- If the harassment results in a tangible employment action (termination, demotion, etc.), the employer is strictly liable
- If no tangible employment action occurs, employers may assert the Ellerth/Faragher affirmative defense

The Ellerth/Faragher Defense Named after two Supreme Court cases, this defense allows employers to avoid liability for supervisor harassment if they can prove:

1. The employer exercised reasonable care to prevent and correct harassing behavior (usually through policies and training)
2. The employee unreasonably failed to take advantage of preventive or corrective opportunities provided by the employer

Coworker and Third-Party Harassment Employers are liable for harassment by coworkers or third parties (such as customers or clients) if they knew or should have known about the harassment and failed to take prompt, appropriate corrective action.

Practical Implications and Strategic Considerations

The evolution of harassment law, particularly in California and New York, has significant implications for both employers and employees. Employers must update their policies and training to reflect the lower thresholds for harassment claims. Employees have broader protections but must still demonstrate that the conduct at issue goes beyond ordinary workplace friction.

When evaluating harassment claims, practitioners should consider the totality of circumstances, document all incidents thoroughly, and understand how recent legal developments in their jurisdiction affect the viability of claims.

2.4 Retaliation

Understanding Retaliation Claims

Retaliation occurs when an employer takes adverse action against an employee for engaging in protected activity. Retaliation claims are often easier to prove than underlying discrimination claims and have become increasingly common in employment litigation.

Protected Activities

The scope of protected activity varies by statute but generally includes:

Filing or Participating in Complaints

- Filing discrimination charges with the EEOC, state, or local agencies
- Participating in discrimination investigations
- Testifying in discrimination proceedings
- Filing internal complaints about discrimination or harassment

Reporting Legal Violations

- Reporting violations of workplace safety laws
- Reporting wage and hour violations
- Reporting environmental violations
- Reporting fraud or other illegal activities

Asserting Legal Rights

- Requesting reasonable accommodations for disabilities
- Taking protected leave (FMLA, state family leave, etc.)
- Refusing to participate in illegal activities
- Asserting rights under collective bargaining agreements

Opposition to Discriminatory Practices

- Objecting to discriminatory treatment of oneself or others
- Intervening to stop harassment
- Refusing to implement discriminatory policies

Key Retaliation Statutes

California Protections California provides extensive retaliation protections through multiple statutes:

Labor Code Section 98.6: Protects employees who file wage claims or cooperate with Labor Commissioner investigations.

Labor Code Section 1102.5: California's Whistleblower Protection Act protects employees who report violations of law to government agencies or their employers. This statute has broad reach and covers reports of suspected violations of any local, state, or federal law.

Fair Employment and Housing Act (FEHA): Prohibits retaliation for opposing discriminatory practices or participating in FEHA proceedings.

New York Protections New York's retaliation protections include:

Labor Law Section 215: Prohibits retaliation for asserting rights under wage and hour laws.

Labor Law Section 740: New York's Whistleblower Protection Act covers employees who report violations of law that create substantial and specific danger to public health or safety.

New York Human Rights Law: Prohibits retaliation for opposing discriminatory practices or participating in discrimination proceedings.

Federal Protections Federal anti-retaliation provisions appear in numerous statutes:

- Title VII (discrimination complaints)
- Fair Labor Standards Act (wage and hour complaints)
- Occupational Safety and Health Act (safety complaints)
- Sarbanes-Oxley Act (corporate fraud reports)

Legal Framework: The McDonnell Douglas Test

Most retaliation claims follow the McDonnell Douglas burden-shifting framework:

Prima Facie Case The plaintiff must establish:

1. Engagement in protected activity
2. Knowledge of the protected activity by the decision-maker
3. Adverse employment action
4. Causal connection between the protected activity and adverse action

Temporal Proximity The timing between protected activity and adverse action is often crucial evidence of causation. While there's no bright-line rule, courts often find strong evidence of retaliation when adverse action occurs within days or weeks of protected activity.

Expanding Definition of Adverse Actions Recent decisions have broadened what constitutes an adverse employment action to include:

- Negative performance evaluations
- Exclusion from meetings or communications
- Changes in job duties or responsibilities
- Hostile treatment by supervisors or coworkers
- Lateral transfers that are materially adverse

Unique Aspects of Retaliation Law

Participation vs. Opposition Clause Protection Many anti-discrimination statutes contain both participation and opposition clauses:

- Participation clause protects formal proceedings (EEOC charges, lawsuits)
- Opposition clause protects informal objections to discriminatory practices

The opposition clause generally requires that the employee's belief about discrimination be reasonable, while participation clause protection applies regardless of the merit of the underlying claim.

Third-Party Retaliation Some jurisdictions recognize claims for third-party retaliation, where an employer retaliates against an employee because of a family member's or associate's protected activity. For example, terminating an employee because their spouse filed a discrimination complaint.

Strategic Considerations

Retaliation claims often have several advantages:

- Lower burden of proof than underlying discrimination claims
- Strong jury appeal (most people understand fairness)
- Often supported by clear temporal evidence
- May proceed even if underlying discrimination claim fails

However, practitioners should be aware of statute of limitations issues, as retaliation claims may have different filing deadlines than underlying discrimination claims.

2.5 Wage and Hour Violations

Overview of Wage and Hour Law

Wage and hour violations are among the most common employment disputes, affecting millions of workers across all industries. These claims can result in significant liability for employers, including back wages, penalties, interest, and attorney's fees.

Key Categories of Violations

Minimum Wage Violations Both federal and state laws establish minimum wage requirements, with employees entitled to the higher of the two rates. Current considerations include:

- Federal minimum wage of $7.25 per hour (unchanged since 2009)

- California's graduated minimum wage system (varying by employer size and location)
- New York's regional minimum wage variations
- Local ordinances that may set higher rates

Overtime Violations The Fair Labor Standards Act (FLSA) requires overtime pay at one and one-half times the regular rate for hours worked over 40 in a workweek. Common violations include:

- Misclassifying employees as exempt from overtime
- Failing to include bonuses, commissions, or other compensation in overtime calculations
- Averaging hours over multiple weeks
- Requiring off-the-clock work

Meal and Rest Break Violations (California) California requires specific meal and rest periods:

- 30-minute meal break for shifts over 5 hours
- 10-minute rest break for every 4 hours worked
- Additional meal break for shifts over 10 hours
- Premium pay of one hour's wages for each missed break

Off-the-Clock Work Employers must compensate employees for all time worked, including:

- Pre-shift preparation time
- Post-shift cleanup or administrative tasks
- Work performed during meal breaks
- Mandatory training or meetings
- Travel time between job sites

Worker Classification Issues

Employee vs. Independent Contractor Misclassification of employees as independent contractors is a significant source of liability. The consequences include unpaid wages, benefits, and tax obligations.

California's ABC Test: Under Assembly Bill 5 (AB5), codified in Labor Code Section 2775, workers are presumed to be employees unless the employer proves all three elements of the ABC test:

- (A) The worker is free from control and direction in performance of the work
- (B) The worker performs work outside the usual course of the hiring entity's business
- (C) The worker is customarily engaged in an independently established trade or occupation

New York's Multi-Factor Test: New York applies a more flexible, multi-factor test focusing on:

- Degree of control exercised by the employer
- Worker's opportunity for profit or loss
- Worker's investment in equipment or materials
- Permanency of the relationship
- Degree of skill required
- Integration of worker's services into employer's business

Exempt vs. Non-Exempt Classifications The FLSA requires that exempt employees meet both salary basis and duties tests:

Salary Basis Test: Employees must receive a predetermined salary of at least $684 per week (federal minimum) that doesn't vary based on hours worked.

Duties Tests: Common exemptions include:

- Executive exemption (managing enterprise or department, supervising others)
- Administrative exemption (office work related to management or business operations)
- Professional exemption (work requiring advanced knowledge in

science or learning)

- Outside sales exemption (primary duty is making sales away from employer's place of business)

California-Specific Requirements and Penalties

Waiting Time Penalties (Labor Code Section 203) When employment ends, California requires immediate payment of final wages (or within 72 hours if no notice given). Failure to pay results in waiting time penalties equal to the employee's daily wage for each day payment is delayed, up to 30 days.

Paystub Requirements (Labor Code Section 226) California requires detailed wage statements showing:

- Gross wages earned
- Total hours worked
- All deductions taken
- Net wages earned
- Pay period dates
- Employee's name and last four digits of SSN
- Employer's name and address

Violations result in penalties of $50 for the first violation and $100 for subsequent violations, plus attorney's fees.

Private Attorneys General Act (PAGA) PAGA allows employees to sue for Labor Code violations on behalf of the state, seeking civil penalties that would otherwise only be recoverable by state agencies. Aggrieved employees receive 25% of any penalties awarded, with the remaining 75% going to the state. Although PAGA actions do not allow recovery of personal damages like lost wages, they can be brought in addition to traditional private claims, making them a powerful supplement in coordinated litigation. See *Kim v. Reins International California, Inc.*, 9 Cal. 5th 73, 259 Cal. Rptr. 3d 769, 459 P.3d 1123 (2020).

New York-Specific Requirements

Spread of Hours Pay New York requires additional compensation when an employee's workday spans more than 10 hours. The employee receives one hour's pay at minimum wage in addition to regular wages.

Frequency of Pay Requirements Manual workers must be paid weekly, while other employees may be paid bi-weekly or semi-monthly. Failure to comply can result in penalties and potential individual liability for corporate officers.

Wage Theft Prevention Act New York requires employers to provide written notice of wage rates, pay dates, and other employment terms at hiring and upon any changes. The notice must be in the employee's primary language if the Department of Labor has made translations available.

Strategic Considerations for Wage and Hour Claims

Wage and hour claims often involve class or collective action procedures, allowing employees to pursue claims on behalf of similarly situated workers. The potential for large monetary recoveries and attorney's fee awards makes these cases attractive to plaintiffs' attorneys.

Employers should regularly audit their pay practices, classification decisions, and timekeeping systems to identify and correct potential violations before they result in litigation.

2.6 Misclassification of Workers

The Critical Importance of Proper Classification

Worker misclassification represents one of the most significant areas of employment law compliance and litigation. The distinction between employees and independent contractors, as well as between exempt and non-exempt employees, has profound implications for wages, benefits, taxes, and legal protections.

Employee vs. Independent Contractor Classification

The rise of the gig economy has intensified scrutiny of worker classification, with devastating financial consequences for employers who misclassify workers.

Consequences of Misclassification When independent contractors are reclassified as employees, employers may face:

- Back wages and overtime payments
- Unpaid payroll taxes and penalties
- Workers' compensation insurance premiums
- Unemployment insurance contributions
- Employee benefits obligations
- Federal and state penalties
- Private lawsuits seeking damages and attorney's fees

California's ABC Test Revolution Assembly Bill 5 (AB5), effective January 1, 2020, revolutionized worker classification in California by codifying the ABC test from the Dynamex decision. This test creates a presumption that workers are employees unless the hiring entity proves all three elements:

(A) *Control Prong*: The worker is free from the control and direction of the hiring entity in connection with the performance of the work, both under the contract and in fact. This examines not just contractual terms but actual working relationships.

(B) *Business Prong*: The worker performs work that is outside the usual course of the hiring entity's business. This is often the most difficult prong to satisfy, as it requires the work to be truly peripheral to the company's core business.

(C) *Independence Prong*: The worker is customarily engaged in an independently established trade, occupation, or business of the same nature as that involved in the work performed. This requires evidence of an ongoing independent business, not just the current work arrangement.

AB5 Exemptions and AB2257 Modifications Recognizing the broad impact of AB5, California has created numerous exemptions for specific professions and modified the law through AB2257. Key exemptions include:

- Licensed professionals (doctors, lawyers, architects)
- Certain creative professionals (writers, photographers, musicians)
- Business-to-business contractors meeting specific criteria
- Professional services contractors earning above certain thresholds

New York's Multi-Factor Approach New York continues to apply a multi-factor economic realities test, examining:

- The degree of control exercised by the employer
- The worker's opportunity for profit or loss
- The worker's investment in equipment or materials
- The permanency of the relationship
- The degree of skill required for the work
- The extent to which the work is integral to the employer's business

This approach provides more flexibility than California's ABC test but creates more uncertainty in borderline cases.

Exempt vs. Non-Exempt Employee Classification

The distinction between exempt and non-exempt employees determines eligibility for overtime pay and other wage and hour protections.

Federal Exemption Requirements Under the Fair Labor Standards Act, exempt employees must satisfy both a salary basis test and a duties test:

Salary Basis Test: Employees must receive a predetermined salary of at least $684 per week ($35,568 annually) that doesn't vary based on the quality or quantity of work performed. The salary must be paid in full for any week in which the employee performs work, regardless of hours worked.

Duties Tests for Common Exemptions:

Executive Exemption: Requires:

- Primary duty of managing the enterprise or a recognized department
- Customary and regular direction of at least two full-time employees
- Authority to hire/fire or significant input into employment decisions

Administrative Exemption: Requires:

- Primary duty of office or non-manual work directly related to management or general business operations
- Exercise of discretion and independent judgment on significant

matters

Professional Exemption: Includes both learned and creative professionals:

- Learned professional: Work requiring advanced knowledge in science or learning, typically acquired through prolonged specialized instruction
- Creative professional: Work requiring invention, imagination, originality, or talent in a recognized field of artistic or creative endeavor

Computer Employee Exemption: Applies to certain computer professionals earning at least $684 per week or $27.63 per hour, whose primary duties involve systems analysis, programming, or related computer work.

Outside Sales Exemption: Requires:

- Primary duty of making sales or obtaining orders/contracts for services
- Customary and regular engagement away from the employer's place of business
- No minimum salary requirement

State-Specific Variations and Enhanced Protections

California's Stricter Standards California generally applies more restrictive interpretations of exemptions:

- Higher salary thresholds for certain exemptions
- More stringent duties test requirements
- "Primary duty" must constitute more than 50% of work time
- Stricter interpretation of "discretion and independent judgment"

New York's Evolving Landscape New York has implemented higher salary thresholds and is considering additional reforms:

- Current salary threshold exceeds federal minimums
- Proposed regulations would further increase thresholds
- Enhanced enforcement mechanisms and penalties

Industry-Specific Classification Challenges

Technology and Gig Economy Companies like Uber, Lyft, and DoorDash face ongoing classification challenges, with different outcomes in different jurisdictions. California's Proposition 22, passed in 2020, created a specific framework for app-based drivers, though its constitutionality remains under challenge.

Construction Industry Construction companies face particular scrutiny over worker classification, with both state and federal agencies conducting targeted investigations. The industry's use of subcontractors creates complex classification issues.

Healthcare Healthcare organizations must carefully analyze relationships with physicians, nurses, and other professionals who may work across multiple facilities or maintain independent practices.

Best Practices for Classification Compliance

Regular Audits and Reviews Employers should conduct periodic audits of worker classifications, examining:

- Actual working relationships vs. contractual terms
- Changes in job duties or responsibilities over time
- Consistency of treatment across similar positions
- Compliance with applicable tests and requirements

Documentation and Contracts Proper documentation should include:

- Clear written agreements reflecting the actual relationship
- Job descriptions accurately describing duties and responsibilities
- Records of how decisions are made regarding worker classification
- Evidence supporting independent contractor relationships (business licenses, insurance, marketing materials)

Proactive Compliance Measures Organizations should:

- Stay current with evolving laws and regulations

- Train managers and HR personnel on classification requirements
- Implement consistent classification policies and procedures
- Seek legal counsel when classification questions arise

2.7 Leave Violations and Accommodation Claims

The Complex Landscape of Leave Laws

Modern employment law includes a patchwork of federal, state, and local leave requirements that create significant compliance challenges for employers and important rights for employees. Understanding these overlapping obligations is crucial for both preventing violations and pursuing claims when rights are violated.

Federal Leave Protections

Family and Medical Leave Act (FMLA) The FMLA provides eligible employees with up to 12 weeks of unpaid, job-protected leave for specific family and medical reasons. Key provisions include:

Eligibility Requirements:

- Employee must work for a covered employer (50+ employees within 75 miles)
- Must have worked for the employer for at least 12 months
- Must have worked at least 1,250 hours in the 12 months before leave
- Must work at a location with 50+ employees within 75 miles

Qualifying Reasons for Leave:

- Birth or adoption of a child
- Serious health condition of employee or immediate family member
- Military family leave for deployment-related issues
- Military caregiver leave for injured service members

Employee Rights and Employer Obligations:

- Continuation of group health insurance during leave
- Restoration to same or equivalent position upon return
- Protection from retaliation for taking or requesting leave
- Advance notice requirements (30 days when foreseeable)
- Medical certification requirements for health-related leave

California Leave Laws

California Family Rights Act (CFRA) California's CFRA provides parallel protections to the FMLA but with some important differences:

- Applies to employers with 5+ employees (compared to FMLA's 50)
- Covers same-sex domestic partners and adult children
- Provides separate leave entitlements from FMLA in some situations
- Recent amendments expand coverage for smaller employers

Pregnancy Disability Leave (PDL) California provides additional leave specifically for pregnancy-related disabilities:

- Up to 4 months of unpaid leave for pregnancy disability
- Applies to employers with 5+ employees
- Separate from and in addition to CFRA leave
- Requires reasonable accommodation for pregnancy-related conditions

California Paid Family Leave (PFL) California's State Disability Insurance program provides partial wage replacement for:

- Bonding with a new child
- Caring for a seriously ill family member
- Military family leave situations
- Benefits funded through employee payroll deductions

New York Leave Protections

New York Paid Family Leave (NYPFL) New York's comprehensive paid family leave program provides:

- Up to 12 weeks of paid family leave
- Benefit amount up to 67% of average weekly wage
- Job protection similar to FMLA
- Gradual phase-in of benefits that reached full implementation in 2021

Covered Reasons:

- Bonding with a new child
- Caring for family member with serious health condition
- Military deployment assistance for family members

New York State Disability Benefits Separate from PFL, New York provides disability benefits for employees unable to work due to their own non-work-related injuries or illnesses.

Disability Accommodation Requirements

Americans with Disabilities Act (ADA) The ADA requires employers to provide reasonable accommodations to qualified individuals with disabilities unless doing so would cause undue hardship. Key concepts include:

Qualified Individual: Someone who can perform the essential functions of the job with or without reasonable accommodation.

Reasonable Accommodation: Modifications that enable a person with a disability to perform the job, including:

- Physical modifications to the workplace
- Equipment or assistive technology
- Modified work schedules or job restructuring
- Reassignment to vacant positions

- Modified policies or procedures

Interactive Process: Both employer and employee have obligations to engage in a good faith interactive process to identify effective accommodations.

Undue Hardship: Accommodations that would impose significant difficulty or expense relative to the employer's size, resources, and business operations.

California Fair Employment and Housing Act (FEHA) California's disability accommodation requirements often exceed federal standards:

- Broader definition of disability
- Stronger interactive process requirements
- More extensive accommodation obligations
- Protection for individuals with medical conditions that may become disabilities

Common Violations and Claims

Denial of Leave Employers may violate leave laws by:

- Refusing to grant eligible leave requests
- Requiring employees to use accrued vacation or sick time when not required
- Counting protected leave against attendance policies
- Failing to maintain health insurance during leave
- Requiring medical certification beyond what's legally permitted

Retaliation for Leave Requests Employees are protected from adverse action for:

- Requesting protected leave
- Taking approved leave
- Opposing illegal leave practices
- Filing complaints about leave violations

Failure to Accommodate Disability accommodation failures include:

- Refusing to engage in the interactive process
- Denying reasonable accommodation requests without proper analysis
- Failing to explore all possible accommodations
- Imposing unnecessary restrictions on leave duration
- Terminating employees instead of providing accommodations

Failure to Restore Position Upon return from protected leave, employers must:

- Restore employee to same or equivalent position
- Maintain same pay, benefits, and working conditions
- Not count protected leave against the employee
- Continue any benefits that accrued during leave

Strategic Considerations for Leave and Accommodation Claims

Documentation Requirements Successful leave and accommodation claims often depend on thorough documentation:

- Written requests for leave or accommodation
- Medical documentation supporting the need
- Records of the interactive process
- Evidence of employer's response or lack thereof
- Communications about return to work or continued accommodation needs

Overlapping Laws and Benefits Practitioners must understand how different leave laws interact:

- FMLA and state family leave laws may run concurrently or separately
- Disability leave may extend beyond family medical leave
- Workers' compensation leave may overlap with other protected leave

- Paid and unpaid leave entitlements may have different requirements

Timing and Notice Issues Leave laws have specific notice requirements and timing provisions:

- Advance notice when leave is foreseeable (typically 30 days)
- Prompt notice for unforeseeable circumstances
- Medical certification deadlines
- Periodic recertification requirements
- Return-to-work notice obligations

Intersection with Other Employment Laws Leave and accommodation claims often intersect with other employment law violations:

- Discrimination based on disability or pregnancy
- Retaliation for asserting rights
- Wage and hour violations during leave periods
- Workers' compensation interactions

2.8 Constructive Discharge

Understanding Constructive Discharge

Constructive discharge occurs when an employee resigns because working conditions have become so intolerable that a reasonable person in the employee's position would feel compelled to quit. Legally, constructive discharge is treated as an involuntary termination, allowing employees to pursue wrongful termination claims even though they technically resigned.

Legal Standard and Elements

To establish constructive discharge, an employee must typically prove:

Objective Intolerability Working conditions must be so difficult or unpleasant that a reasonable person in the employee's shoes would feel compelled to resign. This is an objective standard that considers what a reasonable person would do, not just the individual employee's subjective feelings.

Employer Knowledge and Deliberate Indifference The employer must have known about the intolerable conditions and either:

- Deliberately created the conditions to force resignation
- Failed to remedy known intolerable conditions despite having the ability to do so

Reasonable Opportunity to Remedy In some jurisdictions, employees must give employers a reasonable opportunity to address the problematic conditions before resigning, unless circumstances make such notice futile or dangerous.

Examples of Conditions Supporting Constructive Discharge

Severe Harassment or Discrimination

- Persistent sexual harassment that creates a hostile work environment
- Racial or other discriminatory harassment that the employer fails to address
- Retaliatory conduct designed to force an employee to quit

Dangerous or Unsafe Working Conditions

- Requiring work in conditions that pose serious health or safety risks
- Refusing to address known workplace hazards
- Retaliating against employees who report safety violations

Significant Changes to Job Terms

- Substantial reduction in pay or benefits
- Demotion without justification
- Transfer to undesirable location or shift
- Assignment of menial or degrading tasks unrelated to the position

Isolation and Exclusion

- Systematic exclusion from meetings, communications, or work activities
- Removal of job responsibilities or meaningful work
- Creating an atmosphere of hostility or ostracism

Jurisdictional Differences in Standards

California Approach California recognizes constructive discharge claims and has developed a relatively employee-friendly approach. California courts consider both the objective severity of conditions and whether the employer's conduct was intended to force resignation. The state also recognizes that constructive discharge can occur relatively quickly in cases involving severe harassment or safety violations.

New York Approach New York courts apply a high threshold for constructive discharge claims, requiring that conditions be "so difficult or unpleasant that a reasonable person in the employee's shoes would have felt compelled to resign." New York emphasizes the objective nature of the test and requires clear evidence that the employer knew about the conditions and failed to remedy them.

Federal Courts Federal courts generally apply a strict standard, requiring that working conditions be extraordinarily difficult and that the employer deliberately created intolerable conditions or acted with deliberate indifference to known problems.

Strategic Considerations

Timing of Resignation The timing of resignation relative to intolerable conditions is crucial. Employees who wait too long after conditions improve may have difficulty establishing constructive discharge. Conversely, resigning too quickly without giving the employer opportunity to remedy may weaken the claim.

Documentation Requirements Successful constructive discharge claims require extensive documentation:

- Written complaints to supervisors, HR, or management

- Records of the employer's response or lack thereof
- Evidence of the impact on the employee's health, well-being, or work performance
- Witness statements or corroborating evidence
- Medical records if the conditions affected the employee's health

Relationship to Underlying Claims Constructive discharge is typically not a standalone claim but rather a theory that supports other employment law violations such as discrimination, harassment, or retaliation. The strength of the underlying claim often determines the viability of the constructive discharge theory.

Common Defenses and Challenges

Employer Defenses

- Conditions were not objectively intolerable
- Employee was oversensitive or unreasonable
- Employer took appropriate remedial action
- Employee failed to utilize available complaint procedures
- Resignation was for personal reasons unrelated to working conditions

Evidentiary Challenges

- Proving employer knowledge and intent
- Establishing objective intolerability standard
- Demonstrating causal connection between conditions and resignation
- Overcoming evidence of employee performance problems or misconduct

2.9 Common Overlapping and Hybrid Claims

The Reality of Complex Employment Disputes

Modern employment litigation rarely involves single, isolated claims. Instead, most cases present complex factual scenarios that give rise to multiple, overlapping legal theories. Understanding how different claims interact is essential for developing comprehensive litigation strategies and maximizing recovery for clients.

Typical Claim Combinations and Their Strategic Implications

Sexual Harassment with Discrimination and Retaliation A classic hybrid scenario involves an employee who experiences sexual harassment, reports it, and then faces adverse employment action. This situation typically encompasses:

Sexual Harassment Claim: Based on unwelcome sexual conduct that creates a hostile work environment or involves quid pro quo situations.

Sex Discrimination Claim: Sexual harassment is a form of sex discrimination, but additional discrimination may occur through different treatment based on gender.

Retaliation Claim: When the employer takes adverse action in response to the harassment complaint, this creates a separate retaliation claim that may be easier to prove than the underlying harassment.

Strategic Advantages: This combination provides multiple theories of recovery, different damages calculations, and various procedural advantages. Retaliation claims often have stronger causation evidence (temporal proximity between complaint and adverse action) and may proceed even if the underlying harassment claim faces challenges.

Disability Discrimination with Failure to Accommodate and Constructive Discharge Employees with disabilities often face multiple violations:

Disability Discrimination: Adverse treatment because of the disability itself.

Failure to Accommodate: Employer's refusal to provide reasonable accommodations or engage in the interactive process.

Constructive Discharge: When the lack of accommodation or discriminatory treatment becomes so severe that resignation becomes the only option.

FMLA Violations: If the disability requires time off work, FMLA violations may also occur.

Strategic Considerations: These claims often involve extensive medical evidence and require careful coordination between different legal theories. The failure to accommodate claim may provide the strongest evidence of discrimination, while constructive discharge can transform a resignation into a termination for damages purposes.

Wage and Hour Violations with Retaliation and Misclassification Workers who challenge pay practices often face multiple violations:

Wage and Hour Claims: Unpaid overtime, missed breaks, minimum wage violations.

Misclassification Claims: Being wrongly classified as exempt or as independent contractors.

Retaliation Claims: Adverse action for complaining about pay practices or filing wage claims.

Record-keeping Violations: Failure to maintain proper wage and hour records.

Strategic Benefits: These combinations often involve class or collective action potential, significant monetary damages, and statutory attorney's fees. The retaliation claim may provide individual relief while wage and hour violations create group litigation opportunities.

Procedural Interactions and Complications

Statute of Limitations Coordination Different claims may have different limitations periods:

- Federal discrimination claims require EEOC filing within 180-300 days
- State law claims may have longer periods (1-4 years)
- Wage and hour claims typically have 2-3 year limitations periods
- Retaliation claims may have separate limitation periods from underlying claims

Administrative Exhaustion Requirements Some claims require administrative filings before litigation:

- EEOC charges for federal discrimination claims
- State agency complaints for state discrimination claims
- Labor Commissioner complaints for certain wage claims
- Workers' compensation proceedings for disability-related claims

Damages Calculations and Overlaps Multiple claims may involve overlapping damages:

- Lost wages may be recoverable under multiple theories
- Emotional distress damages may be available for some but not all claims
- Punitive damages availability varies by claim type
- Attorney's fees may be recoverable under some statutes but not others

Substantive Intersections and Reinforcing Evidence

Credibility and Pattern Evidence Multiple claims can provide powerful pattern evidence:

- A series of discriminatory incidents supports both discrimination and harassment claims
- Employer's failure to investigate complaints supports both the underlying claim and retaliation
- Pattern of wage violations across multiple employees strengthens individual claims

Causation Evidence Different claims may provide mutually reinforcing causation evidence:

- Discriminatory comments support both discrimination and retaliation claims
- Temporal proximity between protected activity and adverse action strengthens multiple claims
- Employer's shifting explanations undermine credibility across all claims

Industry-Specific Hybrid Patterns

Healthcare Workers Healthcare employees commonly face:

- Disability discrimination when injured on the job
- Retaliation for reporting patient safety concerns
- Wage and hour violations in demanding work environments
- FMLA violations for work-related injuries

Technology Workers Tech industry employees often encounter:

- Misclassification issues (employee vs. contractor, exempt vs. non-exempt)
- Discrimination and harassment in male-dominated environments
- Retaliation for reporting workplace concerns
- Stock option and compensation disputes

Service Industry Workers Restaurant, retail, and hospitality workers frequently experience:

- Wage and hour violations (unpaid overtime, tip violations)
- Sexual harassment from customers, coworkers, or supervisors
- Retaliation for asserting wage and hour rights
- Discrimination in scheduling, assignments, or advancement

Strategic Approaches to Hybrid Claims

Claim Selection and Prioritization Not every potential claim should be pursued. Strategic considerations include:

- Strength of evidence for each potential claim
- Damages available under different theories
- Procedural advantages or disadvantages
- Jury appeal and comprehensibility

- Settlement leverage provided by different claims

Pleading Strategies Hybrid claims require careful pleading to:

- Avoid inconsistent allegations
- Satisfy different elements for each claim type
- Provide sufficient factual detail for complex scenarios
- Preserve all viable theories while maintaining coherent narrative

Discovery Coordination Multiple claims may require coordinated discovery:

- Personnel files may contain evidence relevant to multiple claims
- Witness testimony may address various legal theories
- Financial records may support both wage and discrimination claims
- Company policies may be relevant to multiple violations

Settlement Considerations Hybrid claims create complex settlement dynamics:

- Multiple claims provide greater settlement leverage
- Different damages theories may appeal to different defendants
- Administrative resolution options may vary by claim type
- Tax treatment of settlements may differ based on claim type

2.10 Emerging Trends and Developments

The Evolving Employment Law Landscape

Employment law continues to evolve rapidly in response to changing workplace dynamics, social movements, technological advances, and legislative reforms. Understanding emerging trends is crucial for practitioners seeking to provide cutting-edge representation and strategic advice.

Post-Pandemic Workplace Changes

Remote Work and Hybrid Arrangements The COVID-19 pandemic fundamentally altered workplace expectations and created new legal issues:

Accommodation Obligations: Remote work requests may constitute reasonable accommodations under disability laws, creating new interactive process obligations for employers.

Wage and Hour Implications: Remote work creates challenges for tracking hours, providing meal and rest breaks, and reimbursing business expenses.

Privacy and Monitoring Issues: Employee surveillance in remote work settings raises new privacy concerns and potential discrimination issues.

Geographic Jurisdiction Questions: When employees work remotely across state lines, determining applicable wage and hour laws, tax obligations, and other legal requirements becomes complex.

Workplace Safety and Health The pandemic heightened focus on workplace safety, creating new areas of potential liability:

- Employee rights to refuse unsafe work
- Accommodation requests related to COVID-19 vulnerability
- Retaliation for reporting safety concerns
- Intersection of workers' compensation and public health measures

Technology and Privacy Developments

Artificial Intelligence and Algorithmic Bias AI use in hiring, performance evaluation, and employment decisions creates new discrimination risks:

- Algorithmic bias in resume screening and candidate selection
- AI-powered performance monitoring systems
- Predictive analytics for employee retention and promotion
- Facial recognition and other biometric technologies in the workplace

Employee Privacy Rights Technology advancement continues to outpace legal frameworks:

- Social media monitoring and its limits

- Location tracking of employee devices
- Email and communication monitoring
- Genetic information privacy
- Biometric data collection and storage

Legislative and Regulatory Developments

Pay Transparency and Equity Increasing focus on wage equality has led to new legal requirements:

- Salary range disclosure requirements in job postings
- Pay equity audits and reporting obligations
- Expanded equal pay laws covering additional protected characteristics
- Restrictions on salary history inquiries

Criminal Background Check Reforms "Ban the box" legislation continues expanding:

- Restrictions on when criminal background checks can be conducted
- Requirements for individualized assessments
- Expanded coverage to private employers
- Integration with fair chance ordinances

Cannabis Legalization Impact As more states legalize cannabis, employment law adapts:

- Limits on testing for off-duty cannabis use
- Medical marijuana accommodation requirements
- Safety-sensitive position exceptions
- Interstate commerce complications

Social Justice and Civil Rights Evolution

Expanded Protected Classes Legislative and judicial developments continue expanding protected categories:

- LGBTQ+ rights expansion (Bostock v. Clayton Cnty., 590 U.S. ___, 140 S. Ct. 1731 (2020) impact)
- Pregnancy accommodation enhancements
- Domestic violence victim protections
- Political activity and belief protections
- Appearance and grooming standard challenges

Unconscious Bias and Systemic Discrimination Legal frameworks are evolving to address systemic and unconscious bias:

- Implicit bias training requirements
- Systemic discrimination claims and remedies
- Intersection of individual and class action approaches
- Data analytics in proving discrimination patterns

Enforcement Trends and Priorities

Government Agency Focus Areas Federal and state enforcement agencies have identified priority areas:

- Wage theft and worker misclassification
- Pregnancy discrimination and accommodation
- LGBTQ+ workplace rights
- Systemic discrimination in hiring and promotion
- Retaliation against workers asserting rights

Private Attorney General Actions Expansion of PAGA-style enforcement mechanisms:

- Employee-initiated enforcement of labor standards
- Qui tam actions for employment law violations
- Collective action alternatives

- Integration with traditional class action procedures

Practical Implications for Practitioners

Staying Current with Rapid Changes The pace of change in employment law requires practitioners to:

- Monitor legislative developments across multiple jurisdictions
- Track agency guidance and enforcement priorities
- Understand technological implications for traditional legal concepts
- Anticipate future developments based on current trends

Client Counseling Adaptations Advising clients requires consideration of emerging issues:

- Risk assessment for new technologies and workplace practices
- Compliance with evolving legal requirements
- Strategic planning for anticipated legal changes
- Cost-benefit analysis of proactive versus reactive approaches

Litigation Strategy Evolution Emerging trends affect litigation approaches:

- New evidence sources and preservation obligations
- Evolving damages theories and calculation methods
- Intersection of traditional claims with new legal theories
- Settlement considerations reflecting changing legal landscape

2.11 Conclusion

The Strategic Imperative of Comprehensive Claim Analysis

Properly categorizing and understanding employment claims is essential to building a strong case and providing effective representation. Each claim type carries unique legal standards, deadlines, evidentiary challenges, and strategic opportunities. The complexity of modern employment law, combined with the reality that most cases involve multiple overlapping claims, requires practitioners to develop sophisticated analytical frameworks and strategic approaches.

Key Takeaways for Effective Practice

Early and Thorough Case Assessment The initial case evaluation sets the foundation for all subsequent strategic decisions. Practitioners must:

- Identify all potential claims arising from the factual scenario
- Understand the interplay between different legal theories
- Assess the strength of evidence supporting each potential claim
- Consider procedural requirements and strategic implications
- Evaluate damages potential under various theories

Jurisdictional Awareness and Comparative Analysis The significant differences between federal, California, and New York employment laws require practitioners to:

- Understand applicable legal standards in each jurisdiction
- Recognize opportunities to forum shop or structure claims advantageously
- Stay current with rapidly evolving state and local laws
- Consider the strategic implications of different legal frameworks
- Anticipate how jurisdictional differences may affect case outcomes

Integration of Substantive Law and Procedural Strategy Successful employment litigation requires seamless integration of substantive legal knowledge with procedural expertise:

- Coordinate statute of limitations and administrative requirements across multiple claims
- Develop pleading strategies that preserve all viable theories
- Plan discovery approaches that efficiently gather evidence for multiple claims

- Consider settlement dynamics created by different claim combinations
- Understand how different claims may affect jury perception and trial strategy

Adaptation to Evolving Legal Landscape Employment law's rapid evolution requires practitioners to:

- Monitor legislative, regulatory, and judicial developments
- Understand how social and technological changes affect legal frameworks
- Anticipate future trends and their implications for current cases
- Adapt traditional legal concepts to new workplace realities
- Counsel clients on emerging risks and opportunities

The Path Forward

Whether handling a straightforward wrongful termination or a complex hybrid case involving discrimination, retaliation, and wage violations, clarity at the outset ensures strategic precision throughout the representation. The investment in thorough initial analysis pays dividends in improved case outcomes, more effective settlement negotiations, and better client service.

The employment law landscape will continue evolving, driven by changing workplace dynamics, technological advancement, and social justice movements. Practitioners who develop strong foundational knowledge while maintaining adaptability to emerging trends will be best positioned to serve their clients effectively in this dynamic practice area.

As we move forward in this guide, the next chapter will examine how to conduct effective client intake and case evaluation, building upon the foundational understanding of claim types developed here. We'll explore practical approaches to gathering information, identifying red flags, requesting key documents, and developing initial case strategies based on the comprehensive framework established in this chapter.

3

Strategic Employment Law Intake

Building the Foundation for Success

A strong employment case begins with a thorough and strategic intake. Whether you're representing an employee or advising a business, the intake process sets the foundation for the factual, legal, and relational aspects of the case. This chapter covers best practices for client interviews, essential documentation, early red flags, and jurisdiction-specific considerations for New York and California.

3.1 The Purpose of the Initial Intake

The initial consultation serves several critical functions that distinguish it from a casual conversation or preliminary screening call. Understanding these purposes helps attorneys maximize the value of this crucial first interaction.

Primary Functions:

Understanding the potential client's story and concerns - This goes beyond surface-level facts. You're gathering the emotional context that drives the client's decision to seek legal help, which often reveals underlying legal theories and damages that may not be immediately apparent.

Identifying legal issues and viable claims - Employment law intersects multiple federal, state, and local statutes. A single incident might trigger claims under Title VII, state fair employment laws, wage and hour statutes, and common law theories simultaneously.

Managing client expectations - Employment litigation is notoriously unpredictable and emotionally taxing. Setting realistic expectations during intake prevents client dissatisfaction and potential malpractice claims later.

Evaluating the credibility and temperament of the client - Courts and juries respond to authentic, credible witnesses. A client who appears evasive, overly emotional, or inconsistent during intake may struggle in deposition or at trial.

Beginning case strategy and issue spotting - Experienced employment attorneys begin formulating strategy during intake, identifying potential defenses, discovery needs, and settlement leverage points.

Determining whether to accept or decline representation - Not every employment dispute merits litigation. The intake helps you identify cases worth pursuing versus those better resolved through other means.

Key Differences Between Employment and Other Practice Areas

Employment intake differs significantly from say a personal injury intake. Employment cases often involve ongoing relationships, complex workplace dynamics, and multiple potential claims arising from the same course of conduct. Unlike a car accident with a clear incident date, employment issues typically develop over months or years, requiring careful timeline construction during intake.

3.2 Preparing for the Interview

Information to Request in Advance

Requesting documents before the initial meeting serves multiple purposes: it demonstrates your professionalism, allows you to review materials beforehand, and helps identify gaps in the client's documentation.

Essential Documents:

Resume or employment application - These establish the client's qualifications and can reveal discrepancies between promised and actual job duties, which may support breach of contract claims.

Offer letter or employment contract - Critical for understanding the employment relationship's terms. Look for at-will disclaimers, arbitration clauses, non-compete agreements, and compensation structures.

Employee handbook or policy documents - These create contractual obligations and establish the employer's own standards for conduct. Violations of company policy can support wrongful termination claims even in at-will states.

Relevant emails, performance reviews, and disciplinary records - Contemporary documents often provide the most reliable evidence of discriminatory animus or pretextual reasons for adverse actions.

Pay stubs and time records - Essential for wage and hour claims. Look for unpaid overtime, misclassification issues, and failure to provide meal or rest breaks.

Termination letter or resignation communication - The employer's stated reason for termination becomes crucial if you later argue pretext. Resignation letters may reveal constructive discharge situations.

Medical records or accommodation requests, if relevant - ADA and state disability accommodation claims require detailed medical documentation and evidence of the interactive process.

Prior complaints or internal grievances - These establish notice to the employer and may support retaliation claims if adverse action followed.

Creating Effective Intake Forms

A tailored intake form streamlines the process and ensures consistency across cases. Include sections for basic demographics, employment history, incident details, damages, and witness information. Consider separate forms for different claim types (discrimination versus wage and hour) to capture claim-specific details.

Sample intake form sections:

- Personal information and contact details
- Employment history with dates and supervisors
- Detailed incident timeline
- Protected characteristics or activities
- Witnesses and supporting documentation
- Damages and ongoing harm
- Prior legal proceedings

3.3 Conducting the Interview: Core Questions

Chronological Narrative

Legal Definition: A chronological narrative is a time-ordered account of events that allows attorneys to identify patterns, establish causation, and spot potential legal theories.

Begin with open-ended questions that allow the client to tell their story naturally:

"Walk me through your employment history with [Company]. When did you start? What was your title and role? Who were your supervisors and coworkers? What were the key events leading up to the issue?"

Why This Matters: Employment discrimination often involves subtle patterns of behavior over time. A chronological approach helps identify these patterns and establishes temporal proximity between protected activity and adverse actions.

Example: A client reports being terminated for "performance issues" but reveals through chronological questioning that the performance concerns began immediately after filing a sexual harassment complaint. This temporal proximity supports a retaliation claim.

Trigger Events

Identify what led to the client seeking legal help. The triggering event often represents the most severe adverse action, but may not be the only actionable conduct.

Key Questions:

- Were they terminated, demoted, reassigned, or retaliated against?
- What reason did the employer give?
- Were there any witnesses to the conduct?
- How did the situation affect your work environment?

Legal Jargon Explained:

Adverse Employment Action - Any action by an employer that materially affects the terms, conditions, or privileges of employment. This includes obvious actions like termination or demotion, but also subtler actions like exclusion from meetings, assignment of menial tasks, or hostile work environment creation.

Pretext - When an employer provides a false or misleading reason for an adverse action to hide discriminatory motives. Establishing pretext often requires showing the stated reason is factually false, wasn't the real reason, or insufficient to justify the action.

Protected Characteristics and Activities

Legal Framework: Federal and state employment laws protect employees from discrimination based on specific characteristics and from retaliation for engaging in protected activities.

Protected Classes Under Federal Law:

- Race, color, national origin (Title VII)
- Sex, including pregnancy and sexual orientation (Title VII)
- Religion (Title VII)
- Age 40+ (ADEA)

- Disability (ADA)
- Genetic information (GINA)

State Law Variations: California's FEHA provides broader protections including sexual orientation, gender identity, military status, and political activities. New York's Human Rights Law similarly expands protected classes and applies to smaller employers.

Protected Activities include:

- Filing discrimination complaints
- Participating in investigations
- Opposing discriminatory practices
- Requesting reasonable accommodations
- Taking protected leave (FMLA, state family leave)
- Whistleblowing on illegal activities

Example Questions:

- Do you belong to any protected class?
- Did you ever request accommodations for a disability or religious practice?
- Have you filed complaints about discrimination, harassment, or wage violations?
- Did you participate in any investigations or protected activities?

Documentation and Evidence

Contemporary documentation often provides the strongest evidence in employment cases. Unlike other practice areas where physical evidence predominates, employment cases typically rely on written communications, personnel records, and witness testimony.

Critical Questions:

- What do you have in writing about these incidents?
- Are there emails, text messages, or audio recordings?

- Do any coworkers support your version of events?
- Did you document incidents as they occurred?
- Are there security cameras or other recordings?

Legal Considerations:

Authentication - All documents must be authenticated for trial use. This typically requires testimony from the author, recipient, or custodian of records.

Hearsay - Out-of-court statements offered for their truth face hearsay challenges. Business records, contemporaneous notes, and party admissions often qualify for exceptions.

Privacy Rights - Recording conversations may violate state privacy laws. California requires two-party consent, while New York permits one-party consent recording.

3.4 Statutes of Limitations - Critical Timing Requirements

Legal Definition: A statute of limitations is a law that sets the maximum time period within which legal proceedings may be initiated after an alleged offense or injury.

Employment law involves complex, overlapping limitation periods that vary by jurisdiction and claim type. Missing a deadline can forever bar otherwise meritorious claims.

Federal Deadlines

EEOC Filing Requirements:

- Title VII, ADA, ADEA claims: 180 days (300 days in states with fair employment agencies)
- EPA claims: 2-3 years depending on willfulness
- FLSA claims: 2-3 years depending on willfulness

Key Timing Issues:

Continuing Violation Doctrine - Allows claims for discriminatory acts outside the limitation period if they're part of an ongoing pattern. However, the Supreme Court's decision in *National Railroad Passenger Corp. v. Morgan*, 536 U.S. 101, 122 S. Ct. 2061, 153 L. Ed. 2d 106 (2002), limited this doctrine significantly.

Discovery Rule - Some statutes begin running when the plaintiff discovers or reasonably should have discovered the violation, rather than when it occurred.

State-Specific Variations

California:

- FEHA claims: 3 years (extended from 1 year in 2019)
- Wage and hour claims: 3-4 years depending on violation type
- Wrongful termination: 2 years

New York:

- NYSHRL claims: 3 years
- NYCHRL claims: 3 years
- Wage and hour: 6 years

Administrative Exhaustion Requirements:

Legal Definition: Administrative exhaustion requires plaintiffs to pursue available administrative remedies before filing suit in court.

Most discrimination claims require filing with EEOC or state agencies before court filing. However, requirements vary:

California: DFEH filing required for FEHA claims, but now allows immediate right-to-sue requests without investigation.

New York: NYSDHR filing required for state claims, with dual-filing options for EEOC claims.

Practical Tip: Always confirm tolling or extension rules, particularly when administrative remedies are involved. Some courts toll limitation periods during administrative proceedings, while others require separate tracking of court filing deadlines.

3.5 Evaluating the Client and the Case

Case Viability Assessment

Legal Strength Analysis:

Elements of Proof - Each claim requires proving specific elements. For Title VII discrimination:

1. Plaintiff belongs to protected class
2. Qualified for position
3. Suffered adverse employment action
4. Circumstances suggest discriminatory motive

Causation Standards - Different claims require different causation standards. Title VII requires "because of" causation, while retaliation claims often require "but for" causation under *University of Texas Southwestern Medical Center v. Nassar*, 570 U.S. 338, 133 S. Ct. 2517, 186 L. Ed. 2d 503 (2013).

Damages Assessment:

Economic Damages - Lost wages, benefits, and future earning capacity. Consider career trajectory, promotion opportunities, and industry standards.

Non-Economic Damages - Emotional distress, reputation harm, and loss of enjoyment of life. These vary significantly by jurisdiction and claim type.

Punitive Damages - Available for intentional discrimination under federal law (with caps) and some state laws without caps.

Example Viability Analysis: A 55-year-old executive terminated during "restructuring" has potential age discrimination claims if younger, less qualified employees retained similar positions. Strong case elements include documented performance, comparative evidence, and discriminatory comments about "fresh blood" or "new energy."

Client Credibility Factors

Positive Credibility Indicators:

- Consistent narrative across multiple interviews
- Contemporary documentation supporting claims
- Corroborating witness accounts
- Reasonable emotional responses to events
- Clear memory of specific dates and details

Red Flag Indicators:

- Inconsistent timelines or narratives between interviews
- Overreliance on emotion with minimal factual support
- Extensive prior litigation history against employers
- Unrealistic expectations about outcomes or damages
- Conspiracy theories or paranoid explanations
- Inability to provide specific examples of claimed discrimination

Credibility Assessment Example: Client claims supervisor made racial slurs but cannot provide dates, witnesses, or context. When pressed for specifics, client becomes defensive and suggests a broader conspiracy. This raises credibility concerns requiring additional investigation.

Employer Analysis

Size and Resources: Employer size affects both legal requirements and practical considerations:

Federal Requirements:

- Title VII: 15+ employees
- ADA: 15+ employees
- ADEA: 20+ employees
- FMLA: 50+ employees

State Variations:

- FEHA (California): 5+ employees for most claims

- NYHRL: 1+ employees (as of 2020)
- Some local ordinances apply to all employers

Resource Considerations: Large corporations typically have experienced employment counsel, HR departments, and substantial settlement funds. Small businesses may lack resources for significant settlements even when liability exists, but may also lack sophisticated defenses.

Insurance Coverage: Many employers carry Employment Practices Liability Insurance (EPLI) that covers discrimination claims. EPLI carriers often control defense and settlement decisions, affecting case strategy.

3.6 Advanced Case Screening Techniques

The Jury Question Test

Ask clients: "If a jury heard your story, what would they think?" This question serves multiple purposes:

- Tests client's ability to articulate their case persuasively
- Identifies potential jury appeal or challenges
- Reveals client's understanding of their situation
- Helps assess damages presentation

Example Application: Client responds: "The jury would see that my boss fired me because I complained about not getting paid overtime." This suggests good jury appeal and clear causation. Contrast with: "The jury would understand that management conspired against me because I knew too much." This response raises credibility concerns.

Avoiding Reverse Engineering

Legal Definition: Reverse engineering occurs when clients attempt to shape facts to fit perceived legal requirements rather than providing accurate accounts.

Warning Signs:

- Client's story changes after learning legal standards

- Convenient timing of events to meet legal requirements
- Sudden "discovery" of discriminatory comments or actions
- Inconsistent details between initial and follow-up interviews

Prevention Strategies:

- Take detailed notes during initial client contact before explaining legal theories
- Ask for specific examples before discussing legal standards
- Request documentation before explaining its relevance
- Use open-ended questions initially, then follow up with specific inquiries

Comprehensive Risk Assessment

Litigation Risks:

- Weak or insufficient evidence
- Credible employer defenses
- Unfavorable precedent in jurisdiction
- Potential counterclaims (defamation, breach of confidentiality)
- Client's ability to withstand discovery process

Financial Risks:

- Case costs versus likely recovery
- Client's ability to contribute to expenses
- Employer's resources and willingness to fight
- Insurance coverage and limits

Reputational Risks:

- High-profile cases affecting attorney reputation
- Ethical concerns with client conduct

- Potential sanctions for frivolous claims

3.7 Declining Representation - Best Practices

You are not obligated to accept every case. Professional responsibility rules permit declining representation for various reasons.

Appropriate Grounds for Declining:

Legal Merit Issues:

- Weak factual foundation insufficient to support claims
- Expired statute of limitations with no tolling exceptions
- Clear employer defenses (legitimate business reasons, documented performance issues)
- Insufficient damages to justify litigation costs

Client-Related Concerns:

- Credibility issues that would undermine case presentation
- Unrealistic expectations despite counseling
- Personality conflicts affecting attorney-client relationship
- Client's inability to participate meaningfully in case

Practical Considerations:

- Conflicts of interest with existing clients
- Capacity or resource constraints in firm
- Geographic limitations affecting case handling
- Lack of expertise in specific legal area

Non-Engagement Letters

Legal Requirement: Many jurisdictions require written non-engagement letters when declining representation after substantive consultation.

Essential Components:

- Clear statement declining representation
- Statute of limitations reminder with specific dates
- Advice to seek other counsel promptly
- Return of any client documents
- Confirmation that no attorney-client relationship exists

Sample Language: "This letter confirms that [Firm] will not be representing you in connection with your employment dispute with [Company]. We recommend that you promptly consult with another attorney, as your claims may be subject to statutes of limitations that could expire as early as [date]. Please be advised that no attorney-client relationship has been established between us."

Ethical Considerations: Avoid providing legal advice beyond declining representation. Don't suggest specific legal theories or strategies, as this may create attorney-client relationships or malpractice exposure.

3.8 Managing Client Expectations - A Critical Success Factor

Unrealistic client expectations represent a primary source of attorney-client disputes and malpractice claims in employment law. Early, honest communication prevents later problems.

Setting Realistic Timeline Expectations

Typical Case Timelines:

- Administrative proceedings: 6-18 months
- Federal court litigation: 18-36 months
- State court litigation: 12-24 months
- Appeals: Additional 12-18 months

Factors Affecting Duration:

- Court scheduling and backlogs

- Discovery complexity and disputes
- Motion practice and summary judgment proceedings
- Settlement negotiations and mediation
- Employer's litigation strategy

Communication Strategy: Explain that litigation is a marathon, not a sprint. Prepare clients for periods of inactivity followed by intense activity. Establish regular communication schedules to prevent anxiety about case progress.

Financial Expectations

Compensation Types:

Back Pay - Lost wages from termination or other adverse action to present. May include benefits, bonuses, and raises client would have received.

Front Pay - Future lost earnings when reinstatement isn't feasible. Requires economic expert testimony and consideration of mitigation efforts.

Emotional Distress - Compensation for psychological harm. Varies dramatically by jurisdiction and requires medical documentation.

Punitive Damages - Available for intentional discrimination under federal law with statutory caps:

- Employers with 15-100 employees: $50,000 cap
- Employers with 101-200 employees: $100,000 cap
- Employers with 201-500 employees: $200,000 cap
- Employers with 500+ employees: $300,000 cap

Attorney's Fees - Available to prevailing plaintiffs under most employment statutes, but subject to reasonableness standards and potential reduction.

Emotional Preparation

Employment litigation is intensely personal and emotionally demanding. Prepare clients for:

Discovery Intrusion: Depositions, document production, and interrogatories that explore personal and professional history in detail.

Public Exposure: Court filings become public records. High-profile cases may attract media attention.

Relationship Impacts: Litigation may affect relationships with former colleagues and industry reputation.

Uncertain Outcomes: Even strong cases face unpredictable juries, adverse rulings, and settlement pressures.

Coping Strategies:

- Recommend counseling or therapy for emotional support
- Establish boundaries around case discussion in personal relationships
- Develop stress management techniques
- Focus on career rebuilding and moving forward

3.9 Administrative Filings and Early Deadlines - Jurisdiction-Specific Requirements

California Procedures

Department of Fair Employment and Housing (DFEH): California recently restructured its civil rights enforcement, transferring investigative functions to the Civil Rights Department (CRD) while maintaining DFEH as the litigation arm.

Filing Requirements:

- FEHA claims require CRD filing before court action
- Three-year filing deadline (extended from one year in 2019)
- Right-to-sue notice available immediately upon request
- No investigation required if immediate right-to-sue requested

Strategic Considerations: The extended three-year deadline provides more flexibility but may create complacency. Immediate right-to-sue requests allow faster court filing but eliminate potential CRD investigation and conciliation benefits.

Practical Filing Tips:

- File electronically through CRD portal
- Include detailed factual allegations
- Request right-to-sue immediately if litigation intended
- Serve copy on employer to start settlement discussions

New York Procedures

Multiple Agency Options:

New York State Division of Human Rights (NYSDHR):

- Handles state law discrimination claims
- One-year filing deadline unless dual-filed with EEOC
- Investigation and conciliation process
- Administrative law judge hearings available

Equal Employment Opportunity Commission (EEOC):

- Federal claims with 300-day deadline in New York
- Dual-filing with state agencies extends deadlines
- Investigation and mediation services
- Right-to-sue required for court filing

New York City Commission on Human Rights (NYCCHR):

- Handles claims under NYC Human Rights Law
- Three-year filing deadline
- Broader protections than state or federal law
- Administrative adjudication with significant remedies

Strategic Filing Decisions: Choice of agency affects timeline, remedies, and litigation strategy. NYCCHR provides broadest protections and longest deadline. EEOC filing preserves federal claims and provides dual-filing benefits.

Coordination with Court Filings

Timing Strategies:

- File administrative charges early to preserve claims
- Coordinate right-to-sue requests with litigation preparation
- Consider settlement leverage from parallel proceedings
- Plan discovery coordination between administrative and court proceedings

Documentation Requirements:

- Maintain copies of all administrative filings
- Track deadlines for multiple proceedings
- Coordinate witness interviews and document production
- Preserve attorney-client privilege across proceedings

3.10 Advanced Intake Considerations

Technology and Privacy Issues

Electronic Communications: Modern workplaces generate extensive electronic evidence. Consider:

- Personal versus company email accounts
- Text messages and instant messaging
- Social media interactions
- Video conferencing recordings
- Company phone records

Privacy Expectations: Employees generally lack privacy expectations in company-provided communications. However, personal devices and accounts may retain privacy protections.

Preservation Obligations: Once litigation is reasonably anticipated, parties must preserve relevant electronic evidence. Failure to preserve can result in sanctions.

Workplace Investigation Considerations

Internal Complaint Procedures: Employers often have internal investigation procedures that may affect legal strategy:

Advantages of Internal Complaints:

- Provides notice to employer
- May resolve issues without litigation
- Creates documented record of employer response
- Satisfies some administrative exhaustion requirements

Disadvantages:

- May alert employer to destroy evidence
- Can provide employer opportunity to develop defenses
- May result in retaliation
- Could waive certain legal claims

Strategic Decision Making: Advise clients on whether to pursue internal procedures based on:

- Employer's track record with investigations
- Client's continued employment status
- Strength of legal claims
- Retaliation risks

Multi-State Employment Issues

Interstate Employment: Many employees work across state lines or for companies with multi-state operations. Consider:

Choice of Law Issues:

- Where work was performed
- Where adverse action occurred
- Company headquarters location
- Contract choice-of-law provisions

Venue Considerations:

- Federal courts have broader venue options
- State courts limited to specific connections
- Forum selection clauses in employment agreements
- Practical considerations (distance, local counsel needs)

Coordination Requirements:

- Multiple state agency filings may be required
- Different limitation periods and procedures
- Varying remedies and damage caps
- Local counsel coordination needs

3.11 Special Considerations for Different Case Types

Wage and Hour Claims

Unique Intake Requirements:

- Detailed time records and pay stubs
- Job duty analysis for exemption status
- Break and meal period documentation

- Travel time and on-call requirements
- Commission and bonus payment records

Class Action Potential: Many wage and hour violations affect multiple employees. Consider:

- Similarly situated employee identification
- Company-wide policy analysis
- Settlement value multiplication
- Notice and opt-out procedures

Whistleblower Claims

Protected Disclosure Requirements:

- Specific legal violations reported
- Reporting procedures followed
- Good faith belief in violation
- Temporal proximity to retaliation

Evidence Preservation:

- Original documents supporting disclosure
- Communications with regulators
- Company response to reports
- Subsequent adverse actions

Executive and High-Level Employee Cases

Unique Considerations:

- Severance agreement analysis
- Non-compete and confidentiality restrictions
- Stock option and equity compensation

- Reputation and industry standing issues
- High-stakes settlement negotiations

Documentation Needs:

- Employment contracts and amendments
- Board meeting minutes
- Executive compensation analysis
- Industry standard comparisons
- Mitigation of damages evidence

3.12 Building the Attorney-Client Relationship

Communication Protocols

Establishing Expectations:

- Response time commitments
- Preferred communication methods
- Regular update schedules
- Emergency contact procedures
- Document sharing protocols

Technology Integration:

- Client portals for document access
- Electronic signature capabilities
- Video conferencing availability
- Mobile communication options
- Security and confidentiality measures

Fee Structure Discussions

Contingency Fee Considerations:

- Percentage rates (typically 33-40%)
- Cost advancement arrangements
- Settlement versus trial percentages
- Fee shifting statute implications
- Expense responsibilities

Hourly Fee Alternatives:

- Blended rate structures
- Task-based billing
- Hybrid contingency-hourly arrangements
- Flat fee components
- Retainer requirements

3.13 Conclusion

The intake phase represents far more than mere fact-gathering - it's a comprehensive evaluation process that determines case viability, client suitability, and strategic direction. A thorough, strategic intake minimizes surprises throughout litigation, enhances case efficiency, and establishes the foundation for a legally sound and emotionally manageable case.

Successful employment attorneys view intake as an investment in case success. The time spent thoroughly evaluating potential clients and their claims pays dividends throughout representation, from discovery through trial or settlement. By implementing systematic intake procedures, maintaining detailed documentation, and setting realistic expectations from the outset, attorneys position themselves and their clients for optimal outcomes.

The intake process also serves as an audition for both attorney and client. Clients evaluate whether the attorney understands their situation and can effectively advocate for their interests. Attorneys assess whether the client's case merits the significant investment of time and resources that employment litigation demands.

Remember that declining representation when appropriate protects both attorney and client interests. A case that shouldn't be pursued often becomes a source of frustration, financial loss, and potential ethical problems. Trust your professional judgment during intake - it's based on experience and expertise that clients lack.

As employment law continues evolving with new statutes, regulations, and court decisions, intake procedures must adapt accordingly. Stay current with legal developments, maintain relationships with administrative agencies, and continuously refine your intake process based on case outcomes and client feedback.

The foundation built during intake supports everything that follows. Invest the time and attention necessary to build it properly, and your cases - and clients - will benefit throughout the representation.

In the next chapter, we'll explore ethical obligations and how to structure the client relationship, including engagement agreements, fee structures, and your duties to the court, client, and opposing counsel.

A strong employment case begins with a thorough and strategic intake. Whether you're representing an employee or advising a business, the intake process sets the foundation for the factual, legal, and relational aspects of the case. This chapter covers best practices for client interviews, essential documentation, early red flags, and jurisdiction-specific considerations for New York and California.

4

Ethical Considerations in Employment Litigation

Employment litigation often involves emotionally charged disputes, complex facts, and evolving laws. Amid these dynamics, your ethical obligations as counsel remain fixed and foundational. Whether you're representing an employee or an employer, clear client relationships, informed consent, and integrity in conduct are essential.

This chapter outlines the key ethical considerations when handling employment cases in New York and California, including how to structure the attorney-client relationship, manage conflicts of interest, and maintain professional responsibility throughout the case.

4.1 Establishing the Attorney-Client Relationship

The Foundation: Written Engagement Agreements

A written engagement letter or retainer agreement is not merely a best practice - it is required under ethical rules in both New York and California. This document serves as the constitutional framework for your professional relationship and provides crucial protection for both attorney and client.

Essential Elements of Engagement Agreements:

Client Identification and Scope Definition Your engagement letter must clearly identify who your client is - a critical distinction in employment law where multiple parties may be involved. For example, when representing a company, specify whether you represent the entity itself, individual managers, or both. The scope of representation should be defined with surgical precision to avoid future disputes about what services are included.

Example: "Attorney represents ABC Corporation in connection with the wrongful termination claim filed by Jane Smith in Los Angeles Superior Court, Case No. 24-CV-12345. This representation does not extend to any related claims that may be filed by other employees or any regulatory investigations by state or federal agencies."

Fee Structure Transparency The fee arrangement must be explained in detail, addressing not just the rate or percentage, but also how fees are calculated, when they are due, and what constitutes a "recovery" in contingency cases.

Key Differences Between New York and California:

In California, Rule 1.5 of the California Rules of Professional Conduct requires that fee agreements be "fair and reasonable." California also mandates specific disclosures for contingency fee agreements, including a statement that the percentage fee will be calculated before or after deduction of costs.

New York Rule 1.5 similarly requires reasonable fees but places additional emphasis on disclosure of the basis for the fee calculation. New York attorneys must also comply with Judiciary Law Section 474-a, which requires written fee agreements for most matters likely to exceed $3,000.

Cost Allocation and Payment Responsibilities Clearly delineate who pays for what expenses. In employment litigation, costs can escalate quickly with expert witnesses, depositions, and document production. Specify whether the client advances costs or whether they are deducted from any recovery.

Termination and Dispute Resolution Provisions Include procedures for ending the representation and resolving fee disputes. This protects both parties and demonstrates professionalism.

Best Practices for Client Onboarding

Plain Language Requirement Legal jargon intimidates clients and can invalidate agreements if the client didn't truly understand the terms. Use everyday language wherever possible.

Poor Example: "Attorney shall provide zealous advocacy pursuant to applicable rules of professional conduct."

Better Example: "Attorney will work diligently to protect your interests while following professional ethics rules."

Client Education Process Schedule a dedicated meeting to review the engagement agreement line by line. This investment of time prevents misunderstandings and demonstrates your commitment to transparency. Document this review in your file with a signed acknowledgment from the client.

Scope Modification Procedures Establish clear procedures for modifying the scope of representation. Employment cases often evolve, with new claims arising or regulatory agencies becoming involved. Your initial agreement should anticipate these possibilities.

4.2 Fee Structures in Employment Cases

Contingency Fees: The Plaintiff's Path

Contingency fee arrangements are the lifeblood of plaintiff-side employment litigation, making legal representation accessible to employees who cannot afford hourly rates. However, these arrangements require careful structuring to comply with ethical requirements and avoid disputes.

Standard Contingency Ranges and Factors

Employment discrimination and wrongful termination cases typically involve contingency fees ranging from 33% to 40% of the total recovery. Several factors influence where your fee falls within this range:

Case Complexity: Simple wrongful termination cases may justify a 33% fee, while complex class actions involving multiple claims and extensive discovery may warrant 40%.

Risk Assessment: Higher-risk cases with uncertain outcomes may justify higher percentages. Cases with strong liability but uncertain damages might fall in the middle range.

Recovery Stage: Some attorneys structure sliding scales based on when recovery occurs - 33% for pre-litigation settlements, 40% for cases requiring trial.

Defining "Recovery" with Precision

The most common source of fee disputes involves what constitutes "recovery." Your agreement must specify whether the contingency percentage applies to:

- Gross settlement amounts before deduction of costs
- Net settlement amounts after costs are deducted
- Non-monetary relief (such as reinstatement or policy changes)
- Attorneys' fees awarded by the court under fee-shifting statutes

Example of Clear Language: "Attorney's fee shall be thirty-five percent (35%) of all monetary recovery obtained through settlement, judgment, or other resolution, calculated on the gross amount before deduction of costs and expenses. If the court awards separate attorneys' fees under applicable fee-shifting statutes, such awarded fees belong entirely to Attorney and are not subject to the contingency percentage."

California-Specific Requirements

California Business and Professions Code Section 6147 requires contingency fee agreements to be in writing and include specific disclosures. The agreement must state whether the contingency percentage is calculated before or after costs are deducted - a critical distinction that can significantly impact the client's net recovery.

California attorneys must also provide clients with a copy of the State Bar's contingency fee disclosure form, which explains the client's rights and the nature of contingency arrangements.

New York Contingency Fee Considerations

New York Judiciary Law Section 474-a requires written agreements for contingency fees and mandates specific disclosures about the client's right to negotiate the fee percentage. New York attorneys should be aware that certain types of cases (such as workers' compensation) have statutory fee limitations.

Hourly Billing: The Defense Standard

Defense counsel and employer-side attorneys typically bill hourly, providing predictable income but requiring careful attention to billing practices and client communication.

Rate Structure and Billing Increments

Establish different rates for different levels of attorney and staff involvement. Partners, associates, paralegals, and support staff should have clearly defined hourly rates. Most firms bill in six-minute increments (0.1 hours), though some use quarter-hour minimums.

Expense Recovery Protocols

Document all recoverable expenses with receipts and detailed descriptions. Common expenses in employment litigation include:

- Court filing fees
- Service of process costs
- Deposition transcript fees
- Expert witness fees
- Travel expenses for depositions or hearings
- Document production and copying costs

Regular Billing Communication

Send detailed monthly invoices that allow clients to understand exactly what work was performed. Include brief descriptions of tasks that justify the time spent.

Good Example: "Review and analyze plaintiff's medical records regarding claimed emotional distress (2.3 hours)."

Poor Example: "Legal research (3.5 hours)."

Hybrid and Alternative Fee Arrangements

Employment law increasingly utilizes creative fee structures that combine elements of hourly and contingency billing or provide fixed fees for specific services.

Limited Scope Flat Fees

These arrangements work well for discrete services such as:

- Reviewing and negotiating severance agreements ($1,500-$3,000)
- Responding to EEOC or DFEH charges ($2,500-$5,000)
- Drafting demand letters ($1,000-$2,500)
- Conducting internal investigations ($5,000-$15,000)

Blended Fee Structures

Some attorneys combine reduced hourly rates with success bonuses, providing predictable income while sharing in favorable outcomes. For example, billing at 75% of standard rates with a 10% contingency fee upon successful resolution.

4.3 Duty of Loyalty and Avoiding Conflicts

The Conflict Check: Your First Line of Defense

Conflict checking in employment law requires particular attention because of the interconnected nature of workplace relationships. A thorough conflict check must examine not just direct adverse parties, but also related entities and individuals who might become involved in the litigation.

Comprehensive Conflict Analysis

Corporate Family Conflicts: When representing or suing a company, check conflicts with parent companies, subsidiaries, and affiliated entities. A discrimination claim against a local restaurant might conflict with representing the parent franchise company in unrelated matters.

Individual Employee Conflicts: Employment cases often involve multiple employees as witnesses or potential plaintiffs. Representing one employee may preclude representation of others with competing interests.

Vendor and Service Provider Conflicts: Companies often use the same law firms for multiple purposes. Representing an employee against a company while simultaneously handling corporate transactions for that company creates an obvious conflict.

Insurance Carrier Considerations: Many employment claims involve insurance coverage disputes. Conflicts can arise between the insured company and the insurance carrier, or between different carriers providing coverage.

Understanding Imputed Conflicts

The concept of imputed conflicts - where one attorney's conflict affects the entire firm - is particularly complex in employment law because of the ongoing nature of many attorney-client relationships.

Firm-Wide Disqualification Rules

Under both California Rule 1.10 and New York Rule 1.10, conflicts are generally imputed throughout the law firm. This means that if any attorney in your firm has represented the employer in any capacity, the entire firm may be disqualified from representing an employee against that employer.

Example: Attorney A at your firm handled a routine contract matter for XYZ Company two years ago. When an employee approaches your firm about suing XYZ Company for discrimination, the entire firm likely has a conflict and cannot take the case.

Screening and Ethical Walls

Some jurisdictions allow the use of ethical screens (also called "Chinese walls") to isolate conflicted attorneys from cases, but this is generally not available for current client conflicts. The screen must be implemented before any confidential information is shared and must include:

- Physical separation of files and attorneys
- Prohibitions on discussing the matter
- Written protocols acknowledged by all firm members

- Notice to affected clients

Waiver and Informed Consent Procedures

When conflicts are waivable, the informed consent process requires more than simply obtaining a signature on a waiver form.

Elements of Effective Conflict Disclosure

Complete Factual Disclosure: Explain exactly what the conflict is, how it arose, and how it might affect the representation. Vague or incomplete disclosures invalidate waivers.

Analysis of Implications: Help the client understand how the conflict might practically affect their case. Will it limit your ability to use certain arguments or evidence? Might it affect settlement negotiations?

Alternative Options: Discuss the client's alternatives, including representation by other counsel or modified representation arrangements.

Ongoing Monitoring: Conflicts can evolve as cases progress. Establish procedures for monitoring potential conflicts and obtaining additional consent if circumstances change.

Non-Waivable Conflicts

Some conflicts cannot be waived under any circumstances:

- Assertion of claims between clients in the same litigation
- Situations where you cannot reasonably believe you can provide competent representation to all clients
- Conflicts prohibited by applicable law

4.4 Confidentiality and Privilege

The Broad Scope of Confidentiality

The duty of confidentiality extends far beyond the attorney-client privilege and encompasses all information relating to the representation, regardless of its source or whether it would be privileged in court.

Information "Relating to Representation"

This broad standard includes:

- Information learned from the client
- Information discovered through investigation
- Information gleaned from documents produced by opposing parties
- Public information gathered in connection with the representation
- Information about the client's business or personal affairs learned in any context

Example: During an employment discrimination case, you learn through discovery that your client has been having an affair with a coworker. Even though this information came from opposing counsel and might be relevant to credibility, you cannot disclose it without client consent because it "relates to the representation."

Attorney-Client Privilege in Employment Context

The attorney-client privilege protects confidential communications between attorney and client made for the purpose of seeking legal advice. In employment law, privilege issues frequently arise in several contexts.

Workplace Communications and Technology

Email and Electronic Communications: Warn clients never to use work email accounts or company devices for attorney-client communications. Employers typically have broad rights to monitor workplace technology, and communications made on company systems are rarely privileged.

Best Practice: Provide clients with a secure, personal email address for all case-related communications and instruct them to never discuss the case using company technology.

Workplace Conversations: Communications between attorney and client at the client's workplace may not be privileged if they can be overheard by colleagues or if the client lacks a reasonable expectation of privacy.

Third-Party Presence: The presence of third parties during attorney-client communications can destroy privilege. Be particularly careful about:

- Family members present during consultations
- Interpreters or translators
- Other employees who might be witnesses
- Union representatives or workplace advocates

Common Privilege Pitfalls in Employment Cases

The Friend or Family Member Exception

Clients often want to include spouses, partners, or close friends in legal consultations. While some jurisdictions recognize limited exceptions for necessary third parties, it's generally safer to meet with clients alone and have them relay information to family members separately.

Joint Client Considerations

When representing multiple employees against the same employer, communications between the attorney and each client may not be privileged in later litigation between those clients. Carefully consider whether joint representation is appropriate and document the privilege implications.

Corporate Client Complications

When representing a company, identify clearly who within the organization can make privileged communications. Generally, only communications with employees authorized to seek legal advice on behalf of the corporation are privileged.

Work Product Protection

Beyond attorney-client privilege, work product protection shields attorney mental impressions, strategies, and certain investigative materials from discovery.

Fact Work Product vs. Opinion Work Product

Fact Work Product: Notes of witness interviews, factual investigations, and document compilations receive qualified protection and may be discoverable upon a showing of substantial need and undue hardship.

Opinion Work Product: Attorney mental impressions, legal theories, strategies, and conclusions receive nearly absolute protection and are rarely discoverable.

Practice Tip: Clearly label documents containing your mental impressions and legal strategies as "Attorney Work Product - Confidential" and keep them separate from purely factual materials.

4.5 Duty of Candor and Truthfulness

Truthfulness to the Court

The duty of candor to the court is absolute and non-negotiable. Employment cases often involve emotional testimony and conflicting accounts of workplace events, making truthfulness obligations particularly important.

Prohibited Conduct Toward Courts

False Statements of Fact: Never make factual assertions you know to be false, even if the client insists they are true. If you discover that a previous factual assertion was incorrect, you have a duty to correct it promptly.

Example: You tell the court that your client was never disciplined at work, but later discover a written warning in the personnel file. You must correct this misstatement immediately.

False Statements of Law: Accurately represent the current state of the law, including adverse authority that is directly on point and controlling. The duty to cite adverse authority is limited to controlling law from your jurisdiction that directly contradicts your position.

Duty to Correct False Testimony: If you learn that your client or a witness has given false testimony, you must take reasonable remedial measures, which may include encouraging the client to correct the testimony or seeking to withdraw from representation.

Professional Dealing with Opposing Counsel

Employment litigation can become contentious, but professional courtesy and honesty in dealings with opposing counsel serve your client's interests and maintain the integrity of the legal system.

Discovery Obligations and Good Faith

Meet and Confer Requirements: Both California and New York require parties to meet and confer in good faith before filing discovery motions. This is not a pro forma requirement - courts expect genuine efforts to resolve disputes.

Document Production Integrity: When producing documents, ensure completeness and accuracy. If you discover that previously produced documents were incomplete, supplement the production immediately.

Deposition Conduct: Prepare clients thoroughly for depositions, but never coach them to give false or misleading testimony. Objections during depositions should be limited and professional.

Client Counseling and Honest Assessment

Your duty of truthfulness to clients requires brutal honesty about case prospects, risks, and potential outcomes.

Realistic Case Evaluation

Liability Assessment: Provide honest assessments of the strength of claims and defenses. Don't inflate prospects to secure representation or maintain client morale.

Example: "While your supervisor's comments were inappropriate and offensive, they may not rise to the level of severe or pervasive harassment required under California law. We have a challenging case on liability, though if we can prove our claims, damages could be substantial."

Damage Calculations: Base damage calculations on realistic assumptions about lost wages, emotional distress, and punitive damages. Avoid inflated settlement demands that undermine credibility.

Settlement Advice: When advising on settlement offers, consider not just the monetary amount but also the client's personal and professional goals, litigation costs, and emotional toll of continued proceedings.

Managing Client Expectations

Timeline Realities: Employment cases often take two to four years from filing to resolution. Prepare clients for the long haul and explain how discovery, motion practice, and court scheduling affect timing.

Cost Considerations: Even in contingency cases, clients may bear costs for expenses, lost wages from time spent on the case, and potential liability for opposing counsel's fees if fee-shifting statutes apply.

Emotional Preparation: Litigation is stressful and invasive. Prepare clients for aggressive discovery, character attacks, and the possibility that private matters may become public record.

4.6 Termination of Representation

Permissive Withdrawal Circumstances

Understanding when you may withdraw from representation protects both attorney and client interests while ensuring continuity of legal services.

Client Non-Cooperation

Failure to Follow Legal Advice: If a client consistently ignores legal advice or insists on pursuing frivolous positions, withdrawal may be appropriate.

Example: Your client in a discrimination case insists on filing a motion for sanctions against opposing counsel despite your advice that the motion lacks merit and could result in sanctions against your client.

Dishonesty or Concealment: If a client lies about material facts or conceals important information, the attorney-client relationship becomes untenable.

Communication Breakdown: When clients become unreachable or refuse to communicate about important case developments, effective representation becomes impossible.

Fee Non-Payment

Establishing Clear Payment Terms: Your engagement agreement should specify payment schedules, consequences of non-payment, and procedures for withdrawal due to fee disputes.

Notice Requirements: Before withdrawing for non-payment, provide written notice and a reasonable opportunity to cure the default. Some jurisdictions require specific notice periods.

Client File Obligations: Even when withdrawing for non-payment, you must provide the client with their file and cannot hold it hostage for unpaid fees.

This includes original documents and work product necessary for the client to continue representation elsewhere.

Mandatory Withdrawal Situations

Certain circumstances require immediate withdrawal, regardless of the impact on the client or the case.

Violation of Ethics Rules

If continuing representation would require violating professional conduct rules, withdrawal is mandatory. This includes situations where new conflicts arise that cannot be waived or where the client insists on illegal conduct.

Client Discharge

Clients have an absolute right to discharge counsel at any time, with or without cause. When discharged, you must withdraw promptly and transition the case smoothly.

Incapacity or Impairment

If your own physical or mental condition materially impairs your ability to represent the client, withdrawal is required.

Procedural Requirements for Withdrawal

Court Approval Process

In active litigation, attorney withdrawal typically requires court approval. Your motion to withdraw must:

- Comply with local court rules regarding form and content
- Provide adequate notice to all parties
- Avoid disclosing privileged information about reasons for withdrawal
- Ensure no prejudice to the client's interests

Client Protection Measures

File Transfer Procedures: Organize and transfer the complete client file, including all documents, correspondence, work product, and case materials necessary for continued representation.

Status Reports: Provide detailed status reports covering all pending deadlines, scheduled hearings, discovery obligations, and strategic considerations.

Third-Party Notifications: Notify courts, opposing counsel, and other relevant parties of the withdrawal according to applicable rules and deadlines.

Trust Account Obligations: Return any unused retainer funds and provide detailed accountings of all client money handled during the representation.

4.7 Limited Scope Representation

Defining Boundaries Clearly

Limited scope representation, also known as "unbundled legal services," allows attorneys to handle specific aspects of a case while leaving other responsibilities to the client. This arrangement requires exceptional clarity about boundaries and expectations.

Common Limited Scope Services in Employment Law

Severance Agreement Review: Many employees seek legal review of severance packages without full representation in negotiations. This service typically includes:

- Analysis of restrictive covenants and their enforceability
- Review of release language and scope
- Assessment of consideration adequacy
- Advice on negotiation strategies the client can implement independently

Sample Scope Language: "Attorney will review the severance agreement provided by client and prepare a written analysis of its terms, including recommendations for potential modifications. Attorney will not communicate with employer or employer's counsel and will not participate in negotiations. Client retains full responsibility for any negotiations or communications with employer."

EEOC/DFEH Charge Preparation: Clients often need help preparing discrimination charges while handling other aspects of their case independently.

Settlement Agreement Review: Clients who negotiate settlements independently may seek legal review before signing the final agreements.

Policy and Handbook Analysis: Employers sometimes seek limited advice on specific policies without retaining counsel for broader employment matters.

Written Scope Agreements

Essential Elements of Limited Scope Agreements

Specific Service Description: Use precise language describing exactly what services you will and will not provide. Avoid general terms that could be interpreted broadly.

Communication Protocols: Specify how you will communicate with the client and whether you will have any contact with opposing parties or courts.

Timeline and Deadlines: Establish clear timelines for the legal service's completion and specify whether you will monitor ongoing deadlines or court dates.

Fee Structure: Limited scope services often use flat fees, but clearly specify what is included and what additional services would require separate agreements.

Termination and Transition: Explain how the limited representation will end and what materials will be provided to the client.

Risk Management in Limited Scope Representation

Malpractice Considerations

Limited scope representation can increase malpractice risks if boundaries are unclear or if clients misunderstand the scope of services. Key risk management strategies include:

Documentation: Maintain detailed records of all advice given and services performed. Document client instructions and decisions that are outside your scope of representation.

Client Education: Ensure clients understand what legal issues are not covered by your representation and recommend obtaining additional counsel for those matters.

Follow-Up Protocols: Establish whether you will provide any follow-up services or reminders about deadlines related to your limited representation.

Competence Requirements

Even in limited scope representations, you must provide competent legal service within the defined scope. This may require additional research or consultation if the limited matter involves unfamiliar legal areas.

4.8 Dual Representation and Class Actions

Challenges of Multiple Client Representation

Representing multiple employees against the same employer presents unique ethical challenges that require careful analysis and ongoing monitoring.

Identifying Potential Conflicts

Damage Disparities: Employees often have different levels of damages based on salary, length of employment, and individual circumstances. In settlement negotiations, this can create conflicts between maximizing recovery for high-damage plaintiffs versus achieving acceptable outcomes for all clients.

Example: In a wage and hour class action, senior managers may have significant overtime claims while entry-level employees have smaller individual damages. Settlement allocation decisions may pit these groups against each other.

Liability Differences: Individual employees may have different levels of evidence supporting their claims, creating conflicts about litigation strategy and settlement positions.

Personal Relationships: Workplace relationships and friendships can complicate multiple representation when discovery reveals information that affects these relationships.

Employment Status Variations: Representing both current and former employees creates conflicts about remedies - current employees may prioritize workplace changes while former employees tend to focus on monetary recovery.

Informed Consent Procedures

Comprehensive Conflict Disclosure

When undertaking multiple representation, disclosure must address:

Potential Areas of Conflict: Explain specific ways interests might diverge as the case progresses.

Settlement Allocation Issues: Describe how settlement funds might be allocated and how decisions about allocation will be made.

Information Sharing: Explain that information learned about one client may be shared with other clients unless privilege applies.

Withdrawal Possibilities: Advise that you may need to withdraw from representing some or all clients if conflicts become non-waivable.

Decision-Making Protocols: Establish procedures for making strategic decisions when clients disagree.

Class Action Considerations

Adequacy of Representation Standards

Class action attorneys face heightened scrutiny regarding adequacy of representation. Key considerations include:

Class Representative Selection: Choose representatives whose interests align with the class and who will actively participate in the litigation.

Settlement Review Process: Court approval requirements for class settlements provide additional protection but require careful documentation of the settlement's fairness.

Notice and Opt-Out Rights: Ensure adequate notice to class members and respect individual decisions to opt out of the class.

Fee Allocation Transparency: Class action fee awards must be reasonable and properly documented. Courts increasingly scrutinize fee applications and require detailed justification for the fee.

4.9 Advertising and Solicitation

State-Specific Advertising Rules

Both California and New York follow modified versions of the ABA Model Rules for attorney advertising, but each has specific requirements and restrictions.

California Advertising Requirements

California Rule 7.3 governs attorney advertising and requires that all communications about legal services be truthful and not misleading. Specific California requirements include:

Written Communications: Must include the lawyer's name and office address, or the name and address of the law firm.

Recorded Communications: Must include the lawyer's name and the fact that the communication is an advertisement.

Testimonials and Endorsements: Permitted but must include disclaimers that results obtained for other clients do not guarantee similar outcomes.

Contingent Fee Advertising: Advertisements mentioning contingent fees must disclose that clients remain responsible for costs regardless of outcome.

New York Advertising Restrictions

New York Rule 7.3 includes additional restrictions on attorney advertising:

Prior Results: Advertisements mentioning prior results must include disclaimers that past results do not guarantee future outcomes.

Specialization Claims: Attorneys cannot claim specialization unless certified in a specialty field recognized by the New York State Bar.

Dramatic Presentations: New York restricts the use of dramatic presentations, including actors portraying lawyers or clients.

Language Requirements: Advertisements in languages other than English must include English translations filed with the court.

Digital Marketing Considerations

Website and Social Media Compliance

Professional Responsibility Online: All online content must comply with advertising rules, including social media posts, blog articles, and website content.

Client Confidentiality: Never post information about current or former clients without explicit written consent, even if the information seems positive or general.

SEO and Content Marketing: Search engine optimization and content marketing must avoid misleading claims about results or expertise.

Online Reviews and Testimonials: Client reviews and testimonials must include appropriate disclaimers and cannot be solicited in ways that violate solicitation rules.

Direct Solicitation Restrictions

Prohibited Solicitation Practices

Both states prohibit direct solicitation of prospective clients in certain circumstances:

In-Person Solicitation: Generally prohibited when the attorney's pecuniary gain is a significant motive, particularly targeting vulnerable individuals.

Targeted Mailings: Restricted when directed at individuals known to need specific legal services, especially following accidents or traumatic events.

Workplace Solicitation: Special restrictions apply to soliciting employees following layoffs, plant closures, or other workplace events.

Permitted Marketing Activities

General Advertising: Broad advertising not targeted at specific individuals is generally permitted if truthful and not misleading.

Referral Programs: Attorney referral programs must comply with fee-sharing and solicitation rules.

Educational Seminars: Educational presentations about employment law are permitted if they provide genuine educational value and avoid direct solicitation.

Professional Networking: Building relationships with other professionals and potential referral sources is encouraged within ethical bounds.

4.10 Technology and Modern Practice Considerations

Electronic Communications Security

Modern employment law practice increasingly relies on technology, creating new ethical obligations around data security and client confidentiality.

Secure Communication Protocols

Email Encryption: Consider using encrypted email services for sensitive client communications, particularly when discussing strategy or confidential information.

Cloud Storage Security: If using cloud-based practice management systems, ensure they include adequate security measures and comply with confidentiality requirements.

Mobile Device Management: Establish protocols for accessing client information on mobile devices, including password protection and remote wipe capabilities.

Video Conferencing Privacy: Ensure video conference platforms used for client meetings include adequate privacy protections and end-to-end encryption.

Document Retention and Destruction

Client File Management

Retention Periods: Establish clear policies for how long client files will be retained after case completion. Consider statute of limitations periods for potential malpractice claims.

Electronic Discovery Obligations: Maintain client files in formats that can be easily accessed and produced if needed for future legal proceedings.

Secure Destruction: When destroying client files, use secure methods that protect confidential information from recovery or disclosure.

Access and Retrieval: Maintain systems that allow efficient retrieval of client information if needed for future reference or legal obligations.

Artificial Intelligence and Legal Technology

AI-Assisted Legal Research

Competence Requirements: Attorneys using AI tools for legal research must understand the limitations and verify the accuracy of AI-generated content.

Confidentiality Concerns: Ensure that AI tools used in practice include adequate confidentiality protections and do not retain or share client information.

Quality Control: Implement quality control measures when using AI-generated content, including independent verification of legal citations and analysis.

Client Disclosure: Consider whether clients should be informed about the use of AI tools in their representation and obtain consent where appropriate.

4.11 Conclusion

Ethical compliance in employment litigation serves as the foundation for effective advocacy and long-term professional success. The emotionally charged nature of workplace disputes, combined with the personal stakes involved for individual clients, makes ethical clarity essential rather than optional.

The key principles discussed in this chapter - clear client relationships, transparent fee arrangements, scrupulous conflict checking, absolute confidentiality, and unwavering truthfulness - provide the framework for navigating complex employment cases while maintaining professional integrity.

Practical Implementation Strategies

Systematic Approach: Develop systematic procedures for intake, conflict checking, and client communication that ensure consistent ethical compliance across all cases.

Ongoing Education: Stay current with changes in professional responsibility rules and employment law developments that affect ethical obligations.

Documentation Habits: Maintain detailed records of ethical decisions, client communications, and conflict analyses to protect both attorney and client interests.

Regular Review: Periodically review engagement agreements, fee structures, and firm policies to ensure continued compliance with evolving ethical standards.

Professional Consultation: When facing complex ethical issues, consult with professional responsibility experts or state bar ethics hotlines rather than attempting to resolve difficult questions in isolation.

The investment in ethical compliance pays dividends through enhanced client relationships, improved case outcomes, and protection from professional liability. In employment litigation, where reputations and careers are often at stake, ethical excellence distinguishes exceptional advocates from merely competent practitioners.

The next chapter will explore evidence gathering and preservation techniques that build upon this ethical foundation to create compelling factual presentations that serve client interests while maintaining professional integrity.

5

Evidence Collection and Preservation in Employment Litigation

The strength of any employment case hinges on the quality and completeness of its evidence. Before discovery begins, proactive evidence gathering and preservation can shape the trajectory of a claim - bolstering credibility, supporting key legal theories, and safeguarding against spoliation defenses. This chapter explores best practices for collecting, preserving, and organizing evidence in employment litigation in New York and California, with guidance on dealing with electronically stored information (ESI), witness coordination, and employer obligations.

Spoliation: The destruction, alteration, or failure to preserve evidence that is relevant to litigation. Courts may impose sanctions ranging from monetary penalties to adverse inference instructions, where the jury is told they may assume the destroyed evidence would have been unfavorable to the party that destroyed it.

5.1 The Importance of Early Evidence Collection

Why It Matters

Early evidence collection serves multiple strategic purposes that can determine the success or failure of an employment case. First, it establishes a factual timeline that transforms abstract legal claims into concrete narratives supported by documentation. Without this chronological foundation, cases often devolve into credibility contests between competing stories.

Second, early collection confirms or challenges the client's narrative before committing to expensive litigation. Many clients have incomplete recollections or may inadvertently mischaracterize events. Documentary evidence either supports their account, requiring only minor adjustments to the legal strategy, or reveals significant discrepancies that demand a full case reassessment.

Third, comprehensive evidence gathering helps determine whether to proceed with litigation or pursue early settlement. Strong documentary evidence creates leverage in negotiations, while weak evidence may counsel toward prompt and early resolution before discovery expenses mount.

Finally, thorough preparation strengthens leverage during mediation and negotiations. Opposing counsel recognizes well-prepared cases and may offer more favorable settlements to avoid the costs and risks of trial.

Key Differences Between New York and California Evidence Laws

New York Approach: New York follows traditional common law evidence rules with some statutory modifications. The state has adopted a more restrictive approach to electronic evidence, requiring clear authentication and chain of custody documentation. New York courts are particularly strict about hearsay exceptions and require substantial foundation for business records.

California Approach: California has embraced more liberal evidence rules, particularly regarding electronic communications. The California Evidence Code Section 1552 creates a broader exception for business records, and courts are generally more accepting of social media evidence and electronic communications with minimal authentication requirements.

Practical Impact: In New York, practitioners must invest more time in evidence authentication and foundation work. In California, the focus shifts toward volume and comprehensiveness rather than technical perfection in evidence presentation.

Common Pitfalls and How to Avoid Them

Missing or Destroyed Evidence: The most devastating pitfall occurs when critical evidence disappears before preservation. This often happens when clients continue using devices normally after consulting counsel but before receiving preservation instructions.

Solution: Implement immediate preservation protocols during the initial client interview. Provide written instructions that clients can reference later, as verbal advice is often forgotten or misremembered.

Client Inadvertent Deletion: Clients routinely delete emails and texts as part of normal device maintenance, not understanding their evidentiary value.

Solution: Explain that seemingly irrelevant communications may provide crucial context. For example, a casual email about weekend plans might establish that the client was expected at work during a claimed medical leave, undermining the client's disability discrimination claims.

Failure to Preserve Devices or Cloud Accounts: Modern employment often involves multiple devices and cloud services that clients may not immediately consider.

Solution: Create comprehensive device and account inventories during intake. Include work devices, personal devices used for work, cloud storage accounts, and social media platforms where work-related communications occurred.

Over-reliance on Verbal Claims: Clients often focus on dramatic verbal exchanges while overlooking documentary evidence that contradicts their narrative.

Solution: Emphasize that employment litigation typically turns on documents rather than testimony. A single email contradicting the client's version of events can destroy an otherwise strong case.

5.2 Key Categories of Evidence in Employment Cases

1. Employment Documents

Offer Letters and Employment Contracts: These establish the foundational employment relationship and often contain crucial terms regarding compensation, duties, and termination procedures. In California, these documents frequently include mandatory arbitration clauses that may limit litigation options. New York has recently restricted mandatory arbitration in some employment contexts, creating different strategic considerations.

Example: An offer letter promising "permanent employment" may contradict an employer's later at-will termination defense, particularly in New York where such language can create implied contract rights.

Non-Disclosure Agreements (NDAs): Modern NDAs often contain broad confidentiality provisions that may impede evidence gathering. Recent legislative changes in both states have limited NDA enforceability in harassment cases. For instance effective November 17, 2023, New York amended its General Obligations Law § 5-336 to broaden restrictions on NDAs in settlement agreements related to workplace misconduct, while California's SB 331, effective since 2022, further limits the use of NDAs in employment-related agreements.

Job Descriptions: Often overlooked, these documents establish essential job functions crucial for disability accommodation claims and can reveal discriminatory language or requirements.

Employee Handbooks and Workplace Policies: These create contractual obligations and establish notice of prohibited conduct. Inconsistent policy enforcement often provides evidence of discriminatory treatment.

Disciplinary Records and Performance Evaluations: These documents frequently reveal pretext in discrimination cases. Sudden performance problems following protected activity often indicate retaliation.

Payroll Records and Benefits Documents: Essential for wage and hour claims, these records also establish employment status and benefits eligibility that may support discrimination claims.

2. Communications

Email Communications: The backbone of most modern employment cases. Email preservation requires attention to both sent and received messages, including those in trash or archive folders.

Legal Jargon - Authentication: The process of proving that evidence is genuine and reliable. For emails, this typically requires testimony about the sender's identity, the recipient's receipt, and the accuracy of the content.

Slack, Teams, and Other Platform Messages: These platforms create informal communication environments where discriminatory attitudes often surface. Unlike email, these platforms may have shorter retention periods and different preservation challenges.

Text Messages: Courts distinguish between screenshots and original data. Screenshots can be easily manipulated, while forensic extraction of original data provides stronger authentication. Both New York and California courts have admitted screenshot evidence, but original data extraction is always preferable.

Social Media Evidence: Relevant posts may establish the client's emotional state, provide timeline information, or contradict damage claims. However, privacy settings and authentication requirements create collection challenges.

Key Difference: California courts are more liberal in admitting social media evidence, while New York requires more substantial authentication and relevancy showings.

3. Timekeeping and Wage Data

Timecards and Punch Records: Essential for wage and hour claims, these records often reveal systematic violations affecting multiple employees, supporting class action claims.

Paystubs and Direct Deposit Records: These establish actual payment patterns and may reveal illegal deductions or misclassification issues.

Meal and Rest Break Records: Particularly important in California, where detailed break requirements create substantial liability exposure. California Labor Code Section 512 requires specific break timing and documentation that many employers fail to maintain properly.

Bonus, Commission, and Incentive Data: Often complex calculations that require expert analysis. These records may reveal discriminatory payment patterns or contract violations.

4. Medical and Accommodation Documentation

Doctor's Notes and Medical Records: Support disability discrimination and FMLA claims. HIPAA privacy protections create collection challenges that require careful attention to authorization procedures.

Accommodation Request Documentation: The interactive process under the Americans with Disabilities Act (ADA) creates extensive documentation requirements. Employers must engage in good faith discussions about reasonable accommodations, and this process generates crucial evidence.

Legal Jargon - Interactive Process: Under the ADA, employers must engage in an informal process with disabled employees to identify reasonable accommodations. This process must be conducted in good faith and documented appropriately.

HR Correspondence: Often contains candid assessments of accommodation feasibility and employee performance that may contradict later litigation positions.

5. Incident Reports and Internal Investigations

Internal Complaint Filings: Document the employee's efforts to resolve issues internally, supporting constructive notice arguments in harassment cases.

Investigative Reports: Often contain witness statements and factual findings that may support or undermine the employee's claims. These reports may be protected by attorney-client privilege if conducted by counsel.

Legal Jargon - Constructive Notice: Knowledge that an employer is presumed to have based on circumstances that would alert a reasonable employer to potential problems, even without direct notification.

6. Witness Identification and Coordination

Current Employees: Often reluctant to cooperate due to fear of retaliation. Early identification and careful approach strategies are essential.

Former Employees: May be more willing to cooperate but may have incomplete information or their own litigation interests.

Third-Party Witnesses: Clients, contractors, and vendors may provide crucial testimony without employment-related conflicts of interest.

5.3 Documenting the Timeline

Creating a comprehensive chronology early in case development serves multiple purposes: it identifies evidence gaps, reveals patterns of discriminatory conduct, and provides a framework for organizing discovery requests.

Essential Timeline Elements:

Hiring and Promotion Dates: Establish the employment relationship and career progression. Sudden changes in advancement patterns following protected activity often indicate discrimination.

Performance Benchmark Documentation: Regular performance reviews create objective baselines for assessing later criticism. Sudden negative evaluations following discrimination complaints often reveal pretext.

Incident Documentation: Each alleged discriminatory act must be precisely dated and contextualized within the broader employment relationship.

Complaint and Response Timeline: Document all internal complaints and employer responses. Delayed or inadequate responses may support hostile work environment claims.

Termination or Adverse Action Dating: Precise timing often reveals retaliatory motivation, particularly when adverse actions occur shortly after protected activity.

Post-Employment Communications: Settlement offers, reference requests, and continued contact may provide evidence of employer knowledge of wrongdoing.

Timeline Analysis Techniques: Look for patterns rather than isolated incidents. Discrimination cases often succeed based on cumulative evidence rather than single dramatic events. Identify gaps where documentation is missing and prioritize evidence gathering in those areas.

5.4 Preservation Obligations for Clients

Employee-Side Preservation Strategies

Immediate Preservation Instructions: Provide clients with written preservation instructions during the initial consultation. Verbal instructions are often forgotten or misunderstood, leading to inadvertent spoliation.

Device Inventory and Backup Procedures: Create comprehensive inventories of all devices and accounts where relevant information might exist. This includes work devices, personal devices used for work purposes, cloud storage accounts, and social media platforms.

Employer-Owned Device Limitations: Clients often misunderstand their rights regarding employer-owned devices. Generally, employees have no right to remove information from employer devices, but they may photograph or transcribe relevant information before returning devices.

Legal Jargon - Litigation Hold: A formal process requiring preservation of all potentially relevant documents and data when litigation is reasonably anticipated. Failure to implement proper litigation holds can result in spoliation sanctions.

Secure Storage Requirements: Instruct clients to backup relevant information to secure, non-shared locations. Cloud storage shared with employers or family members may create access or privilege issues.

Employer-Side Obligations

Triggered Preservation Duties: Employers must implement litigation holds when litigation is reasonably anticipated, which may occur before formal complaints are filed. EEOC charges, internal complaints, or attorney demand letters typically trigger preservation obligations.

Scope of Preservation: Employer obligations extend beyond obvious custodians to include HR personnel, IT staff, and any employees with relevant information. Over-inclusive preservation is generally safer than under-inclusive approaches.

Sanctions for Failure: Federal Rule of Civil Procedure 37(e) and state equivalents provide courts with broad sanctioning authority for spoliation.

Sanctions range from monetary penalties to adverse inference instructions that can be case-dispositive.

Key Difference Between States: California state courts apply more stringent spoliation standards than federal courts, while New York state courts generally follow federal precedents more closely.

5.5 Electronically Stored Information (ESI)

Modern employment litigation is dominated by electronic evidence, requiring sophisticated preservation and collection strategies.

ESI Sources and Challenges

Email Servers: Corporate email systems often have complex retention policies and multiple backup systems. Understanding these systems early prevents evidence loss and reduces collection costs.

Collaboration Platforms: Slack, Microsoft Teams, Zoom recordings, and project management tools create new categories of discoverable information with unique preservation challenges.

Mobile Device Evidence: Work-related communications on personal devices create complex privilege and privacy issues. California has stronger employee privacy protections than New York, affecting collection strategies.

Cloud Storage Complications: Multi-jurisdictional cloud storage may implicate international privacy laws and create complex authentication requirements.

ESI Preservation Letters

Timing and Recipients: Send preservation letters immediately upon case evaluation, before filing formal complaints. Recipients should include opposing counsel, HR departments, and IT personnel.

Scope Definition: Clearly define temporal scope, custodians, and data types. Over-broad requests may be ignored as unduly burdensome, while under-inclusive requests may miss crucial evidence.

Sample Preservation Language: "Please preserve all documents, electronically stored information, and tangible items relating to [employee name]'s employment, including but not limited to emails, text messages, instant messages, social media communications, performance evaluations, disciplinary records, and any recordings or surveillance footage from [date] to present."

Follow-Up and Compliance: Monitor compliance through discovery requests and depositions. Document any spoliation for potential sanctions motions.

5.6 Third-Party Evidence Collection

Subpoena Practice

Third-Party Subpoenas: When information exists outside your client's control, subpoenas provide formal collection mechanisms. Common targets include former coworkers, medical providers, and government agencies.

Subpoena Scope and Limitations: Balance comprehensiveness with proportionality requirements. Over-broad subpoenas invite objections and delay, while narrow subpoenas may miss relevant evidence.

Legal Jargon - Proportionality: A discovery standard requiring that the burden and expense of discovery be proportional to the case's significance and the parties' resources.

FOIA and Public Records Requests

Government Investigation Files: EEOC, OSHA, and state agency investigations often produce relevant evidence unavailable through traditional discovery.

Strategic Timing: File FOIA requests early, as government response times can be lengthy. Some agencies provide expedited processing for active litigation.

Privacy and Redaction Issues: Government agencies often redact personal information, potentially limiting their evidentiary value. Understand redaction policies before relying on government records.

5.7 Audio, Video, and Surveillance Evidence

Recording Laws and Admissibility

California Two-Party Consent Rule: All parties to a conversation must consent to recording. Violations constitute criminal conduct under Penal Code Section 632, and recordings are generally inadmissible.

Exceptions and Workarounds: California law provides limited exceptions for recording criminal conduct or where one party reasonably believes recording is necessary for self-protection.

New York One-Party Consent: Participants may record conversations without other parties' knowledge. However, civil admissibility still requires relevance and authentication.

Strategic Considerations: Even legal recordings may create ethical issues or damage client credibility. Consider whether recording benefits outweigh potential costs.

Employer Surveillance Systems

Video Surveillance: Workplace cameras are increasingly common and may capture discriminatory conduct or contradict witness testimony.

Computer Monitoring: Keystroke logging, screen capture, and internet monitoring create detailed employee activity records that may support or undermine various claims.

GPS and Location Tracking: Company vehicles and devices often include tracking capabilities that establish employee locations and activities.

Privacy Expectations: Employee privacy rights vary significantly between California and New York. California provides stronger privacy protections, while New York follows more traditional employer-friendly approaches.

5.8 Expert Witness Evidence Development

Economic Experts

Lost Wage Calculations: Complex calculations requiring consideration of promotion prospects, benefit values, and tax implications. Early expert involvement helps establish damage ranges for settlement discussions.

Future Earnings Analysis: Particularly important for younger plaintiffs with long career prospects. Experts consider industry trends, skill development, and career trajectory probabilities.

Pension and Retirement Benefit Losses: Often overlooked but potentially substantial, particularly for public sector employees with defined benefit plans.

Vocational Rehabilitation Experts

Career Impact Assessment: Evaluate how termination or discrimination affects long-term career prospects beyond immediate wage loss.

Reasonable Accommodation Analysis: In disability cases, experts may opine on accommodation feasibility and costs.

Mitigation of Damages: Assess plaintiff's efforts to minimize losses through job searches and retraining.

Psychological and Medical Experts

Emotional Distress Documentation: Quantify psychological harm from discrimination or harassment. Requires careful coordination with treating physicians to avoid privilege issues.

Causation Analysis: Distinguish workplace-related psychological harm from pre-existing conditions or other life stresses.

Treatment and Prognosis: Establish ongoing treatment needs and long-term psychological impact for damage calculations.

IT Forensics Experts

Data Recovery: Recover deleted files, emails, and other electronic evidence. May reveal attempts to conceal evidence.

Metadata Analysis: Electronic document metadata can establish creation dates, authorship, and editing history that may contradict witness testimony.

Tampering Detection: Identify alterations to electronic evidence that may support spoliation claims or undermine opposing evidence.

5.9 Case File Organization and Management

Digital Case Management Systems

Cloud-Based Platforms: Tools like Clio, MyCase, and CaseText provide secure, accessible case management with built-in document organization and calendaring features.

Security Considerations: Ensure compliance with attorney confidentiality requirements and client data protection obligations. Both New York and California have specific requirements for lawyer data security.

Collaboration Features: Modern case management systems facilitate multi-attorney collaboration and client access while maintaining security and privilege protections.

Document Organization Strategies

Chronological Organization: Arrange documents by date to support timeline development and pattern recognition.

Custodian-Based Filing: Organize by document source to facilitate privilege review and authentication preparation.

Issue-Based Categories: Group documents by legal theory (discrimination, retaliation, wage and hour) to support motion practice and trial preparation.

Discovery Production Preparation: Maintain production-ready document sets with appropriate privilege logs and confidentiality designations.

5.10 Privilege and Confidentiality Considerations

Attorney-Client Privilege

Client Communications: Protect all attorney-client communications from discovery. Be particularly careful with email communications that may be forwarded or copied to third parties.

Joint Defense Agreements: When representing multiple plaintiffs, establish clear privilege protections through formal agreements.

Waiver Risks: Inadvertent disclosure or third-party presence during communications may waive privilege. Implement protocols to prevent waiver.

Work Product Protection

Litigation Strategy: Protect attorney mental impressions, legal strategies, and case analysis from discovery.

Expert Communications: Draft expert communications carefully to maintain work product protection while complying with disclosure requirements.

Investigation Materials: Attorney-directed investigations may qualify for work product protection, but routine HR investigations typically do not.

Confidentiality Agreements and Protective Orders

Settlement Confidentiality: Many employment settlements include confidentiality provisions that may limit evidence use in related cases.

Discovery Protective Orders: Negotiate appropriate protections for sensitive business information while preserving access to relevant evidence.

Employee Privacy Rights: Balance discovery needs with employee privacy rights, particularly regarding medical information and personal communications.

5.11 Technology and Evidence Preservation Trends

Emerging Technologies

Artificial Intelligence Monitoring: Some employers use AI to monitor employee communications and behavior, creating new categories of potential evidence.

Biometric Data: Timekeeping systems increasingly use biometric data, raising privacy concerns and creating detailed work pattern evidence.

Social Media Analytics: Employers may monitor employee social media activity, creating potential evidence of discriminatory motivation or employee conduct.

Cloud Computing Challenges

Multi-Jurisdictional Data Storage: Cloud data may be stored across multiple jurisdictions with varying privacy laws and discovery obligations.

Third-Party Provider Cooperation: Cloud service providers may resist discovery requests, requiring subpoenas and potentially lengthy litigation to obtain evidence.

Data Retention Variations: Different cloud services have varying retention periods and deletion policies that may affect evidence availability.

5.12 Cost-Benefit Analysis in Evidence Collection

Resource Allocation Strategies

Early Case Assessment: Conduct preliminary evidence review to identify strong and weak case elements before investing in expensive collection efforts.

Proportional Discovery: Focus resources on evidence most likely to impact case outcome rather than comprehensive collection of marginally relevant materials.

Settlement Impact: Consider how evidence collection efforts may affect settlement negotiations and timing.

Cost Control Measures

Phased Discovery: Implement discovery in phases, beginning with most accessible and relevant evidence before pursuing expensive or complex collection efforts.

Technology-Assisted Review: Use automated tools to reduce manual document review costs in large-document cases.

Expert Timing: Engage experts at optimal times to minimize costs while maximizing impact on case development and settlement negotiations.

5.13 Conclusion

Effective evidence gathering is a proactive, ongoing process that requires strategic thinking, technical knowledge, and careful attention to legal requirements. The differences between New York and California law create varying challenges and opportunities that must be considered from case inception through resolution.

Success in employment litigation increasingly depends on mastering electronic evidence collection while maintaining traditional litigation skills. The investment in proper evidence collection early in case development typically pays dividends throughout the litigation process, whether the case resolves through settlement or proceeds to trial.

What is preserved early can shape negotiations, inform case strategy, and withstand scrutiny in court. Whether representing plaintiffs seeking justice or defendants managing exposure, controlling the narrative begins with controlling the facts through comprehensive, strategic evidence collection.

The next chapter will explore legal research and strategy development, examining how to interpret and leverage the evidence gathered through the frameworks established in this chapter. We will focus on transforming raw evidence into compelling legal arguments that support favorable case outcomes.

6

Legal Research and Strategic Development in Employment Law

Once the facts are gathered and the preliminary case theory is formed, the next step is to refine the legal arguments. This involves researching applicable laws, interpreting judicial precedent, identifying procedural considerations, and developing a strategic roadmap from complaint to resolution. Employment cases in New York and California are shaped not only by statutes but by an evolving body of case law that informs how judges and juries evaluate claims.

This chapter explores how to conduct focused legal research and build strategic frameworks tailored to the jurisdiction, forum, and facts of the case.

6.1 Mapping Claims to Legal Theories

Understanding Statutory Causes of Action

After identifying the client's grievance, the critical first step is mapping it to one or more legal causes of action. This process requires understanding the nuanced differences between federal, state, and local laws, each offering distinct advantages and limitations.

Discrimination Claims

The landscape of discrimination law varies significantly between jurisdictions:

Title VII (Federal) applies to employers with 15 or more employees and covers discrimination based on race, color, religion, sex, or national origin. The statute requires exhaustion of administrative remedies through the EEOC, with strict filing deadlines of 180 days (300 days in states with approved agencies). Title VII's remedies are capped, with punitive and compensatory damages limited based on employer size - ranging from $50,000 for employers with 15-100 employees to $300,000 for employers with more than 500 employees.

California's Fair Employment and Housing Act (FEHA) provides broader protections than Title VII, covering employers with five or more employees and including additional protected categories such as sexual orientation, gender identity, military status, and genetic information. FEHA allows for unlimited compensatory and punitive damages, making it particularly attractive for plaintiffs. The statute also permits individual liability for supervisors and managers who engage in discriminatory conduct.

New York Human Rights Law (NYHRL) underwent significant amendments in 2019, expanding protections and lowering the burden of proof for plaintiffs. The law now covers all employers regardless of size for sexual harassment claims and prohibits discrimination in ways that were previously permitted under federal law. Unlike Title VII, NYHRL does not cap damages and allows for attorney's fees in successful cases.

Example: Consider Maria, a pregnant employee terminated after requesting maternity leave. Under Title VII's Pregnancy Discrimination Act, she must prove the termination was because of her pregnancy. Under FEHA, California's broader interpretation might make this easier to establish, particularly given California's strong public policy favoring pregnancy accommodation. Under NYHRL, the recent amendments create an even more favorable landscape, requiring only that pregnancy be "a motivating factor" rather than the sole cause of termination.

Retaliation Claims

Retaliation protection varies dramatically across jurisdictions:

California Labor Code Section 1102.5 protects employees who report violations of law to government agencies or refuse to participate in illegal activities. This statute is broadly construed and includes protection for internal complaints about legal violations. The law covers any employee of any employer and provides for reinstatement, back pay, and attorney's fees.

New York Labor Law Section 215 specifically protects employees who file wage and hour complaints or testify in related proceedings. However, New York's general whistleblower protections are found in different statutes depending on the type of complaint, creating a more complex analytical framework.

Federal retaliation protections exist under various statutes (Title VII, FLSA, Sarbanes-Oxley) but often require proof that the protected activity was a "but-for" cause of the adverse action, a higher standard than many state laws require.

Harassment Claims

The legal framework for harassment claims has evolved significantly, particularly in California and New York:

FEHA requires that harassment be "severe or pervasive" but California courts have been increasingly willing to find harassment actionable even based on single incidents if sufficiently severe. The statute also creates individual liability for harassers and requires employers to take reasonable steps to prevent harassment.

NYCHRL adopted a more plaintiff-friendly standard in its 2019 amendments, requiring only that harassment be "more than petty slights or trivial inconveniences." This represents a significant departure from the federal "severe or pervasive" standard and makes harassment claims substantially easier to pursue in New York.

Wage Violations

Wage and hour law presents complex overlapping federal and state requirements:

Fair Labor Standards Act (FLSA) establishes minimum wage and overtime requirements but allows states to provide greater protections. The statute includes a two or three-year statute of limitations (depending on willfulness) and provides for liquidated damages equal to the unpaid wages.

California Labor Code provides extensive wage protections including meal and rest break requirements, waiting time penalties for final pay delays, and Private Attorney General Act (PAGA) enforcement mechanisms. California's "piece rate" requirements, daily overtime provisions, and strict timekeeping requirements often result in larger recoveries than federal law alone.

New York Labor Law (NYLL) includes broad overtime protections and significant penalty provisions. The state's recent amendments expanded overtime eligibility and increased penalties for violations, making New York wage claims increasingly valuable.

Contract-Based Claims

Employment contract claims require careful analysis of the employment relationship and applicable law:

Breach of Contract claims depend heavily on whether the employment is at-will or governed by an express contract. In California, the covenant of good faith and fair dealing is implied in all contracts, providing additional protection for employees. New York recognizes the covenant more narrowly, typically requiring an express contractual relationship.

Implied Contract theories vary significantly between jurisdictions. California courts are more willing to find implied contracts based on personnel manuals, verbal assurances, or established practices. New York courts require clearer evidence of mutual intent to modify the at-will relationship.

Tort-Based Theories

Courts approach employment torts with varying degrees of skepticism:

Intentional Infliction of Emotional Distress (IIED) requires conduct that is "extreme and outrageous" and causes severe emotional distress. California courts have been somewhat more receptive to IIED claims in employment contexts, particularly when combined with discrimination or harassment. New York courts typically require truly shocking conduct that goes beyond typical workplace conflicts.

Defamation and Compelled Self-Defamation theories arise when employees are forced to disclose embarrassing information to prospective employers. California recognizes compelled self-defamation more readily than many jurisdictions, while New York requires clear evidence that the employer intended to force such disclosure.

Important Practice Note: Courts are often reluctant to expand employment cases into tort law unless the facts clearly warrant it. Judges frequently dismiss tort claims as duplicative of statutory remedies or insufficiently egregious for tort liability.

6.2 Key Research Tools and Resources

Statutory Research Strategies

California Resources

Westlaw's California materials and Continuing Education of the Bar (CEB) publications provide comprehensive coverage of California employment law. The California Labor Code is frequently amended, requiring careful attention to effective dates and transitional provisions. Government Code Section 12900 et seq. (FEHA) should be read in conjunction with regulations promulgated by the California Civil Rights Department (formerly the Department of Fair Employment and Housing).

Key California Research Tip: Always check for recent amendments, as California's legislature frequently updates employment laws. The state's "urgency" provisions mean some changes take effect immediately upon signing rather than on January 1st.

New York Resources

McKinney's Consolidated Laws provides annotated versions of New York employment statutes. The New York Labor Law and Executive Law Section 290 (NYHRL) form the backbone of state employment protections. Pay particular attention to local ordinances, as New York City's Human Rights Law often provides broader protections than state law.

Federal Resources

Cornell Legal Information Institute (LII) provides free access to federal statutes and regulations. However, for comprehensive research, subscription services like Westlaw or Lexis remain essential for case law analysis and ensuring current good law.

Case Law and Judicial Trends

Verification and Currency

Always use Westlaw KeyCite or Lexis Shepard's to verify that cases remain good law. Employment law evolves rapidly, and yesterday's controlling precedent may be today's overruled decision.

Local Practice Guides

California Practice Guide: Employment Litigation (Continuing Education of the Bar) provides practical insights into how California courts approach common employment issues. The guide includes forms, strategic considerations, and recent developments.

Sattler's Employment Discrimination in New York offers similar guidance for New York practitioners, with particular attention to the interplay between state, federal, and local laws.

Appellate Decisions and Trends

State court websites increasingly provide searchable databases of recent decisions. Federal circuit courts of appeal publish opinions that may signal future Supreme Court review or emerging legal trends.

Strategic Research Approach: Focus on decisions from the specific appellate district or federal circuit where your case will be heard. A favorable decision from the California Court of Appeal's Second Appellate District may not be persuasive to judges in the Ninth Circuit or New York's Second Department.

Agency Guidance and Interpretive Resources

EEOC Materials

EEOC enforcement manuals provide detailed guidance on federal employment laws. Opinion letters, while not binding, offer insight into the Commission's interpretation of ambiguous statutory provisions. The EEOC's recent guidance on artificial intelligence in hiring and workplace harassment investigations reflects evolving enforcement priorities.

California Civil Rights Department (CRD)

The CRD (formerly DFEH) publishes regulations, enforcement guidance, and settlement agreements that illuminate California's approach to employment law. The department's recent focus on pay equity and harassment prevention provides valuable insight into enforcement trends.

New York State Division of Human Rights

NYS Division of Human Rights decisions and regulations offer guidance on state law interpretation. The Division's administrative law judges' decisions, while not binding on courts, provide insight into how state investigators and hearing officers analyze discrimination claims.

6.3 Choosing the Right Forum

State vs. Federal Court Considerations

The choice between state and federal court involves multiple strategic considerations beyond simple jurisdictional requirements.

Advantages of State Court

California and New York state courts are generally more favorable to employee plaintiffs than federal courts. State court juries in urban areas often demonstrate greater sympathy for employment claims, and state judges are typically more familiar with complex state employment statutes.

California state courts have developed extensive case law interpreting FEHA and the Labor Code in employee-friendly ways. State court discovery rules may be more liberal, and the availability of PAGA claims in state court provides unique strategic advantages.

New York state courts, particularly in New York City, often feature juries with diverse employment experiences who may be more sympathetic to workplace discrimination claims. The state's recent statutory amendments create a more favorable legal landscape than federal alternatives.

Advantages of Federal Court

Federal courts offer more predictable scheduling, often moving cases to trial more quickly than overburdened state court systems. Federal judges may be more willing to grant summary judgment on weak claims, benefiting defendants but potentially eliminating frivolous aspects of plaintiff cases.

Diversity jurisdiction requires complete diversity of citizenship and an amount in controversy exceeding $75,000. This threshold is often easily met in employment cases given the potential for emotional distress damages, punitive damages, and attorney's fees.

Removal Issues and Strategy

Defense Removal Strategy

Defense counsel frequently seek removal to federal court when state law claims appear vulnerable or when federal court offers procedural advantages. Common removal grounds include:

Federal Question Jurisdiction exists when a federal cause of action is pleaded. However, plaintiffs can sometimes avoid removal by pleading only state law claims, even when federal claims might be available.

Diversity Jurisdiction requires that no plaintiff share citizenship with any defendant and that the amount in controversy exceed $75,000. Defendants must remove within 30 days of service under 28 U.S.C. Section 1446, and all defendants must consent to removal.

Strategic Removal Considerations: Defense counsel may prefer federal court for its perceived neutrality and efficiency, while plaintiff counsel often prefer state court for more favorable law and potentially sympathetic juries.

Defeating Removal

Plaintiff counsel can prevent removal by:

- Naming local defendants to destroy diversity
- Pleading damages below the federal threshold (though this may limit recovery)
- Including claims that are exclusively state law matters
- Ensuring prompt service on all defendants to limit removal timing

6.4 Evaluating Legal Precedent

Hierarchical Analysis of Authority

When analyzing precedent, understand the hierarchical structure of legal authority:

Binding Authority includes decisions from higher courts in the same jurisdiction. A California Supreme Court decision binds all California state courts, while a Ninth Circuit decision binds federal district courts within the circuit.

Persuasive Authority includes decisions from other jurisdictions, lower courts, or parallel courts. These decisions may influence judicial thinking but do not compel particular outcomes.

Key Analytical Framework

Recent Decisions Priority

Focus on recent decisions from the relevant appellate district or federal circuit. Employment law evolves rapidly, and older decisions may not reflect current legal standards. For example, California's 2018 amendment to Government Code Section 12964.5 significantly changed workplace harassment law, making pre-2019 decisions less reliable guides.

Issue-Specific Research

Look for interpretive guidance on key issues such as:

Burden Shifting Analysis: The McDonnell Douglas framework varies in application across jurisdictions. California courts may be more willing to find pretext, while federal courts often require stronger evidence of discriminatory intent.

Retaliation Causation Standards: The Supreme Court's decision in *University of Texas Southwestern Medical Center v. Nassar*, 570 U.S. 338, 133 S. Ct. 2517, 186 L. Ed. 2d 503 (2013), established a "but-for" causation standard for federal retaliation claims, but many state laws use more plaintiff-friendly standards.

Summary Judgment Standards: California and New York courts are often less willing to grant summary judgment in employment cases than federal courts, reflecting different approaches to factual disputes and credibility determinations.

Distinguishing Unfavorable Cases

When confronting adverse precedent, consider multiple distinguishing factors:

Factual Distinctions: Highlight material factual differences between your case and unfavorable precedent. Employment cases are highly fact-specific, and seemingly minor differences may support different legal outcomes.

Procedural Posture: A case decided on summary judgment may not control when additional discovery has revealed new facts. Similarly, decisions on motions to dismiss may not bind courts considering motions for summary judgment.

Jurisdictional Differences: Federal circuit splits create opportunities to argue for more favorable interpretations. State law differences may make out-of-state decisions less persuasive.

Example: In defending against a motion for summary judgment on a retaliation claim, distinguish cases where the temporal proximity between protected activity and adverse action was greater, where the plaintiff had performance issues, or where the employer presented stronger business justifications.

6.5 Strategic Use of the Burden-Shifting Framework

The McDonnell Douglas Test in Practice

Most discrimination and retaliation claims follow the McDonnell Douglas burden-shifting framework, but its application varies significantly across jurisdictions and factual contexts.

Prima Facie Case Requirements

The employee must establish:

1. Membership in a protected class (for discrimination) or engagement in protected activity (for retaliation)
2. Satisfactory job performance
3. Adverse employment action
4. Circumstances suggesting discrimination or retaliation

Strategic Considerations for Prima Facie Cases

Protected Class Membership: This element is usually straightforward for characteristics like race or gender but may require more development for less obvious protected activities or classes.

Job Performance: Document positive performance reviews, lack of discipline, or comparative performance data. Be prepared to address any performance issues honestly while contextualizing them within the discriminatory environment.

Adverse Employment Action: Courts increasingly recognize that adverse actions extend beyond termination to include changes in duties, exclusion from meetings, or creation of hostile work environments.

Causation and Circumstances: Temporal proximity between protected activity and adverse action creates an inference of retaliation, but other circumstantial evidence may be necessary when timing is less compelling.

Employer's Burden of Production

The employer must articulate a legitimate, non-discriminatory reason for the adverse action. This burden is relatively light - the employer need not prove the reason was actually motivating, only that it is legitimate and could explain the action.

Common Employer Justifications:

- Performance deficiencies
- Violation of company policies
- Economic necessity/reorganization
- Personality conflicts or poor cultural fit
- Attendance or punctuality issues

Employee's Pretext Showing

The employee must demonstrate that the employer's stated reason is pretextual - either false or not the actual motivation for the adverse action.

Effective Pretext Arguments:

Pattern-Based Evidence: Demonstrate systematic discrimination through statistical analysis, comparative treatment of similarly situated employees, or evidence of broader discriminatory practices.

Timing and Sequence: Connect the chronology of events to show discriminatory motive. Document how the employer's attitude or treatment changed after learning of protected characteristics or activities.

Comparative Evidence: Identify similarly situated employees outside the protected class who received more favorable treatment under comparable circumstances. Be specific about job duties, performance levels, and disciplinary history.

Shifting Explanations: Document instances where the employer's justification for adverse action changed over time or varied between decision-makers.

Example: Sarah, an African American sales manager, was terminated allegedly for missing sales targets. Pretext evidence might include:

- White colleagues with similar or worse performance who were not terminated
- Performance improvement plans offered to others but not Sarah
- Derogatory comments about diversity initiatives by her supervisor
- The company's history of discrimination settlements
- Changes in the supervisor's attitude after Sarah complained about discriminatory comments

Advanced Strategic Considerations

Mixed Motive Analysis: In cases involving both legitimate and illegitimate motivations, focus on whether discrimination was a motivating factor rather than the sole cause. California and New York law often provide more favorable mixed-motive standards than federal law.

Individual vs. Institutional Discrimination: Consider whether to frame the case as individual bias by specific managers or systemic institutional discrimination. Each approach has different evidentiary requirements and strategic implications.

6.6 Early Strategic Decisions

Demand Letter Considerations

The decision whether to send a demand letter requires careful strategic analysis:

Advantages of Demand Letters:

- May facilitate early settlement without litigation costs
- Demonstrates good faith effort to resolve disputes
- May trigger additional penalties (California waiting time penalties)
- Provides opportunity to test employer's response and potential defenses

Risks of Demand Letters:

- May prompt employer to develop stronger defenses
- Could result in preemptive lawsuit by employer
- May limit surprise in subsequent litigation
- Could affect statute of limitations calculations

California-Specific Considerations: In wage cases, a demand letter may trigger Labor Code Section 203 waiting time penalties, potentially doubling the employee's recovery. However, the demand must be proper and specific to invoke these penalties.

New York Considerations: Demand letters may be particularly effective given New York's strong public policy against employment discrimination and the availability of attorney's fees in successful cases.

Administrative Exhaustion Requirements

EEOC Requirements: Title VII, ADA, and ADEA claims require filing charges with the EEOC within 180 days (300 days in states with approved agencies). The EEOC must issue a right-to-sue letter before federal court litigation can commence.

State Agency Requirements:

- California requires DFEH complaints for FEHA claims, though recent amendments allow for immediate court filing in some harassment cases
- New York requires complaints to the Division of Human Rights for NYHRL claims, with some exceptions

Strategic Timing: Consider whether administrative proceedings will strengthen or weaken your case. Agency investigations may uncover additional evidence but could also provide employers opportunities to develop stronger defenses.

Individual vs. Class/Representative Actions

PAGA Actions in California: Private Attorney General Act claims allow individual employees to seek penalties on behalf of the state for Labor Code violations. PAGA actions cannot be compelled to arbitration and often result in significant settlements.

Class Action Considerations: Rule 23 class actions require:

- Numerosity (though no specific number required)
- Commonality of legal or factual issues
- Typicality of representative claims
- Adequacy of representation

New York Class Actions: Rule 23 class actions may be particularly effective for wage violations under NYLL, given the statute's penalty provisions and attorney's fee awards.

Strategic Analysis: Evaluate whether individual recovery potential justifies class action complications, or whether class treatment provides leverage for settlement.

Defendant Selection Strategy

Individual Liability:

- FEHA allows individual liability for supervisors, managers, and co-workers who engage in discrimination or harassment

- NYCHRL similarly permits individual liability for discriminatory conduct
- Federal law generally does not impose individual liability under Title VII

Corporate Structure Considerations: Consider naming parent companies, subsidiaries, or related entities to increase recovery potential and settlement leverage. Analyze corporate relationships, common ownership, and operational integration.

Strategic Implications: Additional defendants increase discovery costs but may provide additional settlement pressure and recovery options.

6.7 Preemption and Exclusive Remedies

Federal Preemption Doctrines

ERISA Preemption: The Employee Retirement Income Security Act preempts state law claims relating to employee benefit plans. However, the preemption analysis is complex and fact-specific.

Complete Preemption: ERISA completely preempts state law claims that relate to covered employee benefit plans, requiring removal to federal court even when only state claims are pleaded.

Conflict Preemption: State laws that conflict with ERISA's regulatory scheme may be preempted even if they don't directly regulate benefit plans.

Savings Clause: ERISA's savings clause preserves state insurance regulation, creating exceptions to preemption for certain state laws.

LMRA Preemption: The Labor Management Relations Act preempts state law claims that require interpretation of collective bargaining agreements. However, state law claims may survive if they can be resolved without interpreting the CBA.

Workers' Compensation Exclusivity

Workers' compensation exclusivity doctrines bar tort claims for workplace injuries but include exceptions for:

Intentional Conduct: Employers may lose exclusivity protection for deliberate infliction of harm or conduct substantially certain to cause injury.

Public Policy Exceptions: Some states recognize exceptions when employers terminate employees for filing workers' compensation claims or exercising other protected rights.

Dual Capacity Doctrine: Employers may face liability in capacities other than as employers (e.g., as product manufacturers).

Strategic Considerations: Carefully analyze whether workplace injuries trigger exclusivity doctrines or whether exceptions apply to preserve tort remedies.

6.8 Anticipating Employer Defenses

Common Defense Strategies

Legitimate Business Reasons: Employers typically assert non-discriminatory reasons for adverse actions:

- Performance deficiencies supported by documentation
- Policy violations with consistent enforcement
- Economic necessities requiring workforce reductions
- Restructuring or reorganization requirements

Counter-Strategy: Develop evidence showing these reasons are pretextual, inconsistently applied, or developed post hoc to justify discriminatory decisions.

Administrative Exhaustion Failures: Employers often challenge whether plaintiffs properly exhausted administrative remedies:

- Untimely EEOC charges
- Failure to include all defendants in administrative complaints
- Scope limitations on right-to-sue letters

Counter-Strategy: Research exceptions to exhaustion requirements, such as futility or continuing violations doctrines.

Failure to Mitigate Damages: Employers argue that employees failed to minimize damages through reasonable job search efforts.

Counter-Strategy: Document job search activities, applications submitted, and obstacles to mitigation such as employer retaliation or market conditions.

After-Acquired Evidence: Employers may discover employee misconduct that would have justified termination had it been known earlier.

Counter-Strategy: Argue that after-acquired evidence should not bar liability but may only limit remedies, and challenge the severity or relevance of alleged misconduct.

Procedural Defense Challenges

Jurisdiction and Venue: Employers may challenge court jurisdiction or argue for venue transfer.

Standing: Particularly in representative actions, employers may challenge whether plaintiffs have standing to represent others.

Statute of Limitations: Employment statutes have varying limitation periods that may bar some claims.

Counter-Strategies: Develop continuing violation theories, equitable tolling arguments, or discovery rule applications to overcome limitations defenses.

6.9 Drafting a Strategic Legal Roadmap

Comprehensive Case Planning

Claims Assessment Matrix: Develop a systematic approach to evaluate potential claims:

Strength of Legal Theory: Rate each potential claim based on applicable law and supporting facts. Consider whether controlling precedent supports or undermines each theory.

Evidentiary Support: Assess available evidence for each claim and identify gaps requiring additional investigation or discovery.

Damages Potential: Estimate potential recovery for each claim type, considering statutory damages, emotional distress, punitive damages, and attorney's fees.

Strategic Value: Consider how each claim contributes to overall case leverage, settlement discussions, and trial presentation.

Jurisdiction and Venue Analysis

Federal vs. State Court: Based on research into judicial tendencies, jury pools, and applicable law, determine optimal forum selection.

Geographic Considerations: Within chosen court system, analyze venue options for strategic advantages in jury composition, judicial assignment, or procedural rules.

Removal Planning: If filing in state court, anticipate removal attempts and plan strategies to defeat or exploit removal.

Discovery Strategy Development

Essential Evidence Identification: Catalog documents, communications, and testimony necessary to prove each claim and anticipate employer defenses.

Timing Considerations: Plan discovery sequence to build momentum, preserve evidence, and maximize settlement leverage.

Cost-Benefit Analysis: Balance discovery costs against potential recovery and settlement value.

Settlement Analysis Framework

Valuation Methodology: Develop systematic approach to case valuation considering:

- Economic damages (back pay, front pay, benefits)
- Non-economic damages (emotional distress, reputation harm)
- Punitive damages potential
- Attorney's fees and costs

- Litigation risks and uncertainties

Settlement Timing: Identify optimal settlement windows based on discovery milestones, motion practice, and trial preparation costs.

Leverage Assessment: Understand what motivates opposing parties and how to maximize settlement pressure through strategic case development.

Risk Assessment and Contingency Planning

Client-Related Challenges: Identify potential client credibility issues, unrealistic expectations, or cooperation problems that could affect case outcomes.

Factual Vulnerabilities: Acknowledge weaknesses in facts or evidence that could undermine case strength or settlement value.

Procedural Risks: Anticipate motion practice, discovery disputes, or other procedural challenges that could affect case timeline or outcomes.

Financial Considerations: Plan for litigation costs, potential fee-shifting implications, and client financial constraints that might affect case strategy.

6.10 Implementation and Evolution of Strategy

Dynamic Strategy Management

Regular Strategy Reviews: Schedule periodic case assessment meetings to evaluate how new information, legal developments, or changed circumstances affect original strategic decisions.

Milestone-Based Adjustments: Use key case events (discovery responses, depositions, motion rulings) as opportunities to reassess and refine strategy.

Opposition Response Analysis: Monitor opposing counsel's tactics and adjust strategy based on their apparent weaknesses, strengths, or preferences.

Documentation and Communication

Strategy Memoranda: Create written strategy documents that can be updated and shared with clients, co-counsel, or referring attorneys.

Client Communication: Regularly update clients on strategic developments, risks, and opportunities while managing expectations about outcomes and timelines.

Team Coordination: In cases involving multiple attorneys or support staff, ensure all team members understand current strategy and their roles in implementation.

6.11 Conclusion

Effective legal research and strategic development transform reactive lawyering into proactive case-building. Understanding the nuanced differences between federal, state, and local employment laws enables practitioners to select optimal legal theories and forums for their clients' claims. Comprehensive research into applicable statutes, case law, and agency guidance provides the foundation for strategic decision-making throughout the litigation process.

The key to successful employment law practice lies in recognizing that strategy is not static - it must evolve in response to new facts, legal developments, and opposing counsel's tactics. By developing systematic approaches to case evaluation, forum selection, and strategic planning, practitioners can maximize their clients' recovery potential while efficiently managing litigation risks and costs.

Knowing which laws apply, how judges interpret them, and what defenses to expect provides crucial advantages in negotiations, court proceedings, and arbitration. The investment in thorough legal research and strategic planning during the early stages of case development pays dividends throughout the litigation process, leading to better outcomes for clients and more efficient case resolution.

In Chapter 7, we'll explore how to translate your legal strategy into a well-crafted complaint, including jurisdictional pleading requirements, forum considerations, and techniques for building momentum from the first filing.

7

Drafting and Filing Employment Complaints

A well-drafted complaint is the cornerstone of a successful employment lawsuit. It not only initiates litigation but also sets the tone, shapes the narrative, and influences the court's first impression. In employment cases - where credibility, emotion, and statutory nuance often collide - precision, clarity, and strategic foresight are essential.

This chapter walks you through the structure, content, and procedural requirements for drafting and filing complaints in New York and California, with attention to federal versus state court distinctions, claim integration, and preserving leverage.

7.1 Strategic Role of the Complaint

The complaint serves several core purposes extending just starting a lawsuit. Understanding these functions helps attorneys craft more effective pleadings that serve both immediate procedural needs and long-term strategic goals.

Primary Functions:

- **Notice Function**: Formally notifies the defendant of the specific claims against them, fulfilling due process requirements
- **Procedural Trigger**: Initiates the lawsuit and triggers critical procedural timelines, including statutes of limitations and discovery deadlines
- **Issue Framing**: Establishes the legal and factual framework that will guide the entire litigation
- **Leverage Creation**: Signals to the opposing party the seriousness and strength of the case, potentially influencing settlement negotiations
- **Motion Defense**: Provides the foundation for surviving early dismissal motions

The Dual Nature of Effective Complaints

A persuasive complaint strikes a delicate balance between legal sufficiency and compelling storytelling. Legal sufficiency means meeting all procedural requirements and pleading standards to survive motions to dismiss. Compelling storytelling involves presenting facts in a way that builds sympathy for the plaintiff and demonstrates clear wrongdoing by the defendant.

Example of Weak vs. Strong Opening:

Weak: "Plaintiff was employed by Defendant from 2020 to 2023 and was terminated."

Strong: "For three years, Plaintiff Maria Rodriguez excelled as Defendant's top-performing sales manager, consistently exceeding quotas and mentoring junior staff. That all changed when she reported her supervisor's pattern of sexual harassment to HR - within two weeks, Rodriguez found herself terminated for allegedly 'failing to meet performance standards' that she had surpassed for years."

7.2 Choosing the Right Venue: Strategic Forum Selection

The choice between state and federal court can significantly impact case outcomes, making venue selection one of the most critical strategic decisions in employment litigation.

State Court vs. Federal Court Analysis

California State Court Advantages:

- **FEHA Protection**: The Fair Employment and Housing Act (FEHA) provides broader protections than federal law in many areas
- **Removal Avoidance**: Cases filed under purely state law claims are harder for defendants to remove to federal court
- **Jury Composition**: State court juries may be more employee-friendly, particularly in certain counties
- **Discovery Rules**: California state court discovery rules can be more favorable for plaintiffs in certain circumstances
- **Damage Awards**: State courts may be more generous with emotional distress and punitive damages

New York State Court Advantages:

- **Employee-Friendly Precedent**: New York state courts have developed extensive employee-friendly case law
- **NYCHRL Benefits**: New York City Human Rights Law provides even broader protections than state and federal law
- **Procedural Benefits**: Notice pleading standards under CPLR 3013 are often more forgiving than federal Twombly/Iqbal standards
- **Local Knowledge**: State judges may have more familiarity with local employment practices and norms

Federal Court Considerations:

Federal court becomes mandatory when:

- **Federal Claims**: You plead federal causes of action such as Title VII, Americans with Disabilities Act (ADA), Family and Medical Leave Act (FMLA), or Fair Labor Standards Act (FLSA)
- **Diversity Jurisdiction**: Complete diversity exists between parties

and the amount in controversy exceeds $75,000

Key Differences in Practice:

Discovery Scope: Federal courts often have more restrictive discovery rules, while state courts may allow broader fact-finding.

Motion Practice: Federal courts apply stricter pleading standards under Twombly and Iqbal, requiring "plausible" claims rather than mere notice.

Case Management: Federal courts typically move faster due to stricter case management rules and scheduling orders.

Removal Considerations and Prevention Strategies

Understanding Removal: Removal allows defendants to transfer a case from state court to federal court if federal jurisdiction exists. This is a powerful defense tool that can significantly alter case dynamics.

Prevention Strategies:

- **Pure State Claims**: Plead only state-law claims when possible to avoid federal question jurisdiction
- **Amount Limitation**: In diversity cases, consider limiting damages to stay below the $75,000 threshold (though this may not be practical in serious cases)
- **Remand Preparation**: Be prepared to file a motion to remand immediately if removal occurs
- **Strategic Pleading**: Avoid language that suggests federal claims or constitutional violations

Example of Removal-Resistant Pleading: Instead of alleging "Defendant violated Plaintiff's civil rights," specify "Defendant violated California Government Code Section 12940 by discriminating against Plaintiff based on her pregnancy."

7.3 Jurisdiction and Venue Allegations: Building the Foundation

Proper jurisdictional and venue allegations are essential but often overlooked elements that can make or break a case.

Subject Matter Jurisdiction

State Court Jurisdiction:

- **General Jurisdiction**: State courts have broad authority to hear most employment disputes
- **Specific Statutes**: Must cite specific state employment statutes (e.g., FEHA, NYHRL) that grant jurisdiction

Federal Court Jurisdiction:

- **Federal Question**: Cases arising under federal employment laws (Title VII, ADA, FMLA)
- **Diversity Jurisdiction**: Complete diversity of citizenship plus amount in controversy exceeding $75,000

Personal Jurisdiction Requirements

Personal jurisdiction ensures the court has authority over the defendant. In employment cases, this typically involves:

Individual Defendants: Must show sufficient contacts with the forum state, usually satisfied by employment within the state

Corporate Defendants: May be based on:

- Principal place of business
- State of incorporation
- Conducting substantial business in the forum state
- Employing workers in the forum state

Venue Specifications by Jurisdiction

California Venue Rules (CCP § 395):

- County where contract was made or performed (employment

relationship)

- County where defendant resides or has principal place of business
- County where wrongful acts occurred

New York Venue Rules (CPLR 503):

- County where plaintiff resides at time of filing
- County where defendant resides or has principal place of business
- County where a substantial part of events occurred

Example Venue Allegation: "Venue is proper in Los Angeles County pursuant to Code of Civil Procedure Section 395 as Defendant maintains its headquarters in Los Angeles County, Plaintiff performed work in Los Angeles County, and the discriminatory acts alleged herein occurred in Los Angeles County."

7.4 Structuring the Complaint: Building Block Approach

1. Caption Requirements

The caption provides essential case identification and must include:

Complete Party Information:

- Full legal names (not "doing business as" names unless specifically relevant)
- Individual capacity vs. official capacity designations
- Corporate designations (Inc., LLC, etc.)

Court Identification:

- Specific court name and jurisdiction
- Department or division if required
- Case number field (left blank for initial filing)

Document Title Examples:

- "Complaint for Damages and Injunctive Relief"
- "Verified Complaint for Wrongful Termination and Discrimination"
- "Class Action Complaint for Wage and Hour Violations"

Jury Trial Demand: Can be included in caption or as separate section. Example: "DEMAND FOR JURY TRIAL" prominently displayed.

2. Introduction or Preliminary Statement

While optional, a strong introduction frames the entire case and should be used strategically.

Effective Introduction Elements:

- **Human Element**: Focus on the plaintiff as a person, not just an employee
- **Clear Wrongdoing**: Establish obvious unfairness or illegality
- **Stakes**: Convey why this case matters
- **Theme**: Establish recurring themes like betrayal, retaliation, or discrimination

Sample Introduction: "This case involves the systematic harassment and ultimate termination of Sarah Chen, a dedicated software engineer who dared to speak up about her company's toxic culture of discrimination against Asian-American employees. Despite five years of exemplary performance reviews and multiple promotions, Chen found herself labeled a 'troublemaker' and pushed out within months of filing an internal complaint about racist comments from her supervisor. This lawsuit seeks to hold ABC Tech Corporation accountable for violating California's Fair Employment and Housing Act and to ensure that other employees don't suffer the same fate."

3. Parties Section: Establishing the Players

Plaintiff Information Must Include:

- Full legal name and any aliases used in employment
- Current residence (for venue purposes)
- Employment dates and positions held

- Current employment status

Defendant Information Requirements:

- **Corporate Defendants**: Full corporate name, state of incorporation, principal place of business, local address
- **Individual Defendants**: Full name, title, role in alleged misconduct, current address if known
- **Jurisdictional Facts**: Number of employees (critical for federal law coverage), business operations, relationship to other defendants

Sample Party Allegations: "Defendant ACME CORPORATION is a Delaware corporation with its principal place of business in San Francisco, California. At all relevant times, ACME employed more than 50 employees and was subject to the California Fair Employment and Housing Act. ACME operates retail stores throughout California and maintains its corporate headquarters at 123 Main Street, San Francisco, California 94105."

4. Jurisdiction and Venue: Legal Foundation

This section must clearly establish why this court can and should hear the case.

Subject Matter Jurisdiction Example: "This Court has subject matter jurisdiction over this action pursuant to California Government Code Section 12965, which grants the superior courts jurisdiction over actions brought under the Fair Employment and Housing Act. This Court also has jurisdiction over supplemental state law claims pursuant to California Code of Civil Procedure Section 410.10."

Personal Jurisdiction Example: "This Court has personal jurisdiction over Defendants because they conduct substantial business activities in California, employ California residents, and the discriminatory acts alleged herein occurred in California."

5. Factual Allegations: Telling the Story

The factual section is where cases are won or lost. It must be both legally sufficient and emotionally compelling.

Organizational Strategies:

Chronological Approach: Best for cases with clear timeline of events

- Start with hiring and early positive performance
- Progress through protected activity and employer's knowledge
- Detail adverse actions and causal connections
- Conclude with damages and ongoing harm

Thematic Approach: Useful for complex cases with multiple types of misconduct

- Group similar incidents together
- Show patterns of behavior
- Emphasize escalation over time

Key Factual Elements to Include:

Background and Context:

- Plaintiff's qualifications and performance history
- Company policies and stated values
- Workplace culture and environment
- Plaintiff's protected characteristics or activities

Specific Incidents:

- Exact dates, times, and locations when possible
- Direct quotes when available
- Witnesses present
- Documentation or evidence created

Causation Elements:

- Temporal proximity between protected activity and adverse action
- Comparative treatment of similarly situated employees
- Departures from normal procedures or policies
- Direct evidence of discriminatory intent

Sample Factual Allegation: "On March 15, 2023, immediately following Plaintiff's return from FMLA leave, Supervisor Johnson called Plaintiff into his office and stated, 'I hope you're not planning on having any more kids because we can't keep covering for people who aren't committed to the job.' When Plaintiff responded that such comments were inappropriate, Johnson replied, 'Well, maybe this job isn't the right fit for someone with your priorities.' This conversation was overheard by Administrative Assistant Mary Williams, who later confirmed these statements to Plaintiff."

6. Causes of Action: Legal Framework

Each cause of action should be pled as a separate count with specific elements addressed.

Standard Format for Each Count:

- Title clearly identifying the claim
- Incorporation of previous allegations by reference
- Specific statutory citation
- Elements of the claim with supporting facts
- Identification of liable defendants
- Specific damages or relief sought

Sample Count Structure:

COUNT ONE: DISCRIMINATION IN VIOLATION OF CALIFORNIA GOVERNMENT CODE SECTION 12940(a)

"Plaintiff incorporates by reference paragraphs 1 through 45 as though fully set forth herein.

"At all relevant times, Defendants were employers within the meaning of Government Code Section 12940, employing more than five employees.

"Defendants discriminated against Plaintiff because of her pregnancy, a protected characteristic under Government Code Section 12940(a).

"Defendants' discriminatory conduct included but was not limited to: [specific acts].

"As a direct and proximate result of Defendants' unlawful discrimination, Plaintiff has suffered and continues to suffer damages including lost wages, benefits, and emotional distress.

"Defendants' conduct was willful, malicious, and oppressive, justifying an award of punitive damages."

7. Damages: Quantifying the Harm

The damages section must be comprehensive yet realistic, covering all categories of harm.

Categories of Employment Damages:

Economic Damages:

- **Back Pay**: Wages lost from termination or demotion to date of trial
- **Front Pay**: Future lost earnings if reinstatement is not feasible
- **Benefits**: Health insurance, retirement contributions, stock options
- **Bonuses and Commissions**: Lost incentive compensation
- **Mitigation**: Reductions for income earned elsewhere

Non-Economic Damages:

- **Emotional Distress**: Pain, suffering, humiliation, anxiety, depression
- **Reputation Damage**: Harm to professional standing
- **Loss of Enjoyment**: Impact on personal life and relationships

Punitive Damages:

- Available when conduct is malicious, oppressive, or in reckless disregard of plaintiff's rights
- Requires clear and convincing evidence standard
- Subject to constitutional limitations (typically 9:1 ratio to compensatory damages)

Statutory Damages and Fees:

- **Attorney's Fees**: Available under most employment statutes

- **Costs**: Filing fees, deposition costs, expert fees
- **Pre and Post-Judgment Interest**: Compensation for delay in payment

Sample Damages Allegation: "As a direct and proximate result of Defendants' unlawful conduct, Plaintiff has suffered damages in an amount to be proven at trial, including but not limited to: lost wages and benefits in excess of $150,000; emotional distress damages; punitive damages; pre and post-judgment interest; costs of suit; and reasonable attorney's fees as provided by Government Code Section 12965."

8. Prayer for Relief: The Ask

The prayer for relief summarizes all requested remedies and should be comprehensive.

Sample Prayer for Relief: "WHEREFORE, Plaintiff respectfully requests that this Court enter judgment in her favor and against Defendants as follows:

1. For compensatory damages in an amount to be proven at trial, but not less than $200,000;
2. For punitive damages according to proof;
3. For pre and post-judgment interest at the maximum rate allowed by law;
4. For reasonable attorney's fees and costs as provided by Government Code Section 12965;
5. For injunctive relief requiring Defendants to implement policies and training to prevent future discrimination;
6. For such other and further relief as this Court deems just and proper."

9. Demand for Jury Trial

Include a clear, unambiguous demand for jury trial.

Sample Language: "Plaintiff hereby demands a trial by jury on all issues so triable."

7.5 State-Specific Pleading Standards: Navigating Different Requirements

Understanding the distinct pleading requirements in each jurisdiction is crucial for avoiding dismissal and maximizing strategic advantage.

California: Fact Pleading Requirements

California follows a "fact pleading" standard that requires more specificity than federal notice pleading.

Key Requirements:

- **Ultimate Facts**: Must allege facts that directly support each element of each cause of action
- **Not Conclusions**: Avoid legal conclusions without factual support
- **Not Evidence**: Don't plead evidentiary details that belong in discovery

California-Specific Considerations:

Code of Civil Procedure Section 425.10: Governs general damages and must be pled with specificity

Code of Civil Procedure Section 425.11: Requires separate notice for punitive damages with supporting facts showing malice, oppression, or fraud

Information and Belief: Use sparingly and only when facts are peculiarly within defendant's knowledge

PAGA Claims: Private Attorneys General Act claims require prior notice to employer and state agencies, plus separate pleading as distinct cause of action

Sample California Fact Pleading: "On January 15, 2023, at approximately 2:00 p.m., in the conference room at Defendant's San Jose facility, Supervisor Martinez told Plaintiff, 'You people always want special treatment,' referring to Plaintiff's request for a religious accommodation. This statement was made in the presence of three other employees: John Smith, Jane Doe, and Robert Johnson. Following this meeting, Defendant denied Plaintiff's accommodation request without engaging in the interactive process required by law."

New York: Notice Pleading with Substance

New York follows notice pleading under CPLR 3013 but requires sufficient facts to give fair notice of the claim.

Key Requirements:

- **Fair Notice**: Defendant must understand what they're accused of doing
- **Material Elements**: Must allege facts supporting each material element of each cause of action
- **Liberal Construction**: Courts interpret pleadings liberally in favor of plaintiffs

New York-Specific Considerations:

NYHRL and NYCHRL: When filing in New York City, cite both state and city human rights laws for maximum protection

Verified Pleadings: Consider verification when personal knowledge supports stronger impact

Special Damages: Must be specifically pled, including lost wages and benefits

Sample New York Pleading: "Defendant discriminated against Plaintiff based on her disability in violation of New York Executive Law Section 296 and New York City Administrative Code Section 8-107 by refusing to provide reasonable accommodations, subjecting her to harassment, and ultimately terminating her employment because of her disability-related needs."

Federal Court: Twombly/Iqbal Plausibility Standard

Federal courts require "plausible" claims that go beyond mere possibilities.

Key Requirements:

- **Plausibility**: Factual allegations must make the claim plausible, not just possible
- **Non-Conclusory**: Must include factual allegations, not just legal conclusions
- **Context**: Facts must be sufficient to move claim from conceivable to

plausible

Twombly/Iqbal Impact on Employment Cases:

Discrimination Claims: Must plead facts suggesting discriminatory intent, not just the adverse action, plus protected class membership

Retaliation Claims: Must show causal connection between protected activity and adverse action with specific facts

Harassment Claims: Must plead severity and pervasiveness with concrete examples

Sample Federal Pleading: "Defendant's discriminatory intent is evidenced by the following facts: (1) Plaintiff was the only pregnant employee in her department; (2) within one week of announcing her pregnancy, her supervisor began assigning her less desirable projects; (3) her supervisor told a coworker that 'pregnant women can't handle the pressure'; (4) despite positive performance reviews, she was terminated two weeks before her maternity leave was scheduled to begin; and (5) she was replaced by a male employee with less experience."

7.6 Multiple Plaintiffs or Defendants: Complex Party Dynamics

Employment cases often involve multiple parties, each presenting unique strategic considerations.

Multiple Plaintiffs: Strength in Numbers vs. Complexity

Advantages of Multiple Plaintiffs:

- **Pattern Evidence**: Multiple victims strengthen pattern and practice claims
- **Cost Sharing**: Litigation expenses shared among plaintiffs
- **Settlement Leverage**: Employers may pay more to resolve multiple claims
- **Efficiency**: One case instead of multiple lawsuits

Challenges and Considerations:

- **Conflicting Interests**: Plaintiffs may have different goals or damage amounts
- **Confidentiality**: Some plaintiffs may want privacy while others seek publicity
- **Discovery Complications**: Multiple depositions and document productions
- **Settlement Dynamics**: One plaintiff's willingness to settle may affect others

Joinder Requirements: Plaintiffs can be joined if they share:

- Common questions of law or fact
- Claims arising from same transaction or occurrence
- Relief sought doesn't conflict

Sample Multiple Plaintiff Allegations: "Plaintiffs JANE DOE and JOHN SMITH were both employed by Defendant in its marketing department, both suffered discrimination based on their age, and both were terminated as part of Defendant's systematic pattern of replacing older workers with younger employees."

Multiple Defendants: Casting a Wide Net

Strategic Considerations for Multiple Defendants:

- **Individual Liability**: Supervisors and managers may be personally liable under state laws
- **Corporate Structure**: Parent companies, subsidiaries, and related entities
- **Insurance Coverage**: Different defendants may have different insurance
- **Settlement Dynamics**: Multiple defendants may point fingers at each other

Types of Employment Defendants:

Corporate Employers:

- Primary defendant in most cases
- Liable under respondeat superior theory
- May have deepest pockets for damages

Individual Supervisors and Managers:

- Personal liability under FEHA and NYCHRL
- May have limited assets but insurance coverage
- Can provide testimony against corporate defendant

Staffing Agencies and Contractors:

- Joint employer liability possible
- Especially relevant in temporary and contract work

Parent Companies and Affiliates:

- Integrated enterprise doctrine
- Single employer analysis
- Successor liability

Sample Multiple Defendant Structure: "Defendant ABC CORPORATION is liable as Plaintiff's direct employer. Defendant JOHN SUPERVISOR is individually liable under Government Code Section 12940 for his personal participation in the discriminatory conduct. Defendant XYZ HOLDINGS, INC., ABC Corporation's parent company, is liable as a joint employer under the integrated enterprise doctrine based on common ownership, interrelated operations, centralized control of labor relations, and common management."

7.7 Filing and Service Requirements: Procedural Compliance

Proper filing and service are essential procedural requirements that can make confidence or break a case before it begins.

California Filing and Service Requirements

Electronic Filing:

- Most California counties require electronic filing through approved systems
- Original signatures still required on certain documents
- Filing fees vary by county and type of case

Service Requirements:

- **Time Limit**: Must serve within 60 days of filing (CRC Rule 3.110)
- **Methods**: Personal service preferred, substituted service allowed
- **Process Servers**: Consider using registered process servers for important cases
- **Proof of Service**: Must be filed promptly after service

California Service Options:

Personal Service: Direct hand delivery to defendant

- Most reliable method
- Creates strongest legal presumption
- Required for certain types of relief

Substituted Service: Service at home or business when personal service not possible

- Must follow specific requirements
- Additional mailing required
- Court may question adequacy

Service by Mail: Available in limited circumstances

- Requires acknowledgment of receipt
- Not recommended for hostile defendants
- May delay case if not returned

Sample California Service Paragraph: "Service may be made on Defendant ABC CORPORATION by serving its registered agent for service of process, CT CORPORATION SYSTEM, at 818 West Seventh Street, Suite 930, Los Angeles, California 90017."

New York Filing and Service Requirements

Electronic Filing (NYSCEF):

- Mandatory in most counties
- Some courts still require paper copies
- Specific formatting requirements

Service Time Limits:

- **General Rule**: Must serve within 120 days (CPLR 306-b)
- **Extensions**: Available on motion showing good cause
- **Consequences**: Dismissal possible for failure to timely serve

New York Service Methods:

Personal Service: Hand delivery to individual defendant **Corporate Service**: Service on registered agent or designated officer **Substituted Service**: Delivery to suitable person at residence or business plus mailing

Notice of Commencement:

- Required in some New York courts
- Must be served along with summons and complaint
- Provides additional case information to court

Sample New York Service Language: "Service upon Defendant ACME CORPORATION may be made by delivering a copy of the summons and complaint to any officer, director, managing agent, or cashier thereof, or to any other agent authorized by appointment or by law to receive service."

Federal Filing and Service Requirements

Federal Rules of Civil Procedure Rule 4:

- Governs all aspects of federal service
- More flexible than many state rules
- International service provisions available

Federal Service Methods:

Waiver of Service: Defendant agrees to waive formal service

- Saves costs and time
- Extends defendant's time to respond
- Not available for all defendants

Personal Service: Direct delivery by marshal or private process server

Corporate Service: Service on registered agent or officer

State Law Methods: Federal courts can use state law service methods

Sample Federal Service Provision: "Service may be effected by any method authorized by Federal Rule of Civil Procedure 4, including service pursuant to the law of the state in which service is made."

7.8 Sample Opening Paragraphs: Setting the Tone

The opening paragraphs of a complaint set the tone for the entire case. Here are examples across different types of employment cases:

Discrimination Case Opening

"Plaintiff MARIA GONZALEZ dedicated fifteen years of her career to rising through the ranks at Defendant TECH INNOVATIONS CORP, earning consistent promotions and praise for her leadership abilities. That trajectory came to an abrupt halt when she was passed over for a long-promised promotion in favor of a less qualified male colleague, then subjected to a campaign of harassment designed to force her resignation. This case seeks to hold Tech Innovations accountable for its systematic discrimination against women in leadership roles."

Retaliation Case Opening

"When DAVID CHEN discovered that his employer was systematically underpaying female employees, he faced a choice: stay silent or speak up. Chen chose to report the pay disparities to Human Resources, believing his company would want to correct the problem. Instead, Chen found himself branded a troublemaker, stripped of meaningful assignments, and ultimately terminated in clear retaliation for his protected disclosure. This lawsuit seeks justice for Chen and deterrence to prevent similar retaliation against other employees who dare to speak up about workplace violations."

Harassment Case Opening

"For eighteen months, SARAH WILLIAMS endured a hostile work environment where sexual comments, unwanted touching, and explicit materials were part of her daily experience at Defendant CONSTRUCTION PLUS, INC. Despite multiple complaints to supervisors and Human Resources, the harassment not only continued but escalated, ultimately forcing Williams to resign from a job she loved to escape the toxic environment. This case demonstrates how Construction Plus failed in its legal duty to maintain a workplace free from sexual harassment."

Wage and Hour Case Opening

"Every day for three years, JAMES RODRIGUEZ worked more than ten hours managing Defendant RETAIL EMPIRE's busy downtown store, handling everything from customer service to inventory management. Despite working far beyond forty hours per week, Rodriguez was classified as 'exempt' and denied overtime pay - a misclassification that cost him thousands of dollars in wages. This lawsuit seeks to recover Rodriguez's stolen wages and ensure that Retail Empire properly compensates all its hardworking employees."

7.9 Amending the Complaint: Adapting to New Information

Complaints often need modification as cases develop, making understanding of amendment procedures crucial.

Amendment as of Right

Federal Court (FRCP 21(a)):

- One amendment allowed before responsive pleading
- Must be filed within reasonable time
- No court permission required

California:

- One amendment allowed before demurrer or answer
- Must not add entirely new causes of action
- Relates back to original filing date

New York:

- One amendment allowed before responsive pleading
- Liberal allowance for technical corrections
- Substantial changes may require permission

Amendment by Leave of Court

When amendment as of right is not available, court permission is required.

Standards Applied:

- **Liberal Grant**: Courts generally favor amendment when justice requires
- **No Prejudice**: Amendment should not unfairly prejudice defendant
- **Good Faith**: Amendment must not be for improper purposes
- **Statute of Limitations**: New claims may need to relate back to original filing

Strategic Considerations for Amendment:

Discovery Developments: New facts learned in discovery may support additional claims

Legal Developments: Changes in law may create new theories of liability

Defendant's Response: Defenses raised may suggest need for additional claims

Settlement Posture: Additional claims may provide leverage in negotiations

Sample Motion for Leave to Amend: "Plaintiff respectfully moves for leave to file a First Amended Complaint to add a claim for violation of the Family and Medical Leave Act based on facts discovered during Defendant's deposition testimony. The proposed amendment relates to the same core operative facts as the original complaint, will not prejudice Defendant, and is made in good faith to present all viable claims arising from Defendant's conduct."

Relation Back Doctrine

New claims in amended complaints may "relate back" to the original filing date if they arise from the same operative facts.

Benefits of Relation Back:

- Avoids statute of limitations problems
- Preserves original filing date for discovery cutoffs
- Maintains priority over subsequent filings

Requirements for Relation Back:

- Same operative facts as original complaint
- Fair notice to defendant of new claims
- No prejudice from delay

7.10 Advanced Strategic Considerations

Anticipating Defenses

Effective complaint drafting anticipates likely defenses and addresses them proactively.

Common Employment Defenses:

Legitimate Business Reasons: Employer claims adverse actions were for lawful reasons

- **Counter-Strategy**: Plead facts showing pretext, such as timing, comparator evidence, or departures from policy

After-Acquired Evidence: Employer discovers post-termination misconduct that would have justified termination

- **Counter-Strategy**: Focus on front-pay limitations rather than liability, emphasize deterrent effect

Same Decision Defense: Employer claims same decision would have been made absent discriminatory motive

- **Counter-Strategy**: Plead facts showing discrimination was motivating factor, argue burden-shifting

Economic Necessity: Employer claims financial reasons for layoffs or restructuring

- **Counter-Strategy**: Plead facts about selection criteria, comparator treatment, timing of financial claims

Preserving Claims and Evidence

Document Preservation Demands: Include request for litigation hold in complaint or immediately after filing

Witness Identification: Plead facts that identify key witnesses without revealing privileged strategy

Statute of Limitations: Ensure all viable claims are included to avoid later limitations problems

Related Proceedings: Consider impact of EEOC charges, workers' compensation claims, unemployment proceedings

Settlement Positioning

A well-drafted complaint positions the case for favorable settlement discussions.

Damage Quantification: Provide enough specificity to demonstrate significant exposure without limiting recovery

Injunctive Relief: Include requests for policy changes that may be valuable to employer

Publicity Concerns: Consider employer's reputation interests in framing public aspects of case

Multiple Defendants: Create dynamics that encourage finger-pointing and separate settlement discussions

7.11 Technology and Modern Practice

Electronic Filing Systems

California: Most counties use different systems, requiring familiarity with local requirements

New York: NYSCEF is standard but formatting requirements vary by court

Federal: CM/ECF system is universal but local rules add variations

Document Production and ESI

Modern complaints should anticipate electronic discovery issues:

- **Preservation Obligations**: Triggering defendant's duty to preserve electronic evidence
- **Social Media**: Considering relevance of online activity and communications
- **Mobile Devices**: Addressing personal device use for business communications

Privacy and Confidentiality

GDPR and State Privacy Laws: Consider impact on discovery of personal information

Confidentiality Agreements: Address enforceability and scope of employment agreements

Public Records: Consider impact of filing in publicly accessible court systems

7.12 Conclusion and Strategic Synthesis

A persuasive, well-structured complaint is more than a procedural step - it is a tactical document that frames the litigation battlefield. The complaint serves multiple masters: satisfying technical pleading requirements, telling a compelling human story, positioning the case for favorable resolution, and laying the groundwork for successful motion practice and discovery.

Key Strategic Principles:

Integration: Every paragraph should serve both legal sufficiency and persuasive storytelling goals

Anticipation: Consider likely defenses, motion practice, and settlement dynamics from the outset

Flexibility: Draft to preserve maximum strategic options while meeting immediate pleading requirements

Jurisdiction-Specific: Tailor approach to specific requirements and opportunities in chosen forum

Evidence-Based: Ground every allegation in discoverable evidence while maintaining compelling narrative

By anchoring your claims in statute, tailoring to jurisdiction, and aligning facts with theory, you position your case for early settlement success or durable litigation strength. The complaint is your first opportunity to advocate for your client - make it count.

The foundation laid in the complaint will support every subsequent phase of litigation, from surviving motions to dismiss through trial preparation and settlement negotiations. Invest the time and attention necessary to craft a complaint that serves your client's interests throughout the entire litigation process.

8

Surviving Motions to Dismiss in Employment Litigation

After the complaint is filed, one of the first and most common procedural hurdles is a motion to dismiss. Whether it's a Rule 12(b)(6) motion in federal court, a demurrer in California state court, or a CPLR 3211 motion in New York, these early challenges are designed to test the legal sufficiency of the complaint - not the underlying facts.

This chapter equips you to anticipate, defend against, and strategically respond to motions to dismiss in employment litigation, ensuring your claims survive and proceed to discovery.

8.1 Purpose and Nature of Motions to Dismiss

Federal Rule 12(b)(6) and State Equivalents

These motions assert that - even assuming all facts alleged are true - the complaint fails to state a claim upon which relief can be granted. The motion to dismiss serves as a legal filter, allowing courts to eliminate legally insufficient claims before costly discovery begins.

Key Principle: The motion does not test evidence, credibility, or weigh competing narratives. Instead, it asks whether the complaint, if everything alleged were true, would entitle the plaintiff to relief under the law.

Common Grounds for Dismissal

Dismissal may be based on:

Legal insufficiency of the claims: The complaint fails to allege facts that would support a viable legal theory. For example, alleging age discrimination without stating the plaintiff's age or that they are over 40 years old under the Age Discrimination in Employment Act (ADEA).

Failure to plead required elements: Each cause of action has specific elements that must be alleged. A Title VII discrimination claim requires allegations of protected class membership, adverse employment action, and causal connection between the two.

Claims barred by statute of limitations or preemption: Employment claims have strict filing deadlines. For instance, EEOC charges must typically be filed within 180 or 300 days depending on the jurisdiction, and subsequent lawsuits must be filed within 90 days of receiving a right-to-sue letter.

Defects on the face of the pleading or attached documents: When documents attached to the complaint contradict the allegations, courts may dismiss based on those documents. For example, if an employment contract attached to the complaint shows the plaintiff was an at-will employee, claims alleging wrongful termination in violation of contract may fail.

8.2 Common Grounds for Dismissal in Employment Cases

Failure to Exhaust Administrative Remedies

Employment discrimination claims typically require exhaustion of administrative remedies through the Equal Employment Opportunity

Commission (EEOC) or state fair employment agencies. Courts frequently dismiss complaints when:

- No EEOC charge was filed
- The lawsuit raises claims not included in the EEOC charge
- The plaintiff failed to wait for a right-to-sue letter

Example: A plaintiff files a sexual harassment lawsuit but their EEOC charge only mentioned race discrimination. The sexual harassment claims would likely be dismissed for failure to exhaust administrative remedies.

Insufficient Allegations of Protected Activity

Retaliation claims require that the plaintiff engaged in protected activity, such as filing an EEOC charge or opposing discriminatory practices. Complaints often fail when they don't clearly articulate what protected activity occurred.

Weak Pleading: "Plaintiff complained about workplace issues and was subsequently terminated."

Strong Pleading: "On March 15, 2024, Plaintiff filed a written complaint with Human Resources alleging that her supervisor was making racially discriminatory comments about customers. Two weeks later, Plaintiff was terminated for alleged poor performance."

Failure to Establish Protected Class Status

Discrimination claims require membership in a protected class. Courts dismiss complaints that fail to clearly establish this element.

Example: An age discrimination complaint that states "Plaintiff is an older worker" without specifying that the plaintiff was over 40 years old (the threshold for ADEA protection) may be dismissed.

Inadequate Causation Allegations

Employment claims often fail when complaints don't adequately connect protected activity or class membership to adverse employment actions.

Insufficient: "Plaintiff was terminated shortly after filing an EEOC charge."

Sufficient: "Plaintiff was terminated three days after filing an EEOC charge, despite receiving positive performance reviews for two years and being told by her supervisor that 'troublemakers don't last long here.'"

8.3 Responding to a 12(b)(6) Motion (Federal Court)

Legal Standard: Twombly and Iqbal

The Supreme Court's decisions in *Bell Atl. Corp. v. Twombly*, 550 U.S. 544 (2007) and *Ashcroft v. Iqbal*, 556 U.S. 662 (2009) established the "plausibility standard" for federal pleadings. This standard requires more than "labels and conclusions" or "a formulaic recitation of the elements."

Plausibility Standard Explained: Courts must be able to draw a reasonable inference that the defendant is liable for the misconduct alleged. The complaint must contain sufficient factual content to support a plausible claim for relief.

Practical Application: Instead of simply alleging "Defendant discriminated against Plaintiff because of her race," the complaint should include specific facts such as: "Defendant's manager told Plaintiff that 'people like you' weren't suited for leadership positions and consistently assigned Plaintiff to less desirable shifts while promoting less qualified white employees."

Response Strategy

Emphasize well-pleaded facts: Focus on specific, concrete allegations rather than legal conclusions. Highlight temporal proximity between protected activity and adverse actions, discriminatory statements, and statistical evidence of disparate treatment.

Distinguish legal conclusions from factual allegations: Courts accept factual allegations as true but disregard legal conclusions. "Defendant discriminated" is a legal conclusion, while "Defendant's supervisor used racial slurs when addressing Plaintiff" is a factual allegation.

Argue that factual disputes should be resolved at summary judgment: Remind the court that Rule 12(b)(6) motions are not the appropriate vehicle for resolving factual disputes or credibility determinations.

Cite favorable precedent: Use circuit-specific and district-specific case law that favors broad construction of employment protections. Many circuits have held that employment discrimination claims should rarely be dismissed at the pleading stage due to their fact-intensive nature.

Leverage administrative filings: Reference EEOC charges, internal complaints, or other administrative filings that support the complaint's plausibility and demonstrate the employer's knowledge of alleged misconduct.

Amending the Complaint

If the court grants dismissal with leave to amend, act promptly and strategically:

Cure specific deficiencies: Address each point raised by the court's dismissal order. If the court found insufficient causation allegations, add specific facts connecting protected activity to adverse actions.

Don't just add more facts: Focus on adding the right facts that address legal deficiencies. More detail isn't always better if it doesn't advance the legal theory.

Consider strategic additions: Use the amendment opportunity to add claims, parties, or theories that strengthen the overall case.

8.4 Responding to a Demurrer (California State Court)

Legal Standard: Fact-Pleading vs. Notice Pleading

California follows a fact-pleading standard, which differs significantly from federal notice pleading. Under California law, complaints must contain allegations of "ultimate facts" rather than mere conclusions.

Ultimate Facts Defined: These are the essential facts that directly support each element of the cause of action, as distinguished from evidentiary facts (specific details) or legal conclusions.

Comparison to Federal Standard: While federal courts require only enough facts to make a claim plausible, California requires pleading of ultimate facts that constitute the cause of action.

Example of Proper California Pleading: Instead of alleging "Defendant harassed Plaintiff" (legal conclusion), the complaint should state "Defendant's supervisor made unwelcome sexual advances toward Plaintiff on multiple occasions, including touching Plaintiff's shoulders and making comments about her physical appearance" (ultimate facts).

Procedural Requirements

Timing: Opposition briefs are typically due within 15 days of service, though local rules may vary. Some courts require meet-and-confer efforts before filing a demurrer.

Hearing Practice: Unlike federal motions which are often decided on the papers, California demurrers frequently involve oral argument where attorneys can address the court's concerns directly.

Burden on Defendant: The demurring party must specify exactly which allegations are insufficient and why. General attacks on the entire complaint are improper.

Best Practices for Opposition

Reframe allegations constructively: Take the court through the complaint paragraph by paragraph, highlighting how the factual allegations satisfy each element of the cause of action.

Emphasize liberal construction: California courts are required to liberally construe pleadings and resolve doubts in favor of the pleader. Remind the court of this obligation.

Argue against discovery substitute: If the complaint contains substantial factual detail, argue that the demurrer is an improper attempt to avoid discovery and resolve factual disputes on the pleadings.

Distinguish contrary cases: Employment defendants often cite cases from other areas of law where pleading requirements are stricter. Distinguish these cases and emphasize the fact-intensive nature of employment claims.

Amending After Demurrer

California courts generally allow at least one opportunity to amend unless the complaint is clearly incurable. Key considerations:

Liberal amendment policy: California Code of Civil Procedure Section 473 favors liberal allowance of amendments to serve the interests of justice.

Address structural issues: Don't just add more facts - fix fundamental legal problems identified by the court.

Don't waste the opportunity: Courts may not offer additional chances to amend, so ensure the amended complaint addresses all deficiencies.

8.5 Responding to a Motion to Dismiss Under CPLR 3211 (New York)

Grounds for Dismissal

New York's CPLR 3211 provides several grounds for dismissal, with the most common in employment cases being:

CPLR 3211(a)(1) - Documentary evidence: The defendant attaches documents that conclusively negate the claims. For example, a signed separation agreement with a release clause may defeat subsequent discrimination claims.

CPLR 3211(a)(5) - Statute of limitations: Claims are time-barred. New York employment discrimination claims typically must be filed within one year of the discriminatory act or within one year of filing a complaint with the New York State Division of Human Rights.

CPLR 3211(a)(7) - Failure to state a cause of action: The complaint doesn't contain sufficient factual allegations to support a legally cognizable claim.

Legal Standard: Notice Pleading

New York follows a notice pleading standard similar to the pre-Twombly federal standard. The test is whether the complaint gives fair notice of the transactions, occurrences, or series of transactions or occurrences intended to be proved.

Liberal Construction: New York courts construe pleadings liberally and give plaintiffs the benefit of every possible favorable inference.

Four Corners Test: Courts look only at what appears on the face of the complaint to determine whether it states a cause of action.

Response Strategy

Emphasize liberal construction: New York's pleading standard is more forgiving than the federal Twombly/Iqbal standard. Emphasize that pleadings are construed in the light most favorable to the plaintiff.

Focus on notice function: Argue that the complaint provides adequate notice of the claims and that any deficiencies can be addressed through discovery or amendment.

Distinguish documentary evidence: If the defendant relies on CPLR 3211(a)(1), argue that the documents don't conclusively negate the claims or that factual issues exist regarding the documents' interpretation or validity.

Use affidavits strategically: While courts prefer to resolve factual disputes at summary judgment, affidavits can sometimes help clarify ambiguous allegations or provide context for the complaint's allegations.

Comparative Analysis: Federal vs. California vs. New York

Pleading Standards:

- **Federal:** Plausibility standard (Twombly/Iqbal) - requires factual content allowing reasonable inference of liability
- **California:** Fact-pleading standard - requires ultimate facts supporting each cause of action element
- **New York:** Notice pleading - requires fair notice of the transaction or occurrence

Amendment Opportunities:

- **Federal:** Leave to amend should be freely given when justice requires (Rule 15)
- **California:** Liberal amendment policy under CCP Section 473

- **New York:** Amendment favored to prevent dismissals on technical grounds

Burden on Moving Party:

- **Federal:** Must show complaint fails plausibility standard
- **California:** Must specify which allegations are legally insufficient
- **New York:** Must show failure to state cause of action from complaint's four corners

8.6 Advanced Tactics for Surviving Dismissal

1. Plead Facts, Not Just Labels

The distinction between factual allegations and legal conclusions is crucial across all jurisdictions.

Poor Example: "Plaintiff was harassed and discriminated against because of her gender."

Strong Example: "On multiple occasions between January and March 2024, Plaintiff's supervisor made sexually explicit comments about her appearance, including stating that she 'dressed like she wanted attention from men' and asking whether she 'enjoyed being the only woman in the office.' When Plaintiff reported these comments to Human Resources on March 15, 2024, she was told that her supervisor was 'just being friendly' and no investigation was conducted. Two weeks later, Plaintiff was terminated for alleged performance issues despite receiving 'meets expectations' ratings on her most recent performance review."

2. Anchor Claims to Specific Statutory Provisions

Reference exact statutory language and elements to demonstrate legal sufficiency.

Example for California FEHA Claim: "Defendant's conduct violated California Government Code Section 12940(j)(1), which prohibits harassment based on sex, by creating a hostile work environment through repeated unwelcome sexual comments and conduct."

Example for Title VII Retaliation: "Defendant's termination of Plaintiff violated Title VII Section 704(a), 42 U.S.C. § 2000e-3(a), which prohibits retaliation against employees who oppose discriminatory practices, as Plaintiff was terminated in direct response to her internal complaint about racial discrimination."

3. Establish Temporal Proximity and Causation

Employment claims often succeed or fail based on the strength of causation allegations.

Timing is crucial: Plead specific dates and timeframes to establish temporal proximity between protected activity and adverse actions.

Strengthen with context: "Two weeks after Plaintiff filed an internal complaint about age discrimination, she was placed on a performance improvement plan - the first negative performance action in her five-year employment history."

Include discriminatory statements: "When Plaintiff's supervisor learned of her EEOC charge, he told her that 'employees who file complaints against the company usually don't work out' and that she should 'start looking for another job.'"

4. Use Comparative Evidence Effectively

Comparator evidence shows disparate treatment and strengthens discrimination claims.

Specific examples: "Three male employees with similar or worse attendance records were not disciplined, while Plaintiff was terminated for missing two days of work due to a documented medical condition."

Statistical context: "During the relevant time period, Defendant terminated four of its five female engineers while retaining all twelve male engineers, despite comparable or superior performance ratings among the terminated women."

5. Address Affirmative Defenses Preemptively

Anticipate common defenses and address them in the complaint where possible.

Statute of limitations: "Plaintiff filed her EEOC charge within 180 days of the last discriminatory act and received her right-to-sue letter on [date], making this lawsuit timely filed within 90 days."

After-acquired evidence: "Defendant's alleged discovery of performance issues occurred only after Plaintiff's protected activity and appears to be pretextual, as similar issues by male employees were not investigated or disciplined."

6. Leverage Pattern Evidence

Show that discriminatory conduct was part of a broader pattern rather than isolated incidents.

Example: "Plaintiff's termination was part of Defendant's pattern of discriminating against older workers, as evidenced by Defendant's termination of six employees over age 50 in the past year while hiring younger replacements for similar positions."

8.7 Strategic Claim Organization

When to Consolidate Claims

Group similar legal theories under a single cause of action when facts substantially overlap and legal elements are similar.

Example of Proper Consolidation: Combine Title VII sex discrimination and California FEHA sex discrimination claims under one heading since they involve the same facts and similar legal standards.

Benefits of Consolidation:

- Reduces redundancy and improves readability
- Presents a unified theory of liability
- Simplifies motion practice and discovery

When to Split Claims

Separate causes of action when they involve distinct facts, elements, or legal theories.

Wage and Hour vs. Discrimination: These claims involve different facts, statutes, and damages calculations. Splitting allows for targeted defenses and clearer damage theories.

Different Time Periods: If discrimination and retaliation occurred at different times with different actors, consider separate claims to avoid confusion.

Benefits of Splitting:

- Allows targeted defense strategies
- Enables clearer damages calculations
- Provides backup theories if some claims fail
- Facilitates partial summary judgment motions

Claim Sequencing Strategy

Lead with strongest claims: Place your most legally solid claims first to create a strong initial impression.

Group related theories: Keep related claims together (e.g., all discrimination claims, then all retaliation claims).

End with damages: Conclude with claims that aggregate or enhance damages, such as punitive damages or attorney's fees.

8.8 Strategic Considerations in Accepting Dismissal

When Voluntary Dismissal May Be Beneficial

Sometimes accepting dismissal without prejudice or stipulating to dismissal with leave to amend serves the client's interests:

Avoid adverse precedent: If the court signals it will grant dismissal with prejudice, voluntary dismissal preserves the right to refile.

Buy time for development: Dismissal allows time to gather additional evidence, secure witness cooperation, or await related administrative proceedings.

Forum shopping: Dismissal may allow refiling in a more favorable jurisdiction or removal to federal court.

Administrative coordination: Preserves claims while awaiting EEOC right-to-sue letters or other administrative developments.

Critical Safeguards

Always confirm that voluntary dismissal won't prejudice statute of limitations or tolling status:

Check filing deadlines: Ensure adequate time remains to refile after addressing deficiencies.

Preserve tolling: Some jurisdictions toll statutes of limitations during pending litigation; dismissal may restart the clock.

Consider res judicata: Voluntary dismissal without prejudice typically doesn't create res judicata issues, but confirm under applicable law.

Document the record: Ensure the dismissal order clearly states it's without prejudice and preserves the right to refile.

8.9 Potential Outcomes and Next Steps

Possible Court Rulings

Complete dismissal with prejudice: All claims dismissed with no right to amend. Consider immediate appeal if grounds exist.

Complete dismissal without prejudice: All claims dismissed but plaintiff may amend. Analyze deficiencies and determine whether amendment can cure problems.

Partial dismissal: Some claims survive while others are dismissed. Focus resources on surviving claims while considering whether to amend dismissed claims.

Denial of motion: All claims survive. Prepare for answer, discovery, and motion practice on the merits.

Preserving Appellate Rights

Object to erroneous rulings: Ensure proper objections are on the record to preserve issues for appeal.

Request findings: In bench rulings, ask the court to clarify its reasoning for potential appellate review.

Consider interlocutory appeals: Some dismissal orders may be immediately appealable, particularly those involving immunity or jurisdictional issues.

Document the record: Ensure transcripts are prepared and the record is complete for any potential appeal.

Post-Dismissal Case Management

Amendment deadlines: Courts typically set short deadlines for amended pleadings. Use the time efficiently to address deficiencies comprehensively.

Discovery planning: If some claims survive, begin discovery planning immediately to maintain momentum.

Settlement considerations: Partial dismissals may create settlement opportunities by clarifying the scope of remaining liability.

Case evaluation: Use the court's ruling to reassess case strengths and weaknesses for future strategic decisions.

8.10 Conclusion

Motions to dismiss are gatekeeping mechanisms that test the framing - not the truth - of a case. Success requires understanding the distinct pleading standards across jurisdictions, crafting complaints that satisfy legal elements with specific factual allegations, and responding strategically to challenges.

The key to surviving dismissal lies in thorough preparation during the complaint drafting phase. By anticipating likely attacks and aligning your complaint with statutory elements while providing detailed factual support, you can shield your case from early termination and gain momentum going into discovery.

Remember that employment law's fact-intensive nature generally favors allowing cases to proceed past the pleading stage. Courts recognize that employment discrimination and retaliation claims often depend on circumstantial evidence and credibility determinations that are inappropriate for resolution on a motion to dismiss.

Use dismissal challenges as opportunities to strengthen your case theory and factual development. Even successful oppositions to dismissal motions provide valuable insights into the court's perspective and potential weaknesses that should be addressed in discovery and trial preparation.

In Chapter 9, we will explore the discovery process in depth - how to draft effective requests, manage employer resistance, and uncover the documentation and testimony that prove your case.

9

Discovery in Employment Litigation

Discovery is the heart of employment litigation. It is where legal theories are tested against real-world evidence - documents, testimony, and data that can confirm or dismantle your client's claims. A well-executed discovery plan can transform a plausible complaint into a winning case - or expose weaknesses that demand settlement or revision of strategy.

This chapter walks you through the essential tools and tactics for conducting discovery in employment cases in New York and California, with emphasis on best practices for interrogatories, document requests, depositions, and protective orders.

9.1 Purpose and Scope of Discovery

Goals

Discovery serves multiple strategic purposes in employment litigation. First, it allows you to gather evidence supporting your client's claims or defenses by uncovering documents, communications, and witness testimony that may not be readily apparent from the initial pleadings. Second, discovery helps identify witnesses and potential experts who can strengthen your case or undermine your opponent's position. Third, it provides an opportunity to assess the credibility of key players, including supervisors, HR personnel, and other employees who may testify at trial. Fourth, discovery allows you to lock in testimony for use in summary judgment motions or at trial, preventing witnesses from changing their stories later. Finally, it helps evaluate damages and settlement value by revealing the full scope of harm suffered and the employer's conduct.

Scope

Under both state and federal rules, parties may obtain discovery regarding any non-privileged matter that is relevant to a claim or defense and proportional to the needs of the case. The proportionality requirement, emphasized in Federal Rule 26, requires courts to consider the importance of the issues at stake, the amount in controversy, the parties' relative access to relevant information, the importance of discovery in resolving the issues, and whether the burden or expense of the proposed discovery outweighs its likely benefit.

Key Differences Between Federal and State Rules:

In federal court, Rule 26(b)(1) limits discovery to information that is "relevant to any party's claim or defense and proportional to the needs of the case." This represents a significant narrowing from the former standard that allowed discovery of information "reasonably calculated to lead to the discovery of admissible evidence."

In New York state courts, CPLR Article 31 generally follows the federal approach but may be more liberal in certain respects. New York courts often apply a broader relevance standard, particularly in employment cases where patterns of discriminatory conduct may be relevant even if not directly related to the plaintiff's specific claims.

California state courts follow the California Code of Civil Procedure, which allows discovery of "any matter, not privileged, that is relevant to the subject matter involved in the pending action." California's scope is traditionally broader than the current federal standard, though courts increasingly consider proportionality factors.

9.2 Key Discovery Tools

Employment litigation relies on four primary discovery tools, each serving distinct strategic purposes. **Interrogatories**are written questions that must be answered under oath within a specified time period (typically 30 days). They are particularly useful for obtaining factual details and identifying witnesses and documents. **Requests for Production of Documents** seek tangible items, documents, and electronically stored information (ESI) relevant to the case. **Requests for Admission** ask parties to admit or deny specific facts, helping to narrow issues for trial and establish foundations for other evidence. **Depositions** involve oral testimony taken under oath before a court reporter, allowing attorneys to assess witness credibility and lock in testimony.

9.3 Drafting Effective Discovery Requests

Interrogatories

Interrogatories should be crafted to elicit specific factual details that support your legal theories. In discrimination cases, ask about the decision-making process for the adverse employment action, including who was involved, what factors were considered, and whether similar situations were handled differently. For retaliation claims, inquire about the timeline between protected activity and adverse action, and whether the employer was aware of the protected activity.

Avoid compound questions that ask multiple things in a single interrogatory, as they may be objected to as vague or ambiguous. Instead of asking "Describe all conversations between plaintiff and her supervisor regarding her performance, attendance, and complaints about discrimination," break this into separate interrogatories for each topic.

Avoid legal conclusions by focusing on factual inquiries. Rather than asking "Was plaintiff terminated because of her race?" ask "Identify all reasons for plaintiff's termination and all persons involved in the decision to terminate plaintiff."

Customize to case type. In wage and hour cases, focus on work schedules, break periods, overtime calculations, and classification decisions. In harassment cases, inquire about complaint procedures, prior complaints against the alleged harasser, and the employer's response to complaints.

Example Interrogatories:

For a discrimination case: "Identify each person who participated in the decision to terminate plaintiff, including their title, role in the decision-making process, and the specific input they provided."

For a wage and hour case: "Describe plaintiff's regular work schedule during the period from [date] to [date], including start times, end times, break periods, and any variations from the regular schedule."

Requests for Production

Document requests should cast a wide net while remaining specific enough to avoid overbreadth objections. Target key categories of documents that are likely to contain relevant evidence.

Personnel files should include not just the official personnel file, but also supervisor files, payroll files, and any electronic records maintained by HR or management. Request "all documents maintained in any file, whether electronic or hard copy, relating to plaintiff's employment."

Performance evaluations and disciplinary records can reveal pretextual reasons for adverse actions or patterns of discriminatory treatment. Include formal reviews, informal feedback, disciplinary warnings, performance improvement plans, and any communications about performance issues.

Complaints and investigations related to harassment, discrimination, or retaliation should encompass complaints made by or about plaintiff, complaints involving the same supervisors or decision-makers, and the employer's investigative files and reports.

ESI requests must be specific about format, time range, and custodians. Rather than requesting "all emails," specify "all emails sent or received by [specific individuals] during [date range] containing the terms [specific keywords] or relating to [specific subject matter], produced in native format with metadata preserved."

Example Document Requests:

Broad but targeted: "All documents, including but not limited to emails, text messages, memoranda, notes, reports, and electronic files, relating to any complaint of discrimination, harassment, or retaliation made by or against any employee in plaintiff's department from January 1, 2020 to present."

Specific ESI request: "All emails and electronic communications between [Manager A] and [HR Director] from [date] to [date] containing any of the following terms: plaintiff's name, 'pregnancy,' 'maternity leave,' 'accommodation,' or 'termination,' produced in native format with all metadata preserved."

Requests for Admission

Use requests for admission strategically to establish key facts that support your case or eliminate the need to prove basic elements at trial. They are particularly effective for authenticating documents, establishing dates and timelines, and confirming employment relationships.

Example Requests for Admission:

Document authentication: "Admit that Exhibit A is a true and correct copy of the employee handbook in effect during plaintiff's employment from [date] to [date]."

Timeline establishment: "Admit that plaintiff was terminated on [specific date]."

Policy acknowledgment: "Admit that defendant maintained a written anti-discrimination policy during plaintiff's employment."

9.4 Depositions: Planning and Execution

Who to Depose

Plaintiff deposition (for defense attorneys) should focus on establishing the elements of plaintiff's claims, exploring alternative explanations for adverse actions, and assessing damages. Prepare to challenge plaintiff's credibility by exploring inconsistencies between the complaint, EEOC charge, and deposition testimony.

Supervisor and decision-maker depositions are critical for understanding the employer's stated reasons for adverse actions and exploring potential pretextual explanations. Focus on their knowledge of plaintiff's protected characteristics or activities, their role in decision-making, and any departures from normal procedures.

HR representative depositions should cover the employer's policies and procedures, complaint handling, and knowledge of legal requirements. HR witnesses often have the most knowledge about company-wide practices and how plaintiff's situation compares to other employees.

Coworker depositions can provide crucial testimony about workplace culture, discriminatory comments or conduct, and plaintiff's work performance. They may also have knowledge of how similarly situated employees were treated.

Rule 30(b)(6) depositions allow you to obtain testimony from a corporate representative on specific topics. The corporation must designate a witness and ensure they are prepared to testify on the designated topics. This is particularly useful for obtaining testimony about company policies, decision-making processes, and statistical information.

Third-party depositions might include treating physicians in disability discrimination cases, former employees who witnessed relevant events, or vendors who interacted with the workplace.

Deposition Strategy

Begin with background questions to establish the witness's role, tenure, and knowledge of relevant events. This helps assess credibility and creates a foundation for more specific questioning.

Use open-ended narrative questions initially to allow witnesses to tell their story in their own words. Follow up with specific questions to pin down details and explore inconsistencies.

Establish clear timelines by walking through events chronologically. This helps identify gaps in testimony and potential inconsistencies.

Look for contradictions between the witness's deposition testimony and other evidence, including documents, other witness testimony, or prior statements.

Seek admissions that support your case theory. Even adverse witnesses may admit facts that help your case when asked directly.

Assess demeanor and credibility for trial preparation. Note whether the witness is evasive, argumentative, or sympathetic, as this will inform your trial strategy.

Videotape important depositions if you anticipate the witness may be unavailable for trial or if their demeanor is particularly compelling or damaging.

9.5 Discovery from Employers

What to Request

Personnel files should include the complete employment record, not just the official personnel file. Many employers maintain multiple files on employees, including supervisor files, payroll files, benefits files, and electronic records in human resources information systems (HRIS). Request "all files, records, or documents, whether maintained electronically or in hard copy, relating to plaintiff's employment."

Performance documentation includes formal performance reviews, informal feedback, disciplinary actions, performance improvement plans, coaching notes, and any communications about work performance. This documentation often reveals whether performance issues were documented before or after protected activity, suggesting potential retaliation.

Complaints and investigations encompass not only formal complaints filed through HR channels, but also informal complaints to supervisors, reports from exit interviews, and third-party reports of problematic behavior. Include complaints involving the same supervisors or decision-makers to establish patterns of discriminatory or retaliatory conduct.

Email communications should target key custodians likely to have relevant communications, including plaintiff's direct supervisors, HR personnel, and senior decision-makers. Use specific search terms related to the plaintiff, the adverse employment action, and the protected characteristics or activities at issue.

Policies and procedures include employee handbooks, anti-discrimination policies, complaint procedures, and any updates or revisions during the relevant time period. Changes to policies following plaintiff's complaints may indicate awareness of problems or attempts to prevent liability.

Payroll and compensation data includes timecards, pay stubs, overtime records, bonus calculations, commission statements, and benefits information. In wage and hour cases, this data is essential for calculating damages. In discrimination cases, it may reveal pay disparities compared to similarly situated employees.

Leave and accommodation records include requests for family and medical leave, disability accommodations, religious accommodations, and pregnancy-related leave. The employer's response to these requests often forms the basis for discrimination or retaliation claims.

Redaction and Privacy Issues

Employers frequently assert privacy concerns to limit document production, particularly regarding personnel information about non-party employees. While employers have legitimate interests in protecting employee privacy, courts generally require production of relevant information with appropriate protections.

Common redaction issues include third-party employee names, Social Security numbers, medical information, and salary data for non-party employees. Challenge redactions that remove context necessary to understand the documents, such as redacting names of comparator employees or decision-makers.

Protective orders can facilitate broader production by providing confidentiality protections that address the employer's privacy concerns while preserving your access to relevant information. Negotiate protective order terms early in the discovery process to avoid production delays.

9.6 ESI (Electronically Stored Information) Discovery

ESI Protocols

Modern employment litigation heavily relies on electronic evidence, making ESI discovery protocols essential. **Rule 26(f) conferences** (or state equivalents) should address ESI issues early, including the scope of preservation obligations, search methodologies, and production formats.

Keyword searches must be carefully crafted to capture relevant communications while avoiding over-inclusive results that increase costs. Work with ESI vendors or IT professionals to develop effective search terms and test their results on sample data sets.

Date ranges should encompass the relevant time period with appropriate buffers. For retaliation claims, include communications before the protected activity to establish baseline treatment and after the adverse action to capture retaliatory conduct.

Custodians are individuals likely to have relevant ESI in their possession, custody, or control. Include not only obvious custodians like supervisors and HR personnel, but also IT staff who may have system backups, executives who may have high-level communications, and coworkers who witnessed relevant events.

Production formats significantly impact the usefulness of produced ESI. Native format production preserves metadata and allows for more sophisticated analysis, while PDF production may be easier to review but loses important technical information.

Sources to Target

Email systems including Microsoft Outlook, Gmail, and other enterprise email platforms contain the most valuable communications in employment cases. Include both sent and received messages, as well as draft messages that may reveal intent.

Instant messaging platforms like Microsoft Teams, Slack, WhatsApp, and other workplace communication tools are increasingly important sources of evidence. These platforms often contain more informal communications that may include discriminatory statements or admissions.

HRIS and payroll systems contain structured data about employment decisions, performance ratings, compensation changes, and leave requests. This data can reveal patterns of treatment and support statistical analyses.

Surveillance and monitoring systems including badge access logs, GPS tracking data, computer usage logs, and video surveillance may provide objective evidence of workplace events or employee behavior.

Mobile devices belonging to supervisors or decision-makers may contain relevant text messages, emails, or other communications, though courts vary in their willingness to order production from personal devices.

9.7 Handling Objections and Discovery Disputes

Common Objections

Relevance objections argue that requested information does not relate to the claims or defenses in the case. Counter these objections by explaining the connection between the requested information and your legal theories, citing specific factual allegations in your pleadings.

Overbreadth objections claim that discovery requests are too broad in scope, time period, or subject matter. Respond by demonstrating that the scope is proportional to the importance of the issues and the amount in controversy, and offer to narrow the requests if appropriate.

Undue burden objections assert that responding to discovery would be too expensive or time-consuming. Challenge these objections by requesting detailed cost estimates and proposing alternative approaches, such as sampling methodologies or cost-shifting arrangements.

Privilege objections protect attorney-client communications, work product, and other privileged materials. Require detailed privilege logs that identify the basis for each privilege claim and challenge overly broad assertions of privilege.

Vagueness objections claim that discovery requests are unclear or ambiguous. Respond by providing clarifying definitions or offering to meet and confer about the intended scope of requests.

Tactics for Resolving Disputes

Meet and confer requirements mandate good faith efforts to resolve discovery disputes before court intervention. Document these efforts carefully, as courts may sanction parties who fail to meet and confer in good faith.

Deficiency letters formally notify opposing counsel of inadequate responses and provide specific deadlines for supplementation. These letters create a record of the dispute and demonstrate your efforts to resolve issues without court intervention.

Motions to compel seek court orders requiring compliance with discovery requests. Include detailed explanations of the relevance and proportionality of requested information, document meet and confer efforts, and propose reasonable limitations if appropriate.

Protective orders can resolve disputes by providing confidentiality protections that address legitimate concerns while preserving access to relevant information.

State-specific requirements vary significantly. California Code of Civil Procedure Section 2016.040 requires informal resolution efforts before filing discovery motions. New York courts often require pre-motion conferences for discovery disputes, and local rules may specify particular procedures for dispute resolution.

9.8 Protective Orders and Confidentiality

When Protective Orders Are Needed

Sensitive business information including trade secrets, customer lists, financial data, and strategic plans may require confidentiality protections to encourage full disclosure while protecting legitimate business interests.

Personal information such as medical records, Social Security numbers, and private communications may trigger privacy concerns that necessitate protective measures.

High-profile cases involving public figures, senior executives, or matters likely to attract media attention often require protective orders to prevent harmful publicity.

Litigation strategy may benefit from confidentiality protections that prevent opposing parties from using discovery responses in other litigation or sharing information with competitors.

Key Protective Order Provisions

Confidentiality designations should include multiple levels of protection, such as "Confidential" for sensitive business information and "Attorneys' Eyes Only" for highly sensitive materials like trade secrets or medical records.

Access limitations specify who may review protected materials, typically including counsel of record, designated in-house attorneys, expert witnesses, and court personnel. Consider whether parties themselves should have access to certain categories of information.

Use restrictions limit how protected information may be used, typically restricting use to the pending litigation and prohibiting disclosure to third parties or use for business purposes.

Return or destruction requirements specify what happens to protected materials at the conclusion of litigation, including deadlines for return or certification of destruction.

Inadvertent disclosure provisions address what happens when protected materials are inadvertently produced without proper designation, typically providing procedures for clawback and return.

9.9 Discovery Timelines and Deadlines

Effective discovery management requires careful attention to procedural deadlines and strategic timing. **Federal Rule 26(d)** generally prohibits discovery before the parties' Rule 26(f) conference, while state rules may have different timing requirements.

Interrogatory deadlines typically require responses within 30 days of service, though parties may agree to extensions. Plan interrogatory service strategically to allow time for follow-up document requests based on the responses.

Document production deadlines depend on the scope and complexity of requests, but courts generally expect reasonable compliance timelines. Large ESI productions may require months to complete, making early service essential.

Deposition scheduling should consider witness availability, document review needs, and trial preparation requirements. Key depositions should be scheduled early enough to allow follow-up discovery based on the testimony.

Discovery cutoff dates established by court scheduling orders are strictly enforced. Plan backwards from the cutoff date to ensure adequate time for all necessary discovery, including time to resolve disputes and compel compliance.

Expert witness deadlines often occur near the end of the discovery period and may require earlier fact discovery to support expert opinions. Coordinate fact and expert discovery timelines to ensure experts have access to necessary information.

9.10 Conclusion

Discovery is not just procedural - it's strategic. It is where legal theories meet real-world data and where early missteps can be costly. Mastering the discovery process in employment cases requires technical skill, attention to detail, and the ability to anticipate the opponent's tactics.

The most successful employment attorneys view discovery as an investment in case development rather than a necessary burden. They use discovery not only to gather evidence supporting their claims, but also to assess case strengths and weaknesses, evaluate settlement value, and prepare for effective trial presentation.

Understanding the nuances of federal versus state discovery rules, crafting precise and strategic discovery requests, and effectively managing ESI and privilege issues will distinguish your practice and improve outcomes for your clients. The stronger your factual record through discovery, the stronger your settlement posture and trial readiness.

Remember that discovery is an iterative process. Early responses and productions often reveal new avenues for investigation, requiring follow-up discovery to develop emerging theories or challenge new defenses. Build flexibility into your discovery plan and maintain aggressive but professional advocacy throughout the process.

In Chapter 10, we'll dive deeper into managing ESI, including metadata preservation, email threading, and forensic tools for uncovering altered or deleted files.

10

Electronic Discovery in Employment Litigation

In modern employment litigation, electronically stored information (ESI) is often the most valuable - and the most complex - category of evidence. From emails and chat messages to timekeeping systems and cloud storage, ESI can make or break a case. Proper handling of ESI requires early planning, technical know-how, and close attention to evolving legal standards in both New York and California.

This chapter provides practical guidance for identifying, preserving, requesting, and leveraging ESI in employment cases, with emphasis on metadata, forensics, and defensible production protocols. The digital age has fundamentally transformed how employment disputes are litigated, making electronic discovery expertise not just helpful, but essential for successful representation.

10.1 Understanding ESI in the Employment Context

Electronic discovery, commonly known as e-discovery, refers to the process of identifying, collecting, and producing electronically stored information in litigation. Unlike traditional paper discovery, ESI presents unique challenges related to volume, technical complexity, and preservation requirements.

What Constitutes ESI

The scope of ESI in employment cases is vast and continues to expand as workplace technology evolves. Key categories include:

Communication Records

- Emails and attachments from corporate servers, personal accounts, and cloud platforms
- Text messages and iMessages, including those on personal devices used for work
- Messaging apps such as Slack, Microsoft Teams, WhatsApp, and Telegram
- Social media communications, particularly LinkedIn messages and Facebook workplace groups
- Voice messages and audio recordings from phones or applications

Scheduling and Time Management

- Calendars and schedules from Outlook, Google Calendar, or other platforms
- Timekeeping and payroll software data showing hours worked, overtime, and attendance
- Project management tools like Asana, Trello, or Monday.com
- Expense tracking and reimbursement systems

Multimedia Evidence

- Audio and video files, including Zoom recordings, Teams meetings, and training sessions
- Security camera footage from workplace premises
- Phone recordings where legally permissible

- Digital photographs from company events or workplace conditions

System Data

- Web browser history showing accessed websites during work hours
- Remote access logs demonstrating when employees worked from home
- File access logs showing who opened, modified, or deleted documents
- Network activity logs from corporate servers

Metadata and Hidden Information

- File metadata showing creation dates, edits, and deletions
- Email headers revealing routing and timing information
- Document revision histories and track changes
- System logs recording user activity and acccss patterns

Sources of ESI

Understanding where ESI resides is crucial for comprehensive discovery. Sources include:

Corporate Infrastructure

- Employer servers and network-attached storage devices
- Regular and archival backups maintained by IT departments
- Cloud-based platforms such as Google Workspace, Microsoft 365, and Dropbox
- Specialized business systems including HR platforms, CRM software, and compliance databases

Individual Devices

- Employee mobile phones, both company-issued and personal devices used for work
- Laptops, tablets, and desktop computers

- Personal cloud storage accounts where work documents may be stored
- Home computers used for remote work during the COVID-19 pandemic and beyond

Third-Party Platforms

- Social media accounts and professional networking sites
- External file sharing services like WeTransfer or shared Google drives
- Communication platforms hosted by third parties
- Backup services and archives maintained by external vendors

10.2 The Legal Duty to Preserve ESI

The preservation duty represents one of the most critical aspects of ESI management, with severe consequences for failure to comply.

Triggering the Duty

The obligation to preserve ESI arises when litigation is reasonably anticipated, not when it is actually filed. This standard, established in federal courts and adopted by many state courts, creates a lower threshold than many practitioners realize. See *Williams v. Russ*, 167 Cal. App. 4th 1215 (2008) that recognized the duty to preserve evidence when litigation is "probable." if if a complaint has not yet been filed. *Zubulake v. UBS Warburg LLC*, 220 F.R.D. 212 (S.D.N.Y. 2003) where Judge Shira Scheindlin held that "[O]nce a party reasonably anticipates litigation, it must suspend its routine document retention/destruction policy and put in place a 'litigation hold' to ensure the preservation of relevant documents." New York State courts take the position that the "duty to preserve evidence arises when a party reasonably anticipates litigation." See *VOOM HD Holdings LLC v. EchoStar Satellite LLC*, 93 A.D.3d 33 (N.Y. App. Div. 1st Dep't 2012).

Thus the obligation arises when:

- An employee files an internal complaint with HR
- A government agency begins an investigation

- Employment counsel is consulted about potential claims
- Settlement discussions commence
- A demand letter is sent threatening litigation

The key distinction between federal and state approaches lies in timing and scope. Federal courts generally apply a more stringent standard, requiring preservation as soon as litigation becomes "reasonably foreseeable." California state courts have adopted similar standards, while New York courts sometimes apply a slightly more lenient approach, focusing on when litigation becomes "pending or imminent."

Obligations for Employers

Employers face particularly complex preservation obligations due to their control over corporate systems and multiple custodians. Upon recognizing the preservation duty, employers must:

Issue Comprehensive Litigation Holds A litigation hold is a formal directive suspending normal document retention and destruction policies. Effective holds must reach all relevant custodians, including:

- Human resources personnel who handled the employee's matters
- Direct supervisors and managers in the employee's chain of command
- IT staff responsible for system maintenance and backups
- Colleagues who worked closely with the employee
- Legal and compliance teams involved in investigations
- Third-party vendors with access to relevant systems

Suspend Automatic Deletion Protocols Most organizations have automatic deletion policies for emails, files, and other data. These must be immediately suspended for all custodians and systems that might contain relevant information. This includes:

- Email auto-deletion after specified periods
- Temporary file cleanup routines
- Backup rotation schedules that might overwrite older data

- System logs that typically cycle after predetermined timeframes

Identify and Preserve Backup Systems Organizations often maintain multiple layers of backup systems, from daily incremental backups to long-term archive storage. All relevant backup systems must be identified and preserved, even if accessing them requires significant technical effort or expense.

Obligations for Plaintiffs

Individual plaintiffs also bear preservation responsibilities, though their obligations are typically less complex than those facing institutional defendants. Plaintiffs must:

Preserve Personal Communications

- Avoid deleting text messages, emails, or social media posts that might be relevant
- Maintain access to personal email accounts and social media profiles
- Preserve mobile devices without altering or updating software that might affect data
- Avoid creating new communications that might contradict their claims

Maintain Device Integrity

- Refrain from modifying metadata through file transfers or format conversions
- Avoid exporting only portions of email threads or message conversations
- Preserve original file formats when possible
- Document any necessary changes to devices or accounts

Consequences of Preservation Failures

Failure to preserve ESI can result in severe sanctions that may determine case outcomes:

Monetary Sanctions Courts may impose fines to compensate the opposing party for additional discovery costs or to punish the offending party. These fines can range from thousands to hundreds of thousands of dollars, depending on the case value and degree of misconduct.

Adverse Inference Instructions Perhaps the most damaging sanction, adverse inference allows the jury to assume that destroyed evidence would have been unfavorable to the party who failed to preserve it. In employment cases, this can be devastating - juries may infer that destroyed emails contained evidence of discrimination or harassment.

Evidence Preclusion Courts may prohibit parties from introducing certain evidence or making specific arguments if they failed to preserve related ESI. This can significantly limit a party's ability to present their case.

Case Dismissal or Default Judgment In extreme cases of intentional destruction or gross negligence, courts may dismiss the entire case or enter default judgment against the offending party.

10.3 Drafting an ESI Preservation Letter

The preservation letter serves as both a formal notice and a protective measure, documenting your client's diligence in requesting preservation while potentially creating evidence of the opposing party's failures.

Essential Components

Specific Identification of ESI Sources Rather than generic requests, effective preservation letters identify particular types of ESI relevant to the case. For example:

- "All emails sent or received by [specific individuals] regarding [employee's name] or [specific project/incident]"
- "All Slack communications in channels accessible to [department] from [date] to [date]"
- "All video recordings from security cameras covering [specific areas] during [timeframe]"

Detailed Timeframe Specifications Define precise date ranges based on case facts:

- Employment period from hire date to termination
- Extended periods covering pre-hire communications if recruitment practices are at issue
- Post-termination periods for retaliation claims
- Specific incident windows for harassment or discrimination claims

Comprehensive Custodian Lists Identify not just obvious custodians but also peripheral individuals who might possess relevant information:

- Executive assistants who manage calendars and communications
- IT personnel who maintain systems and handle technical issues
- Security staff who monitor workplace activities
- External consultants or vendors involved in relevant projects
- Legal counsel who participated in investigations or decision-making

Technical Preservation Requirements Address specific technical aspects:

- Request suspension of auto-delete functions with specific system names
- Warn against overwriting backup tapes or cloud storage archives
- Specify preservation of metadata and native file formats
- Request identification of all email servers, messaging platforms, and storage systems

Strategic Timing Considerations

Send preservation letters as early as possible, ideally before formal discovery begins. Early preservation letters demonstrate good faith and create a stronger foundation for spoliation claims if the opposing party fails to comply. However, timing must be balanced against strategic considerations - sometimes revealing the full scope of your preservation requests too early can alert opponents to destroy evidence before receiving the letter.

Differences Between New York and California Practice

New York practitioners should be aware that state courts may apply different standards for preservation letters compared to federal practice. New York's CPLR Section 3120 provides broader discovery rights than federal rules, potentially supporting more expansive preservation requests.

California practitioners benefit from the state's strong anti-SLAPP statute and broad discovery rules, but must be mindful of privacy protections that may limit ESI requests involving personal devices or accounts.

10.4 Metadata: The Hidden Evidence

Metadata represents the digital equivalent of forensic evidence, providing crucial information about document creation, modification, and handling that is often invisible to casual users but invaluable in litigation.

Understanding Metadata Types

System Metadata This information is automatically generated by computer systems and includes:

- File creation dates and times
- Last modification timestamps
- File size and format information
- Device identification and user account information
- Network location data showing where files were accessed

Application Metadata Generated by specific software applications:

- Microsoft Word track changes and comment history
- Email routing information showing all servers that handled a message
- PDF creation software and security settings
- Database record creation and modification logs

User-Generated Metadata Information deliberately added by users:

- Document properties like author, title, and keywords

- Email priority settings and read receipts
- File tags and categorization information
- Custom fields in database records

Strategic Applications in Employment Cases

Establishing Timelines Metadata can prove when critical events occurred with precision that human recollection cannot match. For example:

- Email metadata showing when a manager learned of a complaint
- Document creation dates proving when performance evaluations were actually prepared
- File modification times demonstrating attempts to alter evidence after litigation was anticipated

Proving Knowledge and Intent Email read receipts and system logs can establish when individuals became aware of specific information:

- Delivery and read confirmations for policy notifications
- System access logs showing when managers reviewed employee files
- Meeting scheduling metadata proving awareness of conflicts or issues

Detecting Tampering and Backdating Metadata inconsistencies can reveal attempts to manipulate evidence:

- Creation dates that precede the software installation date
- Modification times occurring after preservation duties arose
- Inconsistent author information suggesting document fabrication

Supporting Retaliation Claims Temporal proximity between protected activity and adverse actions can be established through metadata:

- Emails scheduling disciplinary meetings shortly after discrimination complaints
- Performance review documents created immediately following protected activity

- Calendar entries showing the timing of decision-making processes

Preservation and Production Considerations

To maximize metadata value, request and produce ESI in native format when possible. Native format preserves all metadata, while PDF conversion typically strips most forensically valuable information. However, native production requires specialized software and technical expertise to review effectively.

Consider the proportionality requirements under Federal Rule 26(b)(1) when requesting native format production. Courts may limit native format requirements to key documents or specific custodians if the burden and expense are disproportionate to the case value.

10.5 Common ESI Challenges in Employment Cases

Employment litigation presents unique ESI challenges that differ significantly from other practice areas due to the personal nature of workplace relationships and the intersection of professional and private communications.

Commingled Personal and Professional Communications

Modern employees routinely use personal devices and accounts for work purposes, creating complex privilege and relevance issues:

BYOD (Bring Your Own Device) Policies Many employers allow or require employees to use personal smartphones and laptops for work. This creates discovery challenges when these devices contain both relevant business communications and privileged personal information.

Personal Email Accounts Employees often use personal Gmail, Yahoo, or other accounts for work-related communications, particularly when working remotely or when company email systems have limitations.

Social Media Intersection Professional networking on LinkedIn, industry discussions on Twitter, and workplace relationships on Facebook can all become relevant to employment disputes.

Technical Complexity and Cost

ESI discovery in employment cases often involves significant technical challenges:

Cloud Storage Proliferation Documents may be scattered across multiple cloud platforms, each with different access methods, retention policies, and technical capabilities.

Mobile Device Forensics Extracting data from smartphones and tablets requires specialized software and expertise, with costs that can quickly exceed the value of the case in smaller employment disputes.

System Integration Issues Modern workplaces use integrated software systems where data flows between HR platforms, payroll systems, and communication tools, making comprehensive collection complex.

Privilege and Privacy Concerns

Employment ESI discovery frequently implicates various privilege and privacy protections:

Attorney-Client Privilege Employment investigations often involve legal counsel, creating privilege issues when employees communicate with attorneys through company systems.

Medical Privacy FMLA requests, accommodation discussions, and workers' compensation communications may contain protected health information subject to HIPAA or state privacy laws.

Personnel File Confidentiality Many states have specific protections for personnel files and employee privacy that may limit ESI discovery scope.

Volume and Proportionality Issues

Employment cases often generate disproportionate ESI volumes compared to damages at stake:

Email Proliferation A single employee may generate thousands of emails over their employment period, requiring expensive review processes that may exceed the value of the case.

Backup System Complexity Large employers may maintain years of backup data across multiple systems, making comprehensive preservation and production prohibitively expensive.

Third-Party Data Costs Cloud platform providers often charge significant fees for legal hold implementation and data production, adding unexpected costs to discovery.

10.6 Using ESI Search Protocols

Effective ESI search protocols can dramatically reduce discovery costs while ensuring comprehensive evidence collection. The key lies in collaborative development of targeted search criteria that capture relevant information without generating excessive false positives.

Developing Effective Search Terms

Industry-Specific Terminology Employment cases require understanding of workplace specific language:

- Performance management terms like "PIP" (Performance Improvement Plan), "coaching," or "corrective action"
- HR terminology such as "progressive discipline," "accommodation," or "interactive process"
- Code words that may indicate bias, such as "cultural fit," "not ready," or euphemisms for protected characteristics

Boolean Search Strategies Combine terms using Boolean operators to create precise searches:

- "harassment AND (complaint OR report)" to capture formal and informal complaints
- "accommodation OR ADA OR disability" to find Americans with Disabilities Act-related communications
- "FMLA OR leave OR medical" with proximity operators to capture leave-related discussions

Proximity and Wildcard Searches Use advanced search techniques to capture variations:

- "discriminat*" to capture "discrimination," "discriminate," "discriminatory"
- Terms within specified word distances, such as "(pregnancy OR pregnant) w/10 (terminate OR termination)"
- Date range restrictions to focus on relevant time periods

Negotiating Search Protocols

Collaborative Approach Work with opposing counsel to develop mutually acceptable search terms that balance comprehensiveness with cost control. This collaborative approach often results in more defensible searches and reduced motion practice.

Iterative Testing Implement search protocols in phases:

1. Initial broad searches to understand data volumes
2. Sample review to assess hit rates and relevance
3. Refined searches based on initial results
4. Quality control checks to ensure nothing important was missed

Documentation Requirements Maintain detailed records of search protocol development, including:

- Initial term proposals and rationales
- Negotiation communications with opposing counsel
- Test results and hit rate analyses
- Final agreed-upon protocols and any modifications

Custodian Selection Strategies

Primary Custodians Focus initial efforts on individuals most likely to possess relevant information:

- The plaintiff employee and their immediate supervisor
- HR personnel who handled the employee's matters
- Decision-makers involved in adverse employment actions

- Witnesses to alleged discriminatory or harassing conduct

Secondary Custodians Expand to additional custodians based on initial findings:

- Colleagues in the same department or work group
- IT staff who maintain relevant systems
- Legal counsel involved in investigations
- Upper management who approved decisions

Third-Party Custodians Consider external sources of relevant information:

- Employment agencies or recruiters involved in hiring processes
- External investigators hired for workplace complaints
- Vendors or consultants with access to relevant information
- Former employees who may have relevant communications

Time Range Considerations

Core Employment Period The basic timeframe typically covers the employee's entire tenure, but specific considerations may expand this period:

- Pre-employment communications for hiring discrimination claims
- Post-termination period for retaliation or continuing harassment claims
- Extended periods for pattern and practice claims involving multiple employees

Incident-Specific Windows Focus on specific timeframes around key events:

- 30-60 days before and after formal complaints
- Performance review periods and disciplinary actions
- Leave requests and return-to-work processes
- Promotion or transfer decisions

Legal Compliance Periods Consider regulatory and statutory timeframes:

- EEOC charge filing deadlines (300 days in most states)
- State fair employment agency deadlines
- Contractual notice periods or waiting requirements
- Statute of limitations periods for specific claims

10.7 Tools for Reviewing and Producing ESI

The choice of review platform and production format can significantly impact both cost and effectiveness of ESI discovery in employment cases.

Review Platform Selection

Enterprise Platforms for Large Cases For cases involving substantial ESI volumes or high stakes, enterprise-level platforms provide comprehensive functionality:

Relativity The most widely used enterprise e-discovery platform offers:

- Advanced analytics and machine learning for document prioritization
- Comprehensive review workflows with quality control features
- Robust security and audit trails for sensitive employment data
- Integration with forensic tools for metadata analysis

DISCO A cloud-based platform particularly effective for:

- Fast deployment without IT infrastructure requirements
- Intuitive user interface reducing training time for review teams
- Strong collaboration features for multi-attorney review teams
- Competitive pricing for mid-sized cases

Everlaw Increasingly popular for employment cases due to:

- Excellent search capabilities and user experience
- Strong customer support and training resources

- Flexible pricing models accommodating different case sizes
- Good integration with common productivity tools

Mid-Market Solutions For smaller employment cases or cost-conscious clients:

Logikcull Designed for simplicity and cost-effectiveness:

- Drag-and-drop upload with automatic processing
- Fixed monthly pricing rather than per-gigabyte charges
- Basic review features sufficient for most employment cases
- Good option for solo practitioners and small firms

Nextpoint Focused on litigation support with:

- Integrated deposition and trial presentation tools
- Reasonable pricing for small to mid-sized cases
- Good customer support and training resources
- Adequate functionality for typical employment disputes

Review Workflow Optimization

Threading and Conversation Analysis Email threading groups related messages into conversations, dramatically reducing review time by eliminating duplicate content. This is particularly valuable in employment cases where email chains about specific incidents may span weeks or months.

Technology-Assisted Review (TAR) Advanced machine learning can help prioritize documents for review:

- Predictive coding to identify likely relevant documents
- Clustering to group similar documents together
- Conceptual searching to find documents related to key topics
- Quality control sampling to ensure adequate recall rates

Workflow Design Structure review processes to maximize efficiency:

- First-pass review for obvious non-responsive documents
- Issue-specific review tracks for different legal theories
- Quality control review for key documents and privilege
- Final production review to ensure appropriate redactions

Production Format Considerations

Native Format Production Preserves all metadata and original functionality:

- Required when metadata is crucial to the case
- Enables opposing parties to conduct their own metadata analysis
- May reveal more information than intended
- Requires specialized software for effective review

PDF Production with Load Files More common format offering good balance of usability and protection:

- Easier for recipients to review without specialized software
- Allows for redactions while maintaining document integrity
- Load files provide basic metadata in structured format
- Searchable text enables keyword searching across the production

Hybrid Approaches Many cases benefit from combined production formats:

- Key documents in native format for full metadata access
- Routine documents as PDF for easier handling
- Spreadsheets and databases in native format to preserve functionality
- Images and multimedia in appropriate native formats

Redaction and Privilege Protection

Automated Redaction Tools Modern platforms offer automated redaction for:

- Social Security numbers and other PII
- Credit card numbers and financial account information
- Phone numbers and addresses
- Custom patterns specific to client needs

Privilege Workflow Implement systematic privilege review:

- First-level screening for obvious privileged communications
- Attorney-client privilege logs with detailed descriptions
- Work product protection for investigation materials
- Common interest privilege for multi-party situations

Quality Control Procedures Prevent inadvertent production through:

- Multiple review passes for privilege screening
- Random sampling for quality assurance
- Technology checks for metadata removal
- Final verification before production delivery

10.8 Forensic Experts: When and Why to Use Them

Computer forensic experts can provide crucial technical expertise in complex employment cases, but their use must be strategically planned and cost-justified.

Appropriate Use Cases

Data Recovery Situations Forensic experts become essential when standard collection methods are insufficient:

Deleted File Recovery When parties have allegedly destroyed relevant evidence:

- Recovering deleted emails from local hard drives or server backups

- Retrieving text messages from mobile devices after deletion
- Accessing file fragments from computer hard drives
- Reconstructing document revision histories

System Forensics Analyzing computer systems for evidence of tampering or unauthorized access:

- Determining when files were actually created, modified, or deleted
- Identifying unauthorized access to computer systems or databases
- Analyzing system logs to establish user activity timelines
- Detecting evidence of remote access or data exfiltration

Mobile Device Analysis Smartphones and tablets present unique forensic challenges:

- Extracting data from encrypted devices
- Recovering deleted messages and call logs
- Analyzing location data and usage patterns
- Accessing cloud-synced information

Authentication and Integrity Challenges

Document Authentication Forensic experts can establish document authenticity through:

- Metadata analysis showing creation and modification history
- Digital signature verification for electronically signed documents
- Hash value calculations proving document integrity
- Comparison analysis to detect alterations or fabrications

Chain of Custody Issues Maintaining proper chain of custody for digital evidence:

- Creating forensic images of devices and storage media
- Documenting all handling and processing steps

- Maintaining tamper-evident storage and handling procedures
- Providing detailed reports of all forensic procedures

Expert Testimony Preparation Forensic experts must be prepared to explain technical concepts to judges and juries:

- Simplifying complex technical processes for lay audiences
- Demonstrating reliability and accuracy of forensic methods
- Withstanding cross-examination on technical details
- Providing clear visual aids and demonstrations

Selection and Management Considerations

Credential Verification Choose experts with appropriate qualifications:

- Relevant technical certifications (CISSP, EnCE, GCFA)
- Litigation experience in employment or similar cases
- Academic background in computer science or related fields
- Professional reputation and peer recognition

Cost Management Forensic analysis can be expensive, requiring careful budget management:

- Clear scope definition to prevent cost overruns
- Regular progress reports and cost updates
- Consider whether forensic analysis is proportionate to the value of the case
- Evaluate potential for cost recovery from opposing parties

Engagement Timing Early engagement often provides better results:

- Immediate preservation reduces data degradation
- Early analysis can inform discovery strategy
- Expert input on preservation letters and discovery requests
- Opportunity to object to opposing party's forensic procedures

Expert Report and Testimony Standards

Federal Rule 702 Compliance Expert testimony must meet Daubert standards:

- Reliable methodology based on accepted scientific principles
- Proper application of methods to case facts
- Relevant expertise and qualifications
- Opinions based on sufficient facts and data

Report Requirements Expert reports must include detailed information:

- Complete methodology description
- All data and materials considered
- Assumptions and limitations of analysis
- Alternative explanations considered and rejected

Cross-Examination Preparation Prepare experts for aggressive cross-examination:

- Challenge to qualifications and experience
- Questions about methodology and reliability
- Alternative interpretations of findings
- Bias and compensation issues

10.9 Spoliation and Sanctions

Spoliation of evidence represents one of the most serious risks in ESI discovery, with consequences that can determine case outcomes regardless of underlying merits.

Legal Standards for Spoliation Claims

Federal Court Standards Under Federal Rule 37(e), courts may impose sanctions for spoliation of ESI only if:

- The party had a duty to preserve the information
- The information was lost due to failure to take reasonable steps to preserve it
- The information cannot be restored or replaced through additional discovery

For severe sanctions like adverse inference instructions or case dismissal, the moving party must prove that the spoliating party acted with intent to deprive the opposing party of the information's use in litigation.

State Court Variations State courts may apply different standards:

New York Approach New York courts generally require proof of:

- Existence of a duty to preserve
- Breach of that duty through negligent or intentional destruction
- Relevance of the destroyed evidence
- Prejudice to the requesting party

California Standards California courts focus on:

- Willful suppression of evidence
- Materiality of the destroyed evidence
- Prejudice to the opposing party
- Availability of alternative remedies

Common Spoliation Scenarios in Employment Cases

IT System Maintenance Routine IT maintenance can inadvertently destroy relevant evidence:

- Backup tape rotation overwriting preserved data
- System upgrades that delete old email archives
- Server maintenance that clears temporary files or logs
- Cloud storage cleanup routines removing old documents

Employee Device Management Personal device issues create frequent spoliation problems:

- Employees upgrading phones without preserving work-related data
- Damaged devices that cannot be forensically analyzed
- Factory resets that eliminate all stored information
- Lost or stolen devices containing relevant communications

Investigation Process Errors Internal investigations may inadvertently create spoliation issues:

- Interviewing employees without preserving their devices first
- Allowing continued access to systems after litigation is anticipated
- Failing to preserve investigation notes and recordings
- Permitting document destruction during active investigations

Preventing Spoliation Claims

Comprehensive Litigation Hold Procedures Develop systematic approaches to litigation holds:

- Standard hold notice templates for different scenarios
- Tracking systems to monitor compliance
- Regular reminders and compliance checks
- Clear escalation procedures for non-compliance

IT Coordination Work closely with IT departments to ensure preservation:

- Suspend automatic deletion routines for identified custodians
- Create forensic images of key systems and devices
- Implement legal hold flags in email and document management systems
- Coordinate with cloud service providers for preservation

Documentation and Training Maintain detailed records of preservation efforts:

- Document all steps taken to preserve relevant information
- Train employees on litigation hold obligations
- Create audit trails showing compliance efforts
- Prepare declarations supporting preservation efforts

Responding to Spoliation Allegations

Investigation and Documentation When faced with spoliation allegations:

- Immediately investigate the scope and cause of any data loss
- Document all efforts made to preserve relevant information
- Gather technical evidence about system capabilities and limitations
- Interview relevant personnel about preservation efforts

Mitigation Strategies Demonstrate good faith efforts to remedy any problems:

- Conduct additional searches for alternative sources
- Engage forensic experts to attempt data recovery
- Provide detailed explanations of technical limitations
- Offer cost-shifting or other remedial measures

Expert Support Use technical experts to support your position:

- IT declarations explaining system limitations
- Forensic analysis showing extent of recoverable data
- Industry standard testimony about reasonable preservation efforts
- Alternative source identification and analysis

Sanctions Practice and Strategy

Motion Practice Considerations Spoliation motions require careful strategic planning:

- Timing considerations balancing investigation needs with

procedural deadlines

- Evidence gathering to support spoliation claims
- Coordination with other discovery motions and case strategy
- Settlement leverage considerations

Damages and Prejudice Arguments Establish concrete prejudice from spoliation:

- Identify specific evidence likely contained in destroyed materials
- Demonstrate how missing evidence affects ability to prove claims
- Calculate additional discovery costs caused by spoliation
- Show impact on case strategy and settlement position

Proportionality Defenses Challenge disproportionate spoliation requests:

- Cost-benefit analysis of preservation requirements
- Technical feasibility of requested preservation measures
- Availability of alternative sources of the same information
- Relevance and importance of potentially destroyed evidence

10.10 Emerging Trends and Future Considerations

The landscape of ESI in employment litigation continues to evolve rapidly, driven by technological advances and changing workplace practices.

Remote Work Impact

The COVID-19 pandemic fundamentally altered workplace ESI landscapes:

- Increased use of personal devices and home networks for work
- Greater reliance on cloud-based collaboration tools
- Blurred boundaries between personal and professional communications

- New challenges in preserving and collecting distributed ESI

Artificial Intelligence and Machine Learning

AI tools are increasingly impacting both workplace operations and litigation:

- Automated decision-making systems in hiring and performance management
- AI-powered document review and analysis tools
- Machine learning algorithms creating new forms of evidence
- Explainability challenges when AI systems make employment decisions

Privacy and Data Protection

Evolving privacy laws create new compliance challenges:

- California Consumer Privacy Act (CCPA) implications for employee data
- European GDPR requirements for multinational employers
- State-level privacy legislation creating patchwork compliance requirements
- Employee privacy expectations in remote work environments

Social Media and Communications Evolution

New communication platforms create ongoing discovery challenges:

- Ephemeral messaging apps that automatically delete content
- Video conferencing platforms with varying retention policies
- Social media platforms with complex privacy and access controls
- Professional networking sites with employment-related content

10.11 Practical Implementation Strategies

Successfully managing ESI in employment cases requires systematic approaches tailored to case-specific needs and client resources.

Case Assessment and Planning

Initial ESI Assessment Every employment case should begin with systematic ESI evaluation:

- Identify likely sources of relevant ESI based on case facts
- Assess technical complexity and potential costs
- Evaluate client's ESI preservation capabilities
- Determine need for technical assistance or forensic experts

Cost-Benefit Analysis Balance discovery comprehensiveness against proportionality requirements:

- Estimate ESI collection and review costs
- Compare potential costs to likely case value
- Identify high-value ESI sources for priority treatment
- Consider phased discovery approaches to manage costs

Technology Planning Select appropriate tools and resources:

- Choose review platforms based on case size and complexity
- Plan for technical assistance needs
- Coordinate with client IT resources
- Establish quality control procedures

Client Communication and Education

Preservation Education Ensure clients understand their preservation obligations:

- Explain litigation hold requirements in accessible terms
- Provide written preservation instructions

- Establish regular check-ins to monitor compliance
- Address technical questions promptly

Cost Transparency Maintain open communication about ESI costs:

- Provide detailed cost estimates for different discovery approaches
- Explain factors that might increase or decrease costs
- Offer alternatives for cost control
- Monitor actual costs against estimates

Strategic Decision-Making Involve clients in key ESI strategy decisions:

- Explain risks and benefits of different approaches
- Discuss settlement implications of discovery findings
- Address privilege and confidentiality concerns
- Coordinate with business operations needs

Quality Control and Risk Management

Documentation Standards Maintain comprehensive records of all ESI activities:

- Document preservation decisions and communications
- Track custodian compliance with litigation holds
- Record all technical procedures and methodologies
- Maintain privilege logs and redaction decisions

Regular Reviews Implement periodic assessments of ESI strategies:

- Review preservation effectiveness and compliance
- Assess discovery progress against case timelines
- Evaluate cost management and budget adherence
- Adjust strategies based on developing case facts

Risk Mitigation Proactively address potential ESI problems:

- Identify spoliation risks early in case development
- Implement redundant preservation measures for critical evidence
- Prepare contingency plans for technical failures
- Maintain expert relationships for emergency situations

10.12 Conclusion

In employment litigation, ESI is not ancillary - it's central. Managing ESI effectively means preserving crucial timelines, proving intent and knowledge, and anticipating digital defenses. Whether you're litigating a harassment claim or a wage dispute, understanding the who, what, and how of digital data is now an essential part of the legal skillset.

The evolution of workplace technology continues to create new challenges and opportunities in employment litigation. Success requires not only technical competency but also strategic thinking about how ESI fits into broader case narratives and settlement dynamics. Practitioners must balance thoroughness with proportionality, ensuring that ESI discovery serves case objectives without creating disproportionate costs or burdens.

The investment in ESI expertise pays dividends throughout the litigation process. Well-preserved and effectively presented electronic evidence can support compelling witness testimony, establish crucial timelines, and demonstrate patterns of behavior that might otherwise remain hidden. Conversely, ESI mismanagement can result in sanctions, adverse inferences, and missed opportunities that undermine even strong underlying claims.

As employment law practice continues to evolve, practitioners who master ESI discovery will find themselves better equipped to serve clients effectively, resolve cases favorably, and navigate the increasingly complex intersection of law and technology in the modern workplace.

In Chapter 11, we'll turn to mediation and settlement conferences, where much of employment litigation is resolved - and where the evidence you've gathered through careful ESI discovery pays strategic dividends in achieving favorable outcomes for your clients.

11

Mediation and Settlement Conferences in Employment Litigation

In employment litigation, the majority of cases settle - often before trial and frequently during structured negotiations such as mediation or mandatory settlement conferences. These proceedings offer a chance to resolve disputes with greater speed, flexibility, and confidentiality than litigation. But successful resolution requires preparation, strategy, and a deep understanding of your case's strengths and weaknesses.

This chapter covers how to prepare for and conduct mediation and settlement conferences in employment cases in New York and California, highlighting best practices for maximizing value and protecting your client's interests.

11.1 Understanding Alternative Dispute Resolution in Employment Cases

Defining Key Terms

Mediation is a voluntary, confidential process where a neutral third party (the mediator) facilitates negotiations between disputing parties. The mediator does not make binding decisions but helps parties reach their own agreement. Unlike arbitration, mediation is non-binding unless the parties reach a settlement.

Settlement conferences are court-supervised proceedings where a judge or court-appointed neutral attempts to help parties resolve their dispute before trial. These may be mandatory or voluntary, depending on local court rules and case circumstances.

Alternative Dispute Resolution (ADR) encompasses various methods of resolving disputes outside traditional litigation, including mediation, arbitration, early neutral evaluation, and settlement conferences.

Why Employment Cases Favor Settlement

Employment disputes present unique characteristics that make settlement particularly attractive. Unlike commercial litigation, employment cases often involve ongoing relationships, reputational concerns, and highly personal claims of discrimination, harassment, or wrongful termination. The emotional toll on employees, combined with employers' desire to avoid negative publicity and potential punitive damages, creates strong incentives for resolution.

Consider the difference between a breach of contract case and a sexual harassment claim. In the contract dispute, the parties may have no ongoing relationship and purely financial interests at stake. In the harassment case, the employee may seek vindication and systemic change, while the employer faces potential exposure to punitive damages, attorney's fees under fee-shifting statutes, and significant reputational harm if the case proceeds to trial.

11.2 Timing of Mediation: Strategic Considerations

When to Mediate

Early Mediation (Pre-Discovery) Early mediation occurs before substantial discovery, often after the initial complaint and answer are filed. This approach works best in straightforward cases with clear facts or when both parties have mutual interests in confidentiality and quick resolution.

For example, in a case involving an executive's termination where the facts are largely undisputed and the dispute centers on severance entitlements, early mediation can avoid the costs and time of extensive discovery. However, early mediation may disadvantage plaintiffs in cases requiring document discovery to prove discrimination or harassment patterns.

Mid-Case Mediation (Post-Initial Discovery) Mid-case mediation occurs after initial disclosures, key depositions, and essential document production. This timing provides stronger leverage and clearer case valuation for both sides.

Consider a wage and hour class action where initial discovery reveals the scope of potential violations and class size. At this stage, both parties have sufficient information to make informed settlement decisions, but before incurring the substantial costs of expert witness preparation and extensive class discovery.

Pretrial Settlement Conference Court-ordered or judge-supervised conferences occur close to trial, often after failed private mediation attempts. These conferences leverage the immediate prospect of trial to motivate settlement but offer limited time for complex negotiations.

Jurisdictional Differences

California Specific Requirements California has implemented several mandatory mediation requirements that practitioners must understand. Under Labor Code Section 2699.3, Private Attorneys General Act (PAGA) cases now require mandatory early mediation before proceeding to court. This requirement reflects California's policy preference for resolving wage and hour disputes efficiently while preserving employees' rights to pursue penalties on behalf of the state.

Los Angeles Superior Court's Mandatory Settlement Conference (MSC) program requires certain employment cases to participate in settlement conferences before trial. The court's ADR programs are designed to reduce trial backlogs while providing parties with meaningful settlement opportunities.

New York Procedural Framework New York courts, including New York City Civil Court and federal courts in the Southern and Eastern Districts, maintain comprehensive ADR panels with specialized employment mediators. These programs recognize that employment disputes benefit from mediators with subject-matter expertise.

Under the Civil Practice Law and Rules (CPLR), settlement conferences may be ordered at preliminary conferences or compliance conferences, giving judges discretion to require settlement discussions when they believe resolution is possible.

The key difference between California and New York approaches lies in timing and mandatory nature. California increasingly requires early intervention in specific case types (like PAGA actions), while New York provides more judicial discretion in timing and participation requirements.

11.3 Choosing the Right Mediator: Critical Success Factors

Essential Qualifications

Subject-Matter Expertise Employment law mediation requires understanding of complex statutory schemes, including Title VII, the Americans with Disabilities Act, the Fair Labor Standards Act, and state-specific employment laws. A mediator familiar with these frameworks can better assess the case's strengths and guide realistic settlement discussions.

For instance, in a discrimination case involving the interactive process under the ADA, a mediator with employment law background will understand the nuances of reasonable accommodation obligations and can help parties craft settlements that address both monetary relief and prospective compliance measures.

Experience Perspective Consider whether you want a mediator with primarily plaintiff-side or defense-side experience. A former plaintiff's attorney may better understand employee motivations and damages calculations, while a defense-oriented mediator might more effectively communicate trial risks to employers.

However, the most effective employment mediators often have experience representing both sides, providing balanced perspectives that enhance credibility with all parties.

Authority and Temperament Employment cases frequently involve high emotions, particularly in discrimination and harassment matters. Effective mediators must demonstrate patience, empathy, and the authority to guide difficult conversations without appearing biased.

Mediator Selection Sources

Private ADR Providers JAMS (Judicial Arbitration and Mediation Services), the American Arbitration Association (AAA), and National Arbitration and Mediation (NAM) maintain rosters of experienced employment mediators. These providers offer comprehensive services but at premium rates.

Court-Sponsored Programs State and federal courts maintain mediator panels offering services at reduced rates. While these mediators may have less specialized employment experience, court programs provide cost-effective options for smaller cases.

Retired Judicial Officers Former judges often serve as mediators in high-value employment cases, bringing judicial authority and trial experience to settlement discussions. Their perspective on likely trial outcomes can be particularly persuasive to both sides.

The Interview Process

When case stakes justify the effort, interview potential mediators about their approach, experience with similar cases, and settlement philosophy. Key questions include: How do they handle emotional clients? What is their typical mediation structure? How do they approach cases with significant power imbalances between parties?

11.4 Client Preparation: Managing Expectations and Emotions

Setting Realistic Expectations

The Non-Binding Nature of Mediation Clients must understand that mediation creates no obligation to settle unless they agree to specific terms. This distinguishes mediation from arbitration, where the arbitrator's decision is typically binding and enforceable like a court judgment.

Compromise as the Goal Unlike litigation, where one party typically "wins," mediation seeks mutually acceptable solutions. Clients expecting complete vindication or maximum damages may need coaching to understand the benefits of compromise, including certainty, privacy, and avoiding trial risks.

Confidentiality Protections Mediation discussions are generally confidential and inadmissible in subsequent litigation under Evidence Code Section 1119 in California and similar protections in New York. This confidentiality allows parties to make settlement offers and admissions without fear they will be used against them at trial.

Emotional Preparation

Validation Needs in Discrimination Cases Employees who experienced discrimination or harassment often seek acknowledgment of wrongdoing beyond monetary compensation. Effective preparation helps clients articulate these needs while understanding employers' reluctance to admit liability.

For example, a client who endured workplace harassment may value an apology or commitment to policy changes as much as financial relief. Preparing the client to express these interests constructively can lead to more satisfying settlements.

Managing Reaction to Initial Offers First offers in employment mediation are typically far below plaintiff's expectations and above defendant's comfort level. Prepare clients for this reality and coach them not to view initial offers as reflective of case value or as personal insults.

Psychological Dynamics

The Need to Vent Many employment clients need to tell their story before engaging in settlement discussions. Effective preparation includes allowing time for this process while helping clients transition from narrative to negotiation.

Anchoring and Adjustment Initial settlement offers create psychological anchors that influence subsequent negotiations. Prepare clients to understand this dynamic and focus on movement toward reasonable resolution rather than fixating on first offers.

11.5 Mediation Brief Preparation: Advocacy Through Persuasion

Essential Components

Factual Foundation Present facts concisely but compellingly, focusing on those most relevant to damages and liability. Unlike trial briefs, mediation briefs should acknowledge factual disputes while emphasizing the strongest evidence supporting your position.

For example, in a wrongful termination case, rather than simply asserting the client was terminated for discriminatory reasons, highlight specific evidence: "Three weeks after Ms. Johnson complained about sexual harassment, her supervisor documented performance issues for the first time in her five-year tenure, despite her recent promotion and positive annual review."

Legal Framework Explain relevant legal standards without excessive citation, focusing on how the law supports your client's position and creates risks for the opposing party. Include recent developments or trends that might influence the value of the case.

Damages Analysis Provide detailed damages calculations with supporting documentation. Break down economic losses (lost wages, benefits, future earnings) and non-economic damages (emotional distress, reputational harm) with reference to comparable settlements or verdicts when available.

Settlement Context Include relevant settlement history, previous demands and offers, and any factors affecting settlement posture. This information helps the mediator understand the negotiation landscape and identify potential breakthrough points.

Strategic Considerations

Tone and Credibility Mediation briefs should be persuasive but not inflammatory. Acknowledging case weaknesses while emphasizing strengths builds credibility with mediators and opposing counsel. This approach differs from trial advocacy, where zealous representation may require more aggressive positioning.

Document Selection Attach only the most critical documents - smoking-gun emails, performance reviews, pay records, or policy violations. Overwhelming mediators with exhibits reduces the impact of truly important evidence.

Confidential vs. Shared Briefs

Shared Brief Strategy Shared briefs visible to all parties set the tone for negotiation and demonstrate preparation and confidence. They allow you to present your case while signaling reasonableness and willingness to engage constructively.

Confidential Brief Advantages Confidential briefs submitted only to the mediator can address sensitive facts, litigation risks, or settlement flexibility without revealing strategy to opponents. These briefs might discuss client financial constraints, weak evidence, or acceptable settlement ranges.

The choice between shared and confidential briefs depends on case dynamics and negotiation strategy. In cases where you want to demonstrate strength and preparation, shared briefs may be more effective. Where you need to discuss sensitive settlement parameters or acknowledge significant risks, confidential submissions protect strategic information.

11.6 Negotiation Strategies During Mediation

Opening Positioning

Anchoring Principles Research in behavioral economics demonstrates that initial offers significantly influence final settlement amounts. However, extreme anchors that lack reasonable justification can undermine credibility and stall negotiations.

For example, in a discrimination case where comparable verdicts range from $50,000 to $200,000, an opening demand of $500,000 might appear unreasonable without extraordinary circumstances. Conversely, a $150,000 opening demand with clear justification based on damages and precedent provides effective anchoring while maintaining credibility.

Justification and Reasoning Support opening demands with specific calculations and precedent. Reference similar cases, jury verdicts, and regulatory penalties to provide objective bases for your position. This approach shifts discussion from arbitrary numbers to principled negotiation.

Leverage Development and Use

Factual Leverage Strong facts create settlement pressure more effectively than legal arguments. Contemporaneous documents, witness testimony, and clear policy violations provide concrete bases for settlement discussions.

Consider the difference between alleging discrimination generally versus presenting an email where a supervisor states, "We need younger blood in this department" shortly before terminating a 55-year-old employee. The specific evidence creates immediate leverage and settlement pressure.

Legal Leverage Reference favorable case law, procedural advantages (such as surviving summary judgment), or fee-shifting statutes that increase defendant's exposure. In employment cases, attorney's fee provisions in many civil rights statutes create significant leverage for plaintiffs with strong cases.

Economic Leverage Present trial cost analyses showing the expense of continued litigation compared to settlement values. For defendants, this includes attorney's fees, expert witness costs, and management time. For plaintiffs, it includes the risk of adverse outcomes and collection challenges.

Responding to Settlement Offers

Lowball Offer Strategy When facing unreasonably low offers, avoid emotional reactions that can derail negotiations. Instead, ask for justification of the offer and provide specific reasons why it fails to account for the value of the case.

Effective response: "Your offer of $10,000 doesn't account for the $45,000 in documented lost wages, let alone the discrimination claim. Can you help me understand how you arrived at that figure?" This approach maintains dialogue while challenging inadequate offers.

Incremental Movement Plan your concession strategy in advance, making meaningful movements that encourage reciprocal responses while preserving negotiation room. Avoid equal concessions that may signal your bottom line prematurely.

Caucus Strategy

Private Session Advantages Caucus sessions allow mediators to explore sensitive issues, test settlement parameters, and provide reality checks without public positioning concerns. Use these sessions to discuss litigation risks honestly and explore creative solutions.

Information Management Control what information you share with mediators during caucus sessions, understanding that experienced mediators will use this information to facilitate settlement while maintaining appropriate confidentiality.

11.7 Special Considerations in Employment Mediation

Confidentiality and Non-Disclosure Provisions

California's Silenced No More Act Senate Bill 331, effective January 1, 2022, significantly restricts confidentiality provisions in discrimination, harassment, and retaliation settlements. The law prohibits confidentiality clauses that prevent disclosure of factual information related to claims, though it allows protection of settlement amounts and terms.

This creates strategic considerations for both sides. Employers can no longer use broad confidentiality clauses to prevent employees from discussing their experiences, while employees retain the ability to seek privacy around financial terms if desired.

Balancing Confidentiality Interests Even within legal constraints, parties may have legitimate confidentiality interests. Craft provisions that protect necessary business information while complying with statutory limitations. Consider separate confidentiality agreements for truly proprietary information unrelated to the underlying claims.

Tax Implications and Settlement Structure

Allocation Strategies Settlement agreements should specify allocations between different types of damages for tax purposes. Wage-related payments are subject to employment tax withholding and reported on Form W-2, while payments for personal injury or emotional distress may qualify for different tax treatment.

IRS Considerations Under Internal Revenue Code Section 104, payments for personal physical injuries or physical sickness are generally excluded from gross income. However, punitive damages and interest payments are typically taxable. Careful allocation can optimize tax consequences for clients.

Professional Consultation Complex settlements warrant consultation with tax professionals to optimize structure and ensure compliance. Document the business reasons for any allocations to support tax positions if challenged.

Non-Disparagement and Restrictive Covenants

Scope and Enforceability Non-disparagement clauses must be carefully drafted to comply with California and New York restrictions on overly broad provisions. Recent legislation in both states limits clauses that might chill legitimate speech about workplace conditions or public policy issues.

Mutual vs. Unilateral Provisions Consider whether non-disparagement provisions should be mutual or apply only to the employee. Mutual provisions may be more acceptable to employees but can create enforcement challenges for employers if corporate representatives make disparaging statements.

Penalties and Enforcement Include reasonable liquidated damages provisions for covenant breaches, ensuring they constitute reasonable estimates of actual damages rather than punitive penalties that courts might refuse to enforce.

Prospective Relief and Systemic Changes

Policy Modifications Employment settlements can include commitments to policy changes, training programs, or other prospective relief that addresses underlying workplace issues. These provisions may be as valuable to employees as monetary relief.

Implementation and Monitoring Consider how prospective relief will be implemented and monitored. Some settlements include third-party monitoring or reporting requirements to ensure compliance with policy changes.

11.8 Finalizing the Settlement Agreement

Essential Contractual Elements

Payment Terms and Structure Specify payment amounts, timing, and method clearly. Consider whether payments will be made in installments and what happens if payments are missed. Include interest provisions for late payments and security mechanisms for larger settlements.

Release Scope and Limitations Draft release provisions carefully, balancing employer's desire for broad protection with employee's interest in preserving rights to file administrative charges or pursue claims unrelated to the settlement. Consider recent developments limiting overly broad releases.

Dismissal Procedures Specify how the underlying litigation will be dismissed and whether the court will retain jurisdiction to enforce the settlement agreement. Retention of jurisdiction can provide efficient enforcement mechanisms if disputes arise.

Court Approval Requirements

PAGA Settlement Approval California Labor Code Section 2699(l) requires court approval of PAGA settlements, including review of the settlement's fairness and adequacy. Courts examine whether the settlement provides appropriate relief to affected employees and serves the public interest.

Class Action Considerations Rule 23 of the Federal Rules of Civil Procedure and corresponding state rules require court approval of class action settlements. This process includes notice to class members and opportunity for objection, adding time and complexity to settlement finalization.

Incompetent Party Protections Settlements involving minors or legally incompetent parties require court approval to protect their interests. This adds procedural requirements but provides important safeguards.

Documentation Best Practices

Precision and Clarity Draft settlement agreements with precision, avoiding ambiguous terms that could lead to enforcement disputes. Define key terms clearly and anticipate potential interpretation issues.

Integration and Modification Include merger clauses stating that the written agreement represents the complete understanding between parties and can only be modified through written amendments signed by all parties.

11.9 Court-Mandated Settlement Conferences

Distinguishing Features from Private Mediation

Structural Differences Court-mandated settlement conferences typically operate under tighter time constraints than private mediation, often lasting only a few hours compared to full-day private mediations. This compressed timeframe requires more focused preparation and streamlined presentations.

Judicial Authority Settlement conferences facilitated by judges or court attorneys carry additional authority that can influence parties' willingness to make concessions. However, judges must be careful not to compromise their ability to preside over the case if settlement fails.

Limited Narrative Opportunity Unlike private mediation, where parties may have extensive opportunities to present their perspectives, court settlement conferences focus more directly on legal and economic issues with limited time for storytelling or emotional processing.

Preparation Strategies

Concise Case Presentation Prepare streamlined case presentations focusing on key liability evidence, damages calculations, and settlement parameters. Assume the neutral has limited time to review extensive materials.

Clear Authority and Parameters Ensure clients and decision-makers attend with clear settlement authority. Court settlement conferences are less conducive to multiple rounds of consultation with absent parties.

Judicial Input on Valuation Be prepared for direct judicial commentary on the case's strengths, weaknesses, and reasonable settlement ranges. While non-binding, judicial observations carry significant weight in settlement discussions.

11.10 When Mediation Fails: Strategic Response

Post-Mediation Analysis

Information Gathering Value Even failed mediations provide valuable information about opponent's case theory, settlement posture, and key concerns. Analyze what you learned about their evidence, damages arguments, and negotiation priorities.

Case Reassessment Use mediation insights to reassess case value, litigation strategy, and trial preparation priorities. Opponent's arguments and evidence presentations may reveal strengths or weaknesses not previously apparent.

Client Relationship Management Debrief thoroughly with clients about the mediation process, what worked, what didn't, and how the experience affects their litigation goals. Some clients become more motivated to settle after understanding the negotiation process, while others become more committed to trial.

Continued Settlement Opportunities

Mediator's Proposal Process If parties are close but cannot bridge the final gap, many mediators will offer to make a confidential recommendation that parties can accept or reject without disclosure to the other side. This process can break deadlocks when both sides are close to acceptable numbers.

Future Settlement Discussions Mediation failure doesn't preclude future settlement discussions. Many cases settle in subsequent negotiations after additional discovery, dispositive motion practice, or as trial approaches.

Strategic Use of Failed Mediation Consider how to use unsuccessful mediation strategically in ongoing litigation. Demonstrated willingness to engage in good faith settlement discussions may influence judicial case management or provide foundation for fee applications if you ultimately prevail.

Renewed Negotiation Timing

Post-Discovery Settlement Additional discovery may strengthen your position or reveal new information that changes settlement dynamics. Plan for renewed settlement discussions after key depositions or document production.

Dispositive Motion Outcomes Summary judgment rulings, whether favorable or unfavorable, often prompt renewed settlement discussions by clarifying the strength of the case and trial prospects.

Trial Proximity Effects Many employment cases settle immediately before trial as the reality of jury decision-making becomes imminent. Maintain settlement readiness even after unsuccessful mediation.

11.11 Advanced Settlement Techniques

Creative Settlement Structures

Non-Monetary Relief Consider settlement components beyond money, including positive references, policy changes, training commitments, or other prospective relief that addresses client concerns about workplace conditions.

Structured Settlements For larger settlements, consider structured payment arrangements that provide tax advantages or address client's long-term financial planning needs. These arrangements can be particularly valuable in cases involving younger plaintiffs with long-term earning potential.

Conditional Settlement Terms Some settlements include conditions tied to future events, such as implementation of policy changes or achievement of workplace diversity goals. These provisions require careful drafting to ensure enforceability.

Multi-Party Settlement Coordination

Individual vs. Collective Settlements In cases involving multiple plaintiffs or related claims, coordinate settlement strategies to maximize leverage while protecting individual client interests. Consider whether individual settlements might undermine collective bargaining power.

Timing and Sequencing Plan the sequence of settlement discussions in multi-party cases, understanding that early settlements may affect leverage and dynamics for remaining parties.

International and Multi-Jurisdictional Considerations

Cross-Border Employment Issues For cases involving international employers or multi-jurisdictional employment relationships, consider how settlement agreements will be enforced across different legal systems and what governing law provisions are necessary.

Regulatory Compliance Ensure settlements comply with employment laws in all relevant jurisdictions, particularly regarding discrimination, wage and hour, and employee mobility restrictions.

11.12 Conclusion

Mediation and settlement conferences offer unique opportunities to resolve employment disputes on the parties' own terms while avoiding the uncertainty, expense, and emotional toll of trial. Success requires the same rigor as litigation preparation: comprehensive fact development, clear legal analysis, realistic damages assessment, and strategic client counseling.

The key to effective employment mediation lies in understanding that these cases involve more than legal claims and monetary damages. They implicate personal dignity, workplace relationships, and often fundamental questions about fairness and equality in employment. Skilled advocates recognize these broader dimensions while maintaining focus on achievable solutions that serve their clients' real interests.

The landscape of employment dispute resolution continues to evolve, with new statutory requirements, changing confidentiality rules, and innovative settlement structures. Staying current with these developments ensures that your mediation practice remains effective and compliant with evolving legal standards.

Remember that settlement is a process, not a single event. Even unsuccessful mediation attempts provide valuable information and may set the stage for future resolution. The investment in thorough preparation and strategic thinking about settlement pays dividends not only in current cases but in building a practice that consistently achieves favorable outcomes for employment clients.

In Chapter 12, we'll examine summary judgment and other dispositive motions - the next critical inflection point in employment litigation where cases are won, lost, or positioned for favorable settlement.

12

Summary Judgment and Dispositive Motions

A motion for summary judgment is often the final gate between litigation and trial in employment cases. Employers regularly use it as a tool to dismiss claims or narrow issues, arguing that no genuine dispute of material fact exists and that they are entitled to judgment as a matter of law. Plaintiffs, in turn, must marshal admissible evidence to survive and proceed to trial.

This chapter explains how to prepare for, respond to, and strategically deploy summary judgment and related dispositive motions in New York and California, as well as in federal court under Rule 56.

12.1 Purpose and Timing of Summary Judgment

What Summary Judgment Accomplishes

Summary judgment serves as a procedural mechanism to resolve cases without the need for a full trial when the facts are either undisputed or legally insufficient to support a claim. Unlike a motion to dismiss, which tests only the legal sufficiency of the pleadings, summary judgment examines the actual evidence developed during discovery.

The motion asks the court to determine whether a reasonable jury could find in favor of the non-moving party based on the evidence presented. If not, judgment is entered as a matter of law, eliminating the need for trial.

Typical Timing and Strategic Considerations

Summary judgment motions are typically filed after discovery is substantially complete but before trial preparation begins in earnest. The timing serves several strategic purposes:

For Defendants (Employers): Filing early can eliminate weak claims before investing in expensive trial preparation. However, filing too early may result in denial if discovery remains incomplete, particularly regarding the employer's decision-making process or internal communications.

For Plaintiffs (Employees): While less common, plaintiffs may seek summary judgment on clear-cut issues like unpaid wages where documentary evidence is overwhelming, or on liability in cases involving clear policy violations.

Legal Standard Explained

The legal standard for summary judgment requires two showings by the moving party:

1. **No Genuine Dispute of Material Fact:** The moving party must demonstrate that even viewing the evidence in the light most favorable to the non-moving party, no reasonable jury could find facts that would support the non-moving party's case.

2. **Entitlement to Judgment as a Matter of Law:** Even if certain facts are assumed to be true, the law requires judgment in favor of the moving party.

A "material fact" is one that could affect the outcome of the case under the applicable substantive law. A "genuine dispute" exists when the evidence would allow a reasonable jury to return a verdict for either party.

12.2 Jurisdictional Differences in Summary Judgment Procedures

Federal Court Under Rule 56

Federal Rule of Civil Procedure 56 governs summary judgment in federal employment cases, including those brought under Title VII, the Americans with Disabilities Act, the Age Discrimination in Employment Act, and the Fair Labor Standards Act.

Key Federal Requirements:

- The motion must be supported by citations to particular parts of materials in the record
- Affidavits or declarations must be made on personal knowledge and set out facts that would be admissible in evidence
- The court must grant summary judgment if the movant shows there is no genuine dispute as to any material fact

Federal Practice Notes: Federal judges have broad discretion in how they handle summary judgment motions. Some courts require extensive briefing with separate statements of undisputed facts, while others prefer streamlined presentations. Local rules often specify formatting requirements, page limits, and timing for responses.

New York State Practice

New York's summary judgment procedure under CPLR 3212 differs from federal practice in several important ways:

Burden of Proof: The moving party must make a prima facie showing of entitlement to judgment as a matter of law, tendering sufficient evidence to demonstrate the absence of any material issues of fact. Only then does the burden shift to the opposing party to produce evidentiary proof in admissible form sufficient to establish the existence of material issues of fact.

Statement of Material Facts: While not explicitly required by statute, New York courts increasingly expect detailed statements of undisputed facts with specific citations to the record, similar to federal practice.

Timing Considerations: New York allows summary judgment motions to be made at any time after issue is joined, but courts may deny premature motions if discovery is incomplete.

Example of New York Approach: In employment discrimination cases, New York courts often apply a more lenient standard for establishing a prima facie case but require stronger evidence of pretext to survive summary judgment. For instance, in a race discrimination case, temporal proximity between protected activity and adverse employment action may be sufficient to raise an inference of retaliation, even without additional evidence.

California State Practice

California's summary judgment procedure under Code of Civil Procedure Section 437c has undergone significant recent changes that affect employment litigation:

Tripartite Burden: California employs a three-step analysis: (1) the moving party must show entitlement to judgment, (2) the opposing party must raise a triable issue of material fact, and (3) the court must determine whether the evidence would allow a reasonable trier of fact to find for the opposing party.

Separate Statement Requirement: California mandates a separate statement of undisputed material facts, with each fact numbered and supported by admissible evidence. The opposing party must respond to each numbered fact specifically.

Discovery Cutoff: California requires that all discovery be completed before the hearing on summary judgment, with specific timing requirements for service and response.

Recent Developments: California's Fair Employment and Housing Act amendments have expanded protections against harassment and discrimination, making summary judgment more difficult for employers in certain contexts. For example, the definition of harassment has been broadened to include conduct that need not be severe or pervasive if it unreasonably interferes with work performance.

Key Differences Between Jurisdictions

Burden Shifting: Federal courts apply a relatively straightforward standard requiring the moving party to show no genuine dispute of material fact. New

York requires a prima facie showing before burden shifts. California employs the most complex tripartite analysis.

Fact Statement Requirements: California mandates numbered separate statements with specific response requirements. Federal and New York practice varies by judge and local rules, though detailed fact statements are increasingly expected.

Discovery Completion: California has strict requirements for discovery completion. Federal and New York courts have more discretion to consider motions even with ongoing discovery, though this often results in denial or continuance.

Evidentiary Standards: All three jurisdictions require admissible evidence, but California courts are particularly strict about the form of declarations and the foundation for documentary evidence.

12.3 Common Summary Judgment Targets in Employment Cases

Discrimination Claims

Employers frequently target discrimination claims that lack sufficient evidence of pretext or fail to establish a prima facie case under the McDonnell Douglas framework.

Typical Employer Arguments:

- Plaintiff cannot establish membership in a protected class or that adverse action occurred under circumstances giving rise to an inference of discrimination
- Employer's stated reason for adverse action is legitimate and unrelated to protected status
- Plaintiff cannot demonstrate the employer's stated reason is pretextual

Example: In an age discrimination case, an employer might argue that a 58-year-old employee was terminated for poor performance documented over several months, not because of age. The employer would present performance reviews, supervisor testimony, and evidence that younger employees with similar performance issues were also terminated.

Plaintiff's Response Strategy: To survive summary judgment, the plaintiff might present evidence that the employer's performance concerns were never communicated before termination, that younger employees with worse performance were retained, or that supervisors made age-related comments around the time of termination.

Harassment Claims

Harassment claims face particular challenges at summary judgment because courts must determine whether conduct was sufficiently severe or pervasive to alter working conditions.

Traditional Standard: Under federal law and many state laws, harassment must be severe or pervasive enough to create a hostile work environment that a reasonable person would find abusive.

Evolving Standards: New York and California have expanded harassment protections. New York's Human Rights Law now prohibits harassment that subjects individuals to inferior treatment because of protected characteristics, even if not severe or pervasive. California has similarly broadened harassment protections under FEHA.

Example of Successful Defense Motion: An employer might argue that three isolated comments over a two-year period, while inappropriate, do not rise to the level of actionable harassment. The employer would emphasize the company's anti-harassment policy, immediate investigation of complaints, and remedial action taken.

Example of Failed Defense Motion: If those same comments were accompanied by exclusion from meetings, assignment of less desirable work, and management's dismissive response to complaints, a court might find sufficient evidence of harassment to deny summary judgment.

Retaliation Claims

Retaliation claims often succeed or fail based on temporal proximity between protected activity and adverse action, though courts require more than mere temporal proximity.

Protected Activity: Must involve opposition to discriminatory practices or participation in EEOC proceedings, internal complaints, or other legally protected conduct.

Causal Connection: Plaintiffs must show the employer knew of protected activity and that it motivated the adverse action. Close temporal proximity can help establish causation, but courts typically require additional evidence.

Example: An employee files an EEOC charge alleging race discrimination and is terminated three weeks later. If the employee can show only temporal proximity, summary judgment for the employer is likely. However, if the employee can also show that the stated reason for termination (poor performance) was never documented before the EEOC charge, or that supervisors made comments about "troublemakers," summary judgment may be denied.

Wage and Hour Claims

Wage and hour claims often involve clear documentary evidence that can support summary judgment for either party.

Common Issues:

- Misclassification of employees as exempt from overtime
- Failure to pay minimum wage or overtime compensation
- Improper deductions from wages
- Meal and rest break violations (particularly in California)

Example of Employer Victory: Where time records clearly show an employee worked standard 40-hour weeks, was paid above minimum wage, and took documented meal breaks, an employer might successfully obtain summary judgment on overtime and meal break claims.

Example of Employee Victory: Where an employer classified workers as independent contractors but controlled their work methods, provided tools and equipment, and required exclusive service, an employee might obtain summary judgment on misclassification and resulting wage claims.

Constructive Discharge Claims

Constructive discharge requires showing that working conditions were so intolerable that a reasonable person would feel compelled to resign.

Legal Standard: The employee must prove that resignation was involuntary and that the employer deliberately created or knowingly permitted working conditions so intolerable that a reasonable employee would feel compelled to quit.

Common Employer Arguments: The resignation was voluntary, the employee failed to utilize internal complaint procedures, or the working conditions, while unpleasant, were not objectively intolerable.

Example: An employee resigns after being demoted, having responsibilities reduced, and being excluded from meetings. If the employer can show the changes were based on legitimate business reasons and that the employee never complained through proper channels, summary judgment might be appropriate. However, if the changes followed immediately after the employee filed a discrimination complaint and were accompanied by hostile conduct, constructive discharge might survive summary judgment.

12.4 Preparing a Motion or Opposition

The Separate Statement of Material Facts

The separate statement serves as the factual foundation for summary judgment and requires careful attention to both substance and form.

Best Practices for Movants:

- Include only material facts that directly support legal arguments
- Use neutral, objective language without argumentative characterizations
- Provide pinpoint citations to specific page and line numbers in depositions, document production numbers, or paragraph numbers in declarations
- Organize facts chronologically or thematically to tell a coherent story

Best Practices for Opposition:

- Respond to each numbered fact specifically, admitting undisputed facts and disputing others with citations to contrary evidence
- Avoid simply denying facts without providing alternative evidence
- Add additional material facts not included in movant's statement, with proper citations

Common Mistakes:

- Including legal conclusions disguised as facts
- Citing to inadmissible evidence such as hearsay or unsworn statements
- Providing general citations to lengthy documents without pinpoint references
- Mixing argument with factual statements

Supporting Evidence Requirements

Summary judgment motions must be supported by admissible evidence that would be acceptable at trial.

Deposition Testimony: Excerpts must be properly authenticated and cited to specific page and line numbers. Remember that a witness's testimony about what someone else said may be hearsay unless it falls within an exception.

Documentary Evidence: Documents must be properly authenticated through witness testimony or other means. Business records require foundation showing they were kept in the regular course of business.

Declarations and Affidavits: Must be based on personal knowledge, state facts that would be admissible at trial, and be made under penalty of perjury. Declarants should identify their position and basis for knowledge.

Expert Testimony: Expert reports must comply with applicable rules for expert disclosure and opinion testimony. Experts must be qualified and their opinions must be relevant and reliable.

Example of Proper Declaration: "I am the Human Resources Director for ABC Company and have held this position for five years. I personally reviewed John Doe's personnel file in preparing this declaration. Based on my review of the file, Mr. Doe received performance evaluations rating his work as 'below expectations' in March 2023 and 'unsatisfactory' in September 2023. I have attached true and correct copies of these evaluations as Exhibits A and B."

Example of Improper Declaration: "Based on information and belief, Mr. Doe was a poor performer who violated company policies." This declaration lacks personal knowledge foundation and includes legal conclusions.

12.5 The McDonnell Douglas Framework at Summary Judgment

Understanding the Three-Step Analysis

The McDonnell Douglas framework, established by the Supreme Court in *McDonnell Douglas Corp. v. Green, supra*, provides the analytical structure for most employment discrimination cases at summary judgment.

Step One - Prima Facie Case: The plaintiff must establish a prima facie case of discrimination by showing: (1) membership in a protected class, (2) qualification for the position, (3) adverse employment action, and (4) circumstances giving rise to an inference of discrimination.

Step Two - Legitimate Non-Discriminatory Reason: The employer must articulate a legitimate, non-discriminatory reason for the adverse action. This burden is relatively light and requires only that the employer produce evidence of a reason, not prove it.

Step Three - Pretext: The plaintiff must show that the employer's stated reason is pretextual, meaning either that it is false or that discrimination was a motivating factor despite the stated reason.

Applying McDonnell Douglas at Summary Judgment

Prima Facie Case Considerations: Courts often find that plaintiffs can establish a prima facie case with relatively minimal evidence, as this stage requires only showing circumstances that give rise to an inference of discrimination.

Example: A 62-year-old employee with satisfactory performance reviews who is terminated and replaced by a 35-year-old typically establishes a prima facie case of age discrimination, even without direct evidence of discriminatory intent.

Employer's Burden of Production: Employers must provide evidence of legitimate reasons for their actions, but need not prove these reasons were the actual motivation.

Common Legitimate Reasons:

- Poor performance documented through evaluations or disciplinary actions
- Economic necessity requiring workforce reduction
- Restructuring or elimination of positions
- Violation of company policies or procedures
- Attendance or punctuality problems

Pretext Analysis: This is typically where summary judgment motions succeed or fail. Courts look for evidence that the employer's stated reason is either false or that discrimination was a motivating factor.

Evidence of Pretext

Temporal Proximity: Close timing between protected activity (such as filing a complaint) and adverse action can suggest pretext, though proximity alone is rarely sufficient.

Comparator Evidence: Showing that similarly situated employees outside the protected class were treated more favorably is powerful evidence of pretext.

Inconsistent Explanations: When an employer provides different explanations for the same action at different times, it may suggest pretext.

Deviation from Policy: Evidence that an employer failed to follow its usual procedures or policies in taking adverse action against the plaintiff.

Direct Evidence: Comments by decision-makers that reflect discriminatory bias, though such evidence is increasingly rare.

Statistical Evidence: In appropriate cases, statistical evidence showing patterns of discrimination across the workforce.

Strategic Considerations for Each Side

For Plaintiffs:

- Focus on inconsistencies in the employer's explanation
- Develop comparator evidence through discovery
- Document any discriminatory comments or conduct
- Show deviations from standard procedures
- Establish temporal relationships between protected activity and adverse actions

For Employers:

- Ensure consistent documentation of performance issues
- Apply policies uniformly across all employees
- Train supervisors to avoid potentially discriminatory comments
- Document legitimate business reasons for employment decisions
- Maintain detailed records of decision-making processes

12.6 Avoiding Summary Judgment Pitfalls

Common Plaintiff Mistakes and How to Avoid Them

Over-Reliance on Pleadings: The complaint alone cannot survive summary judgment. Plaintiffs must submit admissible evidence including declarations, deposition testimony, and documents to support their claims.

Failure to Address Undisputed Facts: Plaintiffs must specifically respond to each of defendant's claimed undisputed facts with citations to contrary evidence. Simply denying facts without evidentiary support is insufficient.

Generalized Arguments: Courts reject conclusory statements and speculation. Arguments must be tied to specific facts supported by admissible evidence.

Inadequate Discovery: Plaintiffs should use Federal Rule 56(d) or state equivalents to seek additional discovery time if necessary to develop evidence for summary judgment opposition.

Example of Effective Opposition: Instead of arguing generally that "the employer's reasons were pretextual," a plaintiff might present evidence that: (1) the stated performance issues were never documented before the discrimination complaint, (2) a younger employee with worse performance metrics was not disciplined, and (3) the plaintiff's supervisor made age-related comments to coworkers.

Common Defendant Mistakes and How to Avoid Them

Overstating the Lack of Dispute: Courts are skeptical of motions that claim no factual disputes exist when reasonable people could disagree about the evidence.

Ignoring Credibility Issues: Summary judgment is inappropriate when witness credibility is central to resolving factual disputes. Courts typically defer credibility determinations to juries.

Inadequate Evidentiary Support: All factual assertions must be supported by admissible evidence. Conclusory statements in briefs are insufficient.

Failure to Address All Claims: A motion that seeks to dismiss only some claims or some theories of liability may be denied if viable claims remain.

Example of Problematic Motion: An employer argues that no harassment occurred based solely on the harasser's denial, ignoring witness testimony and contemporaneous complaints. Courts will likely find credibility issues that preclude summary judgment.

Evidentiary Objections and Procedural Requirements

Hearsay Objections: Be prepared to address hearsay issues in declarations and deposition testimony. Business records and admissions by party opponents are common exceptions.

Authentication: Ensure all documents are properly authenticated through witness testimony or other appropriate means.

Personal Knowledge: Declarations must be based on personal knowledge and identify the declarant's basis for knowledge of stated facts.

Relevance and Materiality: Focus on facts that are material to the legal claims and defenses, avoiding cumulative or irrelevant evidence.

12.7 Oral Argument and Judicial Discretion

California Practice

Tentative Rulings: Many California superior courts issue tentative rulings before oral argument, allowing parties to know the court's preliminary thoughts and prepare targeted responses.

Preparing for Tentatives: Review the tentative ruling carefully and focus oral argument on the court's specific concerns as opposed to repeating written arguments.

Addressing Evidentiary Issues: Be prepared to discuss specific evidentiary objections and authentication issues, as these often arise in tentative rulings.

Material Fact Disputes: Focus on genuine disputes that preclude summary judgment instead of addressing minor factual disagreements that don't affect the legal outcome.

New York Practice

Judicial Discretion: New York courts have broad discretion in granting oral argument, with practices varying significantly by county and individual judge.

Local Variations: Practice rules differ between counties and between individual judges within the same county. Some judges prefer extensive oral argument while others rely primarily on written submissions.

Motion Practice: New York's motion practice tends to be more formal than federal court, with specific requirements for notice and service.

Strategic Considerations: Because oral argument is not guaranteed, written submissions often carry the primary weight in New York summary judgment practice.

Federal Practice

Judicial Variation: Federal judges have significant discretion in whether to hold oral argument on summary judgment motions. Some decide purely on written submissions while others regularly schedule argument.

Case Management: Federal judges often address summary judgment motions during case management conferences or in conjunction with other pending motions.

Preparation Strategy: If argument is granted, focus on the most compelling factual and legal issues instead of comprehensively reviewing all arguments.

Interactive Approach: Federal judges often ask specific questions during argument, so be prepared to address concerns not raised in written submissions.

Effective Oral Argument Strategies

Concise Presentation: Courts typically allow limited time for argument, so focus on the strongest points rather than attempting to cover all issues.

Responsive Advocacy: Address the court's questions directly and concede points when appropriate and do not evade difficult issues.

Factual Focus: Emphasize genuine factual disputes that preclude summary judgment rather than arguing legal points extensively covered in briefs.

Visual Aids: Consider using demonstrative exhibits or timelines to illustrate complex factual scenarios, though keep them simple and clear.

12.8 Strategic Considerations

Partial Summary Judgment

Partial summary judgment allows courts to resolve some claims or issues while leaving others for trial. This can be particularly valuable in complex employment cases with multiple claims.

Benefits for Defendants:

- Eliminates weak claims that might prejudice the jury on stronger claims

- Reduces trial time and complexity
- May encourage settlement by demonstrating case strength
- Can eliminate claims with significant damages exposure

Benefits for Plaintiffs:

- Establishes liability on clear-cut issues
- Simplifies trial presentation
- May increase settlement leverage
- Can eliminate defenses that would complicate trial

Common Applications:

- Wage and hour cases where liability is clear but damages require calculation
- Cases with both individual and class claims
- Multiple discrimination claims where some lack sufficient evidence
- Cases involving both statutory and common law claims

Example: In a case involving both discrimination and unpaid overtime claims, an employer might seek partial summary judgment on discrimination while conceding overtime liability, allowing the court to focus on damages calculation.

Preserving the Record for Appeal

Evidentiary Objections: All objections to evidence must be raised in writing before or during the summary judgment proceeding to preserve them for appeal.

Standard of Review: Remember that appellate courts review summary judgment rulings de novo, giving no deference to the trial court's decision.

Record Development: Ensure the record contains all evidence necessary to support arguments on appeal, including any evidence excluded by the trial court.

Legal Arguments: Preserve all legal arguments in written submissions, as appellate courts typically will not consider arguments raised for the first time on appeal.

Discovery Considerations

Federal Rule 56(d): Allows parties to request additional discovery time if they cannot present facts essential to justify opposition to summary judgment.

State Equivalents: Most states have similar provisions allowing courts to defer ruling on summary judgment pending additional discovery.

Strategic Timing: Consider whether additional discovery might strengthen your position or whether the current record is sufficient.

Specific Discovery Needs: Rule 56(d) motions must identify specific discovery needed and explain why it is necessary to oppose summary judgment.

Example: A plaintiff might need additional time to depose decision-makers identified late in discovery or to obtain documents referenced in recently produced materials.

12.9 Post-Motion Considerations

When Summary Judgment Is Granted

Complete vs. Partial Grant: Understand whether the ruling eliminates all claims or only some, and consider whether remaining claims justify continued litigation.

Settlement Leverage: Even partial grants may significantly affect settlement negotiations by eliminating high-value claims or establishing important legal principles.

Appeal Considerations: Evaluate whether the ruling presents appealable issues and whether immediate appeal is strategic or whether to wait for final judgment.

Cost-Benefit Analysis: Consider litigation costs for remaining claims against potential recovery or exposure.

When Summary Judgment Is Denied

Trial Preparation: Begin intensive trial preparation immediately, as denial often leads to relatively quick trial scheduling.

Settlement Opportunity: Denial may encourage settlement discussions, as it demonstrates the strength of surviving claims.

Focused Discovery: Consider whether limited additional discovery is needed on issues identified during summary judgment briefing.

Motion Practice: Evaluate whether other dispositive motions might be appropriate, such as motions to exclude expert testimony or motions *in limine*.

Settlement Leverage Effects

Defendant Perspective: Successful summary judgment motions demonstrate case strength and may encourage plaintiff settlement. Denied motions may necessitate increased settlement authority.

Plaintiff Perspective: Surviving summary judgment validates claim strength and typically increases settlement demands. However, consider litigation costs and risks of proceeding to trial.

Partial Success: When summary judgment is granted on some but not all claims, both sides may find middle ground for settlement based on remaining exposure and litigation costs.

12.10 Advanced Strategic Considerations

Class Action and Collective Action Implications

Certification Impact: Summary judgment rulings can affect class certification by resolving common issues or demonstrating that individual issues predominate.

Representative Adequacy: In class actions, summary judgment against the named plaintiff may affect their ability to represent the class.

Opt-In Considerations: In FLSA collective actions, summary judgment rulings may influence other potential plaintiffs' decisions to opt in.

Multi-Jurisdictional Considerations

Forum Selection: When cases could be filed in multiple jurisdictions, consider each court's approach to summary judgment in employment cases.

Removal and Remand: Federal removal of state law claims may affect summary judgment strategy, particularly for claims with different standards.

Coordination: In related cases filed in different jurisdictions, coordinate summary judgment strategy to avoid inconsistent rulings.

Technology and E-Discovery Issues

Electronic Evidence: Ensure electronic documents are properly authenticated and that metadata issues are addressed.

Social Media: Consider whether social media evidence supports or undermines summary judgment arguments.

Communication Records: Text messages, emails, and other electronic communications increasingly play important roles in employment litigation.

12.11 Conclusion

Summary judgment represents both the greatest opportunity and the greatest risk in employment litigation. For defendants, it offers the possibility of complete case resolution without the uncertainty and expense of trial. For plaintiffs, surviving summary judgment validates their claims and typically increases settlement leverage substantially.

Success requires thorough preparation, careful attention to evidentiary requirements, and strategic thinking about which issues to emphasize and which to concede. The key is understanding that summary judgment tests not just the legal sufficiency of claims, but the actual evidence supporting them.

Most importantly, remember that summary judgment is not about winning or losing individual legal arguments - it's about whether the evidence, viewed in the light most favorable to the non-moving party, would allow a reasonable jury to find in that party's favor. This standard requires advocates to think like jurors as well as lawyers, considering not just what the law requires but what real people would find persuasive.

The jurisdictional differences between federal, New York, and California practice add layers of complexity that require careful attention to local rules and customs. However, the fundamental principles remain consistent: material facts must be supported by admissible evidence, legal arguments must be grounded in applicable law, and strategic considerations must account for the broader context of the litigation.

In Chapter 13, we'll shift focus to pretrial preparation, including exhibit management, trial brief drafting, motions *in limine*, and final witness preparation - the critical steps that follow successful navigation of the summary judgment stage.

13

Pretrial Preparation in Employment Cases

Once summary judgment is resolved or bypassed, the case moves toward trial preparation. At this stage, both sides must focus on organizing evidence, clarifying legal theories, preparing witnesses, and complying with court rules on pretrial disclosures. Strong pretrial preparation can create leverage for last-minute settlements - or ensure courtroom success if trial proceeds.

This chapter outlines best practices for pretrial preparation in employment cases in New York, California, and federal courts, with an emphasis on exhibit planning, procedural compliance, and strategic readiness.

13.1 The Pretrial Conference

Purpose and Strategic Importance

The pretrial conference serves multiple critical functions beyond mere administrative scheduling. It represents the final opportunity to streamline issues, address pending motions, and explore settlement before the substantial costs and risks of trial. Judges use these conferences to gauge case strength, encourage resolution, and establish firm trial parameters.

The conference aims to streamline issues for trial, address pending motions such as motions *in limine* (pre-trial motions to exclude certain evidence), set deadlines for exhibit exchange and witness lists, establish jury instruction parameters, and explore potential settlement or alternative dispute resolution (ADR).

Court-Specific Procedures and Key Differences

Federal Courts operate under Federal Rule of Civil Procedure 16, which governs scheduling orders and final pretrial conferences. Federal judges typically conduct these conferences 30-60 days before trial, with mandatory joint pretrial statements due 10-14 days prior. The federal system emphasizes efficiency and judicial case management, often resulting in more structured timelines and stricter enforcement of deadlines.

California requires mandatory trial readiness conferences in most counties, governed by local rules that vary significantly by jurisdiction. Los Angeles County, for example, requires parties to file a trial readiness conference statement five days before the conference, while San Francisco has different timing requirements. California courts often focus heavily on settlement discussions during these conferences, reflecting the state's preference for alternative dispute resolution.

New York follows a unique procedure where the final pretrial conference occurs after filing a note of issue and certificate of readiness. The note of issue is a formal declaration that the case is ready for trial, while the certificate of readiness confirms all discovery is complete and outstanding motions resolved. This two-step process gives New York courts greater control over trial scheduling but can create delays if parties dispute readiness.

Joint Pretrial Statements

Each jurisdiction typically requires a joint pretrial statement summarizing claims, defenses, disputed issues, witness lists, and exhibits. These documents serve as roadmaps for trial and often become the foundation for jury instructions. Federal courts generally require more detailed statements, including specific factual contentions and legal theories, while state courts may accept more general summaries.

Example: In a discrimination case, the joint pretrial statement might include: "Plaintiff contends she was terminated because of her pregnancy in violation of the Pregnancy Discrimination Act. Defendant contends plaintiff was terminated for poor performance documented in her personnel file. Disputed issues include whether plaintiff's performance declined after announcing her pregnancy and whether defendant's stated reasons constitute pretext for discrimination."

13.2 Organizing the Case File

A clean, categorized, and indexed case file supports effective pretrial work and demonstrates professionalism to judges and opposing counsel. The organization system you establish now will prove invaluable during trial when you need to locate documents quickly under pressure.

Essential Categories

Pleadings should include the complaint, answer, amended pleadings, and all motions with their supporting documents and court orders. Chronological organization within each category helps track the case's procedural history.

Discovery encompasses depositions (with word-searchable transcripts when possible), interrogatory responses, requests for production responses, and electronically stored information (ESI). Create separate subfolders for each deponent and document requests by category rather than by date served.

Chronology involves developing a comprehensive fact timeline that becomes the backbone of your trial narrative. Include both favorable and unfavorable events to anticipate opposing counsel's arguments. This timeline should reference specific documents and testimony that support each event.

Trial exhibits must be numbered, labeled, and organized for easy retrieval. Many attorneys create parallel numbering systems - one for internal organization and another for court filing requirements.

Witness preparation materials should include witness summaries, examination outlines, and copies of all prior statements or testimony. This prevents inconsistencies and helps witnesses understand their role in the broader case narrative.

Damages documentation requires meticulous organization of pay records, medical records, tax returns, and expert reports. Employment cases often involve complex economic calculations that require clear supporting documentation.

Technology Solutions

Trial management software such as TrialDirector, CaseMap, or cloud-based solutions like NetDocuments can dramatically improve organization in complex cases. These platforms allow multiple team members to access files simultaneously, create automatic cross-references between documents and witnesses, and generate exhibit lists with a few clicks.

However, always maintain physical backup systems. Court technology can fail, and having organized physical binders ensures you can continue effectively regardless of technical difficulties.

13.3 Exhibit Preparation and Disclosure

Exhibit preparation represents one of the most time-consuming yet critical aspects of pretrial preparation. Proper organization and timely disclosure can prevent trial delays and objections that might otherwise exclude crucial evidence.

Exhibit Lists and Disclosure Requirements

All courts require exhibit lists before trial, but requirements vary significantly in detail and timing. These lists must include exhibit numbers, descriptions, Bates numbers when applicable, and any objections.

Federal courts typically require detailed exhibit lists with specific descriptions. For example, rather than listing "Plaintiff's personnel file," the description should read "Personnel file of Jane Smith, pages 001-157, including performance evaluations dated 3/15/2020, 9/20/2020, and 3/10/2021."

California state courts often accept more general descriptions but require comprehensive witness and exhibit exchanges 30 days before trial in most counties. Some California courts allow supplemental exhibit lists up to 10 days before trial for rebuttal exhibits.

New York requires detailed exhibit schedules as part of the note of issue process. The court may exclude exhibits not properly disclosed, making early preparation essential.

Strategic Coordination with Opposing Counsel

Coordinate with opposing counsel to stipulate to foundation and authentication when possible. A stipulation is an agreement between parties that certain facts are true or certain evidence is admissible, eliminating the need for formal proof at trial.

Example: "The parties stipulate that Exhibit 15, consisting of plaintiff's personnel file maintained in the ordinary course of business, is authentic and admissible subject to relevance objections." This stipulation saves time and prevents unnecessary foundation testimony while preserving the right to object on other grounds.

Physical and Electronic Exhibit Organization

Exhibit Binders should be prepared for the court, opposing counsel, witnesses, and your trial team. Include tabs with exhibit numbers prominently displayed and reference sheets for quick navigation. Organization can be chronological, thematic (employment history, disciplinary actions, retaliation incidents, damages), or by legal claim.

Electronic Exhibits are increasingly common as courts modernize. Prepare high-resolution digital files in multiple formats (PDF, JPEG, PowerPoint) and always have technical support available. Test all electronic equipment before trial and have backup systems ready.

Create a master exhibit list that cross-references physical and electronic versions, including file names, storage locations, and any technical requirements for presentation.

13.4 Motions *In Limine*

Motions *in limine* (pronounced "LIM-ih-nay," meaning "at the threshold" in Latin) are pretrial motions requesting the court to exclude or limit certain evidence or arguments before trial begins. These motions prevent prejudicing the jury with improper testimony or documents and can significantly shape trial strategy.

Strategic Purposes

Beyond excluding harmful evidence, motions *in limine* serve several strategic purposes. They force opponents to reveal their intended trial strategy, create opportunities for favorable pretrial rulings, establish clear boundaries for trial conduct, and preserve appellate issues through specific objections.

Common Employment Case Motions

Excluding Prior Lawsuits or Grievances: Employers often seek to exclude evidence of the plaintiff's previous legal disputes, arguing such evidence is more prejudicial than probative. However, plaintiffs may successfully argue that patterns of complaints show ongoing discrimination or a hostile work environment.

Example: "Defendant moves to exclude any reference to plaintiff's 2019 EEOC complaint against her previous employer, as such evidence is irrelevant to the current claims and would unfairly prejudice defendant by suggesting defendant is litigious."

Barring Expert Testimony: Challenges to expert witnesses focus on qualifications, methodology, or disclosure failures. Federal Rule of Evidence 702 and similar state rules require expert testimony to be based on reliable methods and sufficient facts.

Precluding Speculative or Hearsay Testimony: Employment cases often involve workplace rumors or secondhand accounts of discriminatory statements. Motions *in limine* can exclude such testimony while preserving objections for trial.

Limiting Settlement Discussions: Federal Rule of Evidence 408 generally excludes settlement offers and mediation discussions. However, the scope of this protection can be disputed, particularly regarding statements made during negotiations.

Addressing Character Evidence: Rules governing character evidence are complex and context-specific. An employee's criminal history might be excludable under Rule 404 but admissible under Rule 609 for impeachment purposes.

Procedural Considerations

File motions *in limine* according to the court's scheduling order, typically 30-60 days before trial. Some judges decide these motions during pretrial conferences, while others defer rulings until the evidence is actually offered at trial.

Raise all potential objections early to preserve appellate rights. Courts may find that failure to object pretrial constitutes waiver of the objection at trial.

13.5 Witness Lists and Preparation

Effective witness preparation can determine trial outcomes, particularly in employment cases where testimony often involves emotional or traumatic events. The preparation process requires balancing thorough readiness with ethical boundaries regarding coaching witnesses.

Witness List Requirements and Categories

Fact Witnesses include current and former employees, supervisors, HR personnel, and third parties who observed relevant events. List names, contact information, subject matter of testimony, and whether witnesses will testify live or via deposition.

Expert Witnesses require separate disclosure with detailed reports, qualifications, opinions, and methodologies. Employment cases commonly involve economic experts calculating lost wages and benefits, vocational rehabilitation experts assessing future earning capacity, and medical experts documenting emotional distress damages.

Preparation Strategies

Mock Question-and-Answer Sessions help witnesses become comfortable with the courtroom environment and your questioning style. Practice both direct examination (your questions) and anticipated cross-examination from opposing counsel.

Document Review ensures witnesses understand key evidence and can authenticate documents they created or received. Have witnesses review their deposition transcripts, prior sworn statements, and relevant correspondence.

Courtroom Protocol Education includes practical matters such as speaking clearly, listening to complete questions before answering, saying "I don't know" when appropriate, and maintaining professional demeanor under pressure.

Emotional Preparation is particularly important in employment cases involving harassment, discrimination, or retaliation. Discuss potential emotional triggers and coping strategies without coaching witnesses to provide specific answers.

Cross-Examination Anticipation

Prepare clients and friendly witnesses for potentially hostile questioning by conducting realistic practice sessions that simulate the pressure and unpredictability of cross-examination. Role-play difficult scenarios while emphasizing the importance of truthful testimony.

Example: If your client was terminated after a heated argument with their supervisor, prepare them for questions about their temper, communication style, and any workplace conflicts. Practice responses that acknowledge the argument while maintaining the discrimination claim's credibility.

13.6 Drafting Jury Instructions and Verdict Forms

Jury instructions guide fact-finders' interpretation of the law, while verdict forms shape how they deliver decisions. These documents often determine case outcomes as much as the underlying evidence, making careful drafting essential.

Strategic Importance

Well-crafted jury instructions can favor your client's legal theory while poorly drafted instructions may confuse jurors or highlight weaknesses in your case. Instructions also preserve appellate issues, as appellate courts review jury instruction disputes for legal error.

Best Practices and Resources

Model Instructions provide excellent starting points. California's CACI (Judicial Council of California Civil Jury Instructions), New York's PJI (Pattern Jury Instructions), and federal pattern instructions offer tested language for common employment law claims.

Customization for Specific Claims requires adapting model instructions to your case's particular facts and legal theories. Discrimination cases might require instructions on direct evidence versus circumstantial evidence, while retaliation cases need clear causation instructions.

Example: A standard discrimination instruction might read: "An employer discriminates against an employee because of [protected characteristic] if the employer treats the employee differently than other similarly situated employees, and the [protected characteristic] was a motivating reason for the different treatment."

Negotiation with Opposing Counsel can produce agreed-upon language that reduces the risk of reversible error. Courts appreciate cooperative efforts and may be more receptive to jointly proposed instructions.

Verdict Form Alignment ensures that verdict forms match jury instructions and damages claims. Complex employment cases may require special verdict forms that break down different claims and damages categories.

Timing and Procedure

Submit proposed jury instructions according to local rules - typically 30-60 days before trial in federal court and varying timeframes in state courts. Include supporting case citations and explain any departures from model instructions.

13.7 Trial Briefs

Trial briefs serve as roadmaps for judges, summarizing your case theory and anticipated legal issues. Unlike motion briefs, trial briefs are educational rather than argumentative, helping judges understand complex factual patterns and legal frameworks.

Essential Contents

Claims and Defenses Summary should clearly state each party's position without legal argument. Focus on helping the judge understand the case's scope and complexity.

Factual Narrative presents your version of events in a neutral, non-argumentative manner. This narrative should be compelling but not obviously biased, as judges will compare both sides' versions.

Legal Issues Expected at Trial helps judges prepare for evidentiary rulings and instruction conferences. Identify recurring objections, complex evidentiary issues, and novel legal questions.

Evidentiary Disputes should preview anticipated objections and your responses. This preparation helps judges make quick, consistent rulings during trial.

Relevant Case Law should focus on controlling authority and distinguish unfavorable precedents. Avoid overwhelming judges with excessive citations; instead, focus on the most relevant and recent authorities.

Writing and Presentation Tips

Keep trial briefs concise - typically 10-20 pages maximum. Judges appreciate clarity and brevity, particularly when managing busy trial calendars. Use headings, bullet points sparingly, and clear topic sentences to enhance readability.

Submit trial briefs according to local deadlines, typically 1-2 weeks before trial. Some courts require courtesy copies for law clerks who may assist with research during trial.

13.8 Stipulations and Trial Logistics

Effective trial management requires coordination between opposing counsel, court personnel, and witnesses. Courts increasingly encourage collaboration to streamline trial proceedings and reduce unnecessary disputes.

Factual Stipulations

Stipulate to uncontroversial facts to save time and focus jury attention on genuinely disputed issues. Employment cases often involve extensive documentation where basic facts can be agreed upon without compromising either side's position.

Example: "The parties stipulate that plaintiff was employed by defendant from January 15, 2019, through March 3, 2021, and that her final salary was $75,000 annually. The parties further stipulate that plaintiff filed an EEOC complaint on April 15, 2021, and received a right-to-sue letter on August 10, 2021."

Logistical Coordination

Trial Schedule Confirmation includes daily start times, lunch breaks, expected witness availability, and any schedule conflicts. Employment cases often involve working witnesses who need advance notice for trial attendance.

Interpreter and Accommodation Needs must be arranged well in advance. Courts require advance notice for interpreters, and the Americans with Disabilities Act may require specific accommodations for parties, witnesses, or jurors.

Courtroom Technology coordination prevents trial delays and technical difficulties. Test presentation equipment, confirm internet access for cloud-based documents, and have technical support available.

Communication Protocols

Establish clear communication protocols with opposing counsel for witness scheduling, exhibit issues, and settlement discussions. Professional cooperation often leads to reciprocal courtesy and can prevent minor disagreements from escalating into major disputes.

13.9 Jury Selection Preparation

While comprehensive voir dire strategy is covered in Chapter 14, pretrial preparation should include foundational work for effective jury selection.

Preliminary Research and Planning

Juror Questionnaires when allowed by the court can provide valuable information about potential jurors' backgrounds, experiences, and attitudes. Prepare thoughtful questions that reveal bias without being intrusive.

Bias Identification requires developing lists of experiences, attitudes, or characteristics that might favor or disfavor your client. Employment cases often involve workplace experiences that every adult juror has encountered in some form.

Thematic Question Development should align with your case theory and help identify sympathetic jurors. Questions might explore experiences with workplace unfairness, discrimination, or corporate hierarchies.

Example: "Have you or anyone close to you ever felt you were treated unfairly at work because of your age, gender, race, or other personal characteristics?" This question identifies potential bias while introducing discrimination themes.

Client Consultation

Discuss jury selection strategy with your client, exploring what type of juror might be more or less favorable to their story. Consider demographic factors, work experiences, and life circumstances that might influence juror perspectives.

However, avoid stereotyping or making assumptions based solely on demographic characteristics. Effective voir dire requires individual assessment of each potential juror's attitudes and experiences.

13.10 Advanced Pretrial Considerations

Settlement Leverage and Timing

Strong pretrial preparation creates settlement leverage by demonstrating case readiness and trial competence. Opponents may be more willing to negotiate favorably when they see a comprehensive preparation and organizational strength.

Consider timing settlement discussions strategically. Some cases benefit from early resolution before extensive pretrial costs, while others gain leverage as trial approaches and opponents face the reality of trial risks and expenses.

Backup Plans and Contingencies

Prepare for various trial scenarios, including witness unavailability, document authenticity challenges, and unexpected evidentiary rulings. Having backup witnesses, alternative theories, and contingency plans demonstrates thorough preparation and adaptability.

Example: If your primary economic expert becomes unavailable, have documentation ready to admit the expert's report or prepare a substitute witness who can present similar economic analysis.

Professional Development and Learning

Use pretrial preparation as an opportunity for professional development. Shadow experienced trial attorneys, attend courtroom proceedings in similar cases, and participate in trial advocacy training programs.

Many local bar associations offer trial preparation courses specifically focused on employment law cases, covering practical skills such as exhibit preparation, witness examination, and jury communication.

13.11 Conclusion

Pretrial preparation transforms raw facts into persuasive narratives and scattered documents into admissible exhibits that tell compelling stories. Whether your case settles during pretrial conferences or proceeds to trial, thorough preparation signals professionalism, confidence, and control to judges, opposing counsel, and clients.

The foundation you establish during pretrial preparation carries forward into every aspect of trial, from jury selection through closing arguments. Comprehensive organization, strategic thinking, and attention to procedural details create the platform for effective trial advocacy.

Remember that pretrial preparation is iterative rather than linear. New information may require revising witness lists, updating exhibit organization, or modifying legal theories. Flexibility within a structured framework allows you to adapt while maintaining comprehensive readiness.

The investment in thorough pretrial preparation pays dividends throughout the litigation process. Cases with strong pretrial preparation settle more favorably, proceed more smoothly when they do go to trial, and create better outcomes for clients regardless of resolution method.

In Chapter 14, we will explore the dynamics of jury selection and trial strategy, including voir dire techniques, juror profiling, and thematic storytelling that builds on the pretrial foundation established in this chapter.

14

Jury Selection and Trial Strategy

Jury trials in employment cases are won or lost as much during voir dire as during closing arguments. Jurors bring their own beliefs about fairness, work ethic, discrimination, and loyalty to the workplace. Identifying bias, building rapport, and shaping a narrative that resonates with the jury are critical elements of a successful trial strategy.

This chapter outlines practical guidance on jury selection and trial strategy in employment litigation in New York, California, and federal courts, with emphasis on identifying favorable jurors, effective questioning, and courtroom storytelling.

14.1 The Role of Jury Selection in Employment Trials

Employment cases present unique challenges because every juror has workplace experience. Unlike other areas of law where jurors may lack context, employment disputes tap into universal experiences of work relationships, authority structures, and fairness in the workplace. This familiarity can be both an advantage and a disadvantage.

Jurors often draw on their own workplace experiences and may:

- Empathize with whistleblowers or feel suspicious of "complainers"
- Admire corporate order or distrust HR departments
- Bring implicit biases related to race, gender, disability, or class
- Project their own employment frustrations onto the case
- Apply their personal work ethic standards to evaluate parties

The Critical Difference from Other Civil Cases

In personal injury cases, jurors typically lack experience with medical malpractice or car accidents. In employment cases, every juror has been an employee, supervisor, or business owner. This means they arrive with preformed opinions about workplace dynamics, making jury selection exponentially more important.

Voir dire serves three essential functions:

1. **Spot problematic jurors** - Identify those whose experiences or beliefs make them unsuitable
2. **Frame the narrative through questions** - Begin telling your story through strategic inquiry
3. **Begin persuading through subtle priming** - Plant seeds that will bloom during trial

14.2 Voir Dire Rules by Jurisdiction

Understanding jurisdictional differences is crucial for effective jury selection strategy.

Federal Courts

Federal courts generally provide limited voir dire time and restrict attorney-conducted questioning. The judge typically conducts most questioning, though attorneys may submit proposed questions.

Key Federal Considerations:

- **Rule 47(a)** permits the court to examine prospective jurors or allow attorneys to do so

- Most federal judges limit attorney voir dire to 15-30 minutes per side
- Written questionnaires are more readily approved in complex or sensitive cases
- **Batson challenges** (explained below) apply with strict scrutiny

New York State Courts

New York provides more liberal voir dire rules compared to federal court, allowing attorneys greater latitude in questioning prospective jurors.

New York Specific Rules:

- **CPL § 270.15** allows more extensive attorney questioning
- Courts routinely permit 45-60 minutes of voir dire per side
- Individual sequestered questioning available in sensitive cases
- More permissive approach to hypothetical questions

California State Courts

California offers the most expansive voir dire rights, with some of the most attorney-friendly jury selection procedures in the nation.

California Distinctive Features:

- **Code of Civil Procedure § 223** provides broad attorney questioning rights
- No specific time limits, though judges maintain discretion
- Individual voir dire more readily granted
- **Wheeler/Batson** motions (California's version of discriminatory jury selection challenges) strictly enforced

Strategic Implications of Jurisdictional Differences

The venue significantly impacts your jury selection strategy. In federal court, you must accomplish your goals quickly and efficiently. In California, you have time to develop rapport and explore nuanced positions. In New York, you have moderate time but must balance thoroughness with efficiency.

Request expanded voir dire or written questionnaires in sensitive cases involving sexual harassment, race discrimination, whistleblower retaliation, or cases involving high-profile companies or individuals.

14.3 Juror Profiling and Ideal Characteristics

Understanding the Mindset Divide

Employment cases often divide along philosophical lines about work, authority, and personal responsibility. Understanding these divisions helps identify favorable jurors.

Plaintiff-Side Employment Case

Favorable traits:

- **Belief in fairness and accountability** - Jurors who expect employers to follow their own rules
- **Openness to emotional damages** - Those who understand workplace trauma extends beyond lost wages
- **Positive views of workplace diversity** - Support for inclusive workplace policies
- **Willingness to challenge authority** - Comfort with questioning management decisions
- **Union membership or support** - Understanding of collective workplace rights
- **Experience with workplace unfairness** - Personal knowledge of discriminatory treatment

Detailed Profile of Ideal Plaintiff Juror:

Sarah, a 34-year-old teacher, has worked in both private and public schools. She's witnessed colleagues face unfair treatment and believes institutions should protect workers. She's comfortable with emotional intelligence concepts and understands how workplace stress affects families. Sarah questions authority when necessary and believes lawsuits serve an important societal function.

Red flags:

- **Strong loyalty to corporate structure** - "Companies know best" mentality
- **Belief that lawsuits are "money grabs"** - Inherent skepticism about litigation motives
- **History of management roles** - May identify with employer decision-making (context-dependent)
- **Prior negative experiences with workplace complaints** - Cynicism about internal complaint processes
- **Excessive focus on personal responsibility** - Belief that employees should "toughen up"
- **Hostility toward "victims"** - Discomfort with emotional vulnerability

Defense-Side Employment Case

Favorable traits:

- **Preference for personal responsibility narratives** - Belief that individuals control their outcomes
- **Skepticism about emotional distress claims** - View that workplace stress is normal
- **Experience in HR, compliance, or upper management** - Understanding of employer challenges
- **Analytical thinkers** - Focus on facts over emotions
- **Business ownership experience** - Appreciation for employer perspective
- **Military or law enforcement background** - Comfort with hierarchy and rules

Detailed Profile of Ideal Defense Juror:

Robert, a 45-year-old operations manager, has supervised teams for fifteen years. He's dealt with difficult employees, performance issues, and wrongful termination claims. Robert believes most workplace problems stem from miscommunication or unrealistic expectations. He's skeptical of large damage awards and thinks people should resolve issues through proper channels before involving lawyers.

Red flags for defense:

- **History of workplace discrimination** - Personal experience with unfair treatment
- **Strong union sympathies** - Inherent distrust of management
- **Family members in protected classes** - Heightened sensitivity to discrimination
- **Previous positive experiences with employment lawyers** - Comfort with litigation as solution
- **Social justice orientation** - Strong beliefs about workplace equality

The Complexity of Juror Psychology

Juror profiling isn't foolproof. The same characteristic can cut both ways depending on context:

Management Experience Example: A former supervisor might understand employer challenges (good for defense) or might have witnessed discrimination firsthand (good for plaintiff). The key is exploring the *nature* of their management experience through careful questioning.

14.4 Questioning Techniques During Voir Dire

Fundamental Principles

Effective voir dire requires balancing multiple objectives: gathering information, building rapport, beginning persuasion, and identifying bias. The best questions accomplish several goals simultaneously.

Best Practices

Ask open-ended, non-leading questions: Instead of "Do you think lawsuits are frivolous?" ask "What's your general feeling about workplace lawsuits?"

Encourage jurors to speak from personal experience: "Tell me about a time when you had to report something at work" reveals more than abstract questions about reporting policies.

Normalize discomfort: "Many people have strong feelings about discrimination lawsuits. What are your thoughts?" gives permission to express controversial views.

Listen more than you talk: Watch body language, tone, and what's *not* said. A juror who becomes defensive when discussing authority figures reveals important information.

Advanced Questioning Strategies

The Commitment Technique: After exploring attitudes, ask for commitments: "Based on what you've told me about your experiences, do you think you could be fair to both sides in this case?"

The Assumption Question: "This case involves allegations of sexual harassment. Assuming we prove our case, would you be comfortable awarding damages for emotional distress?"

The Worst-Case Scenario: "If the evidence showed that my client made some mistakes but was still the victim of discrimination, could you still find in her favor?"

Sample Plaintiff-Side Questions

Building Empathy and Identifying Allies:

"Have you ever had to report something unfair at work?"

- *Follow-up*: "How did that make you feel? What was the outcome?"

"Do you believe most people are treated equally in the workplace?"

- *Follow-up*: "What makes some workplaces more fair than others?"

"How do you feel about someone suing their employer?"

- *Follow-up*: "Are there circumstances where it's necessary?"

"Have you ever worked in HR or managed people?"

- *Follow-up*: "What's the hardest part about handling employee complaints?"

Exploring Attitudes Toward Damages:

"If someone experiences discrimination at work, what kinds of harm might they suffer beyond lost wages?"

"How would you feel about awarding money for emotional distress if the evidence supported it?"

Sample Defense-Side Questions

Identifying Management-Friendly Jurors:

"Have you ever had to fire someone?"

- *Follow-up*: "What made that decision difficult? What factors did you consider?"

"Do you think lawsuits are filed too easily these days?"

- *Follow-up*: "What would make a lawsuit seem more or less justified to you?"

"How would you feel about awarding emotional damages?"

- *Follow-up*: "What would convince you that emotional harm actually occurred?"

"Have you or someone close to you been accused of discrimination?"

- *Follow-up*: "How did that affect your view of discrimination claims?"

Testing Skepticism Toward Plaintiff Claims:

"Do you think some people are too sensitive about workplace issues?"

"If an employee had performance problems, would that affect your view of their discrimination claim?"

The Art of Follow-Up Questions

The initial question opens the door; follow-up questions reveal character. Consider this exchange:

Attorney: "Have you ever had a conflict with a supervisor?"

Juror: "Yes, a few years ago."

Attorney: "Can you tell me about that?"

Juror: "My boss was playing favorites and giving the good assignments to his friends."

Attorney: "How did you handle that situation?"

Juror: "I went to HR, but nothing really changed. Eventually, I just looked for another job."

Attorney: "Looking back, do you think HR should have done more?"

This sequence reveals the juror's experience with workplace unfairness, their willingness to use formal complaint processes, their view of HR effectiveness, and their problem-solving approach.

14.5 Using Challenges Effectively

Understanding the strategic use of challenges is crucial for optimizing your jury panel.

For Cause Challenges

For cause challenges allow unlimited removal of jurors who demonstrate actual bias or inability to serve fairly. These challenges require a legal basis and judicial approval.

Legal Standards for Cause:

- **Actual bias:** Juror admits they cannot be fair
- **Implied bias:** Relationship or interest that presumes unfairness
- **Statutory disqualification:** Legal impediment to service

Common Employment Case Grounds:

- Current litigation against the defendant company
- Family member works for defendant
- Strong union leadership role in case involving union issues
- Victim of similar discrimination with ongoing emotional impact
- Business partnership with plaintiff or defendant

Making the Record: When challenging for cause, create a clear record. State: "Your Honor, we challenge Juror No. 7 for cause based on her statement that she 'could never vote in favor of someone suing their employer because lawsuits hurt everyone.'"

Peremptory Challenges

Peremptory challenges allow removal without stating reasons, but are limited in number and cannot be used discriminatorily.

Strategic Considerations:

- **Federal courts:** Typically 3 per side in civil cases
- **New York:** Usually 6 per side
- **California:** Generally 6 per side

The Batson/Wheeler Doctrine

Named for *Batson v. Kentucky*, 476 U.S. 79 (1986), this doctrine prohibits discriminatory use of peremptory challenges based on race, gender, religion, national origin, or other protected characteristics. *People v. Wheeler*, 22 Cal.3d 258, 583 P.2d 748, 148 Cal. Rptr. 890 (Cal. 1978) is California's counterpart to Batson. The *Wheeler* decision predates *Batson* and similarly prohibits the discriminatory use of peremptory challenges under the California Constitution.

Three-Step Batson Analysis:

1. **Prima facie case:** Opponent shows pattern suggesting discrimination
2. **Neutral explanation:** Challenging party provides race-neutral

reason

3. **Pretextual determination:** Court decides if explanation is genuine

Practical Batson Considerations:

Always prepare race-neutral reasons for striking any minority juror. Good reasons include:

- Specific statements showing bias
- Body language or demeanor issues
- Experience that creates conflict
- Educational or professional background concerns

Avoid reasons that could apply to non-minority jurors you didn't strike.

Example of Proper Batson Explanation: "Your Honor, we struck Juror No. 12 not because of her race, but because she stated that she believes 'most discrimination claims are exaggerated' and that she's 'skeptical of people who complain about their jobs.' These statements show bias against our client's claims."

14.6 Developing Trial Themes

Your trial theme should emerge during voir dire and resonate throughout the case. Effective themes tap into universal values while distinguishing your case from others.

Plaintiff Themes

Courage to speak up This theme works when your client reported wrongdoing despite potential retaliation. It appeals to jurors who admire moral courage and believe in accountability.

Voir dire development: "Have you ever had to report something you knew was wrong, even though it might cause problems for you?"

Opening statement: "This case is about what happens when someone has the courage to speak up about wrongdoing, and their employer punishes them for it."

Accountability in the workplace Effective when the employer violated clear policies or legal requirements. Appeals to jurors who believe rules should apply equally to everyone.

Voir dire development: "Do you think companies should have to follow their own rules?"

Opening statement: "This case is about holding a company accountable when they say one thing and do another."

David vs. Goliath Powerful when there's a significant power imbalance. Be careful not to overuse this theme, as it can backfire if the plaintiff seems to be seeking an unfair advantage.

Voir dire development: "How do you feel when someone with less power challenges someone with more power?"

Everyone deserves respect and dignity at work Universal theme that works across different types of employment cases. Particularly effective in harassment or hostile work environment cases.

Voir dire development: "What makes a workplace respectful? What crosses the line?"

Defense Themes

Good faith employer Emphasizes that the employer acted reasonably based on available information and legitimate business reasons.

Voir dire development: "If you were running a business, what factors would you consider when making difficult personnel decisions?"

Opening statement: "This case is about a company that tried to do the right thing, made tough decisions based on legitimate business reasons, and is now being unfairly blamed for an employee's disappointment."

No retaliation, just performance-based decisions Distinguishes legitimate employment actions from illegal retaliation. Requires strong documentation and clear timeline.

Voir dire development: "If an employee's performance declined after making a complaint, how would you separate performance issues from potential retaliation?"

Not every bad experience is illegal Manages expectations about what employment law covers. Particularly useful when the plaintiff had genuine workplace difficulties that don't rise to legal violations.

Voir dire development: "We've all had difficult situations at work. When do workplace problems become legal issues?"

Responsibility goes both ways Emphasizes employee obligations and mutual responsibility in the employment relationship.

Voir dire development: "What responsibilities do employees have to their employers? What about employers to employees?"

Anchoring Themes Early

Begin establishing your theme during voir dire through strategic questioning. Return to it during opening statements, weave it through witness examination, and conclude with it during closing arguments. Consistency and repetition help jurors organize evidence around your central narrative.

14.7 Opening Statements: First Impressions

Opening statements in employment cases require careful balance between legal complexity and human story. Jurors need to understand both the legal framework and why they should care about your client.

Purpose and Strategy

Primary objectives:

- **Introduce your client's story** in compelling, human terms
- **Frame the facts through your lens** before opposing counsel does
- **Begin connecting emotionally with jurors** while maintaining credibility
- **Provide roadmap** for evidence presentation
- **Establish expectations** for what you'll prove

Structural Framework

The Three-Act Structure:

Act I - Setup: Introduce your client, the workplace, and the normal state of affairs **Act II - Conflict:** Explain what went wrong and why it matters legally **Act III - Resolution:** Preview how the evidence will prove your case and what justice requires

Essential Tips

Avoid legal jargon: Instead of "adverse employment action," say "they fired her." Instead of "hostile work environment," describe the specific behavior that made work unbearable.

Don't oversell or promise what you can't prove: Every statement creates an expectation. If you can't deliver, your credibility suffers throughout the trial.

Show (don't tell) how evidence supports your client: Rather than "The evidence will show discrimination," say "You'll hear from three witnesses who saw my client's supervisor use racial slurs."

Keep it structured: Use clear chronology, introduce key players early, and highlight turning points that advance your theme.

Plaintiff Opening Example

"Sarah Martinez loved her job as a software engineer at TechCorp. For three years, she received excellent reviews, promotions, and praise from her supervisors. That changed the day she reported sexual harassment by her team leader.

You'll hear how, within weeks of making that report, her assignments disappeared, her access to important meetings ended, and her previously supportive supervisor began documenting every minor mistake. Six months later, they fired her for 'performance issues' that never existed before she spoke up.

This case is about what happens when a company punishes courage instead of protecting it. The evidence will show that TechCorp didn't fire Sarah for performance - they fired her for reporting harassment. And that's illegal retaliation."

Defense Opening Example

"This case is about a company that made a difficult but necessary decision based on legitimate business reasons. David Johnson wants you to believe he was fired because he complained about overtime policies. The evidence will tell a different story.

You'll learn that Mr. Johnson's performance had been declining for months before he made any complaint. You'll see written warnings, missed deadlines, and customer complaints that had nothing to do with his later grievances about overtime.

When TechCorp finally terminated Mr. Johnson, it wasn't retaliation - it was a long-overdue response to an employee who simply wasn't meeting the job requirements. Sometimes the timing of events can seem suspicious, but correlation isn't causation."

14.8 Managing Jury Perception During Trial

Jurors form impressions constantly throughout the trial process. Managing these perceptions requires attention to details beyond the evidence itself.

What Jurors Observe

How your client behaves: Posture, facial expressions, reactions to testimony, interaction with counsel **Your tone and body language:** Confidence, respect for witnesses, courtroom demeanor **Whether your story is consistent:** Alignment between opening promises and evidence presented **Treatment of opposing parties:** Professional courtesy vs. aggressive tactics **Preparation level:** Organization, efficiency, knowledge of case details

Practical Client Preparation

Physical Presentation:

- Conservative, professional attire appropriate to the workplace context
- Consistent grooming and appearance throughout trial

- Alert, engaged posture (not reading, texting, or appearing disinterested)
- Controlled emotional reactions (crying is acceptable if genuine, but not excessive)

Behavioral Guidelines:

- No visible reactions to adverse testimony (head shaking, eye rolling, sighing)
- Respectful attention to all witnesses, including opposing parties
- Minimal note-passing to counsel during testimony
- Appropriate emotional responses that align with testimony

The Authenticity Balance: Coach your client to be genuine while remaining appropriate. Jurors detect false emotion, but they also notice inappropriate reactions. The goal is authentic behavior that supports your case theme.

Attorney Courtroom Presence

During Opening and Closing:

- Maintain eye contact with jurors
- Use appropriate gestures and movement
- Speak conversationally, not rhetorically
- Show confidence without arrogance

During Witness Examination:

- Treat all witnesses with respect, even during vigorous cross-examination
- Avoid theatrical objections or arguments
- Demonstrate command of facts and law
- Show genuine interest in truth-seeking

Managing Difficult Moments:

- Remain calm during adverse rulings

- Handle surprises professionally
- Acknowledge strong opposing points rather than ignoring them
- Use humor carefully and sparingly

14.9 Reframing Adverse Facts

Every employment case has problematic facts. The key is addressing them proactively and within your favorable framework.

The Principle of Honest Advocacy

Jurors reward honesty and fairness over perfection. Attempting to hide obvious problems destroys credibility and allows opposing counsel to score points by "revealing" what you tried to conceal.

Reframing Strategies

Acknowledge and Contextualize: "Yes, there were performance issues. But the timing of discipline changed after she spoke up."

This technique admits the unfavorable fact while immediately providing context that supports your theory of the case.

Distinguish Correlation from Causation: "He made mistakes - but that's not why he was fired. He was fired after complaining about unpaid wages, and his supervisor admitted the timing was 'unfortunate.'"

This approach separates legitimate issues from illegal motivations.

Use Adverse Facts to Support Your Theme: "The company wants you to focus on Mr. Johnson's attendance problems. But ask yourself: if attendance was really the issue, why did they wait until the day after he filed his EEOC complaint to fire him?"

This technique transforms a weakness into evidence supporting your retaliation claim.

Specific Application Examples

Performance Issues in Retaliation Cases:

- Acknowledge pre-existing performance concerns
- Highlight changes in evaluation standards post-complaint
- Emphasize timing and consistency issues
- Compare treatment to similarly situated employees

Credibility Issues with Plaintiff:

- Address dishonesty or exaggeration directly
- Distinguish between imperfect memory and intentional deception
- Use corroborating evidence to support core claims
- Acknowledge human nature of embellishing under stress

Workplace Conflict in Harassment Cases:

- Separate personality conflicts from discriminatory treatment
- Acknowledge difficult workplace relationships
- Focus on protected characteristic-based conduct
- Distinguish equal-opportunity rudeness from discriminatory behavior

Timing Issues: When adverse actions occur long after protected activity:

- Explain intervening events that rekindled retaliatory motive
- Identify continuing effects of original protected activity
- Use pattern evidence to show sustained retaliation
- Address employer's "convenient" timing explanations

14.10 Advanced Jury Psychology Considerations

Understanding Cognitive Biases

Confirmation Bias: Jurors tend to interpret evidence in ways that confirm their initial impressions. This makes voir dire and opening statements crucial for establishing favorable first impressions.

Attribution Theory: Jurors attribute behavior to either personal characteristics or situational factors. Employment cases often turn on whether jurors attribute workplace problems to employee shortcomings or employer misconduct.

Just World Hypothesis: Many people believe that bad things happen to people who deserve them. This bias can hurt plaintiffs who seem to have contributed to their problems.

Hindsight Bias: Jurors may view employer decisions as obviously wrong when evaluating them after the fact, even if they were reasonable when made.

Cultural and Generational Considerations

Generational Differences:

- **Baby Boomers:** Often more deferential to authority, skeptical of discrimination claims
- **Generation X:** Pragmatic about workplace politics, understanding of corporate downsizing
- **Millennials:** More sensitive to discrimination, comfortable with diversity concepts
- **Generation Z:** Highly attuned to power imbalances, social justice oriented

Cultural Attitudes Toward Work:

- **Individualistic vs. Collectivistic:** Some cultures emphasize personal responsibility while others focus on group harmony
- **Power Distance:** Acceptance of workplace hierarchy varies significantly across cultures
- **Uncertainty Avoidance:** Comfort with ambiguous employment situations differs culturally

Managing Diverse Jury Panels

Modern employment cases often involve diverse jury panels with varying cultural backgrounds, work experiences, and generational perspectives. Effective attorneys adapt their approach to connect with different worldviews.

Universal Themes That Cross Cultures:

- Fairness and equal treatment
- Respect for hard work
- Protecting family financial security
- Following established rules and procedures

Avoiding Cultural Assumptions:

- Don't assume attitudes based on demographics
- Use inclusive language and examples
- Avoid cultural stereotypes in jury selection
- Respect different communication styles during voir dire

14.11 Technology and Modern Jury Selection

Social Media Investigation

Permissible Research:

- Public social media profiles
- Professional networking sites
- Publicly available online information
- News articles or court records

Ethical Boundaries:

- No friend requests or fake profiles
- No accessing private information

- No contact with prospective jurors
- Document sources for potential challenges

Practical Applications: Social media can reveal attitudes toward:

- Litigation and lawyers
- Workplace authority
- Political and social issues
- Personal experiences relevant to case themes

Jury Questionnaires in the Digital Age

Modern jury questionnaires can explore online behavior and digital literacy:

- "Do you participate in online discussions about workplace issues?"
- "Have you shared opinions about litigation on social media?"
- "How do you typically get news and information?"

14.12 Post-Selection Strategy Integration

Connecting Voir Dire to Trial Presentation

Information gathered during jury selection should inform every aspect of trial strategy:

Witness Order: Present witnesses in ways that resonate with identified jury attitudes **Demonstrative Evidence:**Choose visuals and technology appropriate to jury comfort levels **Examination Style:** Adapt questioning approaches to jury communication preferences **Closing Arguments:** Reference themes and concepts introduced during voir dire

Ongoing Jury Assessment

Continue evaluating juror reactions throughout the trial:

- Note which jurors ask questions (in jurisdictions permitting)

- Observe body language during key testimony
- Identify juror leaders and followers
- Adjust strategy based on apparent jury concerns

14.13 Common Mistakes and How to Avoid Them

Voir Dire Mistakes

Over-talking: Attorneys often talk too much during jury selection, missing opportunities to learn about prospective jurors.

Leading Questions: Questions that suggest desired answers don't reveal true attitudes.

Ignoring Uncomfortable Answers: When jurors express unfavorable views, explore rather than avoid them.

Failing to Commit: After exploring attitudes, obtain commitments to fairness from acceptable jurors.

Trial Strategy Mistakes

Inconsistent Themes: Changing your story mid-trial destroys credibility.

Ignoring Jury Reactions: Failing to adjust based on observed jury responses.

Over-promising in Opening: Creating expectations you cannot meet during evidence presentation.

Defensive Closing: Spending closing arguments responding to opponent rather than advancing your case.

Conclusion

Jury selection in employment litigation requires combining legal knowledge, psychological insight, and strategic thinking. The employment trial begins long before the first witness takes the stand. By building rapport, identifying bias, and priming the jury for your narrative during voir dire, you establish the foundation for how your client's story will be received.

Effective jury selection isn't about finding the "perfect" jury - it's about identifying jurors who can fairly evaluate your case and eliminating those whose biases make fair consideration impossible. When voir dire is purposeful and integrated into your larger trial strategy, it becomes a quiet but powerful engine of persuasion that influences every subsequent phase of trial.

The intersection of human psychology, legal strategy, and courtroom advocacy makes jury selection both challenging and rewarding. Success requires careful preparation, flexible execution, and constant attention to the human dynamics that ultimately determine trial outcomes.

In Chapter 15, we'll explore direct and cross-examination techniques, witness control, and the use of expert testimony to support or challenge key claims in employment litigation.

15

Direct and Cross-Examination of Witnesses

The courtroom comes to life when witnesses take the stand. In employment cases, direct and cross-examination offer the clearest opportunity to bring your client's story to light - or to dismantle the opposing party's credibility. The effectiveness of this phase depends on preparation, control, and the strategic use of facts and demeanor.

This chapter focuses on how to plan and conduct direct and cross-examinations of plaintiffs, supervisors, HR representatives, expert witnesses, and third parties in employment trials in New York, California, and federal courts.

15.1 The Goals of Witness Examination

Direct Examination Objectives

Direct examination serves as your opportunity to present your case through the witness's own words. Your primary goals include:

Tell your client's or witness's story credibly and clearly. Unlike a legal brief or opening statement, direct examination allows the jury to hear the human voice behind the facts. The witness becomes the vehicle through which you paint a picture of what actually happened, making abstract legal concepts tangible and relatable.

Establish foundational facts and elements of your claims. Every employment law claim has specific elements that must be proven. For instance, in a Title VII discrimination case, you must establish that the plaintiff belongs to a protected class, was qualified for the position, suffered an adverse employment action, and that the circumstances give rise to an inference of discrimination. Direct examination is where you methodically build this foundation through witness testimony.

Humanize your client and build juror empathy. Employment cases often involve technical legal standards, but at their core, they're about human experiences. A successful direct examination transforms your client from a name on a complaint into a real person with hopes, fears, and legitimate grievances that resonate with the jury.

Lay groundwork for damages. In employment litigation, damages can include back pay, front pay, emotional distress, and punitive damages. Direct examination must establish not just that wrongdoing occurred, but how it specifically harmed the plaintiff financially, professionally, and personally.

Cross-Examination Objectives

Cross-examination operates under entirely different principles and serves distinct strategic purposes:

Challenge credibility or consistency. Cross-examination is your opportunity to expose weaknesses in the opposing party's case by highlighting inconsistencies in testimony, demonstrating bias, or revealing motivations to lie or exaggerate.

Highlight contradictions or implausibility. Effective cross-examination can make implausible stories appear even more unrealistic by forcing witnesses to commit to specific details that don't align with common sense or other evidence in the case.

Undermine key defenses or reduce damages. Rather than trying to prove your own case, cross-examination focuses on weakening the opposition's position. You might undermine an employer's claim that termination was based on legitimate performance issues by showing the timing coincided suspiciously with a discrimination complaint.

Control the narrative using leading questions. Unlike direct examination, cross-examination allows leading questions, giving you the power to control the pace, focus, and direction of testimony. You're not asking the witness to tell their story; you're having them confirm yours.

15.2 Preparing for Direct Examination

1. Develop a Narrative Structure

Organize the examination by theme, not just chronology. While chronological order provides clarity, thematic organization can be more powerful. Consider organizing around concepts like "The Golden Period" (when plaintiff was valued), "The Shift" (when discrimination began), and "The Consequences" (retaliation and harm).

Frame your questions to follow the client's emotional and legal journey. The most compelling direct examinations mirror a story arc with beginning, middle, and end. For example: hiring and early success (establishing baseline), onset of problems (building tension), attempts to resolve (showing good faith), escalation (creating urgency), and resolution/consequences (achieving catharsis).

Example Thematic Approach: Instead of asking "What happened on January 15th, then January 20th, then February 3rd," organize around themes:

- "The Respected Employee" (early performance and relationships)
- "When Things Changed" (onset of discriminatory treatment)
- "Fighting Back" (complaints and advocacy)
- "The Price of Speaking Up" (retaliation and consequences)

2. Practice with Purpose

Avoid over-rehearsing to prevent robotic delivery. While preparation is essential, over-rehearsed testimony sounds scripted and loses authenticity. The goal is for witnesses to be comfortable with the topics and sequence, not to memorize specific word-for-word answers.

Focus on tone, confidence, and composure under pressure. Practice sessions should emphasize maintaining appropriate emotional tone - neither too flat nor overly dramatic. Witnesses should learn to pause when upset, speak clearly when nervous, and maintain eye contact with the jury.

Clarify sensitive or emotionally charged topics. Prepare witnesses to handle difficult subjects with honesty rather than avoidance. If there are unfavorable facts, address them during direct examination rather than allowing them to surface during cross-examination where they appear hidden or deceptive.

Practice Example: If your client was terminated for attendance issues but claims the real reason was discrimination, don't avoid the attendance problems. Instead, establish the context: "Ms. Johnson, let's talk about your attendance in 2023. The company records show you were late several times. Can you explain what was happening in your life during that period?" Then allow her to explain the medical issues, family crisis, or other legitimate reasons while acknowledging the attendance problems honestly.

3. Use Documents Strategically

Introduce performance evaluations, complaint emails, medical letters, or HR memos during direct examination. Documents provide concrete evidence that supports testimony, but they must be introduced through witness foundation. The witness must establish that they recognize the document, can identify what it is, and can explain its significance.

Have the witness explain the meaning, timing, and impact in their own words. Don't just mark documents as evidence and move on. Use them as springboards for more detailed testimony about their significance in the overall narrative.

Document Integration Example: "Ms. Rodriguez, I'm showing you what's been marked as Plaintiff's Exhibit 12. Do you recognize this document?" "Yes, that's my performance evaluation from March 2023." "Who conducted this evaluation?" "My supervisor, Mr. Davidson." "Can you read the overall rating on this evaluation?" "It says 'Exceeds Expectations.'" "How did receiving this evaluation make you feel?" "I was proud. I'd worked really hard that year, and it felt good to have my efforts recognized." "When did your next performance evaluation occur?" "Six months later, in September 2023." "What had changed in your work situation between March and September?" "That's when I filed my complaint about Mr. Davidson's inappropriate comments about women in management."

15.3 Conducting Effective Direct Examination

Key Guidelines for Direct Examination

Use open-ended questions exclusively. Direct examination rules prohibit leading questions (except for preliminary matters like name and address). Your questions should invite explanation: "What happened next?" "How did that make you feel?" "Can you describe the meeting?" "What was your understanding of the policy?"

Listen actively and respond - don't interrupt powerful testimony. Sometimes witnesses will provide more compelling testimony than you anticipated. Don't cut off emotional or detailed responses that effectively advance your case just because they weren't in your script.

Keep the focus on the witness, not yourself. Avoid long, complex questions that showcase your knowledge of the facts. The jury should be listening to the witness, not watching you perform. Your role is to guide, not dominate.

Avoid legalese and keep it conversational. Speak in plain English that both the witness and jury can understand. Instead of "Did the defendant engage in conduct constituting a hostile work environment?" ask "Did Mr. Peterson's behavior make it difficult for you to do your job?"

Detailed Flow Example for Plaintiff Direct Examination

Background and Qualifications Phase: This establishes the witness as a real person with legitimate credentials and aspirations.

"Ms. Chen, please tell the jury about your educational background." "I graduated from State University in 2018 with a degree in marketing." "What drew you to marketing?" "I've always been interested in understanding what motivates people to make decisions. Marketing seemed like a field where I could combine creativity with data analysis." "What was your career goal when you graduated?" "I wanted to work for a consumer products company where I could develop campaigns for products that people use every day."

Hiring and Job Duties Phase: This establishes that the plaintiff was a legitimate, qualified employee doing real work.

"How did you learn about the position at ABC Corporation?" "I saw the job posting on LinkedIn. It was exactly what I was looking for - a marketing coordinator role at a consumer products company." "Can you describe the interview process?" "I had three interviews. First with HR, then with the marketing director, Sarah Williams, and finally with the department team." "How did you feel after the interviews?" "Confident and excited. Everyone seemed enthusiastic about my ideas, especially my suggestion about using social media influencers for the new product launch."

Initial Performance and Feedback Phase: This establishes baseline competence and sets up the contrast with later treatment.

"How would you describe your first six months at ABC?" "It was everything I had hoped for. I was working on interesting projects, my supervisor gave me positive feedback, and I felt like I was contributing to the team's success." "Can you give the jury a specific example of positive feedback you received?" "In my three-month review, Sarah told me that my social media campaign for the spring product launch exceeded expectations and generated twenty percent more engagement than the previous year's campaign."

Onset of Discriminatory or Retaliatory Behavior Phase: This is where the legal claims begin to take shape through specific incidents.

"Did anything change in how you were treated at work?" "Yes, after I got engaged in September." "How did your colleagues learn about your engagement?" "I announced it at our monthly team meeting. I was excited and wanted to share the news with people I considered friends." "What was the reaction?" "Most people congratulated me, but Sarah's expression changed. She looked concerned rather than happy." "What happened after that meeting?" "Within a week, Sarah called me into her office for what she called a 'career planning conversation.'" "Can you tell the jury about that conversation?" "She said that while she was happy for me personally, she was concerned about my commitment to the company. She asked about my timeline for having children and whether I planned to continue working after marriage."

Reporting and Employer Response Phase: This establishes that the plaintiff tried to work within the system and shows the employer's response.

"What did you do after this conversation with Sarah?" "I was confused and upset. I knew those questions weren't appropriate, so I decided to talk to HR." "Who did you speak with in HR?" "Janet Morrison, the HR director." "Can you describe that conversation?" "I explained what Sarah had said and asked if it was appropriate for supervisors to ask about employees' family planning. Janet listened and took notes." "What was Janet's response?" "She said she would look into it and get back to me. She also said I shouldn't worry and that these things sometimes get blown out of proportion."

Termination or Adverse Action Phase: This is where the retaliation claim crystallizes through specific adverse actions.

"What happened in the weeks following your meeting with Janet?" "Things got progressively worse. Sarah began excluding me from important meetings, questioning my work more critically, and giving me less desirable assignments." "Can you give the jury a specific example?" "The next month, there was a major client presentation for our biggest account. I had worked on that account since I started, but Sarah assigned the presentation to a newer employee who had never worked with that client." "How did that make you feel?" "Frustrated and humiliated. The other team members knew I was the logical choice for that presentation."

Emotional and Financial Impact Phase: This establishes damages and helps the jury understand the human cost of the discrimination.

"How did these changes at work affect you personally?" "I became anxious and started having trouble sleeping. I would lie awake at night replaying interactions and wondering if I was overreacting or if things were really as bad as they seemed." "Did you seek any professional help?" "Yes, I started seeing a therapist because the stress was affecting my relationship with my fiancé and my overall well-being." "How has losing your job affected you financially?" "It's been devastating. I was unemployed for eight months and had to take a position at a smaller company for significantly less money. My fiancé and I had to postpone our wedding and move to a smaller apartment."

15.4 Preparing for and Conducting Cross-Examination

General Principles of Cross-Examination

Cross-examination operates under fundamentally different rules and strategic considerations than direct examination. Understanding these differences is crucial for effective execution.

Lead with short, declarative questions. Unlike direct examination, cross-examination allows and encourages leading questions. Your questions should suggest the answer you want: "You were aware that Ms. Chen had filed a discrimination complaint, weren't you?" rather than "What did you know about Ms. Chen's complaint?"

Don't ask questions you don't already know the answer to. This is the cardinal rule of cross-examination. Every question should either elicit testimony that supports your case or set up impeachment if the witness gives an unexpected answer. The courtroom is not the place for discovery.

Be firm but respectful - hostile cross may backfire with sympathetic witnesses. While you want to maintain control, overly aggressive cross-examination can make you appear to be bullying the witness, which often generates jury sympathy for the witness rather than skepticism about their testimony.

Keep control through precise questioning. If the witness evades your question, politely redirect: "I understand your concern, but my question was specifically about whether you knew of the complaint. Can you answer yes or no?" If problems persist, ask the judge to instruct the witness to answer the question asked.

Strategic Targeting of Different Witness Types

Cross-Examining Supervisors: Supervisors often make the best cross-examination targets because they typically have the most knowledge about the disputed events and the most to lose if the plaintiff prevails.

Timeline inconsistencies: Supervisors often give deposition testimony months or years before trial. Their recollections may change, providing impeachment opportunities.

Example: "Mr. Davidson, you testified in your deposition that Ms. Rodriguez's performance problems began in January 2023, correct?" "I believe so, yes." "But the performance improvement plan you placed her on wasn't created until March 2023, was it?" "That sounds right." "So for two months, you knew about serious performance problems but took no formal action to address them?"

Motive for discipline: Explore whether the supervisor had personal reasons to want the plaintiff terminated.

Example: "Ms. Rodriguez had filed a complaint about your management style with HR in December 2022, hadn't she?" "She had raised some concerns, yes." "And you were upset about that complaint, weren't you?" "I was concerned about the allegations." "In fact, you told your assistant that Ms. Rodriguez was 'making trouble' for the department, didn't you?"

Prior treatment of other employees: Establish patterns that show inconsistent application of policies.

Example: "You testified that punctuality was very important in your department, correct?" "Yes, we start our day at 8 AM sharp." "But you never disciplined John Martinez for being late, did you?" "John's situation was different." "John was late more than fifteen times in 2023, wasn't he?" "I don't recall the exact number." "And John never filed any complaints about discrimination, did he?"

Cross-Examining HR Personnel: HR representatives can be effective targets because their job is to prevent discrimination, making their failures more significant.

Bias in investigations: Show that the HR investigation was predetermined or superficial.

Example: "Ms. Morrison, when you investigated Ms. Chen's complaint, you interviewed her supervisor Sarah Williams, correct?" "Yes." "You also interviewed two witnesses that Sarah suggested, didn't you?" "I interviewed relevant witnesses." "But you never interviewed the three coworkers that Ms. Chen specifically asked you to speak with, did you?" "I felt I had sufficient information." "And those three coworkers still work for the company today, don't they?" "Yes." "While Ms. Chen, who made the complaint, no longer works there?"

Failure to follow policy: Use the company's own policies against them.

Example: "Your company has a written policy requiring HR investigations to be completed within thirty days, correct?" "That's the guideline, yes." "Ms. Chen's complaint was filed on March 15th, wasn't it?" "Yes." "And you didn't complete your investigation report until May 22nd, did you?" "We wanted to be thorough." "That's sixty-eight days, isn't it?" "I haven't calculated it exactly."

Shifting justifications: Show that the company's explanation for its actions has changed over time.

Example: "When Ms. Chen was terminated, the termination letter stated the reason was 'restructuring,' didn't it?" "Yes." "But in your deposition, you testified that she was terminated for performance reasons, didn't you?" "Both factors played a role." "And today, you've testified that the termination was due to attendance issues, haven't you?" "Her attendance was also a concern." "So the company's explanation for her termination has been restructuring, performance, and attendance - is that your testimony?"

Cross-Examining Employer Decision-Makers: High-level decision-makers often make poor witnesses because they're removed from day-to-day operations but bear ultimate responsibility for company policies.

Awareness of complaints: Establish that decision-makers knew or should have known about discrimination.

Example: "As CEO, you receive monthly reports from HR about employee complaints, don't you Mr. Johnson?" "I receive summaries of significant issues." "Discrimination complaints would qualify as significant issues, wouldn't they?" "Generally, yes." "So you were aware that three separate employees had filed complaints about the same supervisor in 2023, weren't you?" "I may have been briefed on some complaints."

Failure to act: Show that despite knowledge, no corrective action was taken.

Example: "Despite knowing about these complaints, that supervisor received a positive performance review and a salary increase in 2023, didn't he?" "Performance reviews consider many factors." "The question is whether he received a positive review and salary increase. Yes or no?" "Yes."

Retaliation logic: Get decision-makers to admit that their actions could appear retaliatory.

Example: "Ms. Rodriguez was terminated three weeks after filing her EEOC complaint, wasn't she?" "The timing was coincidental." "You understand that employees might see a connection between filing a complaint and being terminated three weeks later, don't you?" "I can see how someone might misinterpret the situation."

Advanced Impeachment Techniques

Using Deposition Transcripts: Depositions provide excellent impeachment material because they represent sworn testimony given closer in time to the events in question.

Proper impeachment sequence:

1. Lock in the trial testimony: "You testified today that you don't recall the conversation, correct?"
2. Direct attention to the deposition: "Do you recall being deposed in this case on June 15, 2024?"
3. Establish the oath: "You were under oath at that deposition, just as you are today?"
4. Read the inconsistent testimony: "I'm going to read from page 47 of your deposition..."
5. Confirm the contradiction: "So your testimony today is different from your deposition testimony, isn't it?"

Highlighting Memory Gaps: Strategic memory lapses often reveal witness bias or preparation.

Example sequence: "You have a clear memory of Ms. Chen's performance problems, don't you?" "Yes, they were significant." "But you don't remember whether she received positive feedback earlier in the year?" "Not specifically." "And you don't recall the specific compliments you gave her work?" "No." "It's interesting that you have detailed memories of negative events but can't recall positive ones, isn't it?"

Demonstrating Motive to Lie: Show that witnesses have personal or professional reasons to slant their testimony.

Example: "If this jury finds that you discriminated against Ms. Chen, that could affect your career, couldn't it?" "I don't believe I discriminated against anyone." "But if a jury disagreed with you, that would reflect poorly on your management skills, wouldn't it?" "I suppose any adverse finding would be concerning." "And your company could face significant financial liability, correct?" "That's possible." "So you have a personal and professional interest in the outcome of this case, don't you?"

15.5 Expert Witness Examination

Expert witnesses require different examination techniques because they're testifying about specialized knowledge rather than personal observations. Their testimony must meet specific legal standards for admissibility and credibility.

Common Types of Experts in Employment Cases

Vocational/Economic Expert: These experts calculate lost wages, future earning capacity, and career trajectory damages. They typically have backgrounds in economics, vocational rehabilitation, or labor market analysis.

Typical testimony areas:

- Lost back pay calculations accounting for raises, bonuses, and benefits
- Front pay projections based on career trajectory and industry standards
- Mitigation of damages analysis (plaintiff's efforts to find comparable work)
- Economic impact of career derailment or reputation damage

Medical Expert: These experts address physical and emotional injuries resulting from workplace discrimination or harassment. They may be physicians, psychiatrists, or psychologists.

Typical testimony areas:

- Diagnosis and treatment of stress-related conditions
- Causation between workplace events and medical symptoms
- Prognosis and future treatment needs
- Impact on daily functioning and quality of life

HR/Policy Expert: These experts analyze whether employers followed industry standards and best practices in their policies and procedures.

Typical testimony areas:

- Industry standards for harassment prevention and response
- Adequacy of company policies and training programs
- Proper investigation procedures and documentation
- Comparison with accepted HR practices

Forensic/ESI (Electronically Stored Information) Expert: These experts analyze digital evidence, including email metadata, document creation dates, and potential evidence tampering.

Typical testimony areas:

- Authentication of electronic documents
- Timeline reconstruction from digital evidence
- Detection of document alteration or deletion
- Recovery of deleted or hidden electronic communications

Direct Examination of Expert Witnesses

Establish Credentials and Objectivity: Expert qualification is crucial for admissibility and credibility. This process, called "qualifying the witness," must establish both technical expertise and impartiality.

Credential establishment example: "Dr. Martinez, please tell the jury about your educational background." "I have a Ph.D. in Industrial Psychology from Stanford University and a master's degree in Human Resources Management." "What is your current position?" "I'm a professor at the University of California's School of Management and director of the Workplace Studies Institute." "How long have you been studying workplace discrimination and harassment?" "For over twenty years, both in academic research and consulting work." "Have you published research on these topics?" "Yes, I've authored three books and over fifty peer-reviewed articles on workplace discrimination, harassment prevention, and organizational behavior."

Objectivity establishment: "Dr. Martinez, how much are you being paid for your testimony in this case?" "I'm being compensated at my standard consulting rate of $400 per hour for time spent on case review and testimony." "Does your compensation depend on the outcome of this case?" "No, I'm paid the same amount regardless of how the case is resolved." "Have you testified for both plaintiffs and defendants in employment cases?" "Yes, I've testified in approximately thirty cases, representing both employees and employers depending on the facts and my professional opinion."

Walk Through Methodology and Conclusions Clearly: Expert testimony must be based on reliable methods and principles. The expert should explain their process in terms the jury can understand.

Methodology explanation example: "Dr. Martinez, how did you determine whether ABC Corporation's harassment investigation was adequate?" "I used a three-step analysis. First, I reviewed the company's written policies and compared them to industry standards and best practices. Second, I examined how those policies were actually implemented in Ms. Chen's case. Third, I evaluated whether the investigation process was likely to uncover relevant facts and protect the complainant from retaliation."

"What materials did you review in forming your opinion?" "I reviewed the company's employee handbook, HR policies, training materials, investigation file, relevant emails and documents, depositions of key witnesses, and the timeline of events."

"Did you consider alternative explanations for the company's actions?" "Yes, I considered whether the company's response could be explained by factors other than discrimination, such as resource constraints, lack of training, or good faith mistakes."

Use Visual Aids When Permitted: Complex expert testimony often benefits from visual aids, but they must be simple and clearly support the testimony rather than distract from it.

Effective visual aids for experts:

- Timeline showing investigation delays compared to company policy
- Comparison showing different treatment of similar complaints
- Economic projections showing lost earnings over time
- Before-and-after medical records showing symptom progression

Cross-Examination of Expert Witnesses

Challenge Assumptions or Inputs: Expert opinions are only as good as the facts and assumptions they're based on. Effective cross-examination identifies and challenges questionable foundation elements.

Challenging assumptions example: "Dr. Rodriguez, your lost wage calculation assumes Ms. Chen would have received the same percentage raises as other employees, correct?" "That's one assumption, yes." "But you're aware that her performance evaluations showed some areas needing improvement, aren't you?" "I reviewed the evaluations." "Employees with performance issues don't always receive the same raises as top performers, do they?" "That can vary by company." "You didn't factor in the possibility that her raises might have been smaller due to performance concerns, did you?" "I used the average raise percentage for all employees in her category."

Explore Alternative Explanations: Show that the expert's conclusions aren't the only reasonable interpretation of the evidence.

Alternative explanation example: "Dr. Williams, you concluded that Ms. Chen's anxiety was caused by workplace discrimination, correct?" "Based on the timing and her reported symptoms, yes." "But you're aware that she was also planning a wedding during this time period?" "That was mentioned in her medical records." "Wedding planning can be a significant source of stress, can't it?" "It can be stressful, yes." "You also noted that she had recently moved to a new apartment?" "Yes." "And that she was caring for an elderly parent with health problems?" "That was also noted." "So there were multiple potential stressors in her life during the relevant time period, weren't there?" "Yes, but the workplace events were the primary factor." "But you can't rule out that these other stressors contributed to her symptoms, can you?"

Highlight Lack of Independence: Show bias through repeat business relationships or financial incentives.

Independence challenge example: "Mr. Thompson, you've testified for the same law firm in twelve previous cases, haven't you?" "I've worked with them on multiple matters." "And they've paid you over $200,000 in consulting fees over the past three years, haven't they?" "I haven't calculated the total." "That represents a significant portion of your annual income, doesn't it?" "My income comes from various sources." "But losing this law firm as a client would significantly impact your finances, wouldn't it?" "I would prefer not to lose any clients."

15.6 Witness Control and Courtroom Management

Effective witness examination requires managing not just the content of testimony, but also the emotional and practical aspects of courtroom dynamics. Different types of witnesses present different challenges that require specific management techniques.

Dealing with Nervous Witnesses

Nervous witnesses can undermine even the strongest cases if their anxiety prevents them from communicating effectively. The key is to create an environment where they can succeed while maintaining authenticity.

Slow down the pacing. Nervous witnesses often feel pressured to answer quickly, leading to mistakes or incomplete answers. Build in natural pauses and speak more slowly yourself to set a calmer rhythm.

Pacing technique example: “Ms. Johnson, I want to ask you about the meeting with your supervisor on March 15th.” [Pause] “Take your time and think about that day.” [Pause] “Where did this meeting take place?”

Reaffirm that ‘telling the truth’ is the only job. Many witnesses worry about giving “perfect” answers or anticipating where questions are leading. Remind them that their only obligation is honesty.

Truth-focused instruction: “Mr. Garcia, if you don’t remember something clearly, it’s perfectly fine to say you don’t remember. If you’re not sure about dates or details, just tell us what you do recall. The most important thing is that your answers are truthful.”

Use documents as anchors. Documents provide nervous witnesses with concrete reference points that can help stabilize their testimony and refresh their recollection.

Document anchoring example: “Ms. Lee, I’m showing you what’s been marked as Exhibit 15. Take a moment to look at it.” [Allow time for review] “Does seeing this email help you remember the conversation you had with your supervisor that day?”

Handling Evasive or Hostile Witnesses During Cross-Examination

Some witnesses will attempt to avoid answering questions directly or will show hostility toward the examining attorney. These situations require firm but professional management.

Politely redirect when witnesses evade. Don't let evasion continue, but address it professionally to avoid appearing confrontational to the jury.

Redirection technique: "I understand you have concerns about the situation, Mr. Peterson, but my question was very specific. Did you or did you not tell Ms. Rodriguez that 'women don't belong in management positions'? Can you please answer yes or no?"

Lock down answers with yes-or-no questions. When witnesses try to give speeches instead of answering questions, force them to commit to specific positions.

Answer-locking example: "Mr. Davis, I'm not asking for your opinion about whether the comment was appropriate. My question is whether you heard Mr. Thompson make that comment. Yes or no?"

Request court intervention when necessary. If a witness continues to be evasive after redirection, ask the judge to intervene.

Court intervention request: "Your Honor, I've asked the witness three times whether he was present at the meeting on March 10th. Could you please instruct the witness to answer the question?"

Common Pitfalls in Witness Examination

Asking compound questions. Compound questions create confusion and give witnesses opportunities to answer only the part they prefer.

Problematic compound question: "After you filed the complaint, did your supervisor start treating you differently and did your coworkers begin excluding you from meetings and social events?"

Better approach: "After you filed the complaint, did your supervisor start treating you differently?" [Get answer] "Did your coworkers begin excluding you from meetings?" [Get answer] "What about social events?"

Badgering sympathetic witnesses. Overly aggressive cross-examination of sympathetic witnesses often backfires by generating jury sympathy for the witness.

Example of problematic badgering: Continuing to press a witness who is clearly upset about testifying regarding traumatic events, or repeatedly challenging minor details when the witness has already acknowledged the main point.

Better approach: Make your point efficiently and move on. If a witness admits to the key fact you need, don't continue hammering them about related details.

Over-explaining during objections. When an objection is made, stop talking immediately. Don't try to argue with the judge or explain why your question should be allowed in front of the jury.

Proper objection response: Judge: "Sustained." Attorney: "I'll move on, Your Honor." [Then ask a different question]

Improper objection response: Judge: "Sustained." Attorney: "But Your Honor, this goes directly to the witness's credibility and I should be allowed to explore..." [This argues the objection in front of the jury]

15.7 Using Demonstratives and Exhibits During Testimony

Visual evidence can significantly enhance witness testimony, but it must be used strategically and in compliance with evidentiary rules. The key is using visuals to support and clarify testimony rather than distract from it.

Effective Types of Demonstratives in Employment Cases

Timeline displays showing progression of events. Employment discrimination cases often involve complex sequences of events over months or years. Visual timelines help juries understand cause-and-effect relationships.

Timeline example elements:

- Plaintiff's hire date and initial positive reviews

- First discriminatory incident
- Subsequent incidents with increasing severity
- Plaintiff's complaint to HR
- Retaliatory actions following complaint
- Termination or other adverse action

Highlighted emails or performance reviews. Key documents become more impactful when important language is highlighted and enlarged for jury viewing.

Effective highlighting technique: Instead of reading an entire email, project it with key phrases highlighted, such as: "We need to find a reason to get rid of her" or "She's been nothing but trouble since she complained."

Side-by-side comparisons showing disparate treatment. Visual comparisons make discrimination more obvious than verbal descriptions alone.

Comparison examples:

- Performance evaluations: Plaintiff's detailed criticism versus coworker's brief positive comments for similar performance levels
- Disciplinary actions: Plaintiff's immediate termination for minor infraction versus coworker's verbal warning for serious misconduct
- Pay stubs: Plaintiff's salary progression versus similarly situated employees

Best Practices for Using Exhibits

Get exhibits admitted before showing them to the jury. This prevents interruptions during testimony and ensures a smooth flow of presentation.

Foundation establishment process:

1. Show the document to the witness
2. Ask if they recognize it
3. Have them identify what it is

4. Establish authenticity (who created it, when, how witness knows it's accurate)

5. Move for admission

6. Only after admission, publish to the jury

Avoid excessive technology use - simplicity wins. Complicated technology can malfunction and distract from your message. Simple, clear visuals are more effective than elaborate presentations.

Simplicity principles:

- Use large, readable fonts
- Stick to essential information only
- Have backup paper copies
- Test all technology before trial
- Have a non-technical alternative ready

Keep visuals visible but not distracting. Once you've made your point with a visual, remove it or move on. Leaving outdated visuals displayed can confuse the jury.

Display management:

- Remove exhibits when finished with them
- Don't leave demonstratives up during unrelated testimony
- Make sure all jurors can see displayed materials clearly
- Position displays so they don't block the witness from jury view

15.8 Mock Examinations and Focus Groups

When time and budget allow, testing your witness examinations before trial can provide invaluable insights into how your case will be received by actual jurors.

Mock Trial Benefits and Implementation

Mock trial or focus group testing reveals jury reactions. Legal professionals often develop blind spots about how lay people will interpret evidence and witness testimony. Mock trials using community members similar to your likely jury pool can reveal these perception gaps.

Mock trial structure:

- Present abbreviated versions of key witness examinations
- Use focus group participants similar to expected jury demographics
- Test both direct and cross-examination approaches
- Evaluate witness credibility and likability
- Assess comprehension of technical or legal concepts

Use feedback to refine tone, question framing, and witness order. Mock trial feedback often reveals that witnesses who seem strong to lawyers may appear less credible to jurors, or that testimony sequences that seem logical may actually confuse lay people.

Common mock trial revelations:

- Witnesses who appear defensive even when telling the truth
- Technical explanations that lose jury attention
- Emotional testimony that seems calculated rather than genuine
- Cross-examination that appears mean-spirited rather than truth-seeking
- Document presentations that are confusing rather than clarifying

Particularly valuable for high-stakes emotional claims or public-facing employers. Cases involving significant damages, punitive damages, or well-known employers benefit most from mock trial testing because jury reactions can be less predictable.

High-stakes considerations:

- Public company defendants may face heightened jury scrutiny
- Large damage requests require careful jury preparation
- Emotional distress claims need authentic presentation

- Retaliation cases require clear cause-and-effect demonstration

Focus Group Methodology

Recruit participants matching likely jury demographics. The jurisdiction's jury pool characteristics should guide focus group recruitment to ensure representative feedback.

Demographic considerations:

- Age range typical of local jury pools
- Educational background mix
- Employment status variety (employed, retired, unemployed)
- Gender balance
- Cultural and ethnic diversity reflecting community

Test specific examination techniques rather than entire case. Focus groups work best when testing discrete elements rather than full trial presentations.

Focused testing examples:

- Alternative approaches to plaintiff's direct examination opening
- Different methods of presenting technical expert testimony
- Variations in cross-examination tone for key defense witnesses
- Comparative effectiveness of different demonstrative aids

15.9 Strategic Considerations

The order and manner of witness presentation can significantly impact jury perception and case outcome. Strategic decisions about witness sequencing and examination techniques should align with overall trial strategy.

Order of Witnesses

Lead strong: Start with your most credible or sympathetic witness. First impressions matter enormously in trial advocacy. Your opening witness sets the tone for your entire case and creates initial jury impressions that subsequent testimony must either reinforce or overcome.

Strong opening witness characteristics:

- High credibility and likability
- Clear, compelling testimony supporting key claims
- Ability to remain composed under cross-examination
- Personal story that resonates with jury values
- Professional presentation and communication skills

Opening witness example: In a discrimination case, consider leading with a former coworker who witnessed discriminatory behavior rather than the plaintiff. This witness has less personal interest in the outcome, may appear more objective, and can establish the foundation for the plaintiff's later testimony about personal impact.

Save impactful emotional testimony for mid- or late-trial when jurors are more invested. Early in trial, jurors are still forming impressions and may be skeptical of emotional appeals. After they've heard factual foundation testimony and become invested in the story, emotional testimony becomes more powerful.

Emotional testimony timing:

- Early trial: Focus on facts, chronology, and credibility establishment
- Mid-trial: Introduce personal impact and emotional consequences
- Late trial: Reinforce emotional themes while maintaining factual foundation

Emotional testimony example: The plaintiff's testimony about personal impact of discrimination should come after witnesses have established that discrimination actually occurred. If jurors don't believe discrimination happened, emotional testimony about its effects will seem manipulative rather than compelling.

End with a clean, concise summary witness if possible. Your last witness should leave jurors with a clear, memorable final impression that reinforces your key themes without introducing new complications.

Effective closing witness characteristics:

- Concise, focused testimony
- Reinforces rather than introduces key themes
- Unlikely to create new issues on cross-examination
- Professional and sympathetic presentation
- Testimony that naturally leads into closing argument themes

Redirect and Rebuttal Examination

Use redirect to clean up confusing or misleading cross-examination. Redirect examination allows you to address damaging cross-examination testimony, but it must be used strategically rather than reflexively.

Effective redirect situations:

- Cross-examination created misleading impressions about key facts
- Important context was omitted during cross-examination
- Witness was prevented from fully explaining important answers
- New subjects were raised during cross-examination that need clarification

Redirect example: Cross-examination: "You admit you were late to work fifteen times in 2023?" Answer: "Yes." Redirect: "Ms. Johnson, you mentioned being late fifteen times. Can you explain to the jury what was causing your tardiness during that period?" Answer: "I was undergoing chemotherapy treatment for breast cancer. The treatments made me nauseous, and sometimes I couldn't leave home until the nausea passed."

Stay focused - don't rehash all of direct examination. Redirect should address specific issues raised during cross-examination, not repeat the entire direct examination. Lengthy redirect examinations suggest weakness and bore the jury.

Focused redirect principles:

- Address only issues raised during cross-examination

- Use precise questions targeting specific misleading impressions
- Avoid repeating testimony that wasn't challenged
- Keep redirect examination brief and focused
- Don't give opposing counsel additional cross-examination opportunities

In rebuttal, bring concise, surgical responses - don't reopen issues unnecessarily. Rebuttal testimony should address specific claims made during the defense case, not relitigate the entire plaintiff's case.

Effective rebuttal characteristics:

- Directly contradicts specific defense testimony
- Addresses new issues raised during defense case
- Brief and focused rather than comprehensive
- Uses credible witnesses with personal knowledge
- Avoids opening new areas for defense sur-rebuttal

Rebuttal example: If defense witness testifies that company policy prohibits discussing salary, rebuttal witness might testify about specific conversations where management encouraged salary discussions, directly contradicting the defense claim without relitigating broader policy issues.

Jurisdictional Differences in Witness Examination

New York State Courts: New York courts tend to be more formal and traditional in their approach to witness examination. Judges often maintain tighter control over the pace and scope of examination.

New York considerations:

- More formal courtroom atmosphere requires professional presentation
- Judges may be less tolerant of lengthy examinations
- Strong preference for clear, direct questions and answers
- Less tolerance for dramatic or emotional presentation styles

- Stricter enforcement of evidentiary rules during examination

California State Courts: California courts often allow more flexibility in examination style and may be more tolerant of innovative presentation techniques.

California considerations:

- More relaxed courtroom atmosphere allows varied presentation styles
- Judges may allow longer examinations if they serve clear purposes
- Greater tolerance for visual aids and technology use
- More acceptance of emotional testimony and personal storytelling
- Flexibility in examination order and witness scheduling

Federal Courts: Federal courts emphasize efficiency and adherence to Federal Rules of Evidence, with less tolerance for time-wasting or repetitive examination.

Federal court considerations:

- Strong emphasis on efficiency and time management
- Strict adherence to Federal Rules of Evidence
- Judges actively manage examination pace and scope
- Less tolerance for cumulative or repetitive testimony
- Preference for streamlined, focused examinations
- Greater emphasis on expert witness reliability standards under Daubert

Cultural and Demographic Considerations

Jury demographic analysis influences examination style. Understanding your likely jury composition should inform decisions about examination tone, complexity level, and cultural references.

Demographic adaptation examples:

- Blue-collar community juries may respond better to straightforward, no-nonsense examination styles

- Highly educated jury pools may tolerate more complex technical testimony
- Culturally diverse communities may require careful attention to language choices and cultural sensitivity
- Age demographics affect attention spans and technological comfort levels

Witness cultural background affects presentation. Witnesses from different cultural backgrounds may require different preparation and examination approaches to present effectively to diverse juries.

Cultural consideration examples:

- Eye contact norms vary across cultures and may affect credibility perceptions
- Communication styles differ in directness and emotional expression
- Authority relationships may influence how witnesses respond to questioning
- Language barriers may require slower pacing and simpler vocabulary

15.10 Advanced Examination Techniques

Impeachment Strategies Beyond Basic Contradiction

Character impeachment through pattern evidence. Beyond specific contradictions, effective cross-examination can undermine witness credibility by establishing patterns of dishonesty, bias, or unreliability.

Pattern impeachment example: Instead of focusing on one inconsistent statement, establish that the witness has given different versions of events to different people at different times, suggesting a pattern of changing stories to suit circumstances.

"Mr. Thompson, you told the EEOC investigator one version of events, didn't you?" "I answered their questions." "You told your supervisor a different version, didn't you?" "I may have emphasized different aspects." "You told the company's lawyer yet another version during your deposition, didn't you?" "I tried to be thorough." "And today, you're telling the jury still another version, aren't you?"

Impeachment through omission. Sometimes what witnesses don't say is as important as what they do say, particularly in formal settings where completeness is expected.

Omission impeachment example: "When you spoke to HR about the incident, you mentioned Ms. Rodriguez's attitude, didn't you?" "Yes." "You mentioned her tone of voice?" "Yes." "You mentioned her body language?" "Yes." "But you didn't mention that she was crying during the conversation, did you?" "I may not have mentioned that specifically." "Even though someone crying during a disciplinary meeting might be relevant information for HR to have?"

Advanced Direct Examination Techniques

Preemptive disclosure of problematic facts. Rather than allowing damaging facts to emerge during cross-examination, strategic direct examination addresses them head-on in a controlled manner.

Preemptive disclosure example: "Ms. Rodriguez, the company's records show that you were late to work several times during your final months of employment. Can you explain what was happening in your life during that period?"

This approach allows the witness to provide context and explanation rather than appearing to hide information that will inevitably be revealed during cross-examination.

Using silence and pacing for emphasis. Strategic pauses can emphasize important testimony and give juries time to absorb significant information.

Pacing technique example: "What did your supervisor say to you?" [Pause for answer] "He told me that women like me should focus on having babies instead of careers." [Extended pause before next question to let impact sink in] "How did that comment make you feel?"

Building to climactic moments. Effective direct examination creates dramatic tension by building toward key revelations rather than leading with the most important information.

Climactic building example: Rather than immediately asking about the discriminatory comment, build the context:

- Establish the setting and participants
- Describe the business purpose of the meeting
- Detail the normal flow of conversation
- Create the moment when everything changed
- Then reveal the discriminatory statement

This approach makes the key testimony more impactful and memorable.

Managing Difficult Legal Standards

Hostile work environment elements. Employment discrimination cases often require establishing that conduct was severe or pervasive enough to alter working conditions. Witness examination must carefully build this legal standard through specific testimony.

Severity and pervasiveness testimony: "Ms. Chen, how often did your supervisor make comments about women in management?" "At least two or three times per month." "Over what time period?" "From about March through September, so about seven months." "How did these comments affect your ability to do your job?" "I became anxious about speaking up in meetings because I was afraid he would make another comment about women not being leadership material."

Causation in retaliation cases. Retaliation claims require showing that adverse action was caused by protected activity. Witness examination must establish temporal proximity and causal connection.

Causation establishment: "When did you file your EEOC complaint?" "March 15, 2023." "When did your supervisor first mention performance problems?" "March 22, 2023, exactly one week later." "In the two years you had worked for him before filing the complaint, had he ever mentioned performance problems?" "Never. In fact, my last performance review was positive."

15.11 Technology and Modern Courtroom Considerations

Electronic Evidence Presentation

Email and text message authentication. Modern employment cases often involve electronic communications that require proper authentication and effective presentation.

Email authentication process:

1. Establish witness familiarity with email systems
2. Have witness identify their email address
3. Show the email and have witness confirm they sent/received it
4. Establish authenticity through content, timing, or other identifying information
5. Address any concerns about potential alteration

Electronic evidence best practices:

- Print emails in format that shows full headers when relevant
- Maintain original metadata when authenticity is disputed
- Use enlargement for key text but maintain context
- Prepare for authentication challenges with technical witnesses

Social media evidence considerations. Social media posts, LinkedIn profiles, and other online evidence require careful handling to establish authenticity and relevance.

Social media authentication:

- Screenshot preservation with URL and timestamp
- Witness testimony about posting habits and account control
- Technical testimony about platform features when necessary
- Foundation for business networking site profiles in employment context

Remote Testimony Considerations

Video deposition presentation. When live testimony isn't available, video depositions can provide effective witness presentation with proper preparation and technology.

Video deposition best practices:

- Edit to remove dead time and irrelevant portions
- Ensure audio quality is excellent
- Provide transcripts for complex testimony
- Test technology extensively before trial
- Have technical support available during presentation

Remote witness testimony challenges. Post-pandemic courts may allow remote testimony in certain circumstances, requiring adaptation of traditional examination techniques.

Remote testimony considerations:

- Technology failures can interrupt examination flow
- Jury connection with remote witnesses may be diminished
- Document presentation becomes more complicated
- Cross-examination control is more difficult
- Credibility assessment may be affected by video quality

15.12 Ethical Considerations in Witness Examination

Preparation Ethics

Appropriate witness preparation boundaries. Lawyers have an obligation to prepare witnesses effectively while avoiding coaching them to give false testimony.

Proper preparation activities:

- Reviewing likely topics and helping witnesses organize their thoughts
- Explaining courtroom procedures and examination format
- Practicing speaking clearly and maintaining composure

- Discussing how to handle "I don't know" and "I don't remember" situations
- Reviewing documents to refresh recollection

Improper preparation activities:

- Suggesting specific answers to anticipated questions
- Coaching witnesses to avoid harmful truths
- Creating false memories through repetitive suggestion
- Promising benefits for favorable testimony
- Threatening consequences for unfavorable testimony

Document review ethics. Showing witnesses documents before testimony is generally appropriate, but the manner and purpose matter for ethical compliance.

Proper document review:

- Refreshing witness recollection about past events
- Explaining document context and business practices
- Helping witnesses understand technical or legal terminology
- Organizing complex document sets for efficient testimony

Improper document review:

- Altering documents before showing to witnesses
- Suggesting interpretations that conflict with document content
- Using documents to create false memories
- Hiding relevant documents that might harm the case

Truthfulness Obligations

Duty to correct false testimony. If an attorney learns that their witness has given false testimony, they have an obligation to address the situation appropriately.

Response to discovered perjury:

- Immediate consultation with ethics authorities or bar counsel
- Potential withdrawal from representation in some circumstances
- Disclosure obligations vary by jurisdiction
- Cannot use known false testimony in argument or brief

Limits on aggressive cross-examination. While zealous advocacy is expected, cross-examination must remain within ethical bounds.

Ethical cross-examination boundaries:

- Cannot ask questions known to be based on false premises
- Must have good faith basis for impeachment attempts
- Cannot harass witnesses beyond legitimate advocacy purposes
- Should not make accusations without evidentiary support

15.13 Conclusion

Direct and cross-examination represent the heart of trial advocacy, where preparation meets performance and legal strategy becomes human drama. These examinations require a delicate balance: clarity without oversimplification, control without aggression, and emotion without manipulation. The most effective trial lawyers understand that witness examination is both art and science - requiring technical mastery of evidentiary rules combined with intuitive understanding of human psychology and jury dynamics.

In employment litigation specifically, witness examination carries additional complexity because the cases often involve workplace relationships, professional reputations, and deeply personal experiences of discrimination or harassment. The stakes are high not just legally, but personally and professionally for all parties involved. Successful examination requires sensitivity to these human elements while maintaining focus on the legal standards that ultimately determine case outcomes.

The differences between direct and cross-examination reflect fundamentally different strategic objectives. Direct examination tells your story through the witness's authentic voice, building credibility and emotional connection with the jury. Cross-examination challenges opposing narratives through controlled questioning that exposes inconsistencies, bias, or implausibility.

Both require extensive preparation, but that preparation must result in presentations that appear natural and spontaneous rather than scripted or rehearsed.

Modern employment litigation also requires adaptation to technological realities, cultural diversity, and evolving workplace norms. Email communications, social media evidence, remote work arrangements, and changing demographic patterns all influence how witnesses must be examined and how their testimony will be received. Successful trial lawyers must remain current with these developments while maintaining mastery of timeless advocacy principles.

The jurisdictional differences between New York, California, and federal courts require tactical adjustments in examination style, pacing, and formality. However, the fundamental principles of effective witness examination - thorough preparation, clear communication, strategic thinking, and ethical practice - remain constant across all jurisdictions.

Perhaps most importantly, effective witness examination serves the broader goal of truth-seeking that underlies our legal system. While advocacy requires presenting your client's case in the most favorable light possible, the examination process should ultimately help juries understand what actually happened and make informed decisions based on reliable evidence. The most successful trial lawyers are those who can advance their clients' interests while contributing to this truth-seeking process.

Mastering witness examination requires continuous learning and practice. Each case presents unique challenges, and each witness requires individualized preparation and examination strategies. The techniques discussed in this chapter provide a foundation, but its successful application requires judgment, experience, and adaptation to specific circumstances. The investment in developing these skills pays dividends not just in trial outcomes, but in the quality of legal representation provided to clients who have entrusted their professional and personal futures to their attorneys' advocacy skills.

In Chapter 16, we'll conclude the trial phase with closing arguments and jury deliberation, where all the pieces of your case - including the witness testimony developed through effective examination - come together for a final persuasive push toward victory.

16

Closing Arguments and Jury Deliberation

After weeks or months of preparation, discovery, motions, and trial, closing arguments offer the final opportunity to shape how the jury interprets the evidence and applies the law. In employment litigation, closings are where your client's narrative must crystallize, themes must converge, and jurors must be moved to action.

This chapter guides you through crafting compelling closing arguments and anticipating the dynamics of jury deliberation in employment trials in New York, California, and federal courts.

16.1 The Role of Closing Arguments

Purpose and Function

Closing arguments serve multiple critical functions that distinguish them from opening statements and witness examination. Unlike opening statements, which preview what you expect to prove, closings allow you to argue what the evidence has actually shown. This distinction is crucial because it permits advocacy rather than mere recitation.

The primary purposes include:

- Tie together facts, exhibits, and witness testimony into a coherent narrative
- Emphasize key legal elements and demonstrate how the evidence satisfies each requirement
- Remind jurors of your overarching theme while connecting it to legal standards
- Discredit the opposition's theory without alienating jurors through personal attacks
- Empower the jury to reach a verdict and fulfill their role as arbiters of justice

Key Difference from Opening Statements: While opening statements must be factual previews, closings permit argument, inference, and interpretation of evidence. You can tell the jury what the evidence means, not merely what it shows.

Jurisdictional Variations

Federal Courts: Generally allow broader latitude in closing arguments, permitting reasonable inferences from evidence and metaphorical language. However, inflammatory rhetoric or arguments not supported by evidence will draw objections and potential mistrial motions.

New York State Courts: Follow similar principles but tend to be more restrictive regarding emotional appeals and personal attacks on opposing counsel or parties. New York courts emphasize that closings must be based on evidence in the record.

California State Courts: Allow vigorous advocacy but maintain strict prohibitions against arguing facts not in evidence. California courts are particularly sensitive to arguments that appeal to bias or prejudice, especially in employment discrimination cases.

16.2 Structuring Your Closing Argument

1. Reaffirm Your Theme

Begin and end with your trial theme - this anchors your case emotionally and intellectually. Your theme should be a simple, memorable phrase that encapsulates the essence of your client's experience and the legal violation.

Examples of Effective Themes:

- "This is a case about what happens when someone speaks up - and how a company tries to silence them." (Retaliation case)
- "This case is about a company that said one thing but did another - preaching diversity while practicing discrimination." (Discrimination case)
- "This is about power and abuse - how someone trusted with authority used it to harm rather than protect." (Harassment case)

Legal Jargon Explained:

- **Theme**: A unifying narrative thread that connects facts to legal theories and emotional impact
- **Anchoring**: A psychological technique where the first and last information presented has disproportionate influence on decision-making

2. Walk Through the Evidence Systematically

Organize your evidence presentation by the legal elements of each claim rather than chronologically. This approach ensures you address every requirement the jury must find to rule in your favor.

For Discrimination Claims, address each element:

- **Protected Class Membership**: Establish your client belongs to a protected category (race, gender, age, disability, etc.)
- **Adverse Employment Action**: Demonstrate termination, demotion, or other tangible job detriment
- **Similarly Situated Comparators**: Show how others outside the protected class were treated differently
- **Causation**: Connect the protected characteristic to the adverse action

For Retaliation Claims, prove:

- **Protected Activity**: Your client complained about discrimination or participated in an investigation
- **Employer Knowledge**: The employer knew about the protected activity
- **Adverse Action**: The employer took negative action against your client
- **Causal Connection**: The timing and circumstances link the complaint to the retaliation

Practical Example: "Let's look at what happened step by step. Ms. Johnson filed her sexual harassment complaint on March 15th. The very next week, her supervisor - who had given her excellent reviews for three years - suddenly found problems with her work. Within six weeks, she was terminated for 'performance issues' that materialized only after she spoke up."

3. Address Weaknesses Honestly

Acknowledging adverse facts builds credibility and prevents the defense from blindsiding the jury. Frame weaknesses within your larger narrative rather than ignoring them.

Effective Approaches:

- **Performance Issues**: "You heard she had performance issues. But look at the timing - those concerns surfaced only after she complained about harassment. For three years, her reviews were stellar. Suddenly, weeks after her complaint, everything changed."
- **Company Policies**: "The company had policies against discrimination. But as their own HR director admitted, those policies weren't followed. Having a policy means nothing if you don't enforce it."
- **Prior Complaints**: "Yes, she had complained before about working conditions. That doesn't make her a troublemaker - it makes her someone who cares enough about her job to try to make things better."

Legal Jargon Explained:

- **Adverse Facts**: Evidence that appears to support the opposing party's position

- **Preemption**: Addressing negative evidence before the opposition can use it against you

4. Discredit the Opposition's Theory

Frame the employer's version as internally inconsistent or implausible without attacking opposing counsel personally. Focus on contradictions in testimony, gaps in documentation, and implausible explanations.

Effective Techniques:

- **Highlight Contradictions**: "The HR manager testified that they thoroughly investigated every complaint. But when shown the complaint form, she couldn't explain why there are no notes, no witness interviews, no follow-up documentation."
- **Question Timing**: "They say the termination was for budget cuts. If that's true, why was her position filled within three weeks? Why was no one else in her department laid off?"
- **Point Out Implausible Explanations**: "The supervisor claims he doesn't remember making those comments. But he remembers every other detail of their conversations. Is his memory really that selective?"

Comparison to Criminal Law: Unlike criminal defense, where you need only create reasonable doubt, employment plaintiffs must prove their case by a preponderance of the evidence. This means your attack on the defense theory must do more than create doubt - it must make your version more likely than theirs.

5. Humanize Your Client

Employment cases are deeply personal. Jurors need to see your client as a real person who suffered genuine harm, not just a legal abstraction seeking money.

Effective Humanization Strategies:

- **Personal Impact**: "This isn't just about losing a job. Ms. Rodriguez had worked there for eight years. She had built relationships, earned respect, provided for her family. In one moment, because she refused to stay silent about harassment, all of that was taken away."

- **Dignity and Credibility**: "She didn't come forward lightly. She knew the risks. But she also knew that staying silent meant the next woman might face the same treatment."
- **Future Consequences**: "The termination didn't just end her job - it damaged her reputation in a small industry where everyone knows everyone."

Legal Jargon Explained:

- **Humanization**: Making the plaintiff relatable and sympathetic to jurors while maintaining focus on legal standards
- **Mitigation**: The plaintiff's obligation to minimize damages by seeking other employment

16.3 Legal Instructions and the Jury Charge

Using Instructions to Your Advantage

Jury instructions define the legal standards the jury must apply. Effective closings translate these often complex legal concepts into plain English while tying them to your evidence.

Key Translation Strategies:

- **Preponderance Standard**: "The judge will tell you that we must prove our case by a preponderance of the evidence. That means more likely than not - just over 50%. If you think there's a 51% chance we're right, that's enough."
- **Mixed Motive Cases**: "The law says it only takes one motivating factor. Even if the employer had other reasons, if discrimination played any part in the decision, that's enough for liability."
- **Constructive Discharge**: "The judge will instruct you about constructive discharge - that's when working conditions become so intolerable that a reasonable person would feel forced to quit. It's like being fired without the formality."

Jurisdictional Differences:

Federal Courts: Use pattern jury instructions that emphasize burden-shifting frameworks in discrimination cases. The McDonnell Douglas standard requires plaintiffs to establish a prima facie case, then shifts the burden to employers to articulate legitimate reasons.

New York: Follows federal standards but emphasizes the New York Human Rights Law's broader protections. New York instructions often include specific language about the law's remedial purpose.

California: Uses CACI (California Civil Jury Instructions) which tend to be more plaintiff-friendly, particularly regarding harassment claims and the definition of severe or pervasive conduct.

Legal Jargon Explained:

- **Prima Facie Case**: A case that, if unrebutted, would entitle the plaintiff to judgment
- **Burden-Shifting**: A framework where the burden of proof moves between parties as different elements are established
- **McDonnell Douglas Standard**: The three-step process for proving discrimination in the absence of direct evidence

Burden of Proof Distinctions

Civil vs. Criminal Standard: Employment cases use the civil standard of preponderance of the evidence, not the criminal standard of beyond a reasonable doubt. This distinction is crucial for jurors who may expect a higher burden.

Effective Explanation: "This isn't a criminal case where we have to prove guilt beyond a reasonable doubt. The standard here is preponderance of the evidence - more likely than not. Think of it as a scale. Our evidence just needs to tip the scale slightly in our favor."

16.4 Damages Argument

Economic Damages

Economic damages compensate for measurable financial losses. These fall into several categories that require different presentation strategies.

Back Pay: Wages lost from termination to trial. Calculate by multiplying the plaintiff's salary by the time period, then subtract any interim earnings or unemployment benefits received.

Front Pay: Future lost earnings when reinstatement isn't feasible. This requires projections about career trajectory, salary increases, and working lifespan.

Benefits: Lost health insurance, retirement contributions, stock options, and other compensation components often overlooked but significant in value.

Practical Example: "Ms. Chen earned $75,000 annually with full benefits. She's been unemployed for 18 months despite diligent job searching. Her back pay alone is $112,500. Add the $18,000 in lost benefits, and we're looking at over $130,000 in concrete losses - before we even consider the emotional harm."

Legal Jargon Explained:

- **Back Pay**: Wages lost between the discriminatory act and trial
- **Front Pay**: Future lost wages when reinstatement isn't appropriate
- **Mitigation**: The plaintiff's duty to minimize damages through reasonable job search efforts

Emotional Distress Damages

Emotional distress damages compensate for psychological harm caused by discrimination or harassment. These damages are often significant but require careful presentation to avoid appearing speculative.

Key Presentation Elements:

- **Medical Evidence**: Testimony from treating physicians, therapists, or psychiatrists about diagnosed conditions like depression, anxiety, or PTSD
- **Personal Testimony**: The plaintiff's own description of how the discrimination affected their daily life, relationships, and self-esteem
- **Corroborating Witnesses**: Family members, friends, or colleagues who observed changes in the plaintiff's behavior or emotional state

Comparison Across Jurisdictions:

Federal Courts: Generally allow emotional distress damages but may require medical evidence for substantial awards. Some circuits are more restrictive about awards without professional treatment.

New York: Permits significant emotional distress awards even without medical treatment, recognizing that discrimination inherently causes psychological harm.

California: Very generous with emotional distress damages, particularly in harassment cases. California recognizes that the nature of workplace discrimination makes it inherently harmful to dignity and emotional well-being.

Effective Argument Structure: "The law recognizes that discrimination doesn't just hurt your wallet - it hurts your soul. Ms. Anderson testified about sleepless nights, anxiety attacks, and feeling worthless. Her doctor confirmed the diagnosis of major depression. This isn't about getting rich - it's about acknowledging the very real harm that discrimination causes."

Punitive Damages

Punitive damages punish defendants and deter future misconduct. They're available only when the defendant's conduct was particularly egregious, willful, or showed reckless indifference to the plaintiff's rights.

Elements to Emphasize:

- **Egregiousness**: The employer's conduct was particularly shocking or offensive
- **Willful Conduct**: The employer knew their actions were wrong but continued anyway
- **Pattern of Behavior**: This wasn't an isolated incident but part of a broader pattern
- **Deterrence Need**: Punishment is necessary to prevent future similar conduct

Jurisdictional Caps and Limitations:

Federal Title VII Cases: Punitive damages are capped based on employer size:

- 15-100 employees: $50,000 maximum

- 101-200 employees: $100,000 maximum
- 201-500 employees: $200,000 maximum
- 500+ employees: $300,000 maximum

New York Human Rights Law: No statutory caps on punitive damages, allowing potentially unlimited awards based on the defendant's conduct and financial condition.

California Fair Employment and Housing Act: No caps on punitive damages, but courts consider the defendant's financial condition and the reprehensibility of the conduct.

Effective Argument: "This company knew exactly what they were doing. They had policies against harassment, but when women complained, they were ignored, transferred, or fired. The HR manager admitted receiving multiple complaints about the same supervisor, but nothing was done. This pattern of indifference demands punishment - not just to compensate Ms. Williams, but to send a message that this behavior won't be tolerated."

16.5 Defense Closings: Strategic Points

Defense Counsel Goals

Understanding defense strategy helps plaintiff's counsel anticipate and counter their arguments. Common defense approaches include:

Reframing the Narrative: Portraying the plaintiff's claims as overreach, exaggeration, or an attempt to blame others for poor performance or personal problems.

Emphasizing Company Compliance: Highlighting policies, training programs, and good-faith efforts to prevent discrimination and harassment.

Focusing on Legitimate Business Reasons: Demonstrating that adverse employment actions were based on performance, budget constraints, or business restructuring rather than discrimination.

Attacking Credibility: Pointing to inconsistencies in the plaintiff's testimony, failure to follow company procedures, or prior complaints about unrelated issues.

Appealing to Personal Responsibility: Suggesting that the plaintiff should have done more to address problems through internal channels or that they're partly responsible for their situation.

Risk of Overreaching

Defense counsel must be careful not to overreach in their attacks on the plaintiff, particularly in discrimination and harassment cases where aggressive tactics can backfire.

Dangerous Defense Strategies:

- **"She just wants a payday"**: This attack on the plaintiff's motives often backfires, especially with diverse juries who may identify with discrimination victims
- **Blaming the victim**: Suggesting that harassment victims "asked for it" or should have handled the situation differently typically alienates jurors
- **Character assassination**: Personal attacks on the plaintiff's lifestyle, relationships, or unrelated past behavior usually generate sympathy rather than skepticism

Effective Counter-Strategies for Plaintiff's Counsel:

- **Anticipate the attack**: Address potential credibility issues in your case-in-chief rather than waiting for the defense to raise them
- **Reframe personal responsibility**: "They want you to blame Ms. Johnson for not stopping harassment. That's not how the law works - employers are responsible for providing a harassment-free workplace"
- **Use overreach against them**: "They spent more time attacking Ms. Rodriguez's character than explaining why she was suddenly terminated after eight years of excellent performance"

16.6 Rebuttal Arguments

Rebuttal provides the final word, but it's limited to responding to arguments made in the defense closing. Effective rebuttal requires discipline and strategic focus.

Permissible Rebuttal Content

Correcting Misstatements: Address factual errors or mischaracterizations of evidence presented by defense counsel.

Responding to New Arguments: Counter arguments raised for the first time in the defense closing.

Refocusing on Central Message: Return the jury's attention to your core theme and strongest evidence.

Clarifying Legal Standards: Correct any misstatements about the law or jury instructions.

Prohibited Rebuttal Content

New Evidence or Arguments: You cannot raise entirely new theories or evidence not addressed in your main closing.

Personal Attacks: Rebuttal cannot be used to attack opposing counsel personally or make inflammatory statements.

Repetitive Arguments: Simply repeating your main closing arguments without addressing the defense response is ineffective and may be limited by the court.

Effective Rebuttal Structure:

1. **Address the most damaging defense arguments first**
2. **Correct any factual misstatements clearly and concisely**
3. **Reconnect corrected facts to your legal theory**
4. **End with moral clarity and a call to action**

Example: "Defense counsel spent considerable time talking about company policies. But having a policy and enforcing it are two different things. Ms. Chen followed every procedure - she reported the harassment to HR, she documented the incidents, she gave the company every opportunity to fix the problem. The company's response? They transferred her to a lesser position and ultimately forced her out. That's not following policy - that's retaliation."

16.7 Jury Deliberation Dynamics

Factors That Influence Jurors

Understanding what motivates jurors helps craft more effective closing arguments. Research and post-trial interviews reveal several key influences:

Witness Credibility and Likability: Jurors make quick judgments about witness truthfulness based on demeanor, consistency, and apparent sincerity. Likable witnesses have more persuasive power, but credibility ultimately matters more than personality.

Clear Timelines and Causation: Jurors appreciate straightforward chronologies that clearly connect discriminatory conduct to adverse employment actions. Confusing timelines or complex causal chains undermine otherwise strong cases.

Internal Consistency: Jurors notice when testimony contradicts earlier statements, documents, or common sense. Consistency builds credibility; contradictions destroy it.

Adherence to Stated Policies: Jurors expect employers to follow their own rules. When companies ignore their stated policies, it suggests bad faith and supports discrimination claims.

Proportionality of Response: Jurors assess whether the employer's response was proportionate to any legitimate concerns. Severe punishment for minor infractions suggests discriminatory motivation.

Common Juror Biases

Anti-Plaintiff Bias: Some jurors are skeptical of lawsuits generally and may view plaintiffs as opportunistic or greedy. This bias is stronger in conservative communities and among jurors with management experience.

Anti-Corporate Bias: Other jurors distrust large institutions and may be more sympathetic to individual employees. This bias is more common among younger jurors and those with limited management experience.

Damage Skepticism: Many jurors are comfortable with economic damages but skeptical of large emotional distress or punitive awards. They may view these as "jackpot justice" unless the conduct was particularly egregious.

Victim Blaming: Some jurors, particularly in harassment cases, may unconsciously blame victims for not doing more to prevent or stop the misconduct.

Addressing Biases in Closing:

- **For anti-plaintiff bias**: Emphasize that your client didn't want to sue but was forced to seek justice when the company failed to act
- **For damage skepticism**: Ground emotional distress arguments in concrete evidence and medical testimony
- **For victim blaming**: Remind jurors that the law places responsibility on employers, not victims

Deliberation Room Dynamics

Foreperson Influence: The jury foreperson often has disproportionate influence on deliberations. Strong personalities or those with perceived expertise may sway others.

Compromise Verdicts: Juries sometimes split the difference, finding liability but awarding lower damages than requested, or finding some claims valid while rejecting others.

Holdout Jurors: Single jurors can sometimes prevent consensus, leading to compromise verdicts or hung juries. Effective closings address multiple perspectives to minimize holdouts.

Group Psychology: Juries often move toward consensus through discussion and compromise. Extreme positions on either side may moderate through deliberation.

16.8 Jury Verdict Forms

Design Principles

Verdict forms should be clear, logical, and easy to follow. Complex forms confuse jurors and may lead to inconsistent verdicts that require correction or retrial.

Key Elements:

- **Simple Language**: Avoid legal jargon and use plain English
- **Logical Progression**: Follow the legal elements in order
- **Clear Instructions**: Explain when to answer subsequent questions based on previous answers
- **Specific Damages Categories**: Separate economic, emotional distress, and punitive damages

Jurisdictional Variations:

Federal Courts: Often use special verdict forms that require specific findings on each element of each claim. This provides clarity but can be complex.

New York: May use general verdict forms that ask only for overall liability and damages, or special verdicts depending on case complexity.

California: Frequently uses special verdict forms with detailed questions about each claim element and damage category.

Strategic Considerations

Walking Through the Form: Subtly guide jurors through the verdict form during closing argument without appearing to instruct them on how to decide.

Consistency Requirements: Ensure that verdict form answers are logically consistent. Inconsistent verdicts may be subject to correction or retrial.

Damage Calculations: Make sure jurors understand how to calculate damages and what evidence supports each category.

Example Guidance: "The judge will give you a verdict form with several questions. If you find that the company discriminated against Ms. Martinez, you'll answer 'yes' to question one. That allows you to consider damages in questions two through four. Question two asks about economic damages - the lost wages and benefits we discussed. Question three concerns emotional distress - the psychological harm she suffered. Question four addresses punitive damages - whether the company's conduct was so egregious that punishment is warranted."

16.9 Post-Closing Practices

Immediate Post-Verdict Conduct

Maintain Composure: Regardless of the verdict, maintain professional composure. Emotional reactions can be seen by jurors and may affect future cases.

Thank the Jury: Brief, genuine thanks to jurors for their service is appropriate regardless of outcome.

Client Consultation: Immediately consult with your client about the verdict and next steps, whether celebrating victory or discussing appeal options.

Juror Interviews

Permissible Contact: Most jurisdictions allow post-trial juror contact if jurors consent and the contact is not harassing or improper.

Valuable Feedback: Juror interviews provide insight into deliberation dynamics, effective arguments, and areas for improvement.

Ethical Limitations: Cannot ask about jury deliberation content in some jurisdictions, and must respect jurors who decline to participate.

Strategic Value: Understanding why jurors reached their decision helps refine closing argument strategies for future cases.

Post-Trial Motions Preparation

Judgment as a Matter of Law (JNOV): Consider whether the verdict is supported by sufficient evidence. Successful JNOV motions are rare but possible when verdicts clearly contradict the evidence.

New Trial Motions: Evaluate potential grounds including inadequate damages, prejudicial error, or jury misconduct.

Remittitur/Additur: Consider whether damage awards are excessive (remittitur) or inadequate (additur) based on comparable cases and evidence presented.

Legal Jargon Explained:

- **JNOV (Judgment Notwithstanding Verdict)**: A post-trial motion arguing that no reasonable jury could have reached the verdict based on the evidence

- **Remittitur**: Court reduction of excessive jury damage award
- **Additur**: Court increase of inadequate jury damage award (less commonly available)

16.10 Practical Considerations and Best Practices

Timing and Pacing

Length Guidelines: Most effective closings in employment cases last 30-60 minutes. Longer arguments risk losing jury attention; shorter arguments may not fully develop themes.

Pacing Strategy: Vary your pace and tone to maintain interest. Build to crescendos at key points, then allow moments for reflection.

Time Management: Allocate time based on claim strength and complexity. Spend the most time on your strongest arguments and most important damages.

Visual Aids and Technology

Exhibit Integration: Use key documents and exhibits strategically, but don't overwhelm jurors with too many visuals.

Timeline Graphics: Simple timelines can help jurors understand the sequence of events and causal connections.

Technology Limitations: Ensure all technology works properly and have backup plans. Technical difficulties can destroy the flow of your argument.

Common Mistakes to Avoid

Over-Arguing: Making every possible argument weakens strong ones. Focus on your best points and make them well.

Personal Attacks: Attacking opposing counsel or parties personally typically backfires and violates professional conduct rules.

New Evidence: Trying to introduce new facts or evidence during closing arguments will draw objections and may result in mistrial.

Ignoring Weaknesses: Failing to address obvious problems in your case allows the defense to blindside the jury.

Emotional Manipulation: While emotion is important, obvious manipulation can backfire. Keep emotional appeals genuine and tied to legitimate legal issues.

Ethical Considerations

Professional Conduct: Maintain civility and professionalism even during vigorous advocacy. Personal attacks on opposing counsel violate ethical rules and harm your case.

Truth and Accuracy: All factual statements must be supported by evidence in the record. Mischaracterizing evidence can result in sanctions and malpractice liability.

Inflammatory Arguments: Avoid arguments that appeal to bias, prejudice, or passion unrelated to the legal issues. Such arguments may result in mistrial or appeal grounds.

16.11 Conclusion

Closing arguments represent the culmination of everything your client has endured and everything you've built as counsel. A strong closing connects the dots between evidence and law, appeals to both logic and justice, and leaves the jury with a clear sense of duty and path to fulfilling it.

The most effective closings in employment litigation combine legal precision with human empathy. They translate complex legal standards into common sense principles while never losing sight of the real person whose life and livelihood hang in the balance. They acknowledge weaknesses honestly while maintaining conviction about the strength of the case.

Remember that jurors want to do the right thing. Your job is to show them what that is and give them the legal and factual tools to achieve justice. As the jury retires to deliberate, your preparation, clarity, and passion will continue to speak in the deliberation room long after your words have ended.

The art of closing argument lies not in perfection, but in authentic advocacy that serves both the law and the client with equal dedication. Master this balance, and you'll not only win cases - you'll make a meaningful difference in the lives of those who trust you with their stories of workplace injustice.

In Chapter 17, we'll explore how to calculate, present, and support damages in employment cases, from economic losses to emotional harm and punitive awards, building on the damages arguments framework established in this chapter.

17

Calculating Damages in Employment Cases

Damages are the financial and emotional spine of any employment lawsuit. They provide the basis for settlement, the target at trial, and the measure of justice for wrongful workplace conduct. Yet, calculating and presenting damages is both an art and a science - requiring legal accuracy, factual clarity, and narrative cohesion.

This chapter outlines the core components of damages in employment cases in New York, California, and federal courts, including how to quantify lost wages, emotional distress, and punitive awards, and how to structure persuasive damages presentations.

17.1 Categories of Damages

Understanding the different types of damages available in employment cases is crucial for building a comprehensive claim. Each category serves a different purpose and has distinct requirements for proof and calculation.

Economic Damages

Economic damages represent the plaintiff's quantifiable financial losses. These are the easiest to calculate and most readily accepted by courts and juries because they have clear monetary values.

Back Pay: Wages lost from the date of wrongful conduct to the date of trial or settlement. This includes not only base salary but also bonuses, commissions, overtime, and other compensation that would have been earned.

Front Pay: Future wage losses when reinstatement is not feasible. Unlike back pay, which looks backward, front pay projects forward and requires more complex calculations involving the plaintiff's remaining work life expectancy.

Lost Benefits: The value of employer-provided benefits such as health insurance, retirement contributions, stock options, and other perquisites. These are often overlooked but can represent substantial value, particularly for long-term employees.

Medical Expenses: Costs for medical or psychological treatment necessitated by the employer's wrongful conduct. This might include therapy sessions, prescription medications, or hospitalization.

Job Search Costs: Reasonable expenses incurred while seeking new employment, including resume preparation, travel for interviews, and career counseling services.

Non-Economic Damages

Non-economic damages compensate for intangible harms that cannot be easily quantified but are nonetheless real and significant.

Emotional Distress: Compensation for psychological harm such as anxiety, depression, humiliation, and loss of self-esteem. Unlike physical injuries, emotional distress requires careful documentation through testimony and expert opinion.

Loss of Enjoyment of Life: Damages for the plaintiff's reduced ability to enjoy activities and relationships due to the employer's conduct. This might include social withdrawal, loss of interest in hobbies, or strained family relationships.

Reputational Harm: Compensation for damage to the plaintiff's professional reputation, particularly relevant in cases involving public termination or false accusations of misconduct.

Punitive Damages

Punitive damages serve a dual purpose: punishing the defendant for particularly egregious conduct and deterring similar behavior in the future. Unlike compensatory damages, punitive damages are not tied to the plaintiff's actual losses but rather to the defendant's culpability.

Purpose and Rationale: Courts award punitive damages when the defendant's conduct was malicious, reckless, or showed conscious disregard for the plaintiff's rights. The goal is to make the punishment meaningful enough to change behavior.

Standards for Award: The conduct must go beyond mere negligence or ordinary workplace disputes. Examples include systematic harassment, retaliation against whistleblowers, or willful violation of employment laws with knowledge of their illegality.

Statutory and Liquidated Damages

Many employment statutes provide for specific penalties beyond actual damages. These serve to strengthen enforcement and provide additional deterrence.

Wage and Hour Penalties: Statutes like the Fair Labor Standards Act (FLSA) and state wage laws often provide for liquidated damages equal to the unpaid wages, effectively doubling the recovery.

Civil Rights Penalties: Laws like California's Fair Employment and Housing Act (FEHA) and New York City's Human Rights Law (NYCHRL) provide for statutory damages in discrimination cases.

Representative Action Penalties: California's Private Attorneys General Act (PAGA) allows employees to recover civil penalties on behalf of the state, creating substantial potential liability for employers.

17.2 Back Pay: The Foundation of Economic Loss

Back pay forms the cornerstone of most employment damage claims. It represents the wages and benefits the plaintiff would have earned but for the defendant's wrongful conduct.

What Back Pay Covers

Base Wages: The plaintiff's regular salary or hourly wages from the date of termination or other adverse action through the date of trial or settlement. This calculation must account for any raises or merit increases the employee would have received.

Variable Compensation: Bonuses, commissions, and incentive payments present particular challenges because they may vary based on performance, company results, or market conditions. Courts typically look to historical patterns and reasonable projections.

Overtime and Premium Pay: For non-exempt employees, back pay includes overtime compensation that would have been earned. This requires analysis of the plaintiff's typical work schedule and overtime patterns.

Shift Differentials and Premiums: Additional compensation for night shifts, weekend work, or hazardous duty must be included if the plaintiff regularly received such payments.

Calculating Back Pay

The basic formula for back pay is straightforward: multiply the plaintiff's compensation rate by the time period of loss. However, several factors complicate this calculation.

Gross vs. Net Calculation: Back pay is calculated on a gross basis before taxes and other deductions. The defendant cannot reduce the award by arguing that the plaintiff would have paid taxes on the income.

Merit Increases and Promotions: If the plaintiff would have received raises or promotions during the back pay period, these must be factored into the calculation. This often requires testimony from supervisors or HR personnel about the company's promotion practices.

Seasonal and Cyclical Variations: For employees whose compensation varies by season or business cycles, the calculation must account for these patterns. A construction worker, for instance, might earn more in summer months.

Mitigation Requirements

The law requires plaintiffs to make reasonable efforts to minimize their damages by seeking comparable employment. This principle, known as the duty to mitigate, can significantly impact back pay calculations.

Comparable Employment Standard: The plaintiff need only seek work that is substantially similar in terms of compensation, responsibility, and working conditions. A senior executive cannot be required to accept an entry-level position.

Geographic Limitations: Courts generally do not require plaintiffs to relocate to distant areas to find work, though they may need to expand their search radius within reason.

Burden of Proof: While the plaintiff has the duty to mitigate, the defendant bears the burden of proving that the plaintiff failed to make reasonable efforts or rejected suitable employment opportunities.

Documentation Requirements: Plaintiffs should maintain detailed records of their job search activities, including applications submitted, interviews conducted, and positions considered. This documentation becomes crucial if the defendant challenges mitigation efforts.

Legal Distinctions Between Jurisdictions

New York: Prejudgment interest is generally awarded on back pay, calculated from the date of termination. The rate is set by statute and changes periodically. New York courts are relatively generous in awarding back pay and typically do not require plaintiffs to accept substantially inferior positions.

California: Prejudgment interest on back pay is discretionary with the court. California courts tend to be more restrictive in requiring mitigation efforts, particularly for higher-paid executives who may have more employment options.

Federal Courts: Under federal employment statutes, back pay awards vary depending on the specific law. Title VII cases allow back pay for up to two years before the filing of the charge with the EEOC, while FLSA cases may include back pay for up to three years in cases of willful violations.

17.3 Front Pay: Projected Future Losses

Front pay compensates for future wage losses when reinstatement is not feasible or appropriate. Unlike back pay, which involves concrete historical losses, front pay requires projecting future earnings and employment prospects.

When Front Pay is Awarded

Alternative to Reinstatement: Courts typically prefer reinstatement as a remedy because it directly addresses the harm caused by wrongful termination. However, when reinstatement would be ineffective or inappropriate, front pay serves as a substitute.

Hostile Work Environment: If the workplace has become so toxic that the employee cannot reasonably return, front pay may be appropriate. This often occurs in harassment cases where the harasser remains employed or in retaliation cases where management has demonstrated continued hostility.

Position Elimination: When the plaintiff's job has been eliminated or substantially changed, reinstatement may be impossible, making front pay the primary remedy.

Loss of Trust and Confidence: In cases involving breach of fiduciary duty or where the employment relationship has been irreparably damaged, courts may conclude that reinstatement would not benefit either party.

Factors Courts Consider

Age and Work Life Expectancy: Younger plaintiffs typically receive larger front pay awards because they have more years of potential earnings ahead of them. Courts use actuarial tables and economic projections to estimate work life expectancy.

Career Trajectory: The plaintiff's likely career progression affects front pay calculations. A employee on a management track would have different earning potential than someone in a lateral position.

Industry and Economic Conditions: Courts consider the overall health of the plaintiff's industry and the likelihood of finding comparable employment. A declining industry might justify a longer front pay period.

Skills and Marketability: The plaintiff's education, experience, and specialized skills influence how quickly they might find new employment and at what compensation level.

Health and Personal Circumstances: Physical or mental health issues that affect employability can extend the front pay period or reduce earning capacity.

Duration and Calculation Methods

Time Period: Front pay awards typically range from six months to several years, though courts have awarded longer periods in exceptional cases. The period should reflect the time reasonably needed to secure comparable employment.

Present Value Calculations: Because front pay represents future earnings, courts typically reduce the award to present value using appropriate discount rates. This accounts for the fact that receiving money today is worth more than receiving it in the future.

Expert Testimony: Economic experts often testify about appropriate discount rates, inflation factors, and economic projections. Their testimony helps courts make informed decisions about complex financial calculations.

Practical Considerations

Tax Treatment: Front pay awards are generally taxable as ordinary income when received, unlike some other damage categories that may receive more favorable treatment.

Interaction with Other Remedies: Front pay awards must be coordinated with other remedies to avoid double recovery. For instance, if a plaintiff receives severance pay from a new employer, this might offset front pay calculations.

Periodic vs. Lump Sum Payment: While courts typically award front pay as a lump sum, they have discretion to order periodic payments in appropriate cases, particularly for very large awards.

17.4 Lost Benefits and Perks

Employee benefits often represent a substantial portion of total compensation, yet they are frequently undervalued in damages calculations. Properly quantifying lost benefits requires understanding both their economic value and tax implications.

Types of Benefits

Health Insurance: Employer-provided health coverage typically represents one of the most valuable benefits. The loss includes both the employer's premium contributions and the employee's loss of group rate advantages.

Retirement Benefits: This category includes employer matching contributions to 401(k) plans, pension accruals, and profit-sharing contributions. For long-term employees, these losses can be substantial.

Stock Options and Equity Compensation: Particularly valuable in technology and startup companies, stock options require complex valuation methods and consideration of vesting schedules.

Life and Disability Insurance: Group life and disability insurance premiums paid by employers represent both immediate economic loss and loss of insurability at group rates.

Paid Time Off: Vacation, sick leave, and personal days have clear economic value equal to the wages that would have been paid during such time.

Education and Training Benefits: Tuition reimbursement, professional development, and training opportunities represent both immediate value and enhanced future earning capacity.

Vehicle and Expense Accounts: Company cars, expense accounts, and other perquisites must be valued at their fair market value to the employee.

Valuation Methods

Employer Cost Method: The most common approach uses the employer's actual cost for providing the benefit. For health insurance, this would be the premium amount paid by the employer.

Replacement Cost Method: This approach looks at what the employee would pay to replace the benefit independently. For group benefits, this is often higher than the employer's cost.

Fair Market Value Method: For perquisites like company cars or club memberships, courts typically use the fair market value of the benefit to the employee.

Tax Considerations: Some benefits are provided on a pre-tax basis, making their after-tax value to the employee lower than their gross cost. Courts must consider these tax implications in valuation.

Special Valuation Issues

Stock Options: Valuing stock options requires sophisticated financial analysis, considering factors such as the underlying stock price, exercise price, time to expiration, volatility, and vesting schedules. The Black-Scholes model is commonly used, though other methods may be appropriate.

Pension Benefits: Defined benefit pension plans require actuarial analysis to determine the present value of lost future benefits. This involves complex calculations considering the employee's age, service time, and life expectancy.

Health Insurance for Family Members: When employer-provided health insurance covers family members, the loss includes coverage for dependents, which can substantially increase the value.

Documentation Requirements

Employee Handbooks and Benefits Summaries: These documents establish the employer's policies and the benefits to which the employee was entitled.

Payroll Records: Pay stubs and payroll records show employer contributions to various benefit programs.

Insurance Certificates and Policies: These documents establish coverage levels and premium costs for insurance benefits.

Stock Option Agreements: For equity compensation, the specific terms of stock option grants, including vesting schedules and exercise prices, are crucial.

17.5 Mitigation of Damages

The duty to mitigate damages is a fundamental principle in employment law that requires plaintiffs to take reasonable steps to minimize their losses. Understanding this doctrine is crucial for both calculating damages and defending against mitigation arguments.

Legal Foundation and Rationale

Purpose: The mitigation doctrine prevents plaintiffs from recovering damages they could have reasonably avoided. It encourages productive behavior and prevents windfall recoveries.

Reasonableness Standard: The plaintiff need only make reasonable efforts to mitigate; they are not required to take extraordinary measures or accept unsuitable employment.

Burden of Proof: While the plaintiff has the duty to mitigate, the defendant bears the burden of proving that the plaintiff failed to make reasonable efforts or unreasonably rejected suitable employment.

What Constitutes Reasonable Mitigation

Job Search Efforts: Plaintiffs should actively seek employment through multiple channels, including online job boards, networking, employment agencies, and direct applications to employers.

Geographic Scope: Courts typically require plaintiffs to search for employment within a reasonable geographic area, usually their current commuting region. Relocation is generally not required unless the plaintiff previously demonstrated willingness to relocate.

Comparable Employment: The plaintiff need only seek positions that are substantially similar in terms of compensation, responsibilities, and working conditions. A reduction in salary of more than 10-15% typically makes a position non-comparable.

Timing Considerations: Mitigation efforts should begin promptly after termination. Unreasonable delays in starting a job search can reduce damage awards.

Factors Courts Consider

Plaintiff's Age and Experience: Older workers and those with highly specialized skills may face greater challenges in finding comparable employment, justifying longer search periods.

Economic Conditions: General economic conditions and industry-specific downturns can affect the reasonableness of mitigation efforts and the time required to find suitable employment.

Health and Personal Circumstances: Physical or mental health issues, family obligations, or other personal circumstances may limit the plaintiff's ability to mitigate damages.

Seasonal Employment: For workers in seasonal industries, courts consider the availability of work during different times of the year.

Practical Mitigation Strategies

Documentation: Plaintiffs should maintain detailed records of their job search activities, including applications submitted, responses received, interviews conducted, and reasons for rejecting any offers.

Professional Networking: Active networking through professional associations, alumni groups, and industry contacts demonstrates reasonable mitigation efforts.

Skills Enhancement: Taking courses or obtaining certifications to improve marketability shows good faith efforts to mitigate damages.

Career Counseling: Using professional career counseling services demonstrates serious commitment to finding new employment.

Common Mitigation Defenses

Failure to Apply for Available Positions: Defendants often argue that suitable positions were available and that the plaintiff failed to apply. This requires proof that the plaintiff knew or should have known about the opportunities.

Unreasonable Job Search Methods: Defendants may argue that the plaintiff's search methods were inadequate, such as relying solely on online applications without networking or other active measures.

Rejection of Suitable Offers: If the plaintiff received and rejected job offers, defendants will argue that suitable employment was available. The plaintiff must show that the rejected positions were not truly comparable.

Inadequate Search Geographic Area: Defendants may argue that the plaintiff unreasonably limited their geographic search area, particularly for highly paid positions.

Jurisdictional Differences

New York: New York courts tend to be relatively generous in defining "comparable employment" and typically do not require plaintiffs to accept positions with significantly lower compensation or status.

California: California courts may be more demanding in mitigation requirements, particularly for executive-level positions where courts expect more extensive search efforts.

Federal Courts: Federal employment statutes generally follow similar mitigation principles, but specific requirements may vary depending on the underlying statute and circuit court precedent.

17.6 Emotional Distress Damages

Emotional distress damages compensate plaintiffs for the psychological harm caused by employment discrimination, harassment, or other wrongful conduct. Unlike economic damages, emotional distress is inherently subjective and requires careful presentation to establish both the existence and value of the harm.

Legal Standards and Requirements

No Physical Injury Requirement: Most employment statutes allow recovery for emotional distress without requiring physical injury or impact. This represents a significant departure from traditional tort law principles.

Reasonable Basis: The emotional distress must have a reasonable basis in the defendant's conduct. Courts will not award damages for distress that is trivial or unreasonable under the circumstances.

Causation: Plaintiffs must establish that their emotional distress was caused by the defendant's wrongful conduct, not by other life circumstances or pre-existing conditions.

Objective and Subjective Components: Courts consider both the objective severity of the defendant's conduct and the subjective impact on the particular plaintiff.

Types of Evidence

Plaintiff Testimony: The plaintiff's own testimony about their emotional state, symptoms, and impact on daily life forms the foundation of most emotional distress claims. This testimony should be detailed and specific, describing particular incidents and their effects.

Medical and Psychological Treatment: Records from physicians, therapists, and counselors provide objective evidence of emotional distress. Prescriptions for antidepressants or anti-anxiety medications can support claims of severe distress.

Lay Witness Testimony: Friends, family members, and coworkers can testify about changes they observed in the plaintiff's behavior, mood, or personality following the defendant's conduct.

Expert Testimony: Mental health professionals can provide diagnosis, prognosis, and opinions about the relationship between the defendant's conduct and the plaintiff's emotional symptoms.

Documentation of Impact: Evidence showing how emotional distress affected the plaintiff's daily life, such as missed work, canceled social activities, or inability to perform routine tasks.

Categories and Value Ranges

Mild Distress ($10,000-$50,000): Short-term anxiety, embarrassment, or upset that resolves relatively quickly without professional treatment. This might include the distress from a single discriminatory comment or brief period of harassment.

Moderate Distress ($50,000-$200,000): More prolonged emotional impact requiring some professional treatment, such as counseling or medication. This category includes cases where the plaintiff experiences ongoing anxiety, depression, or sleep disturbances but continues to function in daily life.

Severe Distress ($200,000+): Major psychological impact requiring extensive treatment, hospitalization, or resulting in diagnosed mental health conditions like PTSD. This includes cases where the plaintiff cannot work, requires long-term therapy, or attempts self-harm.

Factors Affecting Valuation

Duration and Intensity: Longer-lasting and more severe emotional distress typically results in higher awards. Courts consider both the acute impact immediately following the wrongful conduct and any ongoing psychological effects.

Treatment and Recovery: The extent of professional treatment sought and the plaintiff's recovery progress affect damages. Ongoing therapy or medication suggests continued impact.

Impact on Daily Life: Courts consider how emotional distress affected the plaintiff's ability to work, maintain relationships, participate in activities, and enjoy life.

Pre-existing Conditions: Defendants often argue that the plaintiff's emotional distress stems from pre-existing mental health issues rather than the workplace conduct. Plaintiffs must be prepared to address these arguments.

Credibility Factors: The plaintiff's credibility significantly impacts emotional distress awards. Inconsistencies in testimony or exaggerated claims can reduce or eliminate these damages.

Presentation Strategies

Chronological Narrative: Presenting emotional distress evidence in chronological order helps juries understand the progression from the wrongful conduct to the psychological impact.

Specific Examples: Rather than general testimony about feeling "upset," plaintiffs should provide specific examples of how their emotional state affected their daily activities.

Corroborating Evidence: Medical records, prescriptions, and witness testimony help corroborate the plaintiff's subjective testimony about their emotional state.

Visual Evidence: Photographs showing physical manifestations of emotional distress, such as weight loss or changes in appearance, can be powerful evidence.

Common Challenges

Malingering and Exaggeration: Defendants often challenge emotional distress claims as exaggerated or fabricated. Consistent medical records and witness testimony help address these challenges.

Alternative Causation: Defendants may argue that life events other than the workplace conduct caused the plaintiff's emotional distress. Plaintiffs should be prepared to address other stressors while maintaining that the workplace conduct was a substantial contributing factor.

Lack of Treatment: Defendants may argue that the plaintiff's failure to seek professional treatment undermines their claim of severe emotional distress. Plaintiffs should be prepared to explain any barriers to treatment, such as cost or stigma.

17.7 Punitive Damages

Punitive damages serve a dual purpose in employment law: punishing defendants for particularly egregious conduct and deterring similar behavior in the future. Unlike compensatory damages, punitive damages are not tied to the plaintiff's actual losses but rather to the defendant's culpability and ability to pay.

Standards for Award

Conduct Requirements: Punitive damages require more than ordinary negligence or even discrimination. The defendant's conduct must be malicious, reckless, or show conscious disregard for the plaintiff's rights.

Intentional Misconduct: The most common basis for punitive damages is intentional discrimination or harassment where the defendant knew their conduct was wrong but proceeded anyway.

Reckless Indifference: Conduct showing reckless indifference to federally protected rights can justify punitive damages, such as failing to investigate obvious harassment or maintaining discriminatory policies.

Corporate Liability: For corporate defendants, punitive damages typically require proof that managerial agents participated in or condoned the wrongful conduct

Federal Statutory Caps

The Civil Rights Act of 1991 imposed caps on punitive damages under federal employment statutes, based on the employer's size:

15-100 employees: $50,000 maximum combined compensatory and punitive damages **101-200 employees**: $100,000 maximum **201-500 employees**: $200,000 maximum
500+ employees: $300,000 maximum

These caps apply to individual plaintiffs and are separate for each statutory claim. The caps do not apply to intentional age discrimination under the ADEA or to claims under Section 1981.

State Law Variations

California: The Fair Employment and Housing Act (FEHA) does not impose statutory caps on punitive damages, though constitutional due process limits still apply. California courts generally follow federal constitutional guidelines limiting punitive awards to single-digit ratios compared to compensatory damages.

New York: The New York City Human Rights Law and New York State Human Rights Law do not cap punitive damages. New York courts have awarded substantial punitive damages in egregious cases, particularly those involving systematic discrimination or harassment.

Constitutional Limits: The U.S. Supreme Court has established constitutional limits on punitive damages, generally requiring that they not exceed a single-digit ratio to compensatory damages, with 9:1 being the approximate upper limit.

Factors Courts Consider

Degree of Reprehensibility: The most important factor is how reprehensible the defendant's conduct was. Courts consider whether the conduct caused physical harm, involved deception, targeted vulnerable victims, or was repeated over time.

Ratio to Compensatory Damages: Courts examine the relationship between punitive and compensatory damages. Higher ratios may be justified when compensatory damages are small but the conduct is particularly egregious.

Comparable Civil Penalties: Courts may consider what civil penalties the state might impose for similar conduct, using this as a benchmark for appropriate punishment.

Defendant's Financial Condition: The defendant's ability to pay affects the amount necessary to achieve deterrence. A larger corporation may require a larger award to feel the punishment's impact.

Recurrence of Misconduct: Evidence that the defendant has engaged in similar conduct before or since the plaintiff's case can justify higher punitive awards.

Strategic Considerations

Discovery of Financial Information: To support punitive damages claims, plaintiffs typically need discovery of the defendant's financial condition, which can be challenging to obtain and expensive to analyze.

Corporate Structure: Understanding the defendant's corporate structure is crucial for determining whether punitive damages can be imposed and what entity should be liable.

Insurance Coverage: Many employment practices liability insurance policies exclude or limit coverage for punitive damages, which can affect settlement negotiations.

Trial Strategy: Punitive damages claims often require bifurcated trials, with liability and compensatory damages determined first, followed by a separate proceeding on punitive damages.

Practical Impact

Settlement Leverage: The threat of punitive damages can provide significant settlement leverage, particularly when the defendant faces the possibility of substantial awards that may not be covered by insurance.

Institutional Change: Large punitive awards can force institutional changes in defendant organizations, achieving the deterrent effect that the law intends.

Public Policy: Punitive damages serve important public policy goals by making discrimination and harassment financially costly for employers, encouraging prevention efforts.

17.8 Statutory and Penalty Damages

Many employment statutes provide for specific penalties and liquidated damages beyond actual economic losses. These provisions serve to strengthen enforcement, provide additional deterrence, and ensure meaningful remedies even in cases where actual damages are small.

California Statutory Penalties

Waiting Time Penalties (Labor Code § 203): When employers fail to pay final wages promptly upon termination, they owe the employee's daily wage for each day of delay, up to 30 days. For a $200/day worker, this could result in $6,000 in penalties.

Wage Statement Penalties (Labor Code § 226): Employers must provide accurate wage statements with each paycheck. Violations result in penalties of $50 for the first violation and $100 for each subsequent violation, plus attorney's fees.

Meal and Rest Break Penalties: When employers fail to provide required meal or rest breaks, they owe one hour of pay at the employee's regular rate for each violation. For employees who regularly miss breaks, these penalties can accumulate significantly.

PAGA Penalties: The Private Attorneys General Act allows employees to recover civil penalties on behalf of the state. Penalties range from $100 per employee per pay period for initial violations to $200 for subsequent violations.

Frequency of Pay Violations: California requires most employees to be paid at least twice monthly. Violations can result in penalties and create grounds for waiting time penalties upon termination.

New York Statutory Penalties

Spread of Hours Pay: Employees working more than 10 hours in a day must receive one additional hour of pay at minimum wage, regardless of breaks taken during the shift.

Frequency of Pay Requirements: Manual workers must be paid weekly, while other employees must be paid at least twice monthly. Violations can result in penalties and potential waiting time liability.

Liquidated Damages: Under the New York Labor Law, employees can recover liquidated damages equal to 100% of their unpaid wages, effectively doubling their recovery.

Wage Theft Prevention Act: New York requires employers to provide written notice of pay rates, pay dates, and other wage information. Violations can result in significant penalties, particularly in cases involving multiple employees.

Federal Statutory Provisions

Fair Labor Standards Act (FLSA): Provides for liquidated damages equal to the amount of unpaid wages unless the employer proves good faith and reasonable belief that their conduct was lawful.

Family and Medical Leave Act (FMLA): Allows for liquidated damages equal to lost wages and benefits, plus reinstatement and promotion where appropriate.

Worker Adjustment and Retraining Notification Act (WARN): Requires 60 days' pay and benefits for each affected employee when employers fail to provide required notice of plant closings or mass layoffs.

Class and Representative Actions

Multiplication Effect: Statutory penalties can multiply rapidly in class action or representative action contexts, where violations affecting multiple employees result in per-employee penalties.

PAGA as Representative Action: California's PAGA allows individual employees to pursue penalties on behalf of all aggrieved employees, creating potential liability far exceeding individual damages.

Certification Requirements: Class actions involving wage and hour violations often meet certification requirements because they involve common policies affecting multiple employees similarly.

Strategic Considerations

Compliance Audits: The potential for significant statutory penalties makes compliance audits crucial for employers, particularly those with large workforces or complex pay practices.

Settlement Calculations: Statutory penalties must be factored into settlement calculations, often making resolution more expensive than the underlying wage violations.

Statute of Limitations: Different statutes may have different limitation periods, with some California penalties extending back three or four years.

Documentation and Proof

Payroll Records: Accurate payroll records are crucial for both establishing violations and calculating penalties. Missing or inaccurate records often favor the employee's interpretation.

Policy Documentation: Employee handbooks and policy documents can establish the employer's knowledge of legal requirements and the intentional nature of violations.

Time Records: In cases involving meal breaks, rest periods, or overtime, time records become crucial evidence for establishing the scope and duration of violations.

17.9 Use of Expert Witnesses in Damage Presentation

Expert witnesses play a crucial role in employment damage cases, providing specialized knowledge that helps courts and juries understand complex financial and vocational issues. The strategic use of experts can significantly enhance the persuasiveness and credibility of damage claims.

Types of Experts

Economists: Economic experts specialize in calculating wage losses, projecting future earnings, and determining present value of damage awards. They bring sophisticated analytical tools and credibility to complex financial calculations.

Vocational Rehabilitation Experts: These experts assess employability, analyze job markets, and evaluate the impact of discrimination or wrongful termination on career prospects. They are particularly valuable in cases involving front pay or disability discrimination.

Psychologists and Psychiatrists: Mental health experts provide crucial testimony in emotional distress cases, offering professional opinions about diagnosis, causation, and prognosis. They help translate subjective complaints into objective medical evidence.

Industry Experts: Specialists in particular industries can provide context about compensation practices, career advancement patterns, and market conditions that affect damage calculations.

Forensic Accountants: In cases involving complex compensation structures or business valuations, forensic accountants can analyze financial records and calculate damages involving stock options, profit sharing, or business ownership interests.

Economic Expert Testimony

Wage Loss Calculations: Economic experts use sophisticated modeling to project what the plaintiff would have earned but for the defendant's conduct. This involves analyzing historical wage patterns, industry trends, and economic factors affecting compensation.

Present Value Analysis: For front pay awards, experts calculate the present value of future earnings using appropriate discount rates and inflation factors. This ensures that damage awards accurately reflect the time value of money.

Benefits Valuation: Experts can value complex benefit packages, including retirement contributions, health insurance, and stock options. This often requires specialized knowledge of employee benefit law and financial markets.

Statistical Analysis: In class action cases, experts may use statistical sampling and regression analysis to project damages across large groups of employees.

Vocational Expert Testimony

Labor Market Analysis: Vocational experts analyze local job markets to assess the availability of comparable employment and the time reasonably required to secure new positions.

Transferable Skills Assessment: These experts evaluate the plaintiff's skills and experience to determine what types of positions they could reasonably obtain and at what compensation levels.

Disability Impact: In disability discrimination cases, vocational experts assess how the plaintiff's condition affects their employability and earning capacity.

Mitigation Analysis: Vocational experts can testify about whether the plaintiff's job search efforts were reasonable and whether suitable employment opportunities were available.

Mental Health Expert Testimony

Diagnosis and Causation: Mental health experts provide professional diagnoses and opinions about whether the plaintiff's psychological symptoms were caused by the defendant's conduct.

Treatment and Prognosis: Experts can testify about appropriate treatment modalities and the likely duration and cost of ongoing mental health care.

Functional Impact: Mental health experts can explain how psychological symptoms affect the plaintiff's ability to work and enjoy life, helping to quantify intangible damages.

Differential Diagnosis: In cases where defendants argue alternative causation, mental health experts can analyze various potential causes and provide opinions about the relative contributions of different factors.

Presentation Best Practices

Visual Aids: Experts should use clear, professional visual aids such as graphs, charts, and summary tables to illustrate their analyses. Complex calculations should be broken down into understandable components.

Plain Language: Experts must translate technical concepts into language that judges and juries can understand. Avoiding jargon and using analogies can make testimony more accessible.

Foundation and Methodology: Experts must clearly explain their methodology and the basis for their opinions. This includes discussing data sources, assumptions, and alternative approaches considered.

Cross-Examination Preparation: Experts must be prepared to defend their methodologies and assumptions under rigorous cross-examination. This requires thorough preparation and familiarity with contrary analyses.

Reliability and Admissibility

Daubert Standards: Under federal rules and many state courts, expert testimony must meet reliability standards established in *Daubert v. Merrell Dow Pharmaceuticals*, 509 U.S. 579 (1993). This requires that expert opinions be based on reliable methods and sufficient data.

Qualifications: Experts must be qualified by education, training, or experience to offer opinions in their area of testimony. Courts examine both formal credentials and practical experience.

Basis for Opinions: Expert opinions must be based on sufficient facts or data and be the product of reliable principles and methods. Speculation or unsupported assumptions can result in exclusion of testimony.

Cost-Benefit Considerations

Expert Costs: Expert witnesses can be expensive, particularly for complex economic analyses or extensive vocational assessments. The potential damage award must justify the expert costs.

Case Strategy: The decision to use experts should align with overall case strategy. In smaller cases, the cost of experts may exceed their benefit, while in larger cases, expert testimony may be essential for maximum recovery.

Opposing Experts: Plaintiffs should anticipate that defendants will retain their own experts and prepare to address contrary opinions and methodologies.

17.10 Practical Considerations and Trial Strategy

Successfully presenting employment damages requires more than accurate calculations; it demands strategic thinking about how to make complex financial concepts accessible and compelling to judges and juries. The art of damages presentation lies in combining legal precision with narrative coherence.

Organizing Damage Claims

Chronological Framework: Present damages in chronological order, starting with the wrongful conduct and following through to present and future losses. This helps decision-makers understand the causal chain from misconduct to financial harm.

Category-Based Organization: Within the chronological framework, organize damages by category (economic, non-economic, punitive) to ensure comprehensive coverage and avoid double-counting.

Summary and Detail Balance: Provide clear summary figures while maintaining supporting detail. Judges and juries need both the big picture and the ability to verify calculations.

Visual Presentation: Use professional-quality visual aids to illustrate damage calculations, timelines, and comparisons. Complex financial information becomes more accessible when presented graphically.

Establishing Credibility

Documentation Standards: Meticulous documentation enhances credibility. Every damage component should be supported by appropriate records, testimony, or expert analysis.

Conservative vs. Aggressive Estimates: Strike the right balance between maximizing recovery and maintaining credibility. Overly aggressive damage claims can undermine the entire case.

Acknowledgment of Uncertainties: Where calculations involve estimates or projections, acknowledge uncertainties while explaining why your approach is reasonable and conservative.

Consistency Across Claims: Ensure that damage calculations are consistent across different theories of liability and don't create internal contradictions.

Addressing Common Defense Arguments

Mitigation Challenges: Be prepared to address arguments that the plaintiff failed to mitigate damages. Maintain detailed records of job search activities and be ready to explain any gaps or apparent inconsistencies.

Alternative Causation: Defendants often argue that the plaintiff's damages stem from other causes. Develop evidence showing that workplace conduct was a substantial contributing factor, even if other factors were also present.

Pre-existing Conditions: In emotional distress cases, defendants may argue that psychological symptoms preceded the workplace conduct. Medical records and witness testimony can help establish the timeline and causation.

Speculation Arguments: Defendants frequently argue that damage calculations involve too much speculation, particularly for future losses. Expert testimony and conservative methodologies help address these concerns.

Settlement vs. Trial Considerations

Settlement Leverage: Well-documented damage claims provide significant settlement leverage. Defendants often prefer to settle rather than risk larger jury awards, particularly when punitive damages are viable.

Trial Risk Assessment: Consider the risks of trial, including the possibility of defense verdicts or lower-than-expected awards. Factor in litigation costs, time delays, and the emotional toll on plaintiffs.

Structure of Settlement: Consider whether lump-sum or structured settlements better serve the plaintiff's interests. Tax implications and the plaintiff's financial needs should influence this decision.

Release Scope: Ensure that settlement agreements appropriately scope the release of claims while preserving the plaintiff's rights to pursue other potential violations or future conduct.

Jurisdictional Strategy

Forum Selection: Choice of forum can significantly impact damage awards. Federal courts may be limited by statutory caps, while state courts might allow unlimited punitive damages.

Statutory vs. Common Law Claims: Different legal theories may provide access to different damage categories. Strategic pleading can maximize available remedies.

Class vs. Individual Actions: Consider whether individual or class action procedures better serve the client's interests, particularly for statutory penalty claims that can multiply in representative actions.

Technology and Damage Calculations

Spreadsheet Modeling: Sophisticated spreadsheet models can handle complex damage calculations and allow for sensitivity analysis of key assumptions.

Database Management: For cases involving multiple plaintiffs or extensive time periods, database systems can organize and analyze large amounts of financial data.

Document Management: Electronic document management systems are essential for organizing the voluminous records typically involved in employment damage cases.

Trial Presentation Software: Modern trial presentation software can make complex financial information more accessible to judges and juries through interactive displays and real-time calculations.

17.11 Tax Considerations

Tax implications significantly affect both the calculation and ultimate value of employment damage awards. Understanding these implications is crucial for accurate damage calculations and informed settlement negotiations.

Taxability of Different Damage Types

Back Pay and Front Pay: Generally taxable as ordinary income in the year received. Employers must treat these payments as wages subject to employment tax withholding, though this can create complications for former employees.

Emotional Distress Damages: The taxability of emotional distress awards depends on whether they relate to physical injury or sickness. Pure emotional distress damages are generally taxable, while those relating to physical symptoms may be excludable.

Punitive Damages: Almost always taxable as ordinary income, regardless of the underlying claim. This can significantly reduce the net value of punitive awards to plaintiffs.

Liquidated and Statutory Damages: Generally follow the tax treatment of the underlying claim. Wage-related penalties are typically taxable, while civil rights penalties may receive different treatment.

Timing Issues

Year of Receipt: Damage awards are generally taxable in the year received, which can push plaintiffs into higher tax brackets and result in significant tax liabilities.

Installment Payments: Structured settlements can spread tax liability over multiple years, potentially reducing the overall tax burden by avoiding bracket compression.

Interest Components: Prejudgment interest on damage awards is typically taxable as ordinary income separate from the underlying damages.

Employment Tax Issues

FICA and FUTA: Back pay awards are generally subject to Social Security and unemployment taxes, though the specific year for which the taxes are owed can be complex to determine.

Withholding Requirements: Employers paying damage awards must typically withhold income and employment taxes, though former employees may need to make estimated tax payments.

Correction of Earnings Records: Back pay awards may require corrections to Social Security earnings records to properly credit the plaintiff's account for the periods involved.

Strategic Tax Planning

Settlement Structure: Consider structuring settlements to minimize tax impact, such as allocating portions of settlements to non-taxable categories where legally supportable.

Timing of Payments: The timing of damage payments can affect tax liability. Spreading payments across tax years may reduce overall taxes owed.

Professional Tax Advice: Plaintiffs should receive professional tax advice about the implications of damage awards, particularly for large settlements that could trigger alternative minimum tax or other complications.

17.12 Special Situations and Emerging Issues

Employment law continues to evolve, creating new categories of damages and novel calculation challenges. Understanding these emerging areas is crucial for comprehensive damage analysis.

Remote Work and Gig Economy

Home Office Expenses: For remote workers, damages may include reimbursement for home office expenses, internet costs, and equipment that would have been employer-provided.

Gig Worker Classification: As courts increasingly find that gig workers are employees rather than independent contractors, damage calculations must account for benefits and protections that were wrongfully denied.

Technology Costs: Modern workers often rely on personal devices and software for work. Wrongful termination damages may include compensation for work-related technology expenses.

Cryptocurrency and Digital Assets

Stock Options in Cryptocurrency: As more companies offer cryptocurrency-based compensation, valuation becomes complex due to extreme volatility and regulatory uncertainty.

Digital Asset Benefits: Some employers provide benefits in digital assets or tokens, requiring specialized valuation expertise and consideration of tax implications.

Social Media and Reputation

Digital Reputation Harm: Employment disputes increasingly involve damage to online reputation through social media or professional networking sites. Quantifying this harm requires new approaches and expert testimony.

Influencer and Content Creator Issues: For employees who maintain professional social media presence, wrongful termination may damage their personal brand and income streams beyond traditional employment.

Emerging Statutory Frameworks

Pay Equity Laws: New state and local pay equity laws create potential for substantial damages in cases involving systematic pay disparities based on protected characteristics.

Predictive Scheduling: Laws requiring advance notice of work schedules create new categories of penalties and damages for violations.

Biometric Privacy: State laws regulating collection and use of biometric data in employment create new statutory penalty structures.

17.13 International and Multi-Jurisdictional Issues

As employment relationships increasingly cross state and national boundaries, damage calculations must account for complex jurisdictional issues and varying legal standards.

Multi-State Employment

Choice of Law: When employees work in multiple states, determining which state's damage laws apply can significantly affect potential recovery.

Benefits Coordination: Multi-state employees may have complex benefit arrangements that require careful analysis to determine losses.

Tax Complications: Multi-state employment creates complex tax issues for damage calculations, particularly regarding state income tax obligations.

International Employment

Currency Conversion: For employees working internationally, damage calculations may require currency conversion and consideration of exchange rate fluctuations.

Cost of Living Adjustments: International assignments often include cost of living adjustments that must be factored into damage calculations.

Repatriation Costs: Wrongful termination of international employees may include costs of returning to their home country.

Comparative Damage Standards

International Benchmarking: In cases involving multinational employers, damage calculations may benefit from comparison with awards in other jurisdictions.

Treaty Obligations: International treaties and trade agreements may affect available remedies and damage calculations for certain categories of workers.

17.14 Conclusion

Employment damages serve multiple purposes beyond mere compensation: they vindicate rights, deter misconduct, and restore dignity to those who have suffered workplace wrongs. The successful practitioner must master both the technical aspects of damage calculation and the art of persuasive presentation.

Key principles for effective damage advocacy include thorough documentation, conservative but comprehensive calculations, strategic use of expert testimony, and clear presentation that makes complex financial concepts accessible to decision-makers. Understanding jurisdictional differences, tax implications, and emerging legal trends ensures that damage claims remain current and maximally effective.

The landscape of employment damages continues to evolve with changing work patterns, new technologies, and emerging statutory frameworks. Practitioners must stay current with these developments while maintaining focus on the fundamental goal: securing meaningful remedies that address the full scope of harm caused by employment law violations.

Whether calculating back pay for a wrongful termination, valuing emotional distress in a harassment case, or seeking punitive damages for egregious discrimination, the principles outlined in this chapter provide a framework for comprehensive damage analysis. The intersection of legal accuracy, factual precision, and persuasive advocacy determines the ultimate success of employment damage claims.

In Chapter 18, we will examine how to recover attorney's fees and costs, including statutory fee-shifting provisions and best practices for fee petitions, completing the picture of comprehensive relief in employment cases.

18

Attorney's Fees and Costs in Employment Litigation

In employment litigation, the ability to recover attorney's fees and costs is not just a footnote - it's often central to both litigation strategy and settlement negotiations. Fee-shifting provisions in federal and state laws allow prevailing plaintiffs to seek reimbursement for legal work and case expenses, thereby leveling the playing field against well-resourced employers.

This chapter covers how to assess, document, and recover attorney's fees and costs in New York, California, and federal employment cases, including key statutes, lodestar methodology, and practical considerations for fee petitions.

18.1 Understanding Fee-Shifting in Employment Law

The American Rule vs. Fee-Shifting Statutes

Under the traditional "American Rule," each party pays their own attorney's fees regardless of who wins the case. This rule differs from many other countries where the losing party automatically pays the winner's legal costs. However, Congress and state legislatures have carved out significant exceptions for employment law cases, recognizing that individual employees often lack the financial resources to challenge powerful employers.

Fee-shifting statutes serve multiple policy purposes. They encourage private enforcement of important civil rights and labor laws by making it financially feasible for employees to bring legitimate claims. They also deter employer misconduct by ensuring that successful plaintiffs can recover the full costs of vindication. Without these provisions, many meritorious employment claims would never see the inside of a courtroom.

Federal Fee-Shifting Statutes

Most major federal employment statutes include fee-shifting provisions, but each has distinct requirements and limitations:

Title VII of the Civil Rights Act (42 U.S.C. § 2000e-5(k)) This landmark civil rights statute allows courts to award "reasonable attorney's fees" to the prevailing party. The Supreme Court has interpreted this provision to heavily favor plaintiffs over defendants. Prevailing plaintiffs are entitled to fees as a matter of course, while prevailing defendants can only recover fees when the plaintiff's case was "frivolous, unreasonable, or without foundation" - a standard that protects legitimate claims from being chilled by the threat of having to pay the employer's legal bills.

Americans with Disabilities Act (42 U.S.C. § 12205) The ADA's fee provision mirrors Title VII's language and receives similar judicial interpretation. Courts recognize that disability discrimination cases often involve complex medical issues and reasonable accommodation analyses that require substantial legal work, making fee recovery essential for enforcement.

Family and Medical Leave Act (29 U.S.C. § 2617(a)(3)) FMLA allows recovery of "reasonable attorney's fees, reasonable expert witness fees, and other costs of the action" for prevailing plaintiffs. This broader language explicitly covers expert witness fees, which can be substantial in cases involving medical testimony about serious health conditions or the reasonableness of requested leave.

Fair Labor Standards Act (29 U.S.C. § 216(b)) The FLSA's fee provision is particularly employee-friendly, allowing "reasonable attorney's fees and costs of the action" for any employee who recovers unpaid wages. Unlike some other statutes, the FLSA does not require the employee to be the "prevailing party" - any recovery, even a nominal amount, can trigger fee entitlement.

Section 1981 and Section 1983 Civil Rights Claims These Reconstruction-era civil rights statutes rely on 42 U.S.C. § 1988 for fee-shifting authority. Section 1988 uses the same "prevailing party" standard as Title VII but applies to a broader range of civil rights violations, including race discrimination in private employment contracts (Section 1981) and constitutional violations by government employers (Section 1983).

California Fee-Shifting Provisions

California has developed some of the most employee-friendly fee-shifting rules in the nation:

Fair Employment and Housing Act (Gov. Code § 12965(b)) California's primary anti-discrimination statute allows prevailing plaintiffs to recover attorney's fees and costs, with courts explicitly authorized to apply multipliers to increase fee awards based on factors like exceptional results or the contingent nature of the representation. This provision has been interpreted more generously than its federal counterparts, with California courts more willing to award substantial fees even in cases with modest damages.

Labor Code Violations (e.g., §§ 218.5, 1194) Labor Code § 218.5 underwent significant amendments to favor employees in wage and hour disputes. The statute now creates a presumption that employees should recover fees when they prevail on claims for unpaid wages, overtime, or other compensation. This represents a shift from earlier versions that gave courts more discretion to deny fees.

Labor Code § 1194, which governs overtime violations, includes a specific fee provision for minimum wage and overtime claims. The statute's language is mandatory rather than discretionary, stating that courts "shall" award fees to successful plaintiffs.

Private Attorneys General Act (Lab. Code § 2699(g)) PAGA represents a unique enforcement mechanism that allows employees to bring representative actions on behalf of the state to recover civil penalties for

Labor Code violations. The fee provision in PAGA cases covers not only the representative plaintiff's attorney's fees but also the costs of investigating and prosecuting violations across the employer's entire workforce.

New York Fee-Shifting Laws

New York operates under a three-tiered system of employment discrimination laws, each with its own fee provision:

New York Human Rights Law (Exec. Law § 297(10)) The state's primary anti-discrimination statute allows fee awards to prevailing parties, with the same asymmetrical standard favoring plaintiffs that applies under federal law. New York courts have generally followed federal precedent in interpreting what constitutes a "prevailing party" and "reasonable fees."

New York Labor Law (Labor Law §§ 198, 663, 191) Various sections of the New York Labor Law include fee-shifting provisions for wage and hour violations. Section 198 covers prevailing employees in wage payment disputes, Section 663 applies to overtime violations, and Section 191 governs wage payment timing requirements. These provisions are generally interpreted to favor employee recovery.

New York City Human Rights Law (Admin. Code § 8-502(f)) The New York City ordinance provides broader protection than state or federal law and includes a corresponding fee provision. NYC courts have interpreted this provision liberally, consistent with the statute's remedial purpose and broader coverage of discrimination claims.

18.2 The Lodestar Method: Calculating Reasonable Fees

Understanding the Lodestar Formula

The lodestar method represents the dominant approach courts use to calculate attorney's fees across all jurisdictions. The basic formula appears deceptively simple:

Lodestar = Reasonable Hours × Reasonable Hourly Rate

However, each component involves complex factual and legal determinations that can significantly impact the final award.

Determining Reasonable Hours

The "reasonable hours" component requires meticulous documentation and justification. Courts scrutinize time records for several potential problems:

Contemporaneous Documentation Requirement Time records must be created at or near the time the work was performed. Reconstructed time records created after the fact receive heavy scrutiny and may be rejected entirely. The best practice is to maintain detailed daily time records that specify the date, time spent, attorney or staff member performing the work, and a specific description of the task performed.

Avoiding Duplicative Work When multiple attorneys work on a case, courts examine whether their efforts were efficiently coordinated or unnecessarily duplicative. For example, having three attorneys attend the same deposition may be excessive unless the case involves unusual complexity or the deposition covers multiple distinct legal issues requiring different expertise.

Task Appropriateness Courts reduce fees for work performed by over-qualified attorneys or for clerical tasks billed at attorney rates. Administrative tasks like filing documents, scheduling, or basic legal research should be performed by paralegals or junior associates rather than senior partners. However, truly complex legal research, strategic planning, and client counseling justify senior attorney involvement.

Relationship to Success Federal courts often reduce fees for time spent on unsuccessful claims, while some state courts take a more holistic approach. For example, if a plaintiff wins on 2 of 4 claims, a federal court might reduce the total fee award by 25-50%, reasoning that some work was unproductive. California courts, by contrast, may award full fees if the unsuccessful claims were related to the successful ones or helped establish the factual foundation for victory.

Establishing Reasonable Hourly Rates

The "reasonable hourly rate" determination involves analyzing market conditions and attorney qualifications:

Market Rate Analysis Courts look to prevailing rates charged by attorneys of similar experience and skill in the relevant geographic market for comparable legal services. This analysis considers:

- **Geographic Location**: Rates in major metropolitan areas like Manhattan, San Francisco, or downtown Los Angeles substantially exceed rates in smaller cities or rural areas. However, courts also consider where the case was litigated and whether local counsel could have handled the matter competently.
- **Practice Area Specialization**: Employment law specialists may command higher rates than general practitioners, particularly for complex discrimination or wage and hour class actions. However, the premium for specialization must be reasonable and supported by evidence of the attorney's expertise and reputation.
- **Case Complexity**: Routine wage and hour cases may not justify the same rates as complex discrimination cases involving expert testimony, statistical analysis, or novel legal theories.

Attorney Qualifications and Experience Courts examine the attorney's background, including:

- Years of practice in employment law
- Reputation in the legal community
- Case results and published decisions
- Bar admissions and specialized certifications
- Recognition by peer organizations

Supporting Evidence for Rate Determinations Successful fee petitions typically include:

- Declaration testimony from the requesting attorney detailing qualifications and experience
- Evidence of rates charged to paying clients for similar work
- Testimony from other attorneys about prevailing market rates
- Published rate surveys from bar organizations or legal consulting firms
- Court decisions awarding similar rates to comparable attorneys

Enhancements and Multipliers

In exceptional cases, courts may apply multipliers to increase the lodestar amount:

California's Approach to Multipliers California courts, particularly under FEHA, have embraced multipliers more readily than federal courts. Factors supporting multipliers include:

- **Exceptional Results**: Achieving outcomes that significantly exceed normal expectations, such as obtaining substantial punitive damages or precedent-setting relief
- **Contingency Risk**: Recognizing that employment attorneys often work on contingency, bearing substantial risk of non-payment if the case is unsuccessful
- **Public Interest Impact**: Cases that establish important precedents or vindicate significant public policies may warrant enhanced fees

Federal Court Restrictions The Supreme Court's decision in *Perdue v. Kenny* A., 559 U.S. 542 (2010) significantly limited federal courts' ability to apply multipliers, holding that the lodestar calculation already accounts for most relevant factors. Post-Perdue, federal multipliers are rare and require exceptional circumstances not already reflected in the lodestar calculation.

18.3 Preparing an Effective Fee Petition

Strategic Timing Considerations

The timing of fee petitions can significantly impact success rates and recovery amounts:

Post-Judgment vs. Settlement Context Fee petitions filed after favorable judgments typically receive more favorable treatment than those seeking fees as part of settlement negotiations. Post-judgment petitions benefit from clear determinations of prevailing party status and the scope of success, while settlement-related fee claims may face arguments about the strength of the underlying claims.

Procedural Deadlines Federal courts typically require fee motions within 14 days of final judgment under Federal Rule of Civil Procedure 54(d)(2). State courts have varying deadlines, and some allow fee petitions to be filed simultaneously with the underlying motion for summary judgment or other dispositive relief. Missing these deadlines can result in complete forfeiture of fee recovery rights.

Essential Components of Fee Petitions

Attorney Declaration and Qualifications The requesting attorney's declaration serves as the foundation for the entire fee petition. This document should comprehensively address:

- **Professional Background**: Detailed information about legal education, bar admissions, years of practice, and specialized training in employment law
- **Case-Specific Experience**: Explanation of the attorney's role in the case, major strategic decisions, and unique challenges encountered
- **Rate Justification**: Comparison of requested rates to those charged to paying clients and prevailing market rates for similar services

Detailed Billing Records Time records represent the most scrutinized component of fee petitions. Effective billing records should:

- **Avoid Block Billing**: Rather than entry like "Research case law, draft motion, conference with client - 8.5 hours," break down each task separately with specific time allocations
- **Provide Task-Specific Detail**: Entries should describe not just what was done but why it was necessary for the case. For example, "Research recent developments in disability accommodation law to respond to defendant's motion for summary judgment on failure to accommodate claim - 3.2 hours"
- **Demonstrate Efficiency**: Show logical progression of work and avoid duplicative efforts between different attorneys

Cost Documentation and Recovery Recoverable costs typically include:

- **Filing Fees and Court Costs**: All fees paid to courts, including initial filing fees, motion fees, and appeal costs
- **Discovery Expenses**: Deposition transcripts, court reporter fees, and document production costs
- **Expert Witness Fees**: Where permitted by statute, fees paid to expert witnesses for testimony and report preparation

- **Travel and Accommodation**: Reasonable expenses for necessary travel, though courts scrutinize luxury accommodations or excessive per diem rates
- **Technology and Research Costs**: Expenses for legal research platforms, case management software, and document review technology

Supporting Market Evidence Strong fee petitions include external validation of requested rates through:

- **Rate Surveys**: Published surveys from bar associations or legal consulting firms showing prevailing rates in the relevant market
- **Comparable Case Awards**: Court decisions granting similar rates to attorneys with comparable experience and qualifications
- **Expert Testimony**: Declarations from other employment law practitioners regarding market rates and the reasonableness of the requested fees

18.4 Understanding Court Scrutiny and Common Reductions

Typical Grounds for Fee Reductions

Courts approach fee petitions with healthy skepticism, recognizing the potential for inflated or excessive requests:

Excessive Hours Analysis Judges examine whether the total time spent was reasonable given the case's complexity and outcome. Red flags include:

- **Disproportionate Hours**: Spending 200 hours on a case that settles for $5,000 suggests inefficient case management
- **Unnecessary Complexity**: Over-researching straightforward legal issues or pursuing discovery that doesn't advance the case
- **Poor Case Management**: Failing to coordinate multiple attorneys' efforts or allowing junior associates to spend excessive time on tasks that senior attorneys could complete more efficiently

Unsuccessful Claims Reductions Federal courts routinely reduce fees for work on unsuccessful claims, but the analysis can be complex:

- **Related Claims**: If successful and unsuccessful claims arise from the same factual pattern and require similar legal work, courts may award full fees
- **Distinct Claims**: When unsuccessful claims involve separate legal theories or factual allegations, courts may reduce fees proportionally
- **Catalyst Theory**: Even unsuccessful claims may justify fees if they provided leverage for achieving the ultimate resolution

Judicial Discretion and Practical Considerations

Regional and Judicial Variations Different courts and judges apply varying levels of scrutiny to fee petitions:

- **Employment-Friendly Jurisdictions**: Some courts in California and New York have reputations for generous fee awards, while others apply more stringent review
- **Individual Judge Preferences**: Some judges prefer detailed billing records with specific task descriptions, while others focus more on bottom-line reasonableness
- **Case Type Patterns**: Class action settlements often face more scrutiny than individual discrimination cases due to potential conflicts between class members and counsel

Settlement vs. Trial Outcomes Fee awards often differ based on how cases are resolved:

- **Trial Victories**: Clear courtroom victories typically generate the most favorable fee awards, particularly when plaintiffs achieve substantial damages or injunctive relief
- **Settlement Agreements**: Fee awards in settlement cases may be reduced based on arguments about case strength or risk of loss at trial
- **Summary Judgment**: Prevailing on dispositive motions can generate substantial fee awards while demonstrating efficient case resolution

18.5 Settlement Negotiations and Fee Allocation Strategies

Structuring Fee Provisions in Settlement Agreements

The way attorney's fees are addressed in settlement agreements can significantly impact both the amount recovered and the tax consequences for all parties:

Lump Sum Settlements Without Fee Separation Many settlements provide a single payment amount without specifically allocating portions to damages versus attorney's fees. While this approach simplifies negotiations, it can create complications:

- **Tax Implications**: Plaintiffs may be taxed on the entire settlement amount, including the portion effectively paid to their attorneys
- **Fee Calculation Difficulties**: Without clear allocation, it becomes harder to determine whether the attorney's contingency fee percentage is reasonable
- **Potential Conflicts**: Attorneys and clients may have different preferences about how to characterize the settlement payment

Separate Fee Provisions More sophisticated settlements explicitly address attorney's fees through provisions like "Defendant shall pay plaintiff's reasonable attorney's fees and costs as determined by the court" or "Defendant shall pay $X in damages plus reasonable attorney's fees not to exceed $Y." This approach offers several advantages:

- **Preserved Rights**: Maintains the plaintiff's statutory right to seek fee recovery without waiving claims
- **Tax Clarity**: Clearer separation between compensatory damages and fee awards for tax reporting purposes
- **Negotiation Leverage**: Allows the fee determination to proceed even if parties disagree about the amount

Structured Fee Arrangements Some settlements establish specific fee amounts or caps, such as "Defendant agrees to pay attorney's fees in the amount of $50,000" or "Attorney's fees shall not exceed 40% of the total settlement amount." These provisions provide certainty but may result in under-compensation if the case required exceptional effort.

California's Unique Fee Protection Rules

California law provides special protections for attorney's fees in employment cases that don't exist in other jurisdictions:

Prohibition on Fee Waivers Under California Government Code § 12965(b), agreements that waive FEHA attorney's fees are unenforceable unless they are part of a court-approved settlement or meet specific voluntary settlement criteria. This rule prevents employers from pressuring employees to give up fee rights as a condition of settlement.

Good Faith Settlement Requirements California courts scrutinize FEHA settlements to ensure that any fee waiver was truly voluntary and that the plaintiff received adequate consideration. Factors include:

- Whether the plaintiff was represented by counsel during negotiations
- The relationship between the settlement amount and potential damages
- Whether the plaintiff understood the implications of waiving fee rights
- The timing and circumstances of any fee waiver discussions

18.6 Tax Implications and Planning Considerations

The Taxation Challenge for Employment Settlements

Tax treatment of attorney's fees in employment cases presents complex issues that affect both plaintiffs and their attorneys:

Gross Income Inclusion Problem Under general tax principles, plaintiffs must include the entire settlement amount in gross income, even if a portion goes directly to their attorneys. This can create a harsh result where plaintiffs pay taxes on money they never receive.

IRC Section 62(a)(20) Relief The Internal Revenue Code provides some relief through Section 62(a)(20), which allows an above-the-line deduction for attorney's fees in certain employment discrimination cases. However, this provision applies only to specific types of claims and requires careful documentation.

Planning Strategies Effective tax planning for employment settlements includes:

- **Clear Fee Allocation**: Separate allocation of fees and damages in settlement agreements
- **Qualified Settlement Fund**: In appropriate cases, establishing qualified settlement funds that can provide tax advantages
- **Professional Tax Advice**: Encouraging clients to consult tax professionals before finalizing settlement terms

Reporting and Documentation Requirements

Form 1099 vs. W-2 Treatment Settlement payments may be reported on different tax forms depending on their characterization:

- **Back Pay Awards**: Payments for lost wages may be subject to employment tax withholding and reported on Form W-2
- **Compensatory Damages**: Payments for emotional distress or other non-wage damages typically receive Form 1099 treatment
- **Punitive Damages**: Generally taxable income reported on Form 1099

Record-Keeping Requirements Both attorneys and clients should maintain detailed records showing:

- The basis for fee calculations and hourly rates
- Allocation of settlement amounts between different types of damages
- Documentation supporting any tax elections or deductions claimed

18.7 Defense Fee Recovery: Limited Circumstances

The High Bar for Employer Fee Recovery

While employment statutes generally favor employee fee recovery, employers can recover attorney's fees in limited circumstances:

Frivolous Litigation Standard Employers seeking fee recovery must demonstrate that the employee's claims were "frivolous, unreasonable, or without foundation" - a demanding standard that protects legitimate claims from fee-shifting threats.

Objective vs. Subjective Standards Courts apply an objective standard, asking whether a reasonable attorney would have brought the claims based on the available information, rather than focusing on the plaintiff's subjective motivations or purposes.

Policy Considerations The asymmetrical fee-shifting standard reflects Congressional intent to encourage enforcement of employment laws without chilling legitimate claims through the threat of adverse fee awards.

Practical Defense Strategies

Early Case Assessment Defense counsel should evaluate potential fee liability early in the case and document their analysis of:

- Strength of plaintiff's claims on the merits
- Potential damages exposure if plaintiff prevails
- Estimated defense costs through trial
- Settlement value considering fee exposure

Settlement Positioning Understanding fee liability can inform settlement negotiations, as employers face not only potential damages but also substantial fee awards if plaintiffs prevail at trial.

18.8 Best Practices for Maximizing Fee Recovery

From Case Inception to Fee Award

Initial Case Setup Successful fee recovery begins with proper case management from the first client interview:

- **Retainer Agreement Clarity**: Clearly explain fee-shifting statutes and potential recovery to clients
- **Time-Keeping Systems**: Implement detailed time-keeping from day one, with specific task descriptions and regular time entry
- **Cost Tracking**: Maintain detailed records of all case expenses with supporting documentation

Throughout the Litigation Effective practices during case development include:

- **Strategic Efficiency**: Focus legal work on claims with the strongest likelihood of success and fee recovery
- **Staff Utilization**: Use paralegals and junior associates for appropriate tasks while ensuring senior attorney oversight for complex matters
- **Documentation Discipline**: Maintain contemporaneous time records with sufficient detail to justify each entry

Fee Petition Preparation Successful fee petitions require careful preparation:

- **Market Research**: Gather current data on prevailing rates for comparable services
- **Supporting Evidence**: Collect declarations from other attorneys and documentation of fee awards in similar cases
- **Opposition Anticipation**: Prepare responses to likely challenges about rates, hours, or necessity of specific work

Technology and Efficiency Tools

Modern Practice Management Contemporary legal practice offers tools that can improve both efficiency and fee recovery:

- **Time-Tracking Software**: Automated systems that integrate with calendars and document management systems
- **Case Management Platforms**: Comprehensive systems that track deadlines, communications, and case progress

- **Legal Research Efficiency**: Strategic use of research platforms to avoid duplicative or excessive research time

Documentation and Presentation Technology can also enhance fee petition presentation:

- **Detailed Time Reports**: Software that generates comprehensive time summaries organized by task, attorney, or case phase
- **Rate Comparison Tools**: Databases that provide market rate information for different geographic areas and practice specialties
- **Visual Presentation**: Charts and graphs that clearly illustrate work patterns and case progression

18.9 Comparative Analysis Across Jurisdictions

Federal vs. State Approaches

Philosophical Differences Federal and state courts often apply different approaches to fee awards based on underlying policy considerations:

- **Federal Emphasis on Efficiency**: Federal courts tend to scrutinize fee petitions more closely, with emphasis on eliminating excessive or duplicative work
- **State Focus on Access**: Many state courts, particularly in California, emphasize the access-to-justice rationale for fee-shifting and apply more generous standards

Practical Implications These philosophical differences translate into concrete differences in fee recovery:

- **Multiplier Availability**: California courts readily apply multipliers under FEHA, while federal courts rarely enhance lodestar calculations
- **Unsuccessful Claims Treatment**: State courts may award full fees for work on unsuccessful claims if they were related to successful claims, while federal courts more often reduce fees proportionally

Geographic Variations

High-Cost vs. Lower-Cost Markets Geographic location significantly affects both hourly rates and total fee awards:

- **Metropolitan Areas**: Major cities support higher hourly rates but also involve higher overhead costs and more competition
- **Regional Markets**: Smaller markets may have lower rates but also fewer specialized employment attorneys
- **Cross-Border Cases**: Cases involving attorneys from different markets require careful analysis of appropriate rate standards

State-Specific Considerations

California Distinctions

- More generous multiplier standards under FEHA
- Stronger protections against fee waivers in settlements
- PAGA's unique representative action fee provisions
- Liberal interpretation of "prevailing party" status

New York Variations

- Three-tiered system with different standards for state, city, and federal claims
- Generally follows federal precedent but with some state-specific interpretations
- Strong wage and hour fee provisions in Labor Law

Federal Circuit Differences

- Ninth Circuit (California): Generally more liberal approach to fee awards
- Second Circuit (New York): Moderate approach with emphasis on documentation requirements
- Other circuits: Varying standards with some showing more restrictive approaches

18.10 Ethical Considerations and Professional Responsibility

Fee Arrangements and Client Relations

Contingency Fee Agreements Employment cases often involve contingency fee arrangements that raise specific ethical considerations:

- **Reasonableness Standard**: Contingency percentages must be reasonable given the case complexity, risk, and time investment
- **Client Understanding**: Clients must understand both the fee arrangement and potential fee recovery from opposing parties
- **Settlement Allocation**: Clear agreement about how statutory fee awards affect contingency calculations

Conflicts of Interest Fee recovery can create potential conflicts between attorneys and clients:

- **Settlement Negotiations**: Different preferences about fee allocation in settlement discussions
- **Appeal Decisions**: Clients may prefer to accept lower awards while attorneys seek appellate review to increase fees
- **Case Strategy**: Pressure to pursue fee-generating activities versus most efficient case resolution

Professional Standards and Discipline

Documentation Requirements Bar associations and courts expect attorneys to maintain detailed records supporting fee petitions:

- **Contemporaneous Time Keeping**: Regular and detailed time entry with specific task descriptions
- **Cost Documentation**: Receipts and records for all claimed expenses
- **Rate Justification**: Evidence supporting requested hourly rates based on market conditions and attorney qualifications

Candor and Accuracy Fee petitions require complete honesty about:

- **Work Performed**: Accurate description of tasks and time spent
- **Results Achieved**: Honest assessment of success levels and relationship to fee requests
- **Market Conditions**: Realistic evaluation of prevailing rates and competitive positioning

18.11 Future Trends and Developments

Legislative and Judicial Evolution

Expanding Fee-Shifting Provisions Employment law continues to evolve with new fee-shifting provisions:

- **State Innovation**: States like California continue to expand fee recovery rights in employment cases
- **Federal Developments**: Congressional consideration of enhanced fee provisions in various employment contexts
- **Local Ordinances**: Municipal laws increasingly include fee-shifting provisions for employment violations

Technology and Efficiency The legal profession's increasing use of technology affects fee awards:

- **Artificial Intelligence**: Legal research and document review tools may reduce the hours reasonably necessary for certain tasks
- **Alternative Fee Arrangements**: New models beyond hourly billing may affect fee recovery calculations
- **Remote Work**: Changes in legal practice patterns may affect geographic rate determinations

Strategic Considerations for Practitioners

Practice Development Understanding fee recovery enhances employment law practices:

- **Client Development**: Fee-shifting makes representation economically viable for employees with limited resources

- **Case Selection**: Strong fee provisions can justify taking cases with modest damages but significant legal issues
- **Specialization Value**: Expertise in fee recovery adds value to employment law practices

Risk Management Proper fee recovery practices protect both attorneys and clients:

- **Malpractice Prevention**: Detailed documentation and careful fee calculations reduce potential claims
- **Client Relations**: Clear communication about fee arrangements and recovery potential improves client satisfaction
- **Professional Development**: Mastery of fee recovery enhances reputation and referral relationships

18.12 Conclusion

Attorney's fees represent a vital component of employment law practice, serving both practical and policy objectives. They make representation economically viable for employees challenging workplace violations, while simultaneously encouraging compliance with employment laws by ensuring that successful enforcement efforts are adequately compensated.

The complexity of fee recovery - from initial case setup through final fee award - requires careful attention to documentation, market analysis, and strategic planning. Success depends not only on achieving favorable outcomes for clients but also on properly presenting fee petitions that satisfy increasingly sophisticated judicial scrutiny.

Whether preparing comprehensive fee petitions after trial victories or negotiating fee provisions in settlement agreements, employment attorneys must balance efficiency with thoroughness, ensuring that their professional efforts receive fair compensation while serving the broader goal of making employment law enforcement accessible to all workers.

Mastery of fee recovery principles enhances every aspect of employment law practice, from initial client counseling through final case resolution. As employment law continues to evolve, the ability to effectively seek and recover attorney's fees will remain central to successful practice in this vital area of law.

The principles and practices outlined in this chapter provide the foundation for effective fee recovery, but each case presents unique challenges requiring careful analysis and strategic thinking. The investment in developing fee recovery expertise pays dividends not only in individual cases but in building a sustainable practice dedicated to employment law enforcement and worker protection.

19

Post-Trial Motions and Appeals

Trial may feel like the finish line, but in employment litigation, the legal journey often continues into post-trial motions and potentially appeals. Whether seeking to overturn a verdict, reduce a damages award, or defend a hard-won judgment, post-trial practice demands a different set of tools: precision, legal analysis, and procedural discipline.

This chapter covers common post-trial motions in employment cases - including motions for judgment notwithstanding the verdict (JNOV), motions for new trial, and remittitur - as well as appellate strategy in New York, California, and federal court.

19.1 Overview of Post-Trial Motions

Post-trial motions represent the first opportunity to challenge a verdict before it becomes final judgment. These motions serve as both a remedy for trial errors and a strategic tool for litigation positioning. Understanding their purpose, timing, and procedural requirements is essential for employment practitioners.

Purpose and Function

Post-trial motions serve to:

- Challenge the legal or factual basis of the verdict
- Address procedural errors during trial
- Reduce excessive or unsupported damages
- Preserve issues for appeal

These motions function as a critical bridge between trial and appeal, often determining whether appellate review will even be available. In employment cases, where damages can be substantial and liability complex, post-trial motions frequently target specific elements like emotional distress awards, punitive damages calculations, or claims lacking sufficient evidentiary support.

Timing Requirements

The timing of post-trial motions is perhaps their most critical aspect. Courts strictly enforce deadlines, and late filings typically forfeit rights on appeal. The general timeline requires filing within 15 to 30 days post-verdict, though specific rules vary by jurisdiction:

Federal Court: Most post-trial motions must be filed within 28 days of judgment entry (Federal Rule of Civil Procedure 59).

California: New trial motions must be filed within 15 days after notice of entry of judgment, but no later than 180 days after entry of judgment itself (Code of Civil Procedure Section 657).

New York: Post-trial motions must generally be made within 15 days of verdict, though judges may extend this period in their discretion (CPLR 4404).

Strategic Considerations

Post-trial motions require careful strategic analysis. Filing a motion may delay final judgment and extend litigation costs, but it also preserves appellate rights and may result in settlement leverage. In employment cases, defendants often use post-trial motions to demonstrate the strength of their position while creating pressure for reduced settlements.

Consider the examples of *Tulino v. City of New York*, No. 15-cv-7106 (JMF), 2019 WL 3810975 (S.D.N.Y. Aug. 1, 2019); *Rainone v. Potter*, 388 F. Supp. 2d 120 (E.D.N.Y. 2005); and *Emamian v. Rockefeller Univ.*, No. 07 Civ. 3919 (DAB), 2018 WL 2849700 (S.D.N.Y. June 11, 2018), New York cases where a jury awarded substantial emotional distress damages in employment discrimination lawsuits, followed by defense motions for judgment as a matter of law (JNOV) and/or a new trial, leading to remittitur. In these instances, courts denied the JNOV motions but granted remittitur, reducing the damages.The plaintiffs accepted the reduction rather than face a new trial, demonstrating the tactical value of well-crafted post-trial motions.

19.2 Motion for Judgment Notwithstanding the Verdict (JNOV)

The motion for judgment notwithstanding the verdict, known as JNOV from the Latin "judgment non obstante veredicto," represents one of the most challenging post-trial motions to win. This motion essentially asks the court to substitute its judgment for that of the jury, arguing that no reasonable jury could have reached the verdict based on the evidence presented.

Alternative Names and Jurisdictional Variations

The JNOV motion appears under different names across jurisdictions:

- **Federal Court**: Renewed motion for judgment as a matter of law (Rule 50(b))
- **California**: Motion for judgment notwithstanding the verdict
- **New York**: Motion to set aside the verdict (CPLR 4404)

Despite different nomenclature, the fundamental purpose remains consistent: challenging verdicts that lack sufficient evidentiary support.

Legal Standard and Requirements

The JNOV motion faces an extremely high bar. Courts apply the same standard used for directed verdict motions: whether, viewing the evidence in the light most favorable to the verdict winner, any reasonable jury could have reached the same conclusion. This deferential standard reflects the constitutional right to jury trial and the principle that fact-finding remains the jury's province.

Federal Court Requirements: Under Rule 50(b), a party must have made a Rule 50(a) motion for directed verdict during trial to preserve the right to file a post-trial JNOV motion. This requirement ensures that the opposing party had notice of the legal challenge and an opportunity to present additional evidence.

State Court Variations: California and New York do not require a contemporaneous directed verdict motion, though making one strengthens the post-trial motion by demonstrating consistency in legal theory.

Practical Application in Employment Cases

JNOV motions most commonly target liability determinations rather than damages calculations. In employment litigation, successful JNOV motions typically address:

Failure to Establish Prima Facie Case: When plaintiff fails to prove basic elements of discrimination, retaliation, or wrongful termination claims.

Insufficient Evidence of Causation: Particularly in mixed-motive cases where both legitimate and discriminatory reasons may exist for employment actions.

Consider the New York case of *Zimmermann v. Associates First Capital Corp.*, 251 F.3d 376 (2d Cir. 2001), where the Second Circuit reversed the jury verdict for the plaintiff and ordered judgment as a matter of law (JNOV) in favor of the employer, finding that "[a] jury could not reasonably conclude that age was a motivating factor... [t]he record as a whole indicates a legitimate basis for termination."

Consider also the California case of *Begnal v. Canfield & Associates, Inc.*, 78 Cal. App. 4th 66 (2000) where the California Court of Appeal reversed the trial court's grant of JNOV, reinstating the jury's verdict. The appellate court held that, despite the replacement being older, there was substantial evidence supporting the jury's conclusion that age was a motivating factor in the employee's termination, including statistical evidence and testimony suggesting that the employer's stated reasons were pretextual. Consider also *Cheal v. El Camino Hosp.*, 223 Cal. App. 4th 736 (2014) where the trial court granted JNOV for the employer after a jury found for the plaintiff on age and national origin discrimination under FEHA.

Statute of Limitations Issues: When the evidence clearly shows claims were filed beyond statutory deadlines.

Relationship to Other Motions

JNOV motions are often filed alongside new trial motions, providing alternative relief if the primary motion fails. This strategic approach, known as "motion in the alternative," allows courts to choose the most appropriate remedy while preserving all appellate rights.

19.3 Motion for New Trial

The motion for new trial represents the broadest and most flexible post-trial remedy, allowing courts to address various trial errors that may have affected the verdict's fairness or accuracy. Unlike JNOV motions, which challenge the sufficiency of evidence, new trial motions can address procedural errors, attorney misconduct, and evidentiary rulings.

Statutory Authority and Procedural Framework

Federal Court: Rule 59 governs new trial motions, requiring filing within 28 days of judgment entry. The rule grants broad discretion to district courts in evaluating whether a new trial serves the interests of justice.

California: Code of Civil Procedure Section 657 provides specific grounds for new trial motions and requires filing within 15 days of notice of entry of judgment, with an absolute deadline of 180 days after judgment entry.

New York: CPLR 4404(a) allows new trial motions within 15 days of verdict, though judges may extend this period. New York courts have traditionally been more restrictive in granting new trials than federal courts.

Grounds for New Trial Motions

New trial motions encompass a wide range of potential trial errors:

Jury Misconduct: This includes improper communications, consideration of outside evidence, or bias. In employment cases, jury misconduct might involve internet research about the defendant company or discussions of personal employment experiences not in evidence.

For example, in *Akers v. County of San Diego*, 95 Cal. App. 4th 1441 (2002), the trial court conditionally granted a new trial based on **juror misconduct**, finding that a juror had engaged in improper conduct during deliberations that could have influenced the jury's decision. The court offered a remittitur, reducing the jury's award from $250,000 to $150,000, which the plaintiff accepted. The Court of Appeal affirmed, emphasizing the importance of protecting the integrity of the jury deliberation process and ensuring that verdicts are based solely on the evidence presented at trial.

Improper Evidentiary Rulings: Erroneous admission or exclusion of evidence that substantially affected the outcome. Employment cases frequently involve disputes over personnel file admissibility, prior complaint evidence, and expert testimony regarding damages calculations.

Attorney Misconduct: Includes improper arguments, violations of court orders, or prejudicial behavior. This ground requires showing that the misconduct actually influenced the verdict.

Verdict Contrary to Law or Weight of Evidence: This ground overlaps with JNOV motions but allows more discretionary analysis. Courts may grant new trials when verdicts, while supported by some evidence, are against the great weight of evidence.

Excessive or Inadequate Damages: Courts may order new trials limited to damages when awards are clearly excessive or insufficient. This approach preserves liability findings while addressing damages issues.

Newly Discovered Evidence: This ground requires showing that: (1) evidence was discovered after trial, (2) due diligence could not have uncovered it earlier, (3) the evidence is material and not merely cumulative, and (4) it would likely change the outcome.

Standard of Review and Judicial Discretion

Courts possess broad discretion in ruling on new trial motions, particularly regarding factual determinations. This discretion extends to weighing evidence, assessing witness credibility, and evaluating trial fairness. Appellate courts rarely overturn denials of new trial motions unless the trial court clearly abused its discretion.

The discretionary standard creates both opportunities and challenges. While it allows courts to address trial unfairness that might not meet JNOV standards, it also makes appellate reversal difficult when new trial motions are denied.

Partial New Trials

Courts may order partial new trials limited to specific issues, most commonly damages. This approach saves judicial resources while addressing problematic verdict components. In employment cases, partial new trials often focus on:

- Emotional distress damages lacking evidentiary support
- Punitive damages calculations
- Economic loss projections
- Attorney fee determinations

19.4 Motion for Remittitur

Remittitur represents a compromise between overturning verdicts entirely and accepting excessive damages awards. This procedural device allows courts to reduce damages while preserving liability findings, offering plaintiffs a choice between accepting reduced awards or proceeding to new trial.

Legal Foundation and Purpose

Remittitur addresses the constitutional tension between jury trial rights and due process protection against excessive verdicts. Rather than overturning verdicts entirely, remittitur allows courts to cure damages excessiveness while respecting jury liability determinations.

The Supreme Court has established that remittitur does not violate the Seventh Amendment because it preserves the jury's role in determining liability while addressing clearly excessive damages that shock the judicial conscience.

Procedural Mechanics

The remittitur process typically involves several steps:

1. **Court Determination**: The judge determines that damages are excessive based on the evidence presented
2. **Plaintiff Choice**: The court offers plaintiff the option to accept reduced damages or proceed to new trial
3. **Conditional Ruling**: If plaintiff accepts remittitur, judgment enters for the reduced amount; if declined, the court orders new trial on damages

This process preserves both parties' rights while providing efficient resolution of damages disputes.

Common Targets in Employment Cases

Employment litigation frequently involves remittitur motions targeting specific damages categories:

Emotional Distress Awards: Courts scrutinize emotional distress damages for evidentiary support, often requiring medical evidence, expert testimony, or detailed proof of impact. Awards based solely on conclusory testimony may face remittitur.

In *MacMillan v. Millennium Broadway Hotel*, 873 F. Supp. 2d 546 (S.D.N.Y. 2012), a jury awarded the plaintiff $125,000 in emotional distress damages. The court found the award excessive given the limited evidence of emotional distress, which consisted mainly of the plaintiff's and his daughter's vague and conclusory testimony without medical corroboration. The court granted a remittitur, reducing the emotional distress award to $30,000.

Punitive Damages: The Supreme Court's decision in *State Farm v. Campbell*, 538 U.S. 408 (2003) established due process limits on punitive damages, generally requiring single-digit ratios to compensatory damages. Employment cases frequently involve remittitur motions seeking to enforce these constitutional limits.

Economic Damages: Speculative economic loss projections may face remittitur, particularly when based on uncertain career advancement or earnings assumptions. Courts require reasonable certainty in economic damages calculations.

Strategic Considerations

Remittitur creates complex strategic decisions for plaintiffs. Accepting remittitur provides immediate resolution and avoids new trial risks, but may result in significantly reduced recovery. Declining remittitur preserves the possibility of full damages recovery but risks complete loss if the new trial results in defense verdict.

Defense attorneys often prefer remittitur to new trial motions because it guarantees damages reduction while avoiding the uncertainty and expense of retrial.

19.5 Motion for Additur (Less Common)

Additur represents the mirror image of remittitur, seeking to increase damages awards deemed unreasonably low. However, additur availability varies significantly by jurisdiction and faces constitutional limitations not applicable to remittitur.

Jurisdictional Availability

Federal Courts: Additur is not available in federal court due to Seventh Amendment constraints on judicial fact-finding. The Supreme Court has held that increasing jury awards violates the constitutional right to jury trial more directly than reducing excessive awards.

State Courts: Some states, including California, allow additur in limited circumstances. However, even in permissive jurisdictions, additur remains rare and faces strict procedural requirements.

New York: Generally does not recognize additur, though courts may order new trials when damages are clearly inadequate.

Procedural Requirements

When available, additur follows a process similar to remittitur:

1. Court determines that damages are inadequately low based on the evidence
2. Defendant receives the choice to accept increased damages or proceed to new trial
3. Conditional ruling enters based on defendant's decision

Limited Application in Employment Cases

Additur rarely appears in employment litigation because plaintiffs typically seek substantial damages and juries often award significant amounts when finding liability. However, additur might apply when:

- Juries award minimal damages despite clear liability
- Economic damages calculations are artificially reduced
- Emotional distress awards fail to reflect proven impact

19.6 Judgment Entry and Stay of Enforcement

The transition from verdict to final judgment involves critical procedural steps that affect both post-trial motion rights and appellate timing. Understanding judgment entry procedures and enforcement stays is essential for managing post-trial strategy.

Judgment Entry Process

Federal Court: Under Rule 58, judgment must be set forth in a separate document, clearly identifying the prevailing party and relief granted. The judgment entry starts the clock for both post-trial motions and appeals under Federal Rule of Appellate Procedure 4.

California: Code of Civil Procedure Section 664.5 requires judgment entry within specified timeframes, with notice to parties triggering various deadlines.

New York: CPLR 5016 governs judgment entry, requiring clear identification of the relief granted and parties' obligations.

The judgment entry date is crucial because it triggers multiple deadlines running concurrently. Post-trial motions, appeals, and enforcement procedures all depend on accurate judgment entry dating.

Stay of Enforcement Pending Post-Trial Motions

Most jurisdictions automatically stay judgment enforcement while post-trial motions remain pending. This automatic stay prevents plaintiffs from collecting on judgments that may be modified or overturned, while preserving the status quo during motion practice.

Federal Court: Rule 62(b) automatically stays enforcement during the pendency of post-trial motions filed within the prescribed time limits.

State Court Variations: California and New York have similar automatic stay provisions, though specific requirements may vary.

Stay Pending Appeal

Obtaining a stay pending appeal requires meeting more stringent requirements and typically involves posting an appeal bond.

Bond Requirements: Appeal bonds typically must cover the full judgment amount plus interest and costs during the appeal period. In large employment cases, bond amounts can be substantial, sometimes reaching millions of dollars.

Alternative Security: Courts may accept alternative security arrangements, including letters of credit, escrow accounts, or other financial guarantees.

Factors for Stay: Courts consider the likelihood of appeal success, irreparable harm to the appellant, harm to other parties, and public interest factors.

Consider the case of in *Cox v. City of Los Angeles*, 78 Cal. App. 4th 481 (2000), where the California Court of Appeal held that the trial court did not abuse its discretion by setting an appeal bond lower than the full amount of the judgment, considering the defendant's financial situation and other factors.

Similarly, in New York, courts have discretion under CPLR § 5519 to fix the amount and conditions of an undertaking to stay enforcement of a judgment pending appeal. In *In re Nassau County Strip Search Cases*, 783 F.3d 414 (2d Cir. 2015), the Second Circuit acknowledged that district courts have discretion to waive or reduce appeal bonds in appropriate circumstances.

These cases illustrate that while specific details may vary, courts in both jurisdictions can and do consider financial stability and additional security when determining appeal bond requirements.

19.7 Preserving Issues for Appeal

Appellate practice begins at trial through careful preservation of legal issues and procedural objections. Employment attorneys must understand preservation requirements to maintain appellate rights and create comprehensive trial records.

Fundamental Preservation Requirements

To preserve an issue for appellate review, practitioners must:

Object on the Record: Specific, timely objections during trial create the foundation for appellate review. General objections or failures to object typically waive appellate rights.

State Legal Grounds: Objections must identify the specific legal basis for the challenge, whether evidentiary, procedural, or substantive.

Make Necessary Motions: Certain appellate arguments require specific trial motions, such as directed verdict motions for sufficiency of evidence challenges.

Ensure Accurate Record: Jury instructions, verdict forms, and trial transcripts must accurately reflect the positions taken and objections made.

Common Preservation Failures in Employment Cases

Employment litigation involves complex legal issues that create numerous preservation pitfalls:

Failure to Object to Jury Instructions: Inadequate objections to jury instructions often prevent appellate review of instructional errors. Practitioners must object specifically to problematic language and propose alternative instructions.

Inadequate Evidentiary Objections: General evidentiary objections fail to preserve specific grounds for appeal. Each objection should identify the precise rule violated and potential prejudice.

Waiver Through Failure to Move: Certain appellate arguments require specific trial motions, such as motions for directed verdict, motions *in limine*, or requests for specific jury instructions.

Strategic Preservation Decisions

Preservation decisions require balancing trial strategy with appellate rights. Excessive objections may alienate the jury, while insufficient objections waive appellate rights. Experienced employment attorneys develop systematic approaches to preservation that protect appellate rights while maintaining effective trial advocacy.

19.8 Notice of Appeal

The notice of appeal represents the critical first step in appellate practice, triggering appellate jurisdiction and establishing the framework for appellate review. Understanding filing requirements, deadlines, and procedural prerequisites is essential for employment attorneys pursuing or defending appeals.

Filing Deadlines by Jurisdiction

Appeal deadlines are jurisdictional and cannot be extended for most circumstances:

Federal Court: Rule 4 of the Federal Rules of Appellate Procedure requires filing within 30 days after entry of judgment, extended to 60 days when the United States is a party. These deadlines run from judgment entry, not verdict date.

California: Rule 8.104 requires filing within 60 days after notice of entry of judgment, or 180 days after judgment entry if no notice is served. The California Supreme Court has emphasized strict compliance with these deadlines.

New York: CPLR 5513 generally requires filing within 30 days after service of notice of entry of judgment with notice of entry, though specific circumstances may create different deadlines.

Filing Requirements and Procedures

Where to File: Notices of appeal must be filed with the trial court, not the appellate court. This counterintuitive requirement frequently creates confusion for practitioners unfamiliar with appellate practice.

Content Requirements: The notice must identify the parties, the judgment being appealed, and the court to which the appeal is taken. Specific language requirements vary by jurisdiction but generally require clear identification of the appealable order or judgment.

Service Requirements: Notices must be served on all parties in accordance with applicable service rules. Failure to serve properly may result in dismissal of the appeal.

Filing Fees: Appellate filing fees must be paid at the time of filing, though fee waiver applications may be available for indigent parties.

Designating the Record

Appellate courts review trial court proceedings based on the trial record, making record designation a critical component of appellate practice:

Transcript Designation: Parties must identify portions of trial proceedings to be transcribed for appellate review. Strategic decisions about transcript scope can significantly impact appellate costs and timeline.

Exhibit Designation: The appellate record must include relevant trial exhibits, requiring careful selection to support appellate arguments while managing record size and costs.

Timing Requirements: Record designation deadlines typically run concurrently with or shortly after notice of appeal filing, requiring prompt action to preserve appellate rights.

19.9 Appealing Employment Case Verdicts

Employment case appeals present unique challenges and opportunities, often involving complex legal issues, substantial damages, and significant strategic considerations for both parties. Understanding common appellate issues, standards of review, and success rates helps attorneys make informed decisions about pursuing or defending appeals.

Common Appellate Issues in Employment Cases

Employment appeals frequently involve recurring legal issues that reflect the complexity of employment law and the high stakes involved in employment litigation:

Jury Instruction Errors: Employment law involves nuanced legal standards that create frequent instructional disputes. Common issues include:

- Burden of proof instructions in mixed-motive cases
- Damages instructions for emotional distress and punitive damages
- Causation instructions in retaliation cases
- Instructions regarding employer defenses and affirmative defenses

In *Woods v. START Treatment & Recovery Centers, Inc.*, 864 F.3d 158 (2d Cir. 2017), the jury returned a defense verdict. Woods appealed, arguing that the district court erred by instructing the jury that she had to prove her FMLA leave was the "but-for" cause of her termination. The Second Circuit agreed with Woods, holding that the district court applied the incorrect causation standard. The court clarified that FMLA retaliation claims require a "negative factor" or "motivating factor" standard, not a "but-for" standard. Consequently, the appellate court vacated the judgment and remanded the case for a new trial.

Evidentiary Rulings: Trial courts possess broad discretion in evidentiary matters, but employment cases often involve disputed evidence that significantly impacts outcomes:

- Admission of prior complaint evidence
- Expert testimony regarding damages calculations
- Evidence of comparative treatment of other employees
- Personnel file admissibility and scope

Procedural and Discovery Issues: Employment litigation frequently involves extensive discovery disputes that may provide appellate grounds:

- Sanctions for discovery abuse
- Protective order violations
- Failure to preserve electronic evidence
- Scope of privilege protections

Sufficiency of Evidence Challenges: Appeals challenging the sufficiency of evidence supporting liability or damages determinations, though facing deferential review standards.

Standards of Appellate Review

Understanding appellate review standards is crucial for evaluating appeal prospects and crafting effective appellate strategies:

De Novo Review: Legal issues receive fresh appellate consideration without deference to trial court rulings. This standard applies to:

- Statutory interpretation questions
- Constitutional issues
- Summary judgment denials based on legal conclusions
- Jury instruction legal adequacy

Substantial Evidence Standard: Factual determinations receive highly deferential review, requiring appellate courts to uphold findings supported by substantial evidence in the record. This standard applies to:

- Jury verdict challenges
- Factual findings in bench trials
- Damages calculations with evidentiary support

Abuse of Discretion: Discretionary trial court rulings face intermediate review, requiring clear error or abuse of discretion for reversal. This standard applies to:

- Evidentiary rulings
- Discovery sanctions
- New trial motion denials
- Damages remittitur decisions

Strategic Considerations for Appeals

Plaintiff Considerations: Employment plaintiffs face unique challenges in deciding whether to pursue appeals:

Costs and Delay: Appeals typically take 12 to 18 months and involve substantial costs for transcripts, briefs, and attorney fees. Plaintiffs must weigh these costs against potential recovery increases.

Collection Concerns: Appealing may delay collection while defendants seek stays or post appeal bonds. Plaintiffs should evaluate defendants' financial stability and likelihood of remaining collectible during appeal periods.

Settlement Leverage: Filing appeals may create settlement opportunities, as defendants often prefer avoiding appellate uncertainty and additional litigation costs.

Defendant Considerations: Defendants frequently appeal employment verdicts, seeking to:

Reduce Damages: Even unsuccessful appeals may create settlement leverage for damages reduction *Delay Payment*: Appeals automatically stay enforcement in most jurisdictions, providing time value benefits *Establish Precedent*: Defendants may appeal to establish favorable precedent for future cases *Challenge Liability*: Complete reversal eliminates damages exposure and creates precedential value

Success Rates and Practical Expectations

Employment case appeals face challenging success rates that vary significantly by jurisdiction and issue type:

Overall Reversal Rates: Federal appellate courts reverse district court judgments in approximately 10-15% of civil cases, with employment cases falling within this range.

Partial Success: Many appeals result in partial success, such as damages reduction through remittitur or new trials on specific issues. These outcomes may provide significant value even without complete reversal.

Issue-Specific Success: Legal issues receive more favorable appellate treatment than factual challenges, making jury instruction and evidentiary appeals more promising than sufficiency of evidence challenges.

Consider the case of *Diaz v. Tesla, Inc.*, No. 3:17-cv-06748-WHO Owen Diaz, a former contract elevator operator at Tesla's Fremont factory, filed a lawsuit alleging that he was subjected to a racially hostile work environment, including frequent racial slurs and discriminatory drawings. In October 2021, a jury awarded Diaz $6.9 million in compensatory damages and $130 million in punitive damages, totaling $136.9 million. Tesla filed post-trial motions challenging the damages as excessive. The court agreed that the punitive damages were excessive and reduced the total award to $15 million. Diaz rejected the reduced award, opting for a new trial on damages. In April 2023, a second jury awarded Diaz $175,000 in compensatory damages and $3 million in punitive damages, totaling $3.175 million.

This partial success provided substantial value despite unsuccessful liability challenges. This case underscores the importance of proper jury instructions and the court's role in ensuring that punitive damages are proportionate to the harm suffered and the defendant's conduct. The substantial reduction from the initial $136.9 million award to $3.175 million highlights the judiciary's oversight in aligning jury awards with legal standards.

Appellate Strategy Development

Effective appellate strategy requires careful analysis of trial proceedings, preservation issues, and appellate precedent:

Issue Selection: Successful appeals focus on the strongest issues rather than raising every possible argument. Strategic issue selection concentrates appellate court attention on winnable arguments.

Record Development: Appellate success often depends on thorough record development during trial, requiring practitioners to anticipate appellate issues and preserve them appropriately.

Precedent Analysis: Employment law continues evolving through appellate decisions, making careful precedent analysis essential for crafting persuasive appellate arguments.

19.10 Advanced Post-Trial Strategies

Post-trial practice extends beyond individual motions to encompass comprehensive strategies that maximize client outcomes while managing risks and costs. Sophisticated employment practitioners develop integrated approaches that consider immediate post-trial opportunities alongside long-term strategic objectives.

Coordinated Motion Practice

Rather than filing isolated motions, strategic post-trial practice often involves coordinated motion packages that provide multiple paths to relief:

Primary and Alternative Relief: Filing JNOV motions alongside new trial motions provides courts with flexibility in fashioning appropriate relief while preserving all appellate rights.

Conditional Motions: Structuring motions conditionally allows courts to address issues in sequence, such as requesting remittitur conditioned on denial of new trial motions.

Timing Coordination: Coordinating motion filing with settlement discussions may create enhanced leverage for resolution while preserving procedural rights.

Settlement Leverage in Post-Trial Context

Post-trial motions create unique settlement dynamics that experienced attorneys leverage effectively:

Demonstrating Strength: Well-crafted post-trial motions demonstrate the strength of legal positions and create uncertainty about final outcomes.

Risk Allocation: Post-trial settlement discussions often focus on risk allocation, with parties evaluating the likelihood of successful motions or appeals.

Value Preservation: Settlement discussions may focus on preserving value while avoiding appeal costs and delays.

Cost-Benefit Analysis

Post-trial practice requires careful cost-benefit analysis that considers both immediate expenses and long-term strategic value:

Direct Costs: Motion practice, transcript preparation, and potential appeal costs must be weighed against likely recovery or savings.

Opportunity Costs: Extended litigation delays resolution and may impact other business or legal priorities.

Strategic Value: Successful post-trial motions may establish precedent or create leverage for future cases.

Client Counseling and Expectations

Post-trial practice requires clear client communication about procedures, timing, and likely outcomes:

Realistic Expectations: Clients must understand the difficulty of overturning jury verdicts and the deferential standards applied to trial court rulings.

Timeline Projections: Post-trial motions and appeals significantly extend litigation timelines, requiring client planning for extended uncertainty.

Financial Planning: Large judgments may require immediate financial planning, particularly when appeal bonds or enforcement stays are involved.

19.11 Conclusion

Post-trial litigation represents a high-stakes phase where victories can be preserved or verdicts undone. Whether contesting an excessive judgment or defending a jury's award, success depends on preparation, proper preservation, and procedural discipline. For employment lawyers, knowing how to navigate motions and appeals is essential not only for courtroom outcomes, but also for strategic leverage in post-trial settlement and future litigation.

The key principles for effective post-trial practice include:

Procedural Precision: Strict adherence to deadlines and procedural requirements is essential, as late filings typically forfeit important rights.

Strategic Integration: Post-trial motions should integrate with overall case strategy, considering both immediate relief and long-term objectives.

Preservation Focus: Appellate rights depend on proper preservation during trial, requiring systematic attention to objections, motions, and record development.

Cost-Benefit Analysis: Post-trial practice involves significant costs and delays that must be weighed against potential benefits and strategic value.

Client Communication: Clear client counseling about procedures, timelines, and realistic expectations is essential for informed decision-making.

The evolution of employment law through appellate decisions makes post-trial practice particularly important in this area. Successful post-trial advocacy not only serves immediate client interests but also contributes to the development of employment law precedent that benefits future clients and shapes legal practice.

In Chapter 20, we'll explore how to enforce judgments and settlements, including collection procedures, post-judgment interest, and navigating employer resistance.

20

Enforcement of Judgments and Settlements

Winning a verdict or securing a settlement is not the end of the journey - collection and enforcement are the final mile. Employers may delay, avoid, or resist payment, especially if the judgment is large, unflattering, or involves punitive damages. Whether you're enforcing a court judgment or a private settlement, understanding enforcement mechanisms is essential to delivering real-world results for your client.

This chapter explains how to enforce employment case judgments and settlements in New York, California, and federal court, including garnishments, liens, contempt motions, and negotiating resistance.

20.1 Enforcing Settlements

The Foundation: Documentation and Recording

Settlement enforcement begins with proper documentation. A verbal agreement, no matter how detailed or witnessed, provides insufficient foundation for enforcement. The agreement must be reduced to writing, signed by all parties, and preferably incorporated into the court record.

Incorporating Terms into the Record

If settlement is reached during litigation, ensure it is:

- Documented in writing with precise language
- Signed by all parties and their counsel
- Filed with the court or incorporated into the judgment (if appropriate)
- Contains specific performance deadlines and consequences for breach

The distinction between a private settlement agreement and a court-incorporated settlement is crucial. Private agreements require separate breach of contract litigation for enforcement, while court-incorporated settlements can be enforced through contempt proceedings and other judicial remedies.

Enforceability Mechanisms: Jurisdictional Differences

California's Streamlined Approach

California Code of Civil Procedure Section 664.6 provides a unique enforcement mechanism that allows parties to enforce a written settlement agreement via motion, provided it is signed by both sides and submitted to the court. This statute eliminates the need for a separate breach of contract lawsuit, making California particularly plaintiff-friendly for settlement enforcement.

Under Section 664.6, the court retains jurisdiction to enforce the settlement even after the underlying case is dismissed. This means that if an employer defaults on payment terms, you can file a simple motion rather than initiating new litigation. The court may then enter judgment for the unpaid amount plus interest and attorney's fees (if provided in the agreement).

New York's Traditional Framework

New York follows a more traditional approach. Settlements can be enforced through:

1. **Stipulation of settlement** filed in court under CPLR 2104, which

becomes enforceable as a court order

2. **Plenary action** for breach of contract if the settlement was not incorporated into the court record

The key difference is that New York requires either formal court incorporation or separate litigation. A CPLR 2104 stipulation must be filed with the court and signed by the attorneys or parties. Once filed, it has the same effect as a judgment and can be enforced through all available collection remedies.

Federal Court Flexibility

Federal courts have broad discretion in settlement enforcement. Settlements may be enforced under the court's inherent power if the agreement is part of the record, or via a separate breach of contract action if not incorporated into judgment. Federal judges often retain jurisdiction over settlement agreements through specific language in dismissal orders.

The Federal Rules of Civil Procedure do not provide a specific mechanism like California's Section 664.6, so practitioners must rely on contract principles and the court's general equity powers.

Essential Settlement Clauses

Payment Schedule and Deadlines

Specify exact payment amounts, due dates, and acceptable forms of payment. Avoid vague language like "reasonable installments" or "as soon as possible." Instead, use precise terms: "Defendant shall pay $50,000 in five equal installments of $10,000 each, due on the first day of each month beginning January 1, 2025."

Attorney's Fees for Enforcement

Include a provision that the breaching party pays reasonable attorney's fees and costs incurred in enforcement. This serves both as a deterrent and ensures you can recover the costs of collection efforts. Sample language: "In the event of breach, the non-breaching party shall be entitled to recover reasonable attorney's fees and costs incurred in enforcing this agreement."

Jurisdiction Retained for Enforcement

Explicitly state that the court retains jurisdiction to enforce the settlement terms. This prevents defendants from arguing that the court lacks power to enforce the agreement after case dismissal.

Default Remedies and Interest

Specify what constitutes default (e.g., payment more than 10 days late) and the consequences, including interest rates on unpaid amounts. Consider including an acceleration clause that makes the entire remaining balance due upon default.

20.2 Enforcing Judgments

Initial Steps: The Paper Trail

Obtaining Certified Copies

A certified copy of the judgment is required for enforcement. This document, bearing the court clerk's seal, proves the existence and terms of the judgment. Order multiple certified copies initially, as you'll need them for various enforcement actions.

Recording the Judgment

Recording requirements vary by jurisdiction:

- **California**: Record with the county recorder in any county where the debtor owns real property
- **New York**: File a transcript of judgment with the county clerk to create a judgment lien
- **Federal**: May require domestication in state court for certain enforcement actions

Service Requirements

Most jurisdictions require notice to the judgment debtor before beginning enforcement. This notice informs the debtor of their rights and provides an opportunity for voluntary compliance before more aggressive collection methods.

Time Limits and Interest Accrual

Grace Periods

Some jurisdictions provide a brief grace period before enforcement may begin. California allows 30 days from entry of judgment before most enforcement remedies become available. This period allows debtors to arrange payment or seek appellate relief.

Interest Rates and Compounding

Unpaid judgments accrue interest at statutory rates:

- **California**: 10% simple interest per year (Code of Civil Procedure Section 685.010)
- **New York**: 9% per year (CPLR Section 5004)
- **Federal Court**: Based on weekly Treasury yield under 28 U.S.C. Section 1961

Interest compounds substantial value over time. A $100,000 judgment earning 10% annual interest becomes $110,000 after one year and $121,000 after two years. Use accruing interest as leverage in settlement negotiations.

20.3 Collection Tools and Remedies

Wage Garnishment: The Steady Stream

Federal Framework

The Consumer Credit Protection Act limits wage garnishment to 25% of disposable earnings or the amount by which weekly earnings exceed 30 times the federal minimum wage, whichever is less. "Disposable earnings" means gross wages minus legally required deductions (taxes, Social Security, unemployment insurance).

State Variations

While federal law sets the maximum, states may provide greater protection to debtors:

- **California**: CCP Sections 706.010 et seq. generally follow federal limits but provide additional exemptions for low-income earners
- **New York**: CPLR Article 52 allows garnishment of up to 10% of gross

wages or 25% of disposable income, whichever is less

Practical Considerations

Wage garnishment provides steady, predictable collection but faces several limitations. The employer becomes a third party to the collection process and may resist compliance. Additionally, high-level executives often structure compensation to minimize garnishable wages, receiving income through stock options, deferred compensation, or consulting agreements.

Bank Levies: The Quick Strike

Bank levies allow immediate seizure of funds from the judgment debtor's accounts. Success requires precise identification of the bank and account holder name. The levy freezes the account balance as of the service date, but subsequent deposits may not be captured.

Execution Process

1. Obtain writ of execution from the court
2. Serve the writ on the bank with precise account information
3. Bank freezes account and reports balance to court
4. After statutory waiting period, funds are released to creditor

Exemptions and Challenges

Certain funds may be exempt from levy, including Social Security benefits, disability payments, and funds deposited within specific timeframes before levy. Debtors can challenge levies by claiming exemptions or asserting that seized funds are not their property.

Liens: The Long-Term Strategy

Real Property Liens

Judgment liens create security interests in the debtor's real property. While they don't provide immediate payment, they prevent property sale or refinancing without satisfying the judgment.

Recording Requirements

- **California**: Record abstract of judgment with the county recorder

(CCP Section 697.310)

- **New York**: File transcript of judgment with county clerk to create lien (CPLR Section 5203)

Priority and Duration

Judgment liens generally have priority from the date of recording. They may last 10 years or more, depending on state law, and can often be renewed. Property liens are particularly effective against businesses that may need to refinance or sell real estate.

Personal Property Liens

Some states allow liens on personal property, vehicles, or business assets. These require different recording procedures and may have shorter duration periods than real property liens.

Asset Seizure: The Nuclear Option

Asset seizure involves physical taking of the debtor's non-exempt property for sale at public auction. This remedy is expensive, time-consuming, and often yields disappointing results due to exemptions and the difficulty of selling seized property.

Exempt Property

Substantial property categories are exempt from seizure:

- Primary residence (up to statutory limits)
- Necessary household goods and clothing
- Tools of trade or profession
- One motor vehicle (up to value limits)
- Retirement accounts and life insurance

Business Assets

Commercial debtors face fewer exemptions, making asset seizure more viable against business entities. Inventory, equipment, and accounts receivable may all be subject to seizure, though practical challenges remain significant.

Turnover Motions: Court-Ordered Compliance

Turnover motions seek direct court orders requiring the judgment debtor to surrender specific property or funds. These are particularly effective against liquid assets like bank accounts, accounts receivable, or commissions.

Advantages Over Traditional Seizure

Turnover motions avoid the sheriff's department and auction process, allowing direct transfer of assets to satisfy the judgment. They work well for intangible property that is difficult to seize physically.

Requirements and Procedure

The creditor must identify specific property and demonstrate the debtor's ability to comply. Courts may require posting of bonds and provide debtors with exemption hearings before ordering turnover.

20.4 Contempt and Sanctions for Noncompliance

Civil Contempt: Coercive Power

When parties refuse to comply with settlement agreements or court orders, civil contempt provides a powerful enforcement tool. Unlike criminal contempt (which punishes past conduct), civil contempt is coercive - designed to compel future compliance.

Motion Practice

A contempt motion must establish:

1. A clear and unambiguous court order
2. Knowledge of the order by the alleged contemnor
3. Violation of the order's terms
4. The violation was willful or without adequate excuse

Remedies Available

Courts may impose:

- Coercive daily fines until compliance occurs
- Attorney's fees and costs for bringing the motion
- In extreme cases, incarceration until compliance (though this is rare in civil matters)

Federal Rule 70 and State Equivalents

These rules support enforcement of judgments requiring specific acts rather than monetary payments. For example, if a court orders employee reinstatement or policy changes, Rule 70 allows the court to direct that the acts be performed by a third party at the defendant's expense if the defendant fails to comply.

Strategic Considerations

Contempt proceedings can escalate conflicts and should be used judiciously. They work best when the debtor has clear ability to comply but is choosing not to do so. Against truly insolvent debtors, contempt may be counterproductive.

20.5 Government Agency Enforcement

Federal Department of Labor

The U.S. Department of Labor provides enforcement support in cases involving:

- **Fair Labor Standards Act violations** (unpaid overtime, minimum wage)
- **Worker misclassification** under federal standards
- **Family and Medical Leave Act** violations

The DOL can pursue collection independently of private counsel, using administrative remedies not available to private parties. This includes administrative wage garnishments that bypass court proceedings.

California Division of Labor Standards Enforcement (DLSE)

The California Labor Commissioner's Office provides robust enforcement support for wage and hour violations. The DLSE can:

- Issue citations with civil penalties
- Place liens on employer property
- Pursue criminal prosecution for willful violations
- Collect unpaid wages through administrative procedures

Advantages of Agency Enforcement

Government agencies have collection tools unavailable to private parties, including administrative garnishment, tax intercepts, and license suspension. They also have unlimited resources compared to individual plaintiffs.

Coordination with Private Counsel

Private attorneys should coordinate with government agencies to avoid conflicting collection efforts. Some agencies may require assignment of collection rights, while others work cooperatively with private counsel.

New York Department of Labor

The New York DOL Division of Labor Standards enforces state wage and hour laws through:

- Administrative hearings and determinations
- Wage liens against employer property
- Criminal referrals for willful violations
- Collective enforcement actions for pattern violators

20.6 Post-Judgment Discovery

Debtor's Examination: Information Gathering

Post-judgment discovery allows creditors to investigate the debtor's assets, income, and financial condition. The primary tool is the debtor's examination - a court-ordered deposition of the judgment debtor.

Scope of Examination

Creditors may inquire about:

- All assets owned by the debtor
- Income sources and amounts
- Bank accounts and financial institutions
- Recent asset transfers
- Business relationships and partnerships
- Pending lawsuits or claims

Procedural Requirements

- **California**: CCP Section 708.110 requires court order and reasonable notice
- **New York**: CPLR Section 5224 allows examination of debtor and third parties

Compelling Attendance

Debtors who fail to appear for examination may be held in contempt. Some jurisdictions allow body attachments (arrest warrants) for non-appearance, though this remedy is used sparingly.

Third-Party Discovery

Subpoenas to Financial Institutions

Banks, credit unions, and investment firms can be subpoenaed to produce account records and transaction histories. This discovery often reveals hidden assets or recent transfers.

Information Subpoenas (New York)

CPLR Section 5224 allows service of information subpoenas on third parties with knowledge of the debtor's financial condition. This includes accountants, business partners, and vendors.

Practical Limitations

Financial institutions often charge substantial fees for record production. Additionally, bank secrecy laws and privacy regulations may limit the scope of discoverable information.

20.7 Interest and Costs on Judgments

Interest Rate Comparison

California: 10% simple interest per year (CCP Section 685.010)

- Highest rate among major jurisdictions
- Simple interest calculation (no compounding)
- Applies from date of judgment entry

New York: 9% per year (CPLR Section 5004)

- Moderate rate providing reasonable compensation
- Annual compounding in some circumstances
- May be adjusted by court in exceptional cases

Federal Court: Based on weekly Treasury yield (28 U.S.C. Section 1961)

- Fluctuates with market conditions
- Generally lower than state rates
- Updated weekly by Administrative Office of Courts

Strategic Use of Interest

Accruing interest becomes a powerful settlement tool. A $200,000 California judgment grows by $20,000 annually, creating increasing pressure for resolution. Calculate total exposure including interest when presenting settlement demands.

Recoverable Costs

Beyond interest, creditors may recover:

- Filing fees for enforcement motions
- Service of process costs
- Sheriff's fees for levies and seizures
- Court reporter fees for examinations
- Attorney's fees (if provided by statute or agreement)

20.8 Challenges in Enforcement

Asset Protection Schemes

Entity Manipulation

Sophisticated debtors may attempt to frustrate collection through:

- **Shell corporations** with minimal assets
- **Asset transfers** to related entities
- **Business dissolution** followed by reformation under new names
- **Offshore entities** to hide assets beyond easy reach

Fraudulent Transfer Laws

Both state and federal law provide remedies against fraudulent transfers. The Uniform Fraudulent Transfer Act (adopted by most states) allows creditors to void transfers made to hinder collection efforts.

Piercing the Corporate Veil

When individual defendants hide behind corporate entities, piercing the corporate veil may allow collection from personal assets. This requires showing:

- Inadequate capitalization of the corporation
- Failure to observe corporate formalities
- Commingling of personal and corporate assets
- Use of the corporation to perpetrate fraud

Judgment-Proof Defendants

Recognizing Insolvency

Some defendants legitimately lack assets to satisfy judgments. Warning signs include:

- Recent bankruptcy filings
- Multiple judgments from other creditors
- Unemployment or minimal income
- Rental housing with no real property ownership

Strategies for Insolvent Debtors

Even judgment-proof defendants may become collectible over time. Consider:

- Extended payment plans within debtor's means
- Future income garnishment when employment improves
- Asset monitoring for inheritance or windfalls
- Settlement for partial payment to avoid collection costs

Bankruptcy Complications

Automatic Stay

Bankruptcy filing triggers an automatic stay that halts all collection activities. Violation of the stay can result in sanctions against the creditor.

Discharge and Exceptions

Most employment judgments are dischargeable in bankruptcy, but exceptions exist for:

- Willful and malicious injury
- Fraud or embezzlement
- Certain employment-related fines and penalties

Preference Recovery

Payments received within 90 days before bankruptcy filing may be recoverable by the trustee as preferences. This risk should be considered when negotiating payment terms with financially distressed debtors.

20.9 Negotiating Payment Terms

Installment Plans: Practical Solutions

Structuring Payments

When debtors cannot pay lump sums, installment plans provide practical alternatives. Key considerations include:

- **Payment amount** realistic for debtor's income
- **Payment frequency** (monthly, quarterly, annual)
- **Total payment period** balancing collection speed with debtor capacity
- **Security provisions** to protect against default

Acceleration Clauses

Include provisions making the entire balance due upon default. Sample language: "If Debtor fails to make any payment when due and such failure continues for ten (10) days after written notice, the entire unpaid balance shall become immediately due and payable."

Personal Guarantees

For corporate debtors, consider requiring personal guarantees from principals. This provides additional collection sources and demonstrates commitment to the payment plan.

Structured Settlements: Tax and Timing Considerations

Periodic Payment Benefits

Structured settlements involving periodic payments may provide:

- **Tax advantages** through spreading income recognition
- **Investment growth** potential for deferred payments
- **Collection certainty** through funding with annuities or bonds

Funding Mechanisms

Structured settlements typically involve:

- **Qualified assignment** to specialty companies
- **Annuity purchases** providing guaranteed payments
- **Trust arrangements** for asset protection

Employment Law Considerations

Employment settlements face unique tax issues that affect structuring decisions. Legal damages may be excludable from income, while punitive awards are generally taxable. Consider these factors when negotiating payment terms.

20.10 Advanced Enforcement Strategies

Multi-Jurisdictional Enforcement

Sister State Judgments

The Full Faith and Credit Clause requires states to recognize sister state judgments. However, enforcement procedures vary significantly between states, requiring local counsel familiar with collection practices.

International Enforcement

Collecting against international defendants presents substantial challenges:

- **Treaty requirements** for judgment recognition
- **Foreign asset protection** laws favoring debtors
- **Currency and political risks** affecting collection value
- **Higher costs** often exceeding judgment amounts

Technology and Asset Discovery

Digital Asset Tracing

Modern enforcement increasingly involves digital assets:

- **Cryptocurrency holdings** requiring specialized investigation
- **Online business revenues** from e-commerce and digital services
- **Social media evidence** revealing hidden assets or lifestyle inconsistent with claimed poverty

Professional Investigation Services

Consider engaging professional asset investigation services for complex cases. These services can:

- Locate hidden bank accounts and investments
- Trace asset transfers to related parties
- Identify income sources not apparent from basic discovery
- Provide ongoing monitoring for asset acquisition

Ethical Considerations in Enforcement

Professional Responsibility

Attorneys must balance zealous advocacy with ethical obligations:

- **Truthfulness** in representations to courts and opposing parties
- **Proportionality** in enforcement methods relative to judgment amounts
- **Client counseling** regarding costs and likelihood of collection success

Harassment and Abuse

Enforcement activities must not cross the line into harassment. The Fair Debt Collection Practices Act applies to attorney collection activities, requiring:

- **Reasonable communication** timing and frequency

- **Accurate representations** about legal rights and remedies
- **Proper validation** of debt amounts and legal basis

20.11 Conclusion

Enforcing a judgment or settlement is about turning paper victories into real-world justice. With the right combination of procedural tools, asset tracing, and strategic leverage, employment attorneys can ensure that their clients receive not just a favorable ruling - but the compensation they are owed.

The enforcement process requires patience, creativity, and persistent effort. No single remedy works in every case, and successful collection often requires multiple approaches tailored to the specific debtor's circumstances. The key is understanding the full range of available tools and applying them strategically based on the debtor's assets, income, and sophistication level.

Remember that enforcement is not just about collecting money - it's about preserving the integrity of the legal system and maintaining your client's trust in the justice process. A judgment without collection is merely an expensive piece of paper. Effective enforcement transforms legal victories into meaningful relief for wronged employees.

Never underestimate the importance of vigilant enforcement in preserving the integrity of the legal system and your client's trust. The most brilliant legal strategy and compelling trial advocacy mean nothing if the client never receives their compensation.

In Chapter 21, we'll explore the tax implications of employment settlements, including how to allocate damages and structure agreements to minimize tax burdens for clients.

21

Tax Implications of Employment Settlements and Judgments

Securing compensation for your client represents a major victory in employment litigation - but how that compensation is taxed can dramatically affect the final outcome and your client's satisfaction with the resolution. Employment law settlements frequently involve complex combinations of back pay, front pay, emotional distress damages, civil penalties, punitive damages, and attorney's fees, each carrying distinct tax implications that can significantly impact your client's net recovery.

Poor tax planning doesn't just reduce your client's take-home amount - it can trigger IRS audits, create unexpected tax liabilities, generate disputes with state tax authorities, and potentially expose both attorney and client to professional liability claims. Understanding these tax consequences and structuring settlements appropriately has become an essential competency for employment law practitioners.

This chapter provides comprehensive guidance on the tax implications of employment case settlements and judgments across federal, New York, and California jurisdictions, with practical strategies for damage allocation, exposure minimization, and client preparation for tax consequences.

21.1 Overview: Why Tax Treatment Matters in Employment Cases

The tax treatment of settlement proceeds can vary dramatically based on the nature and characterization of damages awarded. Understanding these distinctions is crucial because different components of employment settlements are subject to entirely different tax regimes.

Key Tax Categories for Employment Settlements

Wage-Related Damages are subject to the full panoply of employment taxes, including federal and state income tax withholding, Social Security taxes (6.2% up to the wage base), Medicare taxes (1.45% on all wages, plus 0.9% additional Medicare tax on high earners), and state unemployment insurance taxes. These amounts must be reported on Form W-2 and are treated as ordinary income subject to withholding requirements.

Emotional Distress Damages occupy a complex middle ground in tax treatment. While damages for physical injuries are generally excludable from income under Internal Revenue Code Section 104(a)(2), emotional distress damages are typically taxable unless they arise from or directly result in physical injury or physical sickness with documented medical evidence.

Punitive Damages are always taxable as ordinary income under federal law, regardless of the underlying claim. This treatment stems from the policy that punitive awards are intended to punish wrongdoers rather than compensate for actual losses, making them analogous to windfall income rather than restitution.

Civil Penalties and Liquidated Damages generally receive the same tax treatment as the underlying substantive damages. For example, liquidated damages under the Fair Labor Standards Act for unpaid wages are treated as wage income, while civil penalties under anti-discrimination statutes may be treated as non-wage income.

Attorney's Fees present particularly complex tax issues. Under the traditional "gross income inclusion" rule, plaintiffs are taxed on the entire settlement amount, including portions paid directly to their attorneys.

However, the above-the-line deduction under IRC Section 62(a)(20) provides relief for many employment law claims.

The Stakes of Improper Tax Planning

Consider a wrongful termination settlement of $200,000 allocated entirely as back pay. If properly structured with appropriate allocations for emotional distress and other non-wage damages, the client might save $15,000-25,000 in employment taxes alone. Conversely, improper allocation can trigger IRS scrutiny, state tax audits, and potential penalties for both under-withholding and misreporting.

The goal is straightforward: maximize your client's net recovery while maintaining full compliance with federal and state tax obligations. This requires careful planning, proper documentation, and coordination with qualified tax professionals.

21.2 Federal Tax Framework: IRC Section 104 and Related Provisions

The foundation of settlement taxation lies in Internal Revenue Code Section 104(a)(2), which excludes from gross income "damages (other than punitive damages) received on account of personal physical injuries or physical sickness." However, this exclusion has limited application in most employment cases.

The Physical Injury Requirement

The Tax Court and federal appellate courts have consistently interpreted "personal physical injuries" narrowly. Mere emotional distress, workplace stress, anxiety, depression, or other psychological harm does not qualify for the exclusion unless it manifests in documented physical symptoms or results from an underlying physical injury.

Example: In *Domeny v. Comm'r*, T.C. Memo 2010-9 (U.S. Tax Ct. 2010), Julie Domeny, who suffered from multiple sclerosis (MS), experienced a worsening of her condition due to a hostile work environment, including stress from her supervisor's misconduct. After being terminated during a medically advised leave, she settled with her employer. The settlement included a payment of $16,933, which she excluded from her income under IRC § 104(a)(2), arguing it was compensation for physical sickness. The IRS contested this exclusion. The Tax Court ruled in favor of Domeny, finding that the settlement payment was indeed on account of her physical sickness, as her MS symptoms were exacerbated by her work environment. Therefore, the payment was excludable from gross income under IRC § 104(a)(2).

Also, in *Blackwood v. Comm'r*, T.C. Memo 2012-190, the Tax Court held that damages received for emotional distress, without physical injury, are not excludable from gross income under IRC §104(a)(2). The court emphasized that physical symptoms resulting from emotional distress do not qualify as physical injuries or sickness. In Blackwood's case, the court found that her symptoms were consistent with those typically associated with emotional distress. Moreover, she did not provide medical evidence demonstrating that her symptoms were severe enough to constitute a physical injury or sickness. Unlike in *Domeny v. Commissioner*, *supra*, where the taxpayer's multiple sclerosis was exacerbated by workplace stress and medically verified, Blackwood lacked such corroborating medical documentation.

Taxability Analysis for Common Employment Damages

Back Pay and Front Pay are always taxable as wage income because they represent compensation for services that would have been performed. These amounts are subject to income tax withholding, FICA taxes, and unemployment insurance contributions. The timing of tax liability generally occurs when the settlement is paid, not when the wages would have been earned.

Emotional Distress Without Physical Manifestation is taxable as ordinary income under IRC Section 104(a)(2). This includes damages for humiliation, mental anguish, loss of reputation, and psychological harm that doesn't result in documented physical symptoms. Such damages are typically reported on Form 1099-MISC.

Emotional Distress With Physical Symptoms may be partially or wholly excludable if the physical symptoms are documented through medical evidence and directly caused by the workplace conduct. The key is establishing causation between the discriminatory conduct and specific, diagnosed physical ailments.

Punitive Damages are explicitly excluded from the Section 104(a)(2) exclusion and are always taxable, regardless of the underlying claim.

This includes both common law punitive damages and statutory penalty provisions designed to punish rather than compensate.

Interest on Judgments or Delayed Payments is taxable as ordinary income and must be reported separately, typically on Form 1099-INT. This applies even if the underlying damages might otherwise be excludable.

21.3 Strategic Settlement Structuring for Optimal Tax Treatment

Proper settlement structuring begins during negotiations and requires careful attention to damage allocation, payment mechanics, and reporting requirements. The IRS and courts generally respect parties' reasonable, good-faith allocations of settlement proceeds among different damage categories.

Fundamental Structuring Principles

Explicit Damage Allocation is essential in every settlement agreement. Rather than accepting a lump-sum payment "for all claims," the agreement should specify precise dollar amounts for each category of damages. This allocation should reflect the actual nature of the claim, the evidence presented, and the parties' good-faith assessment of damages in each category.

Sample Allocation Language:

> The parties agree that the $150,000 settlement payment represents compensation as follows:- Lost wages and benefits: $75,000- Emotional distress damages: $50,000- Liquidated damages under FLSA: $25,000

Avoiding Lump-Sum Characterization prevents the IRS from treating the entire settlement as wage income subject to employment tax withholding. Courts have repeatedly held that undifferentiated lump-sum settlements will be characterized based on the nature of the underlying claims, often resulting in less favorable tax treatment.

Distinguishing W-2 vs. 1099 Payments requires careful coordination with the defendant's payroll and tax reporting systems. Wage components must be processed through payroll with appropriate withholding, while non-wage components should be reported on Form 1099-MISC without withholding.

Documentation and Negotiation Strategies

The reasonableness of damage allocations depends on supporting documentation developed during litigation. Emotional distress allocations should be supported by medical records, therapy records, expert testimony, or other evidence of psychological harm. Wage loss calculations should be documented through employment records, expert economic testimony, and mitigation evidence.

Negotiation Tip: Defendants often prefer larger emotional distress allocations because they avoid employment tax obligations on the employer's side. This creates opportunities for win-win structuring that benefits both parties' tax positions.

Example: In a $100,000 discrimination settlement, allocating $40,000 to emotional distress saves the employer approximately $3,060 in FICA taxes (7.65% employer portion) while potentially saving the employee $3,060 in FICA taxes plus reducing income tax withholding obligations.

21.4 Withholding, Reporting, and Payment Mechanics

The mechanics of settlement payments require careful coordination between legal counsel, the defendant's payroll systems, and tax reporting requirements. Improper payment processing can negate careful tax planning and create compliance problems for all parties.

W-2 Reporting Requirements

Scope of W-2 Treatment: Back pay, front pay, vacation pay, severance pay, and other wage substitutes must be processed through the defendant's payroll system with standard withholding requirements. This includes federal and state income tax withholding, Social Security taxes (6.2% up to the annual wage base), Medicare taxes (1.45% on all amounts), and state unemployment insurance taxes where applicable.

Timing Considerations: W-2 income is generally taxable in the year received, not the year originally earned. This can create bunching problems where multiple years of back pay are received in a single tax year, potentially pushing the plaintiff into higher tax brackets.

Withholding Calculations: Payroll systems typically calculate withholding based on the assumption that the settlement payment represents regular periodic wages, which can result in over-withholding. Plaintiffs may need to file for refunds or adjust withholding on other income sources.

1099 Reporting for Non-Wage Damages

Categories Subject to 1099 Reporting: Emotional distress damages, punitive damages, civil penalties (in most cases), and interest payments must be reported on Form 1099-MISC. The defendant must provide copies to both the plaintiff and the IRS by January 31 following the payment year.

No Withholding Requirements: Unlike W-2 payments, amounts reported on 1099-MISC are not subject to withholding. This means plaintiffs receiving substantial 1099 income may need to make estimated quarterly tax payments to avoid underpayment penalties.

Multiple 1099s: Complex settlements may require multiple 1099 forms. For example, interest payments are reported on Form 1099-INT, while other non-wage damages are reported on Form 1099-MISC.

Split Payment Strategies

Separate Checks Approach: Many practitioners prefer having defendants issue separate checks for different damage categories. This approach provides clear documentation of the allocation and simplifies tax reporting for all parties.

Sample Payment Structure:

- Check #1 to plaintiff: Net wage damages after withholding (with W-2)
- Check #2 to plaintiff: Emotional distress damages (with 1099-MISC)
- Check #3 to plaintiff's attorney: Attorney's fees (with 1099-MISC to

attorney)

Direct Payment to Attorneys: When attorney's fees are paid directly to counsel, the defendant typically issues a 1099-MISC to the attorney rather than the client. This can simplify the client's tax situation but requires careful coordination with fee reporting requirements.

21.5 Attorney's Fees: The Gross Income Inclusion Problem and Solutions

The taxation of attorney's fees in contingent fee cases presents one of the most complex areas of settlement tax planning. Understanding these rules is essential for proper client counseling and avoiding unexpected tax liabilities.

The Traditional Gross Income Inclusion Rule

Under traditional tax principles, plaintiffs are taxed on the entire settlement amount, including portions paid directly to their attorneys under contingent fee arrangements. This rule treats the attorney as the plaintiff's agent, making the full recovery taxable to the plaintiff even though the attorney receives a portion directly.

Example: Client receives a $200,000 settlement with a 40% contingent fee. Under the gross income inclusion rule, the client is taxed on the full $200,000 even though they only receive $120,000. The client may then deduct the $80,000 attorney's fee, but this deduction was historically subject to the 2% miscellaneous itemized deduction floor and alternative minimum tax limitations.

The Section 62(a)(20) Above-the-Line Deduction

The American Jobs Creation Act of 2004 added IRC Section 62(a)(20), providing an above-the-line deduction for attorney's fees in certain civil rights and employment law cases. This deduction is particularly valuable because it reduces adjusted gross income and is not subject to itemized deduction limitations.

Qualifying Claims: The deduction applies to claims under:

- Civil rights statutes (Title VII, Section 1983, Americans with Disabilities Act)

- Whistleblower protection laws (Sarbanes-Oxley, False Claims Act)
- Fair Labor Standards Act and other wage and hour laws
- Most state employment discrimination and retaliation statutes

Scope of Deduction: The deduction is limited to the amount of attorney's fees actually paid or incurred and cannot exceed the amount of judgment or settlement includible in gross income for the taxable year.

Best Practices for Fee Allocation

Explicit Fee Provisions in Settlement Agreements should specify not only the total attorney's fee amount but also the legal basis for the fee award. This documentation supports the Section 62(a)(20) deduction and provides clarity for tax reporting.

Sample Fee Language:

> Defendant shall pay Plaintiff's counsel attorney's fees in the amount of $60,000, representing reasonable attorney's fees incurred in prosecuting claims under Title VII of the Civil Rights Act of 1964, as amended.

Separate Fee Payments can simplify tax reporting by having the defendant pay attorney's fees directly to counsel with a separate 1099-MISC. This approach doesn't change the underlying tax treatment but provides cleaner documentation.

Client Tax Planning: Clients should be advised to work with tax professionals when attorney's fees constitute a substantial portion of the settlement. The interaction between the gross income inclusion rule, the Section 62(a)(20) deduction, and other tax provisions can be complex.

21.6 Emotional Distress Damages: The Physical Injury Exception

Emotional distress damages represent a significant component of many employment settlements, but their tax treatment depends critically on whether they arise from or result in physical injury or physical sickness.

The Narrow Physical Injury Exception

The Tax Court has interpreted the "personal physical injuries" requirement of IRC Section 104(a)(2) restrictively. Purely emotional or psychological harm, regardless of its severity, does not qualify for the income exclusion unless it manifests in documented physical symptoms.

Qualifying Physical Manifestations have been recognized in cases involving:

- Documented stress-induced ulcers with medical evidence
- Migraines caused by workplace harassment with physician treatment records
- Sleep disorders resulting from discrimination with sleep study documentation
- Hypertension caused by workplace retaliation with medical monitoring records

Non-Qualifying Emotional Harm includes:

- Anxiety and depression without physical symptoms
- Loss of reputation or professional standing
- Humiliation or mental anguish
- Post-traumatic stress disorder without documented physical manifestations

Documentation Requirements for Physical Symptoms

To support the income exclusion for emotional distress damages that result in physical symptoms, practitioners should develop comprehensive medical evidence during the litigation process.

Essential Documentation:

- Contemporary medical records showing diagnosis and treatment of physical symptoms

- Physician statements linking physical symptoms to workplace conduct
- Treatment records demonstrating ongoing medical intervention
- Expert medical testimony establishing causation between discrimination and physical harm

Timing Considerations: Medical evidence should ideally document physical symptoms arising during or shortly after the discriminatory conduct. Symptoms that develop long after the workplace events may be more difficult to link causally to the employment-related harm.

Strategic Considerations for Emotional Distress Allocations

Reasonable Allocation Requirements: Settlement allocations for emotional distress must be reasonable in relation to the evidence presented. Allocating 90% of a settlement to emotional distress in a straightforward wage and hour case would likely be rejected by the IRS as unreasonable.

Defendant's Perspective: Defendants may be more willing to agree to larger emotional distress allocations because they typically don't affect the defendant's tax position. This creates opportunities for beneficial tax planning that serves both parties' interests.

State Law Variations: Some state employment statutes provide specific damages for emotional distress or mental anguish. Understanding these statutory frameworks can support reasonable allocation arguments.

21.7 Punitive Damages, Civil Penalties, and Interest

Certain categories of employment settlement proceeds are always taxable under federal law, regardless of the underlying circumstances or damage allocation strategies.

Punitive Damages

Universal Taxability: IRC Section 104(a)(2) explicitly excludes punitive damages from the personal injury exclusion. This means punitive damages are always taxable as ordinary income, whether awarded under federal civil rights statutes, state discrimination laws, or common law theories.

Statutory vs. Common Law Punitive Damages: The taxability rule applies equally to traditional punitive damages and statutory penalty provisions designed to punish discriminatory conduct. For example, liquidated damages under the Age Discrimination in Employment Act are treated as punitive damages for tax purposes.

Allocation Strategies: While punitive damages are always taxable, proper allocation can still provide benefits by ensuring appropriate 1099 reporting rather than W-2 treatment with additional employment taxes.

Civil Penalties and Liquidated Damages

The tax treatment of civil penalties and liquidated damages depends on their underlying purpose and statutory framework.

Wage-Related Penalties: Liquidated damages under the Fair Labor Standards Act are generally treated as additional wage income because they're directly tied to unpaid wages. These amounts are subject to employment tax withholding and W-2 reporting.

Punitive Civil Penalties: Statutory penalties designed to punish discrimination or retaliation are typically treated as non-wage income subject to 1099 reporting. Examples include civil penalties under state fair employment laws or federal whistleblower statutes.

Compensatory Civil Penalties: Some statutory penalties are designed to compensate for actual harm rather than punish wrongdoing. These may receive more favorable tax treatment depending on their specific purpose and documentation.

Interest on Judgments and Delayed Payments

Taxability: Interest awarded on judgments or paid on delayed settlement amounts is always taxable as ordinary income, regardless of the tax treatment of the underlying damages. This interest must be reported separately on Form 1099-INT.

Calculation and Allocation: Settlement agreements should specify the interest amount separately from principal damages to ensure proper tax reporting. Post-judgment interest rates are typically set by statute and can be calculated from the judgment date to the payment date.

Strategic Timing: In some cases, accelerated settlement payments can reduce interest obligations and simplify tax reporting, providing benefits to both parties.

21.8 State-Specific Tax Considerations

While federal tax principles provide the foundation for settlement taxation, state tax laws can create additional complexities and opportunities for tax planning.

California State Tax Treatment

Federal Conformity: California generally conforms to federal tax treatment of personal injury damages under IRC Section 104(a)(2). Damages excludable under federal law are typically also excludable for California state income tax purposes.

Section 62(a)(20) Recognition: California recognizes the federal above-the-line deduction for attorney's fees under IRC Section 62(a)(20), providing the same benefits for state tax purposes as federal taxation.

Franchise Tax Board Scrutiny: The California Franchise Tax Board has been particularly aggressive in auditing settlement allocations, especially in high-value cases. Detailed documentation supporting damage allocations is essential for California taxpayers.

Employment Tax Considerations: California's State Disability Insurance (SDI) tax applies to wage income, including back pay and front pay awards. The 2024 SDI rate is 0.9% on wages up to $153,164, adding another layer of employment tax on wage-characterized settlement proceeds.

Unique California Issues:

- California's higher individual income tax rates increase the value of proper tax planning
- Community property laws can affect the taxation of settlement proceeds for married taxpayers

- California's aggressive enforcement posture requires particularly careful documentation

New York State Tax Treatment

Federal Conformity: New York generally follows federal tax treatment for personal injury damages and employment settlements. Amounts excludable under IRC Section 104(a)(2) are typically also excludable for New York state income tax purposes.

Section 62(a)(20) Conformity: New York conforms to the federal above-the-line deduction for attorney's fees, providing parallel benefits for state tax purposes.

Withholding Requirements: New York requires withholding on wage income, including back pay and front pay awards. The state withholding rates depend on the employee's withholding allowances and filing status.

Local Tax Considerations: New York City and Yonkers impose additional local income taxes that apply to settlement proceeds. These taxes can add 3-4% to the effective tax rate for city residents.

Unique New York Issues:

- New York's relatively high state income tax rates make tax planning particularly valuable
- The state's detailed wage and hour laws can affect the characterization of certain settlement components
- New York's whistleblower statutes may provide specific protections affecting tax treatment

Multi-State Considerations

Domicile vs. Workplace: Plaintiffs may be subject to tax in their state of domicile, the state where they worked, or both. Settlement agreements should consider these multi-state tax implications.

Withholding Obligations: Defendants must typically withhold taxes based on the state where the work was performed, but employees may need to file returns in multiple states.

Professional Advice: Multi-state tax issues are particularly complex and typically require coordination with tax professionals familiar with interstate tax obligations.

21.9 Advanced Tax Planning Strategies

Sophisticated employment settlements may benefit from advanced tax planning techniques that go beyond basic damage allocation strategies.

Structured Settlements and Annual Payments

Concept: Rather than receiving a lump-sum payment, structured settlements provide for payments over multiple years, potentially reducing the overall tax burden by spreading income across multiple tax years and avoiding bracket compression.

Advantages:

- Spreading income across multiple tax years can reduce marginal tax rates
- Provides steady income stream for plaintiffs
- Can reduce estimated tax payment obligations
- May provide some protection against plaintiff's spending or investment mistakes

Disadvantages:

- Reduces present value of settlement proceeds
- Creates ongoing compliance and reporting obligations
- May be complicated by changes in tax law
- Requires sophisticated actuarial calculations

Practical Considerations: Structured settlements work best in high-value cases where the tax savings justify the complexity and reduced present value. They require specialized insurance products and careful drafting to ensure compliance with tax requirements.

Qualified Settlement Funds

Purpose: Qualified Settlement Funds (QSFs) under IRC Section 468B provide a mechanism for holding settlement proceeds while resolving allocation and distribution issues. They're particularly useful in class action employment cases or cases with multiple plaintiffs.

Benefits:

- Allows time to develop optimal tax allocation strategies
- Provides flexibility for staggered distributions
- Can simplify complex multi-plaintiff settlements
- May provide administrative advantages for defendants

Requirements:

- Must be established pursuant to court order or government decree
- Requires ongoing tax filings and compliance
- Limited to cases involving multiple claimants or complex distribution issues

Tax-Deferred Investment Strategies

Individual Retirement Account Contributions: Settlement proceeds may provide opportunities for maximizing retirement account contributions, particularly for plaintiffs who haven't been working during litigation.

Tax-Loss Harvesting: Plaintiffs receiving substantial settlements may benefit from coordinating with existing investment portfolios to optimize overall tax positions.

Charitable Giving Strategies: Large settlements may create opportunities for charitable deduction planning, particularly for plaintiffs interested in giving back to advocacy organizations or legal aid societies.

21.10 Practical Implementation Guidelines

Successful tax planning in employment settlements requires systematic attention to documentation, coordination, and client communication throughout the litigation and settlement process.

Early Planning Strategies

Discovery and Damage Development: Tax planning should begin during the discovery phase as damages are developed and quantified. Understanding the likely tax treatment of different damage categories can inform negotiation strategies and settlement priorities.

Expert Witness Coordination: Economic experts calculating damages should understand tax implications and be prepared to support reasonable allocations among different damage categories.

Medical Evidence Development: For cases involving emotional distress claims, early coordination with treating physicians can help develop medical evidence supporting physical symptom documentation.

Settlement Negotiation Integration

Defendant Education: Many defendants and their counsel are unfamiliar with employment settlement tax issues. Educating opposing counsel about tax benefits that serve both parties' interests can facilitate more creative settlement structures.

Joint Tax Planning: In appropriate cases, parties may benefit from joint consultation with tax professionals to develop structures that optimize both parties' tax positions.

Implementation Coordination: Settlement agreements should include specific provisions for payment processing, tax reporting, and coordination between parties' payroll and accounting systems.

Client Communication and Preparation

Early Tax Counseling: Clients should be advised about potential tax consequences early in the litigation process, not just at settlement. This allows for informed decision-making about litigation strategies and settlement priorities.

Estimated Tax Planning: Clients receiving substantial 1099 income may need to make quarterly estimated tax payments to avoid underpayment penalties. This planning should begin immediately after settlement execution.

Professional Referrals: Complex tax issues require coordination with qualified tax professionals. Employment attorneys should develop relationships with CPAs and tax attorneys experienced in settlement taxation.

Documentation and Record-Keeping

Settlement Agreement Provisions: Tax allocation provisions should be detailed, specific, and supported by the litigation record. Generic or boilerplate language should be avoided.

Supporting Documentation: Settlement files should include all documentation supporting tax allocations, including medical records, economic analyses, and expert reports.

Client File Maintenance: Settlement tax issues may arise years after case resolution during IRS audits or state tax examinations. Maintaining comprehensive files is essential for ongoing client support.

21.11 Common Pitfalls and Risk Management

Even experienced employment practitioners can encounter significant tax-related problems in settlement cases. Understanding common pitfalls and implementing risk management strategies is essential for protecting both clients and practitioners.

Frequent Structuring Mistakes

Inadequate Damage Allocation: The most common mistake is failing to provide detailed, reasonable allocations among different damage categories. Lump-sum settlements without allocation invite IRS scrutiny and often result in less favorable tax treatment.

Unreasonable Allocations: While parties have significant flexibility in allocating settlement proceeds, allocations must be reasonable in relation to the evidence and legal theories presented. Aggressive allocations that can't be supported by the litigation record may be challenged by tax authorities.

Withholding Coordination Failures: Failing to coordinate with defendants' payroll systems can result in improper withholding, incorrect tax reporting, or administrative complications that delay settlement payments.

Documentation Deficiencies: Insufficient documentation supporting tax allocations can create problems during subsequent audits or examinations, potentially years after settlement.

Professional Liability Considerations

Scope of Representation: Employment attorneys should clearly define the scope of their representation regarding tax issues. While attorneys can and should provide general guidance about tax implications, complex tax planning typically requires coordination with tax professionals.

Malpractice Prevention: Proper tax planning and client counseling can prevent significant financial harm to clients. Conversely, failing to address obvious tax issues or providing incorrect tax advice can create malpractice exposure.

Documentation of Advice: All tax-related advice and recommendations should be documented in client files, including referrals to tax professionals and limitations on the scope of legal representation.

Audit Defense Preparation

IRS Audit Triggers: Certain factors increase the likelihood of IRS scrutiny, including large settlements, significant emotional distress allocations, substantial attorney's fee deductions, and inconsistent reporting between parties.

Audit Documentation: Settlement files should be maintained with audit defense in mind, including all supporting documentation for tax allocations and clear explanations of the legal and factual basis for settlement terms.

Professional Coordination: Audit defense often requires coordination between employment counsel, tax professionals, and sometimes additional specialists. Establishing these relationships before they're needed is preferable.

21.12 Emerging Issues and Recent Developments

The taxation of employment settlements continues to evolve through new legislation, administrative guidance, and judicial decisions. Staying current with these developments is essential for effective practice.

Legislative Developments

Tax Cuts and Jobs Act Impact: The 2017 Tax Cuts and Jobs Act eliminated or restricted many itemized deductions, making the Section 62(a)(20) above-the-line deduction for attorney's fees even more valuable. The Act also increased standard deductions, potentially affecting the value of various tax planning strategies.

State Legislative Changes: Many states have enacted or are considering legislation affecting the taxation of settlement proceeds, particularly in the areas of whistleblower protections and civil rights enforcement.

Administrative Guidance

IRS Guidance Updates: The IRS periodically issues revenue rulings, private letter rulings, and technical advice memoranda addressing specific settlement taxation issues. Recent guidance has focused on the intersection of employment settlements with other tax provisions.

State Administrative Developments: State tax authorities continue to develop guidance on settlement taxation, often following federal principles but sometimes diverging on specific issues.

Judicial Developments

Circuit Court Decisions: Federal appellate courts continue to refine the boundaries of the personal injury exclusion and the application of various tax principles to employment settlements.

Tax Court Precedents: The Tax Court regularly addresses settlement taxation issues, providing guidance on allocation reasonableness, documentation requirements, and the application of various exclusions and deductions.

21.13 International and Cross-Border Considerations

Employment settlements involving foreign nationals, multinational employers, or international work assignments present additional tax complexities that require specialized attention.

Foreign National Plaintiffs

Tax Treaty Benefits: Foreign nationals may be entitled to reduced tax rates or other benefits under international tax treaties. These treaties can significantly affect the taxation of settlement proceeds.

Residency Determinations: The tax treatment of settlement proceeds may depend on the plaintiff's tax residency status, which can be complex for individuals with connections to multiple countries.

Withholding Requirements: Special withholding rules may apply to payments to foreign nationals, requiring coordination with defendants' international tax compliance systems.

Multinational Employer Considerations

Transfer Pricing Issues: Settlements involving multinational employers may raise transfer pricing questions if settlement payments are allocated among related entities in different countries.

Foreign Tax Credit Implications: Settlement payments may affect the employer's foreign tax credit calculations and overall international tax planning.

Cross-Border Employment

Source of Income Rules: Settlement proceeds may be subject to taxation in multiple countries depending on where the employment services were performed and where the settlement is paid.

Double Taxation Relief: International tax treaties and foreign tax credit provisions may provide relief from double taxation, but require careful planning and compliance.

21.14 Technology and Settlement Administration

Modern employment settlements increasingly rely on technology solutions for payment processing, tax reporting, and ongoing administration. Understanding these systems and their implications is important for effective settlement implementation.

Electronic Payment Systems

ACH and Wire Transfers: Electronic payment systems can provide faster, more secure settlement payments while maintaining proper documentation for tax reporting purposes.

Multi-Party Payment Platforms: Specialized platforms can facilitate complex settlement payments involving multiple recipients, different tax treatment categories, and ongoing reporting requirements.

Tax Reporting Technology

Automated 1099 Generation: Many payroll systems now provide automated generation of 1099 forms for settlement payments, reducing administrative burden while ensuring compliance.

Electronic Filing Requirements: Most tax reporting must now be filed electronically, requiring coordination with defendants' tax compliance systems.

Settlement Administration Services

Third-Party Administrators: Complex settlements may benefit from third-party administration services that handle payment processing, tax reporting, and ongoing compliance requirements.

Qualified Settlement Fund Administration: Specialized administrators can handle the complex requirements of qualified settlement funds, including ongoing tax filings and distribution management.

21.15 Conclusion and Best Practices Summary

In employment law practice, achieving favorable settlement terms represents only part of the victory - ensuring that clients retain the maximum possible amount after taxes is equally important. Poor tax structuring can reduce a plaintiff's net recovery by tens of thousands of dollars, trigger costly audits, and create long-term compliance problems that overshadow the original litigation success.

Effective settlement tax planning requires integration throughout the litigation process, from the initial damage development through the final payment. This integration involves several key principles that should guide every employment settlement.

Early Planning Integration means considering tax implications from the beginning of case development. As damages are calculated and legal are theories developed, practitioners should consider how different damage categories will be taxed and structure discovery and expert testimony accordingly. This early planning creates opportunities for beneficial settlement structuring that might not be available if tax issues are addressed only at the settlement stage.

Reasonable and Supported Allocations form the foundation of defensible settlement structures. Tax authorities generally respect parties' good-faith allocations of settlement proceeds, but those allocations must be reasonable in relation to the evidence presented and legal theories pursued. This requires careful documentation throughout litigation and thoughtful integration of tax considerations into damage development.

Professional Coordination recognizes that employment attorneys cannot and should not attempt to provide comprehensive tax advice on complex settlement structures. Successful tax planning requires coordination with qualified tax professionals who understand both the legal context of employment settlements and the intricacies of federal and state tax law.

Client Communication and Education ensures that clients understand the tax implications of settlement decisions and can make informed choices about settlement priorities. Clients should understand potential tax consequences early in the litigation process, not just at settlement, and should be connected with appropriate tax professionals when circumstances warrant.

Documentation and Risk Management protects both clients and attorneys from future problems that may arise during tax audits or compliance examinations. Proper documentation includes not only the settlement agreement itself but also all supporting materials that justify tax allocations and their treatment.

The tax landscape for employment settlements continues to evolve through legislative changes, administrative guidance, and judicial decisions. Practitioners must stay current with these developments while maintaining focus on the fundamental principles that guide effective settlement tax planning.

Most importantly, practitioners should remember that tax considerations, while important, should serve the broader goal of achieving justice for clients who have suffered employment law violations. The most sophisticated tax planning cannot substitute for achieving fair compensation for workplace wrongs, and tax strategies should enhance rather than complicate the resolution of employment disputes.

21.16 Practical Checklists and Implementation Tools

To ensure systematic application of tax planning principles in employment settlements, practitioners should utilize comprehensive checklists and standardized procedures that address all critical tax considerations.

Pre-Settlement Tax Planning Checklist

Damage Development Phase:

- [ ] Identify all potential damage categories (wages, emotional distress, punitive, etc.)
- [ ] Develop medical evidence for any physical manifestations of emotional distress
- [ ] Calculate back pay and front pay with appropriate documentation
- [ ] Determine applicable statutory penalties and their characterization
- [ ] Assess punitive damage exposure and likely tax treatment
- [ ] Document attorney's fee arrangements and applicable deduction provisions

Expert Witness Coordination:

- [ ] Brief economic experts on tax implications of different damage allocations

- [ ] Ensure medical experts can testify to physical symptoms if relevant
- [ ] Coordinate expert testimony to support reasonable settlement allocations
- [ ] Prepare experts to address tax-related cross-examination questions

Discovery Strategy:

- [ ] Obtain employment records necessary for wage loss calculations
- [ ] Develop medical records supporting physical injury claims
- [ ] Document emotional distress through therapy records, witness testimony
- [ ] Gather evidence supporting punitive damage claims
- [ ] Identify all relevant statutory penalty provisions

Settlement Negotiation Tax Checklist

Initial Settlement Discussions:

- [ ] Educate opposing counsel about mutual tax benefits of proper structuring
- [ ] Identify defendant's payroll and tax reporting capabilities
- [ ] Discuss preliminary damage allocation concepts
- [ ] Assess opportunities for structured payments or delayed distributions

Settlement Agreement Drafting:

- [ ] Include detailed allocation among all damage categories
- [ ] Specify W-2 vs. 1099 reporting for each component
- [ ] Include attorney's fee allocation and payment provisions
- [ ] Address withholding and payment timing issues

- [ ] Include coordination provisions for tax reporting

Pre-Execution Review:

- [ ] Verify reasonableness of all damage allocations
- [ ] Confirm supporting documentation exists for each allocation
- [ ] Review payment and reporting logistics with all parties
- [ ] Obtain necessary client approvals and tax acknowledgments

Post-Settlement Implementation Checklist

Payment Processing Coordination:

- [ ] Provide detailed payment instructions to defendant's payroll department
- [ ] Confirm proper W-2 vs. 1099 treatment for each payment component
- [ ] Verify correct tax withholding calculations
- [ ] Establish timeline for payment processing and tax document delivery

Client Tax Preparation:

- [ ] Advise client of estimated tax payment obligations
- [ ] Provide referral to qualified tax professional if needed
- [ ] Deliver all tax-related settlement documentation to client
- [ ] Explain record retention requirements for potential audits

Documentation and File Management:

- [ ] Maintain complete file of all supporting documentation
- [ ] Preserve expert reports and medical evidence supporting allocations
- [ ] Document all tax-related advice provided to client
- [ ] Establish system for ongoing client support during tax filing period

21.17 Settlement Agreement Tax Language Templates

Effective settlement agreements require precise language that clearly establishes tax treatment intentions while providing flexibility for implementation. The following templates provide starting points for common settlement structures.

Basic Damage Allocation Template

DAMAGE ALLOCATION AND TAX TREATMENT: The parties agree that the total settlement amount of $[AMOUNT] represents compensation allocated as follows, and that such allocation reflects the parties' good faith assessment of the nature and extent of damages in each category based on the evidence presented in this matter:

A. Lost Wages and Benefits: $[AMOUNT] This amount represents compensation for past and future lost wages, salary, bonuses, commissions, and employee benefits that Plaintiff would have received but for Defendant's conduct. This amount shall be subject to applicable payroll tax withholding and shall be reported on Form W-2.

B. Emotional Distress Damages: $[AMOUNT] This amount represents compensation for mental anguish, emotional distress, humiliation, and related psychological harm suffered by Plaintiff as a result of Defendant's conduct. [If applicable: Including compensation for documented physical symptoms resulting from such emotional distress as evidenced by the medical records of Dr. [NAME].] This amount shall be reported on Form 1099-MISC without payroll tax withholding.

C. Civil Penalties/Liquidated Damages: $[AMOUNT] This amount represents [specify statutory basis] penalties/liquidated damages under [cite relevant statute]. This amount shall be reported on Form 1099-MISC without payroll tax withholding.

D. Attorney's Fees and Costs: $[AMOUNT] This amount represents reasonable attorney's fees and costs incurred by Plaintiff in prosecuting the above-entitled matter under [cite relevant fee-shifting statutes]. This amount shall be paid directly to Plaintiff's counsel and reported on Form 1099-MISC to counsel.

The parties acknowledge that the foregoing allocation is based on their good faith assessment of the nature of the claims and damages presented in this litigation and is intended to reflect the substance of the resolution achieved.

Alternative Structured Payment Template

STRUCTURED SETTLEMENT PAYMENTS: In lieu of a lump sum payment, Defendant shall make payments to Plaintiff according to the following schedule, with each payment allocated among damage categories as specified:

Year 1: $[AMOUNT] ([breakdown by category])
Year 2: $[AMOUNT] ([breakdown by category])
Year 3: $[AMOUNT] ([breakdown by category])

Each annual payment shall be made no later than [DATE] of the respective year. Wage components shall be processed through Defendant's payroll system with appropriate withholding. Non-wage components shall be paid without withholding and reported on Form 1099-MISC.

The parties acknowledge that this structured payment approach is intended to spread the tax impact of the settlement over multiple tax years while maintaining the agreed-upon allocation of damages among categories.

Multi-Party Payment Coordination Template

PAYMENT AND REPORTING COORDINATION: Defendant shall issue settlement payments as follows:

1. To Plaintiff: $[NET AMOUNT] representing: Net wages after withholding: $[AMOUNT] Emotional distress damages: $[AMOUNT] [Other non-wage components]: $[AMOUNT]

2. To [LAW FIRM]: $[FEE AMOUNT] representing attorney's fees under [statutory authority]

3. To [TAXING AUTHORITIES]: Withheld amounts as follows: Federal income tax: $[AMOUNT] State income tax: $[AMOUNT] FICA taxes: $[AMOUNT] [Other withholding]: $[AMOUNT]

Defendant shall provide appropriate tax forms (W-2 and 1099-MISC) to all recipients by January 31 following the tax year of payment. Defendant shall coordinate with its payroll department to ensure proper processing of wage components through standard payroll systems.

21.18 Client Counseling Scripts and Communication Templates

Effective client communication about tax issues requires clear, non-technical explanations that help clients understand implications without providing specific tax advice that would fall outside the scope of legal representation.

Initial Tax Discussion Script

"As we develop your case and consider potential settlement, it's important that you understand the tax implications of different types of damages we might recover. Different kinds of compensation are taxed differently, which can significantly affect how much you actually receive.

Wage-related damages like back pay are taxed just like regular wages - with income tax, Social Security, and Medicare taxes taken out. **Emotional distress damages** are usually taxable as regular income, but without the additional Social Security and Medicare taxes. **Punitive damages** are always taxable as regular income.

There are some limited exceptions - for example, if your emotional distress caused documented physical symptoms like ulcers or migraines, some of those damages might not be taxable at all. We'll need medical evidence to support that.

Attorney's fees can be complicated. In most employment cases, you can deduct legal fees from your taxable income, which helps reduce the tax impact.

This is general information about how these rules typically work. For your specific situation, especially if we reach a substantial settlement, I'd recommend consulting with a tax professional who can give you specific advice about your circumstances."

Settlement Conference Tax Briefing

"Before we finalize settlement terms, let's review how the proposed agreement would be taxed:

The $[AMOUNT] wage component will be treated like regular salary - you'll receive about $[NET AMOUNT] after taxes, and you'll get a W-2 form for tax filing.

The $[AMOUNT] for emotional distress will be taxable income, but without Social Security and Medicare taxes, so you'll keep about $[NET AMOUNT]. You'll receive a 1099 form for this.

The $[AMOUNT] in attorney's fees will be paid directly to me, and you can deduct this amount on your tax return, which helps reduce your overall tax burden.

Overall, you'll receive approximately $[TOTAL NET] after taxes. You may need to make quarterly tax payments on the 1099 income to avoid penalties.

Do you have any questions about these tax implications? Would you like me to refer you to a tax professional to discuss your specific situation?"

Post-Settlement Tax Preparation Communication

"Now that your settlement has been finalized, here's what you need to know for tax preparation:

Documents you'll receive:

- W-2 form for the $[AMOUNT] wage component (by January 31)
- 1099-MISC form for the $[AMOUNT] emotional distress damages (by January 31)
- Copy of settlement agreement with damage allocation details

Tax filing considerations:

- You can deduct the $[AMOUNT] attorney's fees on your tax return
- You may need to make estimated tax payments on the 1099 income
- Keep all settlement-related documents for at least three years in case of audit

Professional assistance: Given the complexity of your settlement, I recommend consulting with a tax professional for your specific situation. I can provide referrals to CPAs experienced with employment settlements if you'd like.

My role going forward: I've provided general information about tax treatment, but specific tax advice should come from a qualified tax professional. I'm available to provide copies of settlement documents or answer questions about the legal aspects of our agreement."

21.19 Coordination with Tax Professionals

Employment attorneys must establish clear boundaries regarding tax advice while ensuring clients receive appropriate professional guidance for complex tax issues.

When to Refer to Tax Professionals

Mandatory Referral Situations:

- Settlements exceeding $100,000 with complex allocation issues
- Cases involving potential physical injury exclusions requiring detailed medical evidence
- Multi-state tax implications affecting withholding and filing requirements
- Structured settlements or qualified settlement funds
- International tax issues involving foreign nationals or multinational employers

Recommended Referral Situations:

- Clients with other significant income requiring coordination
- Settlements creating substantial 1099 income requiring estimated tax payments
- Cases where attorney's fee deduction strategies could provide significant benefits
- Clients requesting specific tax planning advice beyond general guidance

Professional Coordination Protocols

Initial Consultation Coordination:

- Provide tax professional with complete settlement agreement and supporting documentation
- Explain legal theories and evidence supporting damage allocations
- Clarify scope of legal representation vs. tax advisory services
- Establish communication protocols for ongoing coordination

Ongoing Collaboration:

- Regular communication during settlement negotiations on tax-advantageous structures
- Joint client meetings when beneficial to coordinate legal and tax strategies
- Shared documentation to ensure consistency in advice and planning
- Coordination on audit defense if tax issues arise post-settlement

Scope of Attorney Tax Guidance

Appropriate Attorney Guidance:

- General explanation of tax treatment for different damage categories
- Discussion of common tax issues in employment settlements
- Explanation of attorney's fee deduction availability
- Basic guidance on record retention and documentation requirements

Beyond Attorney Scope:

- Specific tax return preparation advice
- Detailed estimated tax payment calculations
- Investment or financial planning recommendations
- Representation in tax audits or examinations

21.20 Audit Defense and Post-Settlement Issues

Employment settlements can trigger IRS or state tax authority scrutiny, requiring ongoing attention to potential audit issues and defense strategies.

Common Audit Triggers

Settlement Characteristics That Increase Audit Risk:

- Large settlements with significant emotional distress allocations
- Substantial attorney's fee deductions under Section 62(a)(20)
- Inconsistent reporting between plaintiff and defendant
- Unusual allocation patterns not supported by litigation evidence
- Multiple years of back pay creating income bunching issues

Taxpayer Profile Factors:

- High-income taxpayers claiming large attorney's fee deductions
- Inconsistent income patterns suggesting unreported settlement proceeds
- Previous audit history or compliance issues
- Large changes in reported income from year to year

Audit Defense Preparation

Documentation Requirements:

- Complete settlement agreement with detailed damage allocation provisions
- All supporting documentation justifying allocation decisions
- Expert reports, medical records, and other evidence supporting damage categories
- Correspondence and negotiations demonstrating good faith allocation process
- Attorney's fee agreements and documentation of services provided

Professional Coordination:

- Early involvement of tax professionals experienced in audit defense
- Coordination between employment counsel and tax representatives
- Clear delineation of representation responsibilities during audit process
- Preservation of attorney-client privilege while providing necessary cooperation

Post-Settlement Compliance Issues

Ongoing Client Support:

- Availability to provide settlement documentation for tax filing purposes
- Assistance with audit defense coordination when tax issues arise
- Clarification of settlement terms if questions arise during tax preparation
- Referral to appropriate professionals for ongoing tax compliance needs

Professional Liability Management:

- Clear documentation of scope of representation regarding tax issues
- Appropriate referrals to tax professionals for complex situations
- Maintenance of complete files supporting all tax-related advice provided
- Regular communication with clients about limitations of legal representation in tax matters

21.21 Conclusion: Integrating Tax Planning into Employment Law Practice

The taxation of employment settlements represents a critical component of effective employment law practice that requires systematic attention, professional coordination, and ongoing education. The difference between proper and improper tax planning can be measured not only in dollars retained by clients but also in professional satisfaction and risk management for practitioners.

Successful integration of tax planning into employment practice requires recognition that tax considerations are not ancillary issues to be addressed at settlement but integral components of case development, negotiation strategy, and client counseling. This integration begins with damage development during discovery, continues through expert witness preparation and settlement negotiations, and extends through post-settlement implementation and potential audit defense.

The complexity of settlement taxation should not deter practitioners from addressing these issues but rather should encourage appropriate professional development and collaboration. Employment attorneys need not become tax experts, but they must understand enough about settlement taxation to recognize issues, provide appropriate general guidance, and coordinate effectively with tax professionals when circumstances warrant.

Client service excellence in employment law increasingly requires attention to the full range of consequences flowing from litigation resolution. Clients who achieve favorable legal outcomes but suffer unexpected tax consequences or compliance problems have not been fully served. Conversely, clients who receive comprehensive guidance that maximizes their net recovery while ensuring full compliance experience the kind of professional service that builds lasting relationships and referral sources.

The evolving nature of tax law affecting employment settlements requires ongoing professional development and attention to legislative, administrative, and judicial developments. Employment practitioners should regularly update their knowledge of settlement taxation issues through continuing legal education, professional publications, and coordination with tax professionals.

Risk management considerations also support systematic attention to settlement tax issues. Professional liability exposure can arise from failing to address obvious tax issues, providing incorrect tax advice, or failing to refer clients to appropriate tax professionals when circumstances warrant. Proper documentation of tax-related discussions, appropriate scope of representation clarification, and timely referrals protect both clients and practitioners.

The investment in developing tax planning competency pays dividends through enhanced client outcomes, reduced professional liability exposure, improved settlement negotiation capabilities, and the professional satisfaction that comes from delivering comprehensive, sophisticated legal services.

As employment law continues to evolve through legislative changes, administrative guidance, and judicial decisions, the tax implications of settlements will likewise continue to develop. Practitioners who establish systematic approaches to settlement tax planning, maintain current knowledge of relevant developments, and cultivate professional relationships with qualified tax experts will be best positioned to serve their clients effectively in this complex and evolving area of practice.

In Chapter 22, we will address the equally complex issues surrounding confidentiality provisions, non-disparagement clauses, and other restrictive settlement terms, including their enforceability, ethical implications, and recent legislative restrictions that are reshaping employment settlement practice.

22

Confidentiality, Non-Disparagement, and Other Settlement Clauses

Settlement agreements often include more than just money - they shape narratives, reputations, and future conduct. Clauses like confidentiality and non-disparagement are common, but in recent years, legislatures in New York, California, and at the federal level have imposed limits on their use, especially in employment cases involving harassment, discrimination, and retaliation.

This chapter explores the purpose, enforceability, and evolving legality of confidentiality, non-disparagement, no-rehire, neutral reference, and non-admission clauses in employment settlements.

22.1 Confidentiality Clauses

Purpose and Strategic Considerations

Confidentiality clauses serve multiple strategic purposes in settlement agreements. They prevent public disclosure of the settlement amount or underlying facts, protecting employer reputation and sensitive business information while deterring similar claims or unwanted publicity. For plaintiffs, confidentiality can provide privacy and protection from potential backlash, though it may limit their ability to warn others about workplace misconduct.

The strategic value of confidentiality varies significantly depending on the nature of the case. In trade secret disputes, confidentiality protects legitimate business interests. In harassment cases, however, confidentiality may shield serial offenders and prevent other victims from coming forward, leading to increased legislative restrictions.

Typical Language and Variations

Standard confidentiality language typically reads: "The parties agree to keep the existence and terms of this settlement strictly confidential and shall not disclose any information regarding this matter to any third party, except as required by law or with prior written consent of all parties."

More sophisticated agreements include graduated levels of confidentiality. For instance, parties might agree to keep settlement terms confidential while allowing discussion of general workplace policies. Some agreements permit disclosure to immediate family members, attorneys, accountants, or tax advisors with appropriate confidentiality obligations.

The scope of confidentiality can also vary. Broad clauses prohibit disclosure of "any information related to the dispute," while narrow clauses focus only on financial terms. The trend favors narrower confidentiality provisions that balance legitimate privacy interests with public transparency concerns.

Legal Limits and Jurisdictional Differences

California's Comprehensive Approach

California Code of Civil Procedure Section 1001 represents the most restrictive approach to confidentiality clauses. The statute prohibits confidentiality clauses in settlements involving sexual assault, sexual harassment, workplace harassment or discrimination based on any protected characteristic including race, gender, religion, national origin, disability, age, sexual orientation, or any other protected class, and retaliation for reporting such conduct.

Importantly, parties may not conceal factual allegations related to these claims, meaning that even if settlement terms remain confidential, the underlying facts of misconduct cannot be hidden. This creates a significant limitation on employer protection strategies. However, plaintiffs can request confidentiality, but they must initiate it knowingly and voluntarily after receiving independent legal advice.

The California approach reflects a policy judgment that public awareness of workplace misconduct outweighs private settlement preferences. This has led to increased employer focus on preventing misconduct rather than hiding it through confidential settlements.

New York's Balanced Framework

New York General Obligations Law Section 5-336 takes a more measured approach, barring confidentiality specifically in cases involving sexual harassment and workplace discrimination. The law requires that plaintiffs be given 21 days to consider the confidentiality term and 7 days to revoke after signing, ensuring informed consent.

This cooling-off period acknowledges that settlement negotiations can be emotionally charged and that plaintiffs may need time to fully consider the implications of confidentiality. The revocation period provides an additional safeguard against coerced agreements.

New York's approach differs from California's in its narrower scope, focusing primarily on sexual harassment and discrimination rather than the broader category of workplace harassment based on protected characteristics.

Federal Legislation

The federal Speak Out Act of 2022 specifically bars enforcement of pre-dispute nondisclosure agreements in sexual assault and sexual harassment cases. This means that NDAs signed before any misconduct occurs cannot be enforced to prevent disclosure of sexual misconduct. However, post-dispute settlement agreements may still include confidentiality provisions, subject to state law restrictions.

The federal approach recognizes the coercive nature of pre-dispute NDAs while preserving the ability of parties to negotiate confidentiality as part of settlement discussions where both parties have full knowledge of the allegations.

Comparative Analysis of Jurisdictional Approaches

The key differences between jurisdictions reveal different policy priorities. California prioritizes maximum transparency in workplace misconduct cases, potentially deterring settlements but increasing public awareness. New York balances transparency with party autonomy through procedural safeguards. Federal law targets the most problematic NDAs while preserving settlement flexibility.

These differences create strategic considerations for multi-jurisdictional employers and plaintiffs' attorneys. A California-based company may face broader disclosure requirements than a New York company, even for similar misconduct. This patchwork of laws has led some employers to adopt California-compliant policies nationwide to ensure consistency.

Best Practices for Confidentiality Clauses

Effective confidentiality clauses should be tailored narrowly to avoid enforceability challenges. Rather than blanket confidentiality, consider limiting confidentiality to specific elements like settlement amounts while allowing discussion of workplace policies or safety concerns.

Include specific exceptions for legal, tax, and family disclosures. Standard carve-outs should cover testimony compelled by legal proceedings, subpoenas, government investigations, and required tax reporting. Consider including language like: "Nothing in this confidentiality provision prevents disclosure required by law, court order, or government investigation, or prohibits communication with government agencies regarding potential violations of law."

Use clear, plain language to avoid ambiguity that could lead to enforcement disputes. Define key terms like "confidential information" and specify whether the existence of the settlement itself is confidential or only its terms.

22.2 Non-Disparagement Clauses

Purpose and Strategic Function

Non-disparagement clauses serve as reputational protection mechanisms for both parties, though they typically benefit employers more significantly. These clauses prevent parties from publicly criticizing each other, protecting reputation and future employment prospects while reinforcing settlement finality.

For employers, non-disparagement clauses can prevent negative reviews on employment websites, social media criticism, or public statements that might damage company reputation or deter and impact recruitment efforts. For employees, mutual non-disparagement can protect against negative references or public criticism that might harm future employment opportunities.

The strategic value of non-disparagement clauses has evolved as social media and online review platforms have amplified the potential impact of negative statements. A single negative post can reach thousands of people instantly, making reputation protection more critical but also more challenging.

Typical Language and Enforcement Challenges

Standard non-disparagement language typically provides: "The parties agree not to make any disparaging, derogatory, or negative statements about each other, whether written or oral, to any third party, including but not limited to statements made to media, on social media platforms, or in professional contexts."

However, enforcement of non-disparagement clauses presents significant challenges. Proving that a statement is "disparaging" rather than truthful criticism can be difficult. Courts must balance contractual obligations against free speech rights, particularly when statements relate to matters of public concern.

The definition of "disparaging" itself creates enforcement challenges. Is a factual statement about workplace conditions disparaging if it reflects poorly on the employer? Courts generally require that disparaging statements be false or misleading, not merely negative but truthful.

Legal Restrictions and Public Policy Concerns

California's Protective Framework

California Government Code Section 12964.5 significantly limits employer ability to enforce non-disparagement clauses that restrict disclosure of information about unlawful acts in the workplace. The statute specifically covers harassment, discrimination, and retaliation, recognizing that silencing victims can perpetuate workplace misconduct.

Critically, any agreement subject to this law must include a specific disclaimer stating: "Nothing in this agreement prevents you from disclosing information about unlawful acts in the workplace, such as harassment or discrimination or any other conduct that you have reason to believe is unlawful."

This mandatory language ensures that employees understand their right to report misconduct despite non-disparagement provisions. Failure to include this disclaimer can render the entire non-disparagement clause unenforceable.

New York and Federal Approaches

New York has no direct statutory prohibition on non-disparagement clauses, but courts increasingly scrutinize overly broad clauses that conflict with public policy. New York courts apply a reasonableness standard, examining whether the clause is narrowly tailored to legitimate business interests or overly broad in restricting protected speech.

Federal courts have shown similar skepticism toward broad non-disparagement clauses, particularly in cases involving whistleblower activity or matters of public concern. The National Labor Relations Board has also found that overly broad non-disparagement clauses can violate workers' rights to discuss working conditions.

Enforceability Standards and Best Practices

For non-disparagement clauses to be enforceable, they must be specific and limited in scope. Vague terms like "negative comments" or "unfavorable statements" create ambiguity that courts may resolve against the drafting party. More effective language focuses on false or misleading statements while preserving rights to make truthful disclosures.

Consider language like: "The parties agree not to make false, misleading, or defamatory statements about each other. This provision does not restrict truthful statements required by legal process, made to government agencies, or protected by law."

Avoid clauses that could chill speech on matters of public interest. Non-disparagement provisions that might prevent discussion of workplace safety, discrimination, or other public concerns face heightened scrutiny from courts applying public policy exceptions.

Mutual vs. Unilateral Non-Disparagement

Most non-disparagement clauses are mutual, applying to both employer and employee. However, the practical impact often favors employers, who typically have greater resources and platforms for public statements. Employees may benefit more from provisions that specifically address negative references or social media criticism by company representatives.

Unilateral non-disparagement clauses applying only to employees face greater enforceability challenges, as courts may view them as one-sided and potentially coercive. Mutual clauses appear more fair and are generally more enforceable.

22.3 No-Rehire Clauses

Definition and Strategic Purpose

No-rehire clauses prohibit plaintiffs from applying for or accepting future employment with the defendant employer. These clauses serve multiple purposes: they provide finality to the employment relationship, eliminate potential future conflicts, and may reduce employer concerns about settling cases with employees they view as problematic.

However, no-rehire clauses can significantly impact an employee's future career prospects, particularly in specialized industries or geographic areas where the employer has substantial market presence. This has led to increased legislative scrutiny and restrictions.

California's Restrictive Approach

California Code of Civil Procedure Section 1002.5 represents the most restrictive approach to no-rehire provisions. The statute bans no-rehire provisions in settlements of employment claims unless there is a good-faith finding of employee misconduct or the provision applies only to specific job functions rather than all employment.

The "good-faith finding of misconduct" standard requires more than mere allegations or employer suspicions. There must be credible evidence of actual misconduct that would justify excluding the employee from future employment. This creates a factual inquiry that can complicate settlement negotiations.

The alternative exception for "specific job functions" allows more targeted no-rehire provisions. For example, an employee terminated for financial misconduct might be prohibited from finance-related positions while remaining eligible for other roles within the company.

Other Jurisdictional Approaches

New York and federal courts have no categorical ban on no-rehire clauses, but they may raise public policy concerns in certain contexts. Courts are particularly skeptical of no-rehire clauses in whistleblower cases or where the underlying claim involves protected activity under employment law.

The enforceability of no-rehire clauses often depends on their scope and justification. Broadly written clauses that permanently bar all employment may be viewed as punitive and contrary to public policy, while narrowly tailored provisions addressing specific legitimate concerns are more likely to be enforced.

Alternatives to Absolute No-Rehire Clauses

Given the restrictions on no-rehire clauses, parties should consider alternatives that address employer concerns while preserving employee opportunities. Time-limited no-rehire provisions might prohibit re-employment for a specific period rather than permanently. Department-specific restrictions might address legitimate concerns about workplace dynamics without completely foreclosing employment opportunities.

Some agreements include conditional re-employment provisions that allow future hiring subject to standard application processes and requirements. This approach provides flexibility while ensuring that any future employment decision is based on then-current qualifications and circumstances.

22.4 Neutral Reference Agreements

Purpose and Practical Benefits

Neutral reference agreements represent a compromise solution that benefits both parties in settlement negotiations. These agreements typically require employers to limit reference information to basic employment facts: dates of employment, position held, and sometimes final salary information.

For employees, neutral reference agreements eliminate the risk of negative references that could damage future employment prospects. This is particularly valuable when the employment relationship ended contentiously or when the employee fears retaliation through negative references.

For employers, neutral reference agreements provide clarity and consistency in reference practices while reducing legal risk. Standardized neutral references eliminate the possibility of defamation claims or discrimination allegations based on inconsistent reference practices.

Standard Language and Variations

Typical neutral reference language provides: "Employer agrees to provide a neutral reference consisting of title, dates of employment, and salary verification only. All reference inquiries will be directed to [specific person/department], and no other information will be provided."

Some agreements include additional elements like general job performance ratings or eligibility for rehire status, though these additions can complicate the "neutral" nature of the reference. The trend favors simpler, more limited approaches that minimize potential disputes.

More sophisticated agreements address practical implementation issues. They might specify the format for reference responses, identify who is authorized to provide references, and include procedures for handling informal reference inquiries or networking contacts.

Implementation Challenges

Neutral reference agreements face practical enforcement challenges. Ensuring that all potential reference sources within a company comply with the agreement requires comprehensive internal communication and training. Informal references through professional networks or social media contacts may be difficult to control.

Some agreements address these challenges by including specific notification requirements when the employee applies for positions, allowing the employer to ensure that appropriate personnel handle reference inquiries. Others include penalties for violations of the neutral reference commitment.

Legal Protections and Limitations

Neutral reference agreements must be balanced against qualified immunity statutes that protect employers providing good-faith references. Some states provide legal protection for employers giving truthful references, which can create tension with contractual neutral reference obligations.

The agreements should also address mandatory disclosure requirements. For example, employers may be legally required to disclose certain information about former employees in regulated industries, regardless of neutral reference commitments.

22.5 Non-Admission of Liability

Standard Language and Legal Purpose

Non-admission of liability clauses are virtually universal in settlement agreements. The standard language provides: "This agreement shall not be construed as an admission of wrongdoing, liability, or fault by any party. The parties enter into this agreement to avoid the costs and uncertainties of continued litigation."

These clauses serve critical legal and business purposes. They protect employers from creating precedent for future cases, prevent the settlement from being used as evidence in other litigation, and preserve the employer's public reputation by clarifying that payment does not constitute an admission of wrongdoing.

For plaintiffs, non-admission clauses may initially seem disadvantageous, as they prevent the settlement from serving as validation of their claims. However, these clauses are typically essential for reaching settlement, as most employers will not agree to settlements that include admissions of liability.

Limitations and Exceptions

While courts generally enforce non-admission clauses, they cannot override certain legal obligations. The clauses do not prevent compliance with statutory reporting duties, such as EEOC reporting requirements or safety incident disclosures required by OSHA. They also cannot prevent cooperation with government investigations or whistleblower protections.

Non-admission clauses typically do not prevent the use of settlement agreements in subsequent litigation to prove the existence of a settlement or to enforce the settlement terms themselves. However, they should prevent use of the settlement as evidence of underlying liability.

The effectiveness of non-admission clauses can be limited in cases involving serial misconduct. While the clause may prevent use of a specific settlement as evidence, patterns of behavior evidenced by multiple settlements may still be relevant in subsequent cases, depending on applicable evidence rules.

Strategic Considerations

Non-admission clauses should be carefully drafted to address specific evidentiary concerns. Standard language may not provide adequate protection in complex cases involving multiple parties or related litigation. Consider whether the clause should address public statements, regulatory proceedings, or specific types of future litigation.

For plaintiffs' attorneys, non-admission clauses may be balanced against other settlement terms. While accepting a non-admission clause may limit certain strategic advantages, it may be necessary to achieve other important goals like substantial monetary compensation or workplace policy changes.

22.6 Severability and Integration Clauses

Severability Provisions

Severability clauses ensure that if one provision of a settlement agreement is found invalid or unenforceable, the remainder of the agreement remains in effect. This is particularly important given the evolving legal landscape surrounding settlement agreement provisions.

Standard severability language provides: "If any provision of this agreement is deemed invalid, illegal, or unenforceable by a court of competent jurisdiction, the remaining provisions shall remain in full force and effect, and the invalid provision shall be modified to the minimum extent necessary to make it enforceable."

The strategic importance of severability clauses has increased as legislatures impose new restrictions on settlement provisions. Without severability clauses, the invalidation of a confidentiality provision might void the entire settlement agreement, potentially requiring renegotiation or returning the case to litigation.

Integration and Merger Clauses

Integration or merger clauses establish that the written settlement agreement represents the complete understanding between the parties, superseding all prior negotiations, discussions, or agreements. Standard language provides: "This agreement constitutes the entire agreement between the parties and supersedes all prior negotiations, representations, or agreements relating to the subject matter hereof."

These clauses prevent parties from later claiming that additional terms were agreed upon but not included in the written document. They also prevent enforcement of contradictory terms from earlier drafts or preliminary agreements.

Integration clauses must be carefully drafted to avoid unintended consequences. They should not prevent enforcement of separate agreements that parties intend to remain in effect, such as existing confidentiality agreements or non-compete provisions that are not part of the settlement.

Best Practices for Severability and Integration

Effective severability clauses should include modification language that allows courts to narrow overly broad provisions rather than simply striking them entirely. This approach, sometimes called "blue pencil" authority, can preserve more of the parties' intended agreement.

Consider including specific guidance for courts on how to modify problematic provisions. For example, the clause might specify that overly broad confidentiality provisions should be narrowed to comply with applicable law rather than eliminated entirely.

Integration clauses should be comprehensive but not overly broad. They should clearly identify what prior agreements or understandings are superseded while preserving any separate agreements that the parties intend to remain in effect.

22.7 Whistleblower and Government Reporting Carve-Outs

Legal Requirements and Policy Rationale

Settlement agreements cannot legally prohibit employees from reporting violations of law to government agencies or cooperating with government investigations. Various federal and state laws protect whistleblower activity, and settlement agreements that attempt to restrict such activity may be void as against public policy.

The policy rationale for these protections is clear: public enforcement of employment laws depends on employee willingness to report violations. Settlement agreements that silence employees would undermine the broader legal framework protecting workplace rights.

Federal agencies including the EEOC, NLRB, SEC, OSHA, and DOL have all taken positions that settlement agreements cannot restrict employee rights to file charges or cooperate with investigations. Some agencies have imposed specific requirements for settlement agreement language.

Required Safe-Harbor Language

Effective settlement agreements must include specific language protecting whistleblower and reporting rights. Standard safe-harbor language provides: "Nothing in this agreement prevents Employee from filing a charge or complaint with any government agency, participating in any government investigation, or testifying in any legal proceeding. Employee is not required to notify Company before making any such reports or disclosures."

The language should be comprehensive, covering all relevant government agencies and types of protected activity. Consider including specific references to agencies that are particularly relevant to the type of case being settled.

Some agencies require even more specific language. For example, the NLRB has indicated that settlement agreements should include language specifically preserving rights under the National Labor Relations Act to discuss working conditions with other employees.

Scope of Protected Activity

Whistleblower protections extend beyond formal complaints to government agencies. They typically cover informal communications with agency staff, participation in agency investigations, testimony in enforcement proceedings, and cooperation with congressional investigations.

The protections may also extend to certain types of public disclosure, particularly when employees are reporting violations that pose public safety risks. However, the scope of protection for public disclosure varies by jurisdiction and the nature of the reported violation.

Settlement agreements should not attempt to restrict any activity that might be protected under whistleblower laws. When in doubt, it is better to include broader carve-outs rather than risk invalidating the entire agreement.

Practical Implementation Considerations

While settlement agreements cannot restrict whistleblower activity, they can include provisions requiring employees to comply with applicable procedural requirements for such reports. For example, agreements might remind employees of any internal reporting procedures required by law, while making clear that such procedures are not mandatory.

Agreements should avoid any language that could be interpreted as discouraging protected activity. For example, requiring employees to notify the company before making reports to government agencies could be viewed as chilling protected activity and should be avoided.

Consider including affirmative language encouraging compliance with applicable laws and regulations. This approach demonstrates good faith while avoiding any appearance of restricting protected rights.

22.8 Drafting Checklist for Enforceable Clauses

Jurisdictional Compliance Requirements

Before drafting any settlement agreement provision, attorneys must thoroughly research applicable federal, state, and local law restrictions. The legal landscape is rapidly evolving, and provisions that were enforceable in previous years may now be prohibited or restricted.

Key compliance steps include confirming whether the plaintiff must initiate confidentiality provisions in jurisdictions requiring such initiation, including any required revocation periods, inserting all mandatory disclaimers regarding unlawful acts and whistleblower rights, and ensuring that non-disparagement clauses comply with applicable speech protection laws.

Review recent case law and agency guidance in the relevant jurisdiction, as courts and agencies are actively interpreting new legislation restricting settlement provisions. What appears compliant based on statutory language may be subject to additional restrictions based on recent interpretations.

Language and Clarity Requirements

Settlement provisions should use plain, clear language that can be understood by parties without legal training. Ambiguous language creates enforcement risks and may be interpreted against the drafting party. Define key terms explicitly rather than relying on assumed meanings.

Avoid overbroad language that attempts to restrict more activity than necessary to achieve legitimate business purposes. Courts are increasingly willing to invalidate overly broad provisions, and overbroad language may taint other provisions in the agreement.

Consider including specific examples of permitted and prohibited conduct to clarify the scope of restrictions. While examples cannot cover every situation, they can provide helpful guidance and reduce the likelihood of disputes.

Tailoring to Specific Circumstances

Generic settlement language often fails to address the specific circumstances of individual cases. Consider the nature of the underlying dispute, the parties' ongoing relationship, if any, the potential for future interaction between the parties, and industry-specific considerations that might affect enforcement.

For example, confidentiality provisions in trade secret cases might legitimately be broader than those in harassment cases. Non-disparagement clauses in social media-intensive industries might need specific provisions addressing online activity.

Include attorney's fees provisions for breach of post-settlement terms where enforceable under applicable law. This creates additional incentive for compliance and may make enforcement economically viable even for relatively minor breaches.

Quality Control and Review Processes

Implement systematic review processes to ensure settlement agreement compliance with current law. Consider maintaining checklists specific to different types of cases and different jurisdictions to ensure consistent compliance.

Review agreements with an eye toward potential future changes in law. While agreements cannot anticipate all legal developments, they can be drafted to be more resilient to likely changes in the legal landscape.

Consider including annual review processes for template language to ensure continued compliance as laws evolve. The rapid pace of legal change in this area requires ongoing attention to maintain effective settlement practices.

22.9 Recent Trends and Legislative Shifts

Post-#MeToo Legal Developments

The #MeToo movement has fundamentally altered the legal landscape surrounding employment settlement agreements. Legislatures at federal, state, and local levels have enacted new restrictions on settlement provisions, particularly those that might conceal workplace misconduct or prevent victims from speaking out.

These changes reflect a policy shift away from private resolution of workplace misconduct toward greater public transparency and accountability. The traditional view that settlement agreements serve legitimate privacy interests has been balanced against concerns about protecting future victims and deterring misconduct.

Many employers have proactively adapted their settlement practices in response to these changes, limiting confidentiality provisions even where not legally required and focusing on workplace policy improvements rather than secrecy. This trend suggests that legal restrictions may be driving broader cultural changes in how workplace misconduct is addressed.

Employer Strategy Evolution

Employers increasingly limit confidentiality to financial terms only, allowing discussion of workplace policies and general facts about disputes. This approach reduces legal risk while preserving some protection for settlement amounts and specific internal business information.

Many employers now emphasize policy changes and workplace improvements as part of settlement agreements rather than relying primarily on secrecy and non disparagement. This approach can provide more meaningful resolution for plaintiffs while demonstrating employer commitment to preventing future problems.

The trend toward transparency has also led employers to focus more heavily on prevention and early intervention rather than post-incident damage control. Investment in training, policy development, and complaint procedures may be more cost-effective than extensive litigation and settlement secrecy.

Judicial Skepticism of Broad Clauses

Courts are increasingly wary of boilerplate language in settlement agreements, particularly clauses that broadly restrict employee rights or speech. Judges more frequently scrutinize settlement provisions for compliance with public policy and statutory requirements.

This judicial skepticism extends beyond employment law to other areas where settlement agreements might affect public interests. Courts are more willing to find settlement provisions unenforceable when they conflict with broader policy goals.

The trend suggests that settlement agreement drafting must be more thoughtful and tailored to specific circumstances rather than relying on standard forms. Generic language that might have been acceptable in previous years may now face enforcement challenges.

Plaintiffs' Attorney Response Strategies

Plaintiffs' attorneys increasingly negotiate settlement provisions early in the process rather than treating them as afterthoughts to monetary terms. Understanding the enforceability limits of various clauses allows more effective negotiation of overall settlement packages.

Many plaintiffs' attorneys now push back more aggressively on overreaching settlement provisions, particularly those that might restrict client rights over and above what is legally permissible. This has led to more detailed negotiations over settlement language and their structure.

The evolving legal landscape has also created opportunities for plaintiffs' attorneys to add value by ensuring that settlement agreements comply with current law and protect client interests that might not have been considered in earlier practice.

22.10 Conclusion

Settlement clauses are not mere legal formalities - they define post-litigation reality and can have lasting impacts on both parties long after the dispute is resolved. Whether shielding reputations or protecting rights, each clause must strike a careful balance between enforceability and fairness, taking into account the rapidly evolving legal landscape surrounding employment settlements.

The growing legal scrutiny and statutory restrictions on settlement provisions require lawyers to draft more thoughtfully and specifically rather than relying on broad, generic language. The days of boilerplate settlement clauses that attempt to restrict all possible future activity are ending, replaced by a need for nuanced provisions that address legitimate interests while respecting legal limitations and public policy concerns.

In employment law particularly, the words that close a case can echo long after the ink dries, affecting not only the immediate parties but also workplace culture, future litigation trends, and public understanding of workplace rights. Effective settlement agreement drafting now requires not only legal technical skill but also awareness of broader social and policy implications.

The trend toward transparency and accountability in workplace misconduct cases reflects deeper changes in social attitudes and legal priorities. Settlement agreements must adapt to these changes while continuing to serve their legitimate purposes of providing finality, protecting legitimate interests, and enabling resolution of disputes without the costs and uncertainties of trial.

As the legal landscape continues to evolve, practitioners must stay current with new legislative developments, judicial interpretations, and agency guidance while maintaining focus on crafting agreements that truly serve their clients' long-term interests. The most effective settlement agreements will be those that anticipate future legal developments while addressing current requirements and practical needs.

Success in this environment requires moving away from generic templates toward customized agreements that reflect the specific circumstances of each case, the applicable legal requirements, and the parties' legitimate interests in resolution and moving forward. The additional time invested in thoughtful drafting will be repaid through reduced enforcement disputes and more durable resolutions.

In Chapter 23, we'll address employer retaliation after settlement, including how to recognize, document, and litigate post-settlement misconduct that undermines the agreement or violates employment law protections.

23

Post-Settlement Retaliation and Enforcement Protections

Settlement agreements are intended to bring finality to disputes - but the reality is that some employers engage in post-settlement retaliation, subtly or overtly punishing employees after a claim is resolved. Retaliation may include blacklisting, hostile work environments (if the employee remains employed), or refusal to comply with agreed terms.

This chapter outlines how to identify, respond to, and litigate retaliation that occurs after a settlement or judgment, and how to invoke statutory protections in New York, California, and federal jurisdictions.

23.1 What Is Post-Settlement Retaliation?

Retaliation is any adverse action taken by an employer against an employee because that employee engaged in legally protected activity. Protected activity includes filing discrimination complaints, participating in workplace investigations, or exercising rights under employment laws. The key legal test is whether the employer's adverse action was motivated, at least in part, by the employee's protected conduct.

Retaliation occurs when an employer takes adverse action against an employee for engaging in protected activity, such as:

- Filing a discrimination, harassment, or wage claim
- Participating in an investigation
- Enforcing or discussing a settlement agreement
- Reporting unlawful workplace conduct to a government agency

Post-settlement retaliation happens after resolution of the original claim, often in more covert forms. Unlike pre-settlement retaliation, which typically occurs during active litigation, post-settlement retaliation presents unique challenges because it may appear unrelated to the original dispute and can be more difficult to prove causally connected to the protected activity.

The temporal gap between settlement and retaliation does not insulate employers from liability. Courts have recognized that retaliation can occur months or even years after the initial protected activity, as long as there is sufficient causal connection between the protected conduct and the adverse action.

23.2 Common Forms of Post-Settlement Retaliation

Blacklisting

Blacklisting refers to the practice of informally or formally preventing someone from obtaining employment within an industry or geographic area. In the post-settlement context, this typically manifests as:

Informal reference calls that sabotage future employment: Former employers provide negative or misleading information to prospective employers during informal reference checks. Unlike formal reference letters, these communications often occur off-the-record and can be difficult to detect or prove.

Example: After settling a sexual harassment claim, Sarah applies for positions in her industry. Unknown to her, her former supervisor has been telling hiring managers at competing firms that Sarah was "difficult to work with" and "caused problems" whenever they call for informal references.

Industry-specific whisper campaigns: In close-knit industries where professionals frequently interact, employers may spread negative information about former employees through professional networks, trade associations, or industry events.

Example: In the construction industry, after settling a wage and hour claim, a foreman discovers that potential employers at job sites have been told he's a "troublemaker" who "can't be trusted" by his former employer's network of subcontractors.

Refusal to provide agreed neutral references: When settlement agreements specifically require neutral references but employers either refuse to provide them or provide references that subtly undermine the employee.

Hostile Work Environment (if still employed)

When employees remain with their employer after settlement, they may face a **hostile work environment** - a workplace atmosphere that becomes intimidating, hostile, or offensive due to discriminatory conduct. Post-settlement hostility often includes:

Isolation or exclusion: Deliberately excluding the employee from meetings, team communications, or workplace social interactions. This form of retaliation creates professional isolation that can impair job performance and career advancement.

Example: After settling an age discrimination claim, Robert continues working but finds himself excluded from strategy meetings he previously attended, with colleagues claiming they "forgot" to invite him or that the meetings were "last minute."

Stripping of responsibilities: Removing meaningful job duties, assignments, or decision-making authority as punishment for pursuing legal claims. This differs from legitimate business restructuring because it targets the specific employee who engaged in protected activity.

Example: Following settlement of a disability discrimination claim, Maria's employer removes her project management responsibilities and assigns her only clerical tasks, despite her qualifications and previous performance.

Micromanagement and excessive scrutiny: Subjecting the employee to unreasonable oversight, frequent performance reviews, or documentation of minor infractions that were previously overlooked for other employees.

Failure to Rehire or Consider for Promotion

No-rehire policies are employment policies that permanently bar former employees from returning to work for the company. When these policies are applied specifically because an employee filed legal claims, they constitute retaliation. This is particularly problematic when:

- The settlement agreement did not include a no-rehire clause
- The employee left on good terms aside from the legal dispute
- Similarly situated employees without legal claims are rehired
- The policy is applied inconsistently

Example: After settling a pregnancy discrimination claim and taking a position elsewhere, Jennifer applies to return to her former employer for a promotion. Despite her excellent work history and qualifications, she's told there's a "policy" against rehiring former employees, though she learns that other former employees without legal claims have been rehired.

Breach of Settlement Agreement

Settlement agreements are contracts, and employers who fail to comply with their terms commit **breach of contract**. Common breaches include:

Late payments or omitted benefits: Failing to make agreed-upon payments on time or excluding agreed benefits like health insurance continuation or retirement contributions.

Disregarding confidentiality or non-disparagement terms: While employees are often bound by these clauses, employers who violate their own confidentiality obligations or make disparaging statements about the employee also breach the agreement.

Example: Despite a mutual non-disparagement clause, an employer tells industry colleagues that a former employee who settled a discrimination claim was "just looking for a payday" and "wasn't really discriminated against."

Refusal to Cooperate with Government Investigations

Government investigations by agencies like the Equal Employment Opportunity Commission (EEOC), Department of Labor (DOL), or state civil rights departments may continue even after private settlements. Employers who discourage or prevent former employees from participating in these investigations engage in retaliation.

EEOC investigations often involve pattern-and-practice reviews that examine whether employers have engaged in systemic discrimination. Former employees' testimony can be crucial to these investigations, and employers cannot lawfully interfere with this participation.

Example: After settling an individual claim, the EEOC opens a broader investigation into the employer's practices. The employer contacts the former employee's new employer, suggesting they "might want to reconsider" employing someone involved in "ongoing legal issues."

23.3 Legal Protections Against Retaliation

Federal Law

Title VII of the Civil Rights Act of 1964 (42 U.S.C. § 2000e-3) prohibits retaliation against employees who oppose unlawful employment practices or participate in Title VII proceedings. The statute's protection extends beyond the employment relationship and covers post-settlement conduct.

The **opposition clause** protects employees who oppose practices they reasonably believe to be unlawful, even if those practices are later determined to be lawful. The **participation clause** provides broader protection for employees who participate in formal proceedings, such as filing charges or testifying in investigations.

Americans with Disabilities Act (ADA), **Family and Medical Leave Act (FMLA)**, **Fair Labor Standards Act (FLSA)**, and **Section 1981** each contain their own anti-retaliation provisions with varying standards and remedies.

Section 1981 provides particularly robust protection because it allows unlimited compensatory and punitive damages, unlike Title VII's damage caps. It covers retaliation related to race discrimination and extends to post-employment conduct.

Sarbanes-Oxley Act (SOX), **Dodd-Frank Act**, and **Occupational Safety and Health Act (OSHA)** whistleblower statutes protect employees who report specific types of misconduct and explicitly cover post-employment retaliation.

California Law

Fair Employment and Housing Act (FEHA) Retaliation Protections (Government Code § 12940(h)) provide broader protection than federal law in several respects:

- No damage caps on compensatory damages
- Longer statute of limitations (three years versus federal deadlines of 180-300 days for administrative charges)
- Protection for perceived association with protected activities
- Coverage of independent contractors and unpaid interns

Labor Code § 98.6 specifically protects wage claimants from retaliation, including after claims are resolved. This statute is particularly significant because it covers retaliation related to wage and hour disputes, which are common in post-settlement contexts.

Key difference from federal law: California's statute explicitly states that protection continues "after the claim is resolved," removing any ambiguity about post-settlement coverage.

Labor Code § 1102.5 provides broad whistleblower protection for employees who report violations of law to government agencies or internally. This statute covers a wider range of conduct than federal whistleblower laws and includes protection for reporting violations of any law, regulation, or rule.

New York Law

New York Human Rights Law (NYHRL) Retaliation Provisions (Executive Law § 296(7)) offer protections similar to federal law but with some enhanced features:

- Broader definition of "employer" (four or more employees versus Title VII's 15)
- More generous damage awards
- Stronger protection for opposition conduct

New York Labor Law § 215 covers wage-related retaliation and includes specific protections for employees who file wage claims or participate in wage investigations.

New York City Human Rights Law (NYCHRL) provides the broadest protection against retaliation of any jurisdiction covered in this chapter. The law protects against any action that could dissuade a reasonable person from pursuing legal rights, creating a very low threshold for establishing retaliation.

Key difference: The NYCHRL uses an objective "could dissuade" standard rather than requiring proof that the action actually deterred the employee or others from pursuing legal rights.

23.4 Legal Remedies for Post-Settlement Retaliation

1. Filing a New Administrative Complaint

EEOC Charges: The Equal Employment Opportunity Commission accepts retaliation charges even when the underlying discrimination charge has been resolved. Retaliation is considered a separate violation with its own statute of limitations.

Procedural note: Employees must file EEOC charges within 180 days of the retaliatory act (300 days in states with fair employment practice agencies). The charge must specifically allege retaliation and identify the protected activity that motivated the employer's adverse action.

California Civil Rights Department (CRD) complaints can be filed for retaliation under FEHA within three years of the retaliatory act. California's longer statute of limitations provides significantly more time than federal deadlines.

New York Division of Human Rights (DHR) complaints must be filed within one year for most retaliation claims, though some wage-related retaliation claims have different deadlines.

Strategic consideration: Filing administrative charges can provide investigation resources and potential conciliation opportunities that may resolve matters without litigation.

2. Filing a New Civil Lawsuit

Damages available in retaliation lawsuits typically include:

- **Compensatory damages**: Lost wages, benefits, and other economic losses resulting from the retaliation
- **Emotional distress damages**: Compensation for psychological harm caused by the retaliatory conduct
- **Punitive damages**: Available in cases involving particularly egregious conduct (subject to statutory caps under some laws)
- **Attorney's fees**: Available under most employment statutes when employees prevail

Injunctive relief can include orders requiring employers to:

- Stop retaliatory conduct
- Provide agreed references
- Remove negative information from personnel files
- Reinstate employees to former positions

Example case structure: A retaliation lawsuit might include claims for violation of Title VII's anti-retaliation provision, breach of settlement contract, defamation (for false statements made to prospective employers), and intentional interference with prospective economic advantage.

3. Enforcing the Settlement Agreement

Breach of contract claims arise when employers fail to comply with settlement terms. These claims are typically governed by contract law rather than employment statutes, which can provide different remedies and procedural advantages.

Court enforcement: When settlement agreements are filed with courts, violations can be addressed through motions to enforce rather than separate lawsuits. This process is often faster and less expensive than filing new litigation.

Contempt proceedings: In cases involving court-ordered settlements, employers who violate terms may face contempt of court, which can include monetary sanctions and imprisonment in extreme cases.

Damages for breach: Contract damages typically focus on putting the non-breaching party in the position they would have been in if the contract had been performed, which may differ from statutory employment law damages.

4. Seeking Protective Orders

Restraining orders and **injunctive relief** can provide immediate protection for employees facing ongoing retaliation. These orders are particularly useful when retaliation involves harassment, threats, or interference with new employment.

Workplace protection orders in some jurisdictions specifically address workplace harassment and can include provisions requiring employers to stop retaliatory conduct and maintain professional boundaries.

Example relief: A protective order might require an employer to stop contacting the employee's new employer, provide agreed references, or limit communications to specific business purposes through designated representatives.

23.5 Evidence of Retaliation

Documentary Evidence

Email communications often provide the strongest evidence of retaliatory intent. Look for messages that:

- Reference the employee's legal claims
- Show changes in treatment after settlement
- Demonstrate coordination between managers about the employee
- Reveal discriminatory attitudes or motivations

Example: An email from a supervisor stating "We need to make sure [employee] doesn't think she can come back here after what she put us through" directly evidences retaliatory intent.

Personnel records can show differential treatment through:

- Performance evaluations that suddenly become negative after settlement
- Disciplinary actions that escalate without justification
- Changes in job assignments or responsibilities
- Documentation of incidents that were previously ignored

Temporal Evidence

Timeline analysis is crucial for establishing causal connection between protected activity and adverse action. Key elements include:

- Proximity in time between settlement and retaliation
- Changes in employer behavior after settlement
- Lack of legitimate business reasons for adverse actions
- Consistency of treatment compared to similarly situated employees

Legal standard: While temporal proximity alone rarely proves retaliation, close timing combined with other evidence can establish the necessary causal connection. Courts generally find temporal proximity most persuasive when adverse actions occur within days or weeks of protected activity.

Witness Testimony

Coworker statements can establish:

- Changes in workplace atmosphere after settlement

- Supervisor comments about the employee's legal claims
- Differential treatment compared to other employees
- Knowledge of employer policies or practices

Professional references from industry contacts can demonstrate blacklisting through:

- Reports of negative informal references
- Unusual questions about the employee's legal history
- Employers' refusal to provide agreed references
- Industry reputation damage

Comparative Evidence

Similarly situated employees analysis examines whether employees who did not engage in protected activity received different treatment. Key factors include:

- Job duties and performance levels
- Disciplinary history
- Length of employment
- Qualifications and experience

Example: If an employer refuses to rehire a former employee who settled a discrimination claim, but rehires other former employees with similar qualifications and work history, this suggests discriminatory treatment.

23.6 Preventing Retaliation in Settlement Agreements

Essential Protective Clauses

No retaliation clause should be comprehensive and specific:

Standard language: "Employer agrees not to engage in any act of retaliation, direct or indirect, against Employee for any reason arising out of or relating to this claim or its resolution, including but not limited to retaliation for Employee's participation in any future government investigation or legal proceeding."

Enhanced language: The clause should explicitly cover:

- Direct and indirect retaliation
- Retaliation by agents, employees, or affiliated entities
- Future protected activity, including government cooperation
- Both employment-related and personal retaliation

Reference provisions should specify exact language and procedures:

Neutral reference template: Attach a specific reference letter to the agreement or include precise language that references must contain. Specify who will provide references and through what method (written, verbal, or both).

Example provision: "Employer agrees to provide only the following information in response to reference inquiries: Employee's job title, dates of employment, and final salary. Employer will not provide any negative information about Employee's performance, character, or reasons for separation."

Enforcement mechanisms should include:

Attorney's fees provision: "In any action to enforce this agreement, the prevailing party shall be entitled to reasonable attorney's fees and costs."

Liquidated damages clause: "Employer acknowledges that any breach of the non-retaliation provisions will cause irreparable harm to Employee that cannot be adequately compensated by monetary damages alone. Therefore, Employee shall be entitled to injunctive relief and liquidated damages of $[amount] for each breach."

Jurisdiction and venue clauses: Specify where enforcement actions must be filed to avoid procedural complications.

Advanced Protective Strategies

Monitoring and reporting requirements: Some agreements include provisions requiring employers to report compliance or allowing employees to request confirmation of reference content.

Third-party reference services: In high-risk situations, agreements might require employers to use professional reference services that provide standardized, neutral responses.

Escalation procedures: Include internal dispute resolution mechanisms that address potential retaliation before it escalates to litigation.

23.7 Ethical Considerations

Attorney Responsibilities

Rule 1.1 (Competence) requires attorneys to understand retaliation risks and advise clients accordingly. This includes explaining potential post-settlement risks and incorporating appropriate protective measures.

Rule 1.4 (Communication) mandates that attorneys keep clients informed about retaliation developments and explain legal options clearly.

Rule 8.4 (Misconduct) prohibits attorneys from assisting clients in conduct that violates laws or ethical rules, including covering up retaliation or intimidating witnesses.

Scope of Confidentiality and Non-Disparagement

Legal limitations: Employers cannot contractually waive or limit an employee's right to:

- Report violations of law to government agencies
- Participate in government investigations
- Provide truthful testimony in legal proceedings
- File charges with administrative agencies

Example of problematic clause: "Employee agrees not to discuss this matter with any third party, including government agencies." This language is overly broad and likely unenforceable because it could discourage lawful reporting.

Compliant alternative: "Employee agrees not to make disparaging statements about Employer, provided that this provision does not prohibit truthful testimony in legal proceedings or reports to government agencies as permitted by law."

Protected communications: The National Labor Relations Act and various whistleblower statutes protect certain employee communications regardless of contractual provisions.

Government Investigation Rights

EEOC cooperation: The Equal Employment Opportunity Commission has taken the position that settlement agreements cannot prevent employees from filing charges or cooperating with EEOC investigations. Agreements that attempt to do so may be challenged as contrary to public policy.

State agency cooperation: Most state civil rights agencies have similar policies protecting employee cooperation, even when settlement agreements contain confidentiality provisions.

Best practice: Include specific carve-outs for government cooperation: "Nothing in this agreement prevents Employee from filing charges with or cooperating with investigations by the EEOC, state civil rights agencies, or other government entities."

23.8 Strategic Considerations for Practitioners

Client Education and Preparation

Red flag training: Educate clients about warning signs of potential retaliation:

- Changes in employer behavior or communications
- Unusual reference requests or employer inquiries
- Industry feedback about reputation damage
- Breach of settlement terms

Practical example: Provide clients with a checklist of concerning behaviors and contact information for immediate consultation if retaliation occurs.

Documentation protocols: Establish systems for clients to document potential retaliation:

- Email preservation procedures
- Incident logging methods
- Contact information for potential witnesses
- Reference request tracking

Ongoing Client Relationships

Post-settlement monitoring: Maintain contact with clients during vulnerable periods (typically 6-24 months post-settlement) through:

- Scheduled check-in calls
- Email updates on legal developments
- Availability for urgent consultations
- Referral networks for career counseling

Compliance verification: For high-risk cases, consider requesting periodic compliance reports or reference audits to ensure employers are meeting their obligations.

Timing and Statute of Limitations

Urgent response protocols: Retaliation claims often have short deadlines:

- EEOC charges: 180-300 days depending on jurisdiction
- State administrative charges: Varies by state (one to three years)
- Contract breach claims: Governed by state contract law (typically 3-6 years)

Practice tip: Establish intake procedures that can quickly identify retaliation issues and preserve claim deadlines.

Continuing violation doctrine: In some circumstances, ongoing retaliation may be treated as a continuing violation that extends filing deadlines. However, practitioners should never rely on this doctrine and should file claims promptly.

Leverage and Settlement Strategy

Retaliation as aggravating factor: Post-settlement retaliation can significantly increase damages in subsequent claims and may support punitive damage awards.

Pattern evidence: Retaliation against multiple employees can support class action claims or pattern-and-practice charges with government agencies.

Strategic consideration: Document retaliation carefully as it may be useful in representing other employees or in broader enforcement actions.

23.9 Recent Developments

Increased Enforcement Activity

EEOC priorities: The Equal Employment Opportunity Commission has identified retaliation as a priority enforcement area, with retaliation charges comprising the largest category of charges filed annually (over 55% of all charges in recent years).

State agency expansion: California's Civil Rights Department and New York's Division of Human Rights have expanded their retaliation enforcement, including systematic reviews of post-settlement compliance.

Pattern-and-practice investigations: Government agencies increasingly pursue broad investigations when individual retaliation complaints suggest systemic problems.

Expanded Liability Theories

Third-party retaliation: Courts have recognized claims where employers retaliate against employees indirectly by taking action against family members, business associates, or other third parties.

Example: An employer who terminates an employee's spouse in retaliation for the employee's discrimination claim may face liability for third-party retaliation.

Social media retaliation: New forms of retaliation include negative social media campaigns, online reviews, or digital blacklisting that can be more difficult to detect and prove.

Industry-wide coordination: Some cases involve multiple employers within an industry coordinating to blacklist employees, creating broader conspiracy and antitrust issues.

Technological Evidence

Digital discovery: Electronic communications, social media posts, and digital personnel records provide new sources of evidence for retaliation claims.

Metadata analysis: Time stamps, revision histories, and communication patterns can reveal retaliatory intent and coordination between decision-makers.

Reference tracking: Technology platforms that track reference requests and employer responses can provide objective evidence of blacklisting.

Class Action Developments

Retaliation class actions are becoming more common, particularly in cases involving:

- Systematic blacklisting practices
- Coordinated industry responses to legal claims
- Pattern violations of settlement agreements
- Widespread interference with government investigations

Settlement class protections: Some courts require enhanced anti-retaliation provisions in class action settlements, recognizing the heightened risk of retaliation against class members.

23.10 Comparative Analysis of Jurisdictions

Federal vs. State Protections

Damage limitations: Federal statutes often cap compensatory and punitive damages, while state laws may provide unlimited damages:

- Title VII: Caps range from $50,000 to $300,000 based on employer size
- California FEHA: No caps on compensatory damages
- New York: Varies by statute, generally more generous than federal

Statute of limitations: Significant variations affect strategic decisions:

- Federal EEOC charges: 180-300 days
- California administrative complaints: 3 years
- New York: 1-3 years depending on specific statute

Scope of protection: State laws often provide broader coverage:

- Smaller employers (California and New York cover employers with 4+ employees vs. federal requirement of 15+)
- Broader definitions of protected activity
- Enhanced protection for opposition conduct

Practical Implications for Multi-State Practice

Forum selection: When multiple jurisdictions apply, consider:

- Damage availability and limitations
- Statute of limitations differences
- Procedural advantages
- Local court attitudes toward retaliation claims

Choice of law: Settlement agreements should specify which state's law governs enforcement to avoid conflicts and provide predictability.

Example: A California employee who settles with a New York employer might benefit from California's longer statute of limitations and unlimited damages, making California law preferable for the settlement agreement.

23.11 Conclusion

The fight doesn't always end with a signed agreement. Retaliation after a settlement is not only unethical - it's often illegal and increasingly scrutinized by courts and government agencies. Post-settlement retaliation presents unique challenges because it may be subtle, delayed, and seemingly unrelated to the original dispute, but legal protections continue beyond the settlement date.

Understanding the various forms retaliation can take - from blacklisting and hostile work environments to settlement breaches and interference with government investigations - allows practitioners to better protect their clients and recognize violations when they occur. The legal framework provides multiple avenues for relief, including administrative complaints, civil litigation, contract enforcement, and injunctive relief, each with distinct advantages and procedural requirements.

Effective prevention requires careful drafting of settlement agreements with specific anti-retaliation provisions, reference protocols, and enforcement mechanisms. However, even the best-drafted agreements cannot prevent all retaliation, making ongoing client education and monitoring essential components of post-settlement practice.

The legal landscape continues to evolve, with increased government enforcement, expanded liability theories, and new forms of technologically-enabled retaliation. Practitioners must stay current with these developments while maintaining the fundamental skills of evidence gathering, strategic thinking, and client counseling that effective retaliation practice requires.

By anticipating misconduct, documenting violations, and invoking the right legal remedies, employment lawyers can protect their clients beyond the courthouse and help ensure the dignity and stability that settlements are supposed to deliver. The goal is not just to resolve the immediate dispute, but to create lasting protection that allows employees to move forward in their careers without fear of continued retaliation.

In Chapter 24, the final chapter, we'll address client care after closure, including tax reporting follow-up, career counseling referrals, and re-engagement protocols that support holistic legal practice.

24

Post-Resolution Client Care and Long-Term Success

A favorable judgment or settlement represents a legal milestone, but your client's journey extends far beyond the courtroom victory. Many clients emerge from employment litigation emotionally drained, professionally disoriented, and uncertain about their future trajectory. As counsel, your responsibilities transcend securing legal victory - they encompass preparing your client for comprehensive financial, psychological, and career recovery.

This chapter examines the critical components of post-resolution client care, spanning tax reporting assistance and strategic career planning to sustainable relationship building and holistic advocacy approaches that distinguish exceptional employment law practices.

24.1 Understanding the Emotional Landscape of Litigation

Employment disputes carry unique psychological burdens that distinguish them from other areas of civil litigation. Unlike contract disputes or personal injury cases, workplace conflicts strike at the core of professional identity and economic security. Clients typically experience a complex constellation of emotions including:

Identity Crisis and Professional Displacement: Employment litigation often follows sudden termination or constructive discharge, leaving clients questioning their professional worth and market value. Unlike voluntary career transitions, litigation-induced job loss creates an involuntary rupture in career trajectory that can trigger existential questioning about professional competence and future prospects.

Institutional Betrayal and Trust Erosion: Workplace disputes frequently involve betrayal by colleagues, supervisors, or organizational leadership whom clients previously trusted. This institutional betrayal differs significantly from interpersonal conflicts because it damages fundamental assumptions about workplace fairness and professional relationships, often extending distrust to future employment opportunities.

Litigation Fatigue and Decision Exhaustion: Extended employment disputes create chronic stress through prolonged uncertainty, repetitive depositions, document production demands, and strategic decision-making. This differs from acute stress responses because it involves sustained psychological pressure over months or years, depleting emotional reserves and decision-making capacity.

Reputational Anxiety and Professional Stigma: Clients often fear that litigation history will render them unemployable or professionally radioactive. This anxiety distinguishes employment cases from other litigation because professional reputation directly impacts earning capacity and career advancement opportunities.

Post-Litigation Emotional Letdown: Even successful resolution can trigger unexpected emotional responses similar to post-traumatic stress or achievement depression. Clients may experience anticlimax, purposelessness, or renewed anxiety about future challenges. Recognizing these responses allows proactive intervention through appropriate referrals and continued support.

The distinction between pre-litigation emotional states and post-resolution psychological needs requires different advocacy approaches. Pre-litigation support focuses on crisis intervention and strategic planning, while post-resolution care emphasizes rehabilitation, future-oriented planning, and sustainable recovery strategies.

24.2 Comprehensive Final Deliverables and Strategic Client Briefing

Case closure requires systematic preparation of comprehensive post-resolution documentation that serves both immediate practical needs and long-term strategic purposes. This differs from the conclusion of a simple case because employment law resolutions create ongoing obligations, reporting requirements, and enforcement considerations that extend years after final signatures.

Detailed Outcome Summary and Implementation Roadmap

Settlement vs. Judgment Documentation Differences: Settlement agreements require different documentation than court judgments because they create contractual obligations rather than judicial mandates. Settlement documentation should include detailed performance timelines, breach remedies, and modification procedures, while judgment documentation focuses on enforcement mechanisms, appeal deadlines, and collection procedures.

Payment Structure Analysis: Modern employment settlements often involve complex payment structures that require detailed explanation. Lump sum payments create different tax implications than structured payments spread over multiple tax years. Continuation of benefits, stock option vesting, and pension credit restoration each carry distinct legal and financial consequences requiring separate documentation and explanation.

Contingent Payment Provisions: Many settlements include contingent payments triggered by specific events such as COBRA continuation, outplacement service completion, or non-competition agreement compliance. These provisions require clear documentation because failure to meet conditions can void payment obligations or trigger clawback provisions.

Tax Reporting Guidance and Professional Consultation

Wage vs. Non-Wage Damage Classification: Employment settlements typically include multiple damage categories subject to different tax treatment. Back pay and front pay constitute wage income subject to employment taxes, while compensatory damages for emotional distress may qualify for different treatment under IRC Section 104. Punitive damages generally constitute taxable income without employment tax implications.

Attorney's Fee Reporting Complexities: The American Jobs Creation Act of 2004 created specific reporting requirements for attorney's fees in employment cases. Clients must report gross settlement amounts as income while claiming attorney's fees as above-the-line deductions, creating potential tax liability on attorney compensation. This differs from other litigation contexts where attorney's fees may be excluded from gross income calculations.

State Tax Variation Considerations: State tax treatment of employment settlements varies significantly across jurisdictions. Some states follow federal classifications while others impose different requirements. Clients relocating after resolution may face additional complications requiring specialized tax advice.

Professional Tax Consultation Recommendations: Given the complexity of employment settlement taxation, recommend consultation with tax professionals experienced in employment law matters rather than general practitioners. Provide clients with specific questions to ask potential tax advisors to ensure appropriate expertise levels.

Enforceability Framework and Breach Response Protocols

Settlement Agreement vs. Court Order Enforcement: Settlement agreements create contractual obligations enforceable through breach of contract actions, while court judgments provide additional enforcement mechanisms including wage garnishment, asset seizure, and contempt proceedings. Explain these distinctions because enforcement strategies differ significantly based on resolution structure.

Statute of Limitations for Breach Claims: Settlement agreement breaches typically carry contract statute of limitations periods ranging from three to six years depending on jurisdiction, while judgment enforcement may have different limitation periods. Document these timelines clearly because delayed enforcement can forfeit recovery rights.

Monitoring and Detection Systems: Establish systems for monitoring compliance with ongoing settlement obligations such as neutral references, non-disparagement requirements, or continuation of benefits. Unlike one-time payments, ongoing obligations require active monitoring to detect breaches promptly.

Confidentiality and Communication Guidelines

Non-Disparagement vs. Confidentiality Distinctions: These terms are often confused but create different legal obligations. Non-disparagement clauses prohibit negative statements about former employers while allowing factual disclosure, whereas confidentiality provisions may prohibit any discussion of underlying facts or resolution terms.

Reference Request Protocols: When settlements include neutral reference agreements, provide clients with specific language and procedures for requesting references. Include contact information, approved factual statements, and escalation procedures if neutral reference obligations are breached.

Social Media and Online Presence Guidelines: Modern confidentiality and non-disparagement obligations extend to social media platforms, online reviews, and professional networking sites. Provide specific guidance about LinkedIn updates, Glassdoor reviews, and social media posts that could trigger breach claims.

24.3 Strategic Career Transition Support and Professional Rehabilitation

Employment litigation clients face unique career transition challenges that distinguish them from typical job seekers. Litigation history, potential reputational concerns, and industry-specific considerations require specialized transition support that acknowledges both legal constraints and professional realities.

Career Coaching and Vocational Rehabilitation Referrals

Industry-Specific Career Coaching: Different industries have varying tolerance levels for litigation history and different approaches to reference checking. Technology companies may focus more on skills demonstration than employment history, while financial services firms conduct extensive background investigations. Refer clients to career coaches with industry-specific experience who understand these nuances.

Executive vs. Non-Executive Transition Support: Executive-level clients face different challenges than individual contributors because senior positions involve more extensive background checking, longer hiring processes, and greater scrutiny of employment history. Executive transition support should include board presentation coaching, media training, and reputation management strategies.

Vocational Rehabilitation for Career Pivots: Some clients use litigation resolution as an opportunity for career transitions into different industries or roles. Vocational rehabilitation services can assess transferable skills, identify training needs, and develop transition strategies that leverage litigation experience positively.

Resume and Professional Profile Development

Litigation Gap Explanation Strategies: Employment gaps during litigation require careful explanation that acknowledges time away from work without highlighting legal conflicts. Develop standard language that characterizes gaps as "career transition periods" or "professional development time" while remaining truthful.

LinkedIn Profile Optimization: Professional networking profiles require careful crafting to present litigation gaps positively while complying with confidentiality obligations. Include guidance on industry keyword optimization, connection strategy, and content sharing that demonstrates continued professional engagement.

Reference Strategy Development: When traditional supervisor references are unavailable due to litigation, help clients identify alternative professional references including clients, vendors, industry colleagues, and professional association contacts who can speak to work quality and character.

Professional Development and Skill Enhancement

Continuing Education Strategic Planning: Use resolution periods for strategic skill development that enhances marketability and demonstrates continued professional growth. Identify industry certifications, advanced degrees, or specialized training that address skill gaps or market trends.

Professional Association Re-engagement: Encourage active participation in professional associations, industry conferences, and networking events to maintain professional visibility and demonstrate continued industry engagement despite litigation history.

Volunteer and Board Service Opportunities: Strategic volunteer work can provide recent references, demonstrate leadership capabilities, and fill employment gaps constructively while building new professional networks.

24.4 Mental Health Support and Trauma-Informed Advocacy

Employment litigation often involves workplace harassment, discrimination, or retaliation that creates lasting psychological impact requiring specialized mental health support. Unlike other litigation contexts, workplace trauma affects professional identity, economic security, and future employment relationships simultaneously.

Trauma-Informed Practice Integration

Workplace Trauma vs. General Trauma Responses: Workplace trauma involves betrayal by trusted institutions and colleagues, creating unique psychological responses that differ from other traumatic experiences. Workplace trauma often triggers hypervigilance about future employment relationships, difficulty trusting supervisors, and anxiety about professional competence.

Secondary Trauma from Litigation Process: The litigation process itself can create additional trauma through depositions, document review, and adversarial proceedings that require clients to repeatedly recount traumatic experiences. Recognize signs of secondary trauma including litigation avoidance, emotional numbing, or excessive anxiety about case proceedings.

Cultural and Demographic Considerations: Different demographic groups experience workplace trauma differently based on historical patterns of discrimination, cultural backgrounds, and community support systems. Mental health referrals should consider cultural competency, language preferences, and community-specific resources.

Specialized Mental Health Referrals

Employment-Focused Therapy Specializations: Refer clients to mental health professionals with specific experience in workplace trauma, career transition counseling, or employment-related stress disorders. General therapists may lack understanding of employment law context and workplace dynamics.

Group Therapy and Support Networks: Workplace trauma support groups provide peer connections with others who have experienced similar challenges. These groups offer unique benefits because participants understand employment law contexts and professional concerns that general support groups may not address.

Employee Assistance Program Navigation: When available, EAPs through current or former employers can provide confidential counseling services, but clients may hesitate to use employer-sponsored resources due to confidentiality concerns. Explain EAP confidentiality protections and limitations to help clients make informed decisions.

Stress Management and Coping Strategy Development

Litigation Stress vs. Post-Resolution Adjustment: Stress management needs change significantly between active litigation and post-resolution periods. Active litigation stress focuses on case management and decision-making, while post-resolution stress involves uncertainty about future employment and identity reconstruction.

Professional Identity Reconstruction: Help clients develop new professional narratives that incorporate litigation experience positively rather than viewing it as career damage. This involves reframing advocacy experience, resilience demonstration, and commitment to workplace justice as professional strengths.

Sleep and Wellness Protocol Development: Chronic litigation stress often disrupts sleep patterns, exercise routines, and general wellness practices. Recovery requires intentional reconstruction of healthy lifestyle patterns that support long-term career success.

24.5 Long-Term Client Relationship Development and Strategic Re-engagement

Successful employment law practices recognize that case resolution represents the beginning rather than the end of valuable client relationships. Former clients become referral sources, repeat clients for future issues, and testimonials for practice development efforts.

Follow-Up Communication Protocols

Systematic Check-In Scheduling: Implement systematic follow-up protocols that acknowledge different client needs over time. Three-month check-ins focus on immediate adjustment issues, six-month contacts address longer-term career progress, and annual communications maintain ongoing relationships while identifying new legal needs.

Value-Added Communication Strategy: Follow-up communications should provide value in addition to simple relationship maintenance. Include relevant legal updates, industry news, or professional development resources that demonstrate continued investment in client success rather than purely transactional follow-up.

Privacy and Confidentiality in Ongoing Communications: Maintain appropriate confidentiality standards in ongoing communications while building relationships. Avoid discussing case details in written communications and ensure secure communication channels for sensitive discussions.

Future Legal Service Opportunities

New Employment Legal Review: Many former clients benefit from legal review of new employment contracts, severance agreements, or workplace policies. Offer annual complimentary reviews of new employment documents as relationship maintenance that provides genuine value while identifying potential new legal needs.

Preventive Legal Counseling: Provide guidance on avoiding future workplace conflicts through documentation practices, performance management strategies, and early intervention techniques. This positions your practice as preventive rather than purely reactive legal support.

Contract and Agreement Review Services: Former clients often encounter non-competition agreements, consulting contracts, or partnership agreements requiring legal review. Established relationships facilitate efficient service delivery while maintaining client loyalty.

Referral Network Development

Client-to-Client Referral Systems: Former employment law clients often maintain professional networks that include potential future clients. Develop systems for facilitating appropriate referrals while maintaining confidentiality about previous client relationships.

Professional Network Integration: Integrate former clients into your professional network through LinkedIn connections, professional association introductions, and industry event invitations. This maintains relationships while expanding your professional presence.

Testimonial and Case Study Development: With appropriate permissions and confidentiality protections, develop anonymized case studies and client testimonials that demonstrate practice capabilities while maintaining client privacy.

24.6 Document Retention and Recordkeeping Best Practices

Employment law case resolution creates ongoing document retention obligations for both clients and attorneys that extend significantly after the case is over. These obligations arise from tax reporting requirements, potential future disputes, and ethical responsibilities that distinguish employment law from other practice areas.

Client Document Retention Guidance

Settlement Agreement Preservation: Settlement agreements represent contractual obligations that may require enforcement years after execution. Clients should maintain original agreements in secure, accessible locations with backup copies in separate locations. Digital copies should be stored securely with physical originals retained indefinitely.

Tax Document Organization: Employment settlement taxation creates multi-year reporting obligations requiring systematic document retention.

W-2 and 1099 forms should be retained for seven years minimum, while supporting documentation including settlement agreements and attorney fee calculations should be retained indefinitely for potential audit purposes.

Employment History Documentation: Performance reviews, disciplinary actions, termination documentation, and workplace communications retain value for future employment disputes or reference requests. Advise clients to maintain comprehensive employment files including both positive and negative documentation.

Financial Record Integration: Settlement payments often integrate with existing financial records through bank deposits, investment transfers, or retirement account contributions. Ensure clients understand how settlement documentation connects to broader financial recordkeeping for tax and estate planning purposes.

Attorney Recordkeeping Obligations

Ethical File Retention Requirements: State bar rules impose varying file retention requirements ranging from five to ten years, with some jurisdictions requiring indefinite retention of client files. Review applicable ethical rules and establish systematic retention policies that exceed minimum requirements for employment cases.

Conflict Checking Database Maintenance: Employment law practices often represent multiple clients within the same industries or against the same employers. Maintain comprehensive conflict checking databases that include former client information, opposing parties, and potential future conflicts for extended periods.

Privilege and Confidentiality Protection: Attorney-client privileged communications require permanent protection even after representation concludes. Establish secure storage systems for privileged materials with appropriate access controls and confidentiality safeguards.

Client Trust Account Documentation: Settlement fund handling creates trust account obligations requiring detailed recordkeeping for potential bar audits. Maintain comprehensive trust account records including client authorizations, disbursement documentation, and reconciliation records.

24.7 Ethical Professional Disengagement and Relationship Transition

Proper case conclusion requires careful attention to professional responsibility requirements that govern attorney-client relationship termination while preserving opportunities for future representation and referral relationships.

Formal Disengagement Procedures

Written Termination Communication: Provide formal written communication documenting representation conclusion, case outcome summary, and future contact procedures. This documentation protects both attorney and client by clearly establishing the end of the attorney-client relationship and ongoing obligations.

Original Document Return Protocols: Return all original client documents while retaining appropriate copies for file retention requirements. Document the return process to avoid future disputes about missing materials and ensure clients have necessary documentation for ongoing obligations.

Statute of Limitations Notifications: Identify and communicate all applicable statutes of limitations for potential future claims including breach of settlement agreements, tax disputes, or related employment issues. This notification protects clients from waiving potential claims due to missed deadlines.

Outstanding Fee and Cost Resolution: Address all pending billing issues, outstanding costs, and potential refunds before formal disengagement. Unresolved financial issues can complicate future relationships and create ethical violations if not properly handled.

Transition Planning for Future Representation

Scope of Future Representation: When appropriate, establish parameters for potential future representation including retainer requirements, fee structures, and scope limitations. This prevents misunderstandings about ongoing legal relationships while preserving opportunities for future work.

Referral Protocols for Related Issues: Employment law clients often encounter related legal issues including business formation, contract disputes, or family law matters arising from career transitions. Establish referral protocols for practice areas outside your expertise while maintaining client relationships.

Emergency Contact Procedures: Provide clients with procedures for urgent legal questions or emergency situations that may arise after formal representation concludes. This demonstrates continued commitment to client welfare while establishing appropriate boundaries.

Professional Responsibility Compliance

Client File Audit and Review: Conduct comprehensive file reviews before closure to ensure all client materials are properly organized, privileged materials are identified, and retention obligations are clearly documented. This process prevents future ethical violations and ensures efficient file management.

Billing Audit and Reconciliation: Review all time records, expense allocations, and trust account transactions to ensure accurate billing and proper client fund handling. Address any discrepancies before formal disengagement to avoid future disputes.

Conflict Resolution Documentation: Document resolution of any potential conflicts that arose during representation and establish protocols for addressing conflicts in future representations. This proactive approach prevents ethical violations in subsequent matters.

24.8 Building Comprehensive Holistic Practice Models

Modern employment law practice increasingly demands integrated service delivery that addresses client needs over and above what has been traditional legal representation. Holistic practice models distinguish exceptional firms by providing comprehensive support that addresses the interconnected legal, professional, and personal challenges arising from workplace disputes.

Interdisciplinary Partnership Development

Human Resources Consulting Integration: Partner with experienced HR consultants who can provide workplace policy development, training services, and preventive counseling that complements legal representation.

These partnerships create referral opportunities while expanding service offerings to existing clients.

Career Coaching and Outplacement Services: Formal partnerships with career transition specialists provide seamless service delivery for clients facing employment changes. These relationships should include defined referral protocols, fee-sharing arrangements where ethical, and coordinated service delivery that avoids conflicts of interest.

Mental Health Professional Networks: Develop relationships with trauma-informed therapists, career counselors, and psychiatric professionals who understand employment law contexts. These networks provide appropriate referrals while ensuring clients receive specialized care for employment-related psychological issues.

Financial Planning and Tax Services: Employment settlements create complex financial planning needs requiring specialized expertise. Partner with financial planners and tax professionals experienced in employment law matters to provide comprehensive guidance on settlement fund management, tax optimization, and retirement planning.

Technology Integration and Resource Development

Client Portal and Resource Centers: Develop secure online portals that provide clients with case updates, document access, and educational resources throughout and after representation. These systems improve communication efficiency while providing ongoing value to former clients.

Educational Content and Training Programs: Create webinar series, written guides, and educational workshops addressing common client concerns including workplace rights, career transition strategies, and legal compliance issues. This content demonstrates expertise while providing ongoing value to client relationships.

Mobile Communication and Support Systems: Implement mobile-friendly communication systems that accommodate client preferences and accessibility needs. Modern clients expect responsive communication through various channels including text messaging, video conferencing, and mobile applications.

Practice Management and Growth Strategies

Client Feedback and Service Improvement: Implement systematic client feedback collection through surveys, interviews, and focus groups that identify service gaps and improvement opportunities. Use this feedback to refine service delivery and develop new practice areas responding to client needs.

Community Engagement and Professional Leadership: Engage in community organizations, professional associations, and industry leadership roles that demonstrate expertise while building referral networks. This engagement should align with practice goals while providing genuine community value.

Continuing Education and Professional Development: Maintain cutting-edge expertise through specialized training, industry conferences, and peer collaboration. Employment law evolves rapidly, requiring ongoing education to provide competent representation and innovative service delivery.

24.9 Addressing Common Post-Resolution Client Concerns

Employment law clients typically have recurring questions and concerns following case resolution that require proactive communication and comprehensive guidance. Understanding these common issues allows preparation of standard resources while customizing responses to individual client circumstances.

Confidentiality and Communication Guidelines

"What can I tell future employers about the case?": This question requires careful analysis of specific confidentiality provisions because settlement agreements vary significantly in scope and restrictions. Standard confidentiality clauses typically prohibit disclosure of settlement terms and underlying facts but may allow acknowledgment that disputes were resolved. Non-disparagement provisions are separate from confidentiality and may permit factual statements while prohibiting negative characterizations.

Provide clients with specific language templates for common situations including job interview responses, reference check conversations, and professional networking discussions. For example: "I had a professional disagreement with my former employer that we resolved amicably through legal processes. I'm excited to focus on new opportunities and contributing to your organization."

"Can I discuss the case with colleagues or friends?": Personal relationships typically fall outside confidentiality restrictions, but clients should understand that confidential information shared with others may lose legal protection. Advise clients to limit discussions to trusted individuals and avoid social media posts or public discussions that could be construed as confidentiality violations.

Background Check and Employment Screening Concerns

"Will litigation appear on background checks?": The answer depends on the structure of the case's resolution and public filing requirements. Court judgments typically become public records accessible through background checks, while private settlements generally remain confidential unless specifically disclosed. However, some background check services search legal databases that may capture complaint filings even if cases were subsequently settled confidentially.

Explain the distinction between criminal background checks, employment verification, and civil litigation searches because employers use different screening levels depending on position requirements and industry standards. High-security positions may involve more comprehensive searches than standard employment screening.

"How should I explain employment gaps?": Litigation periods create employment gaps requiring careful explanation that remains truthful while presenting clients positively. Develop standard language emphasizing professional development, career transition planning, or family obligations depending on individual circumstances and gap duration.

Ongoing Legal Obligations and Compliance

"What if my former employer breaches the settlement agreement?": Settlement breach remedies depend on specific agreement terms and may include monetary damages, injunctive relief, or contract rescission. Explain the difference between material and minor breaches because remedy availability varies based on breach severity and impact.

Establish protocols for breach detection and response including documentation requirements, notice provisions, and communication procedures. Many settlement agreements require written notice and cure periods before formal breach claims can be pursued.

"Can my former employer retaliate for filing the lawsuit?": Post-litigation retaliation can occur through negative references, industry communications, or interference with future employment opportunities. While settlement agreements often include non-retaliation provisions, enforcement can be challenging and may require additional legal action.

Advise clients to document potential retaliation including screenshots of social media activity, witness statements about negative communications, and evidence of interference with employment opportunities. This documentation becomes crucial if additional legal action becomes necessary.

Tax Implications and Financial Planning

"What taxes will I owe on the settlement?": Tax obligations depend on damage classifications and payment structures within settlement agreements. Back pay and front pay constitute wage income subject to employment taxes, while compensatory damages may qualify for different treatment depending on underlying claims and documentation.

Punitive damages generally constitute taxable income without employment tax implications, while attorney fees create above-the-line deduction opportunities under specific circumstances. State tax implications vary significantly and may differ from federal treatment.

"Should I make estimated tax payments?": Large settlement payments may require estimated tax payments to avoid underpayment penalties, particularly when settlements include multiple tax years or create significant income spikes. Coordinate with tax professionals to calculate appropriate payment amounts and deadlines.

"How should I invest or manage settlement funds?": Settlement fund management requires consideration of immediate needs, long-term financial goals, and potential tax optimization strategies. Recommend consultation with financial advisors experienced in windfall management who can provide comprehensive planning guidance.

Career Planning and Professional Development

"When should I start looking for new employment?": Job search timing depends on multiple factors including financial needs, market conditions, industry-specific considerations, and personal readiness. Some clients benefit from immediate job searches to maintain professional momentum, while others need recovery time to address litigation-related stress or skill development needs.

Consider industry-specific hiring patterns, seasonal variations, and economic conditions when advising clients about optimal timing for job search activities. Technology companies may hire continuously while education positions follow academic calendars.

"Should I change industries or career paths?": Career transition decisions require careful analysis of transferable skills, market opportunities, financial implications, and personal interests. Some clients use litigation resolution as catalysts for positive career changes, while others prefer returning to familiar industries and roles.

Provide resources for career assessment, industry research, and transition planning while acknowledging that major career changes involve additional time and financial commitments that may not be appropriate for all clients.

Reference and Networking Strategies

"How do I handle reference requests?": Reference strategies depend on settlement agreement provisions, available references, and industry norms. When traditional supervisor references are unavailable, help clients identify alternative professional references including clients, vendors, colleagues, and industry contacts.

Prepare clients for reference conversations by providing guidance on appropriate responses to common questions while complying with confidentiality obligations. Practice interview techniques that address employment gaps and litigation history positively without violating settlement terms.

"Should I maintain professional relationships with former colleagues?": Professional relationship maintenance requires balancing networking benefits with potential confidentiality risks and emotional considerations. Former colleagues may provide valuable references and networking opportunities, but relationships may be complicated by litigation history and workplace dynamics.

Advise clients to approach colleague relationships carefully, focusing on professional networking rather than discussing litigation details or workplace conflicts that led to legal action.

24.10 Transformative Practice Development and Client Legacy

Excellence in employment law practice extends over and above successful case resolution to encompass transformative client relationships that restore dignity, rebuild careers, and create lasting positive impact. This approach distinguishes exceptional practitioners by focusing on comprehensive client welfare rather than purely transactional legal services.

Client Dignity and Professional Restoration

Employment litigation often damages client confidence, professional identity, and career trajectory in ways that legal victories alone cannot repair. Transformative practice acknowledges these broader impacts and addresses them through comprehensive support that surpass simple traditional legal representation.

Professional Identity Reconstruction: Help clients develop new professional narratives that incorporate litigation experience as evidence of courage, integrity, and commitment to workplace justice rather than career damage. This reframing process requires ongoing support and reinforcement through multiple interactions and communications.

Industry Reputation Rehabilitation: When appropriate, develop strategies for rebuilding professional reputation within industry communities through thought leadership, professional association participation, and strategic networking that demonstrates continued expertise and professional engagement.

Mentorship and Peer Support Facilitation: Connect former clients with mentors, peer support networks, and professional communities that provide ongoing encouragement and career development opportunities. These relationships often prove more valuable than formal services in sustaining long-term career success.

Practice Legacy and Community Impact

Exceptional employment law practices create lasting positive impact that go further than individual client representation to influence workplace culture, legal precedent, and community awareness of employment rights and responsibilities.

Systemic Change and Legal Precedent: Identify opportunities for advancing employment law through strategic litigation, amicus brief participation, and professional association involvement that creates broader positive impact over and above the resolution of the individual's case.

Community Education and Awareness: Develop educational programs, speaking engagements, and written resources that increase community awareness of employment rights while positioning your practice as a thought leader and trusted resource.

Professional Development and Mentorship: Contribute to professional development of other employment law practitioners through continuing education programs, mentorship relationships, and practice management resources that elevate the entire profession.

Sustainable Practice Growth and Client Satisfaction

Transformative practice approaches create sustainable competitive advantages through exceptional client satisfaction, referral generation, and professional reputation development that distinguish practices in competitive legal markets.

Client Satisfaction and Loyalty Measurement: Implement comprehensive client satisfaction measurement systems that track both immediate case satisfaction and long-term career outcomes. Use this data to refine service delivery and demonstrate practice value to potential clients.

Referral Network Development and Management: Cultivate systematic referral networks including former clients, professional colleagues, and community partners that provide sustainable practice growth through trusted relationships rather than marketing expenditures.

Professional Reputation and Market Positioning: Develop distinctive market positioning based on comprehensive client care, transformative outcomes, and community impact that differentiates your practice from competitors focused purely on legal technical services.

Conclusion: From Transaction to Transformation

Employment law practice at its highest level transforms client trauma into stepping stones for future success while creating lasting positive impact that extends well beyond the individual's case resolution. This transformation requires comprehensive understanding of client needs, systematic service delivery processes, and genuine commitment to client welfare that distinguishes exceptional practitioners from purely transactional legal service providers.

The investment in comprehensive post-resolution client care generates significant returns through client loyalty, referral generation, professional satisfaction, and community impact that justify the additional time and resources required. More importantly, this approach fulfills the highest aspirations of legal practice by using professional skills to create genuine positive change in client lives and community welfare.

By implementing the strategies, systems, and approaches outlined in this chapter, employment law practitioners can elevate their practices from successful legal representation to transformative client advocacy that creates lasting positive impact for individuals, workplaces, and communities. This transformation represents the ultimate goal of employment law practice: using legal expertise to create a more just and equitable workplace environment for all participants and stakeholders.

Final Practice Integration Note: The concepts and strategies presented throughout this comprehensive guide work synergistically to create exceptional employment law practices that serve clients, communities, and the legal profession with distinction. Integration of these approaches requires systematic implementation, ongoing refinement, and genuine commitment to client welfare that transcends traditional legal service delivery to encompass holistic advocacy and transformative client relationships.

Congratulations on completing this examination of employment law practice in New York, California and the Federal Courts.

Glossary of Employment Law Terms

A

ADA (Americans with Disabilities Act): Federal law prohibiting discrimination against individuals with disabilities in employment, public accommodations, and other areas.

ADEA (Age Discrimination in Employment Act): Federal law prohibiting employment discrimination against individuals age 40 and older

Administrative Exhaustion: The requirement that a plaintiff must complete administrative proceedings (e.g., filing with EEOC, DFEH/CRD, or DHR) before bringing a lawsuit in court.

Adverse Employment Action: Any negative action taken by an employer that materially affects the terms, conditions, or privileges of employment, such as termination, demotion, suspension, or significant changes in job duties.

Affirmative Defense: A defense that admits the basic facts alleged by the plaintiff but asserts additional facts that justify the employer's conduct or bar the claim (e.g., statute of limitations, after-acquired evidence).

At-Will Employment: The default employment relationship in most U.S. states, allowing either party to terminate the employment relationship at any time, for any lawful reason, or no reason at all.

B

Back Pay: Wages, salary, benefits, and other compensation that an employee would have earned from the date of wrongful termination or adverse action until judgment, settlement, or reinstatement.

Bona Fide Occupational Qualification (BFOQ): A narrow exception to anti-discrimination laws that permits employers to make employment decisions based on protected characteristics when such characteristics are reasonably necessary to the normal operation of the business.

Burden-Shifting Framework: The analytical structure used in discrimination and retaliation cases, typically following the McDonnell Douglas test: (1) plaintiff establishes prima facie case, (2) defendant articulates legitimate reason, (3) plaintiff proves pretext.

C

CFRA (California Family Rights Act): California law providing eligible employees with unpaid family and medical leave.

Class Action: A lawsuit brought by one or more plaintiffs on behalf of a larger group of similarly situated individuals who share common legal or factual issues.

Collective Action: Under the Fair Labor Standards Act (FLSA), a lawsuit brought by one or more employees on behalf of themselves and other "similarly situated" employees for wage and hour violations.

Compensatory Damages: Monetary awards intended to compensate the plaintiff for actual losses, including lost wages, benefits, and emotional distress.

Constructive Discharge: A resignation that occurs when working conditions become so intolerable that a reasonable person would feel compelled to quit, legally treated as a termination.

Contingency Fee: A fee arrangement where the attorney receives a percentage of any recovery obtained for the client, typically ranging from 25% to 40% in employment cases.

D

DFEH/CRD (Department of Fair Employment and Housing/Civil Rights Department): California state agency that investigates discrimination complaints (now called Civil Rights Department).

Defamation: False statements that harm a person's reputation, which can occur in employment contexts through negative references, workplace gossip, or public statements about an employee's performance or character.

Demurrer: California's version of a motion to dismiss, challenging the legal sufficiency of the complaint without addressing the truth of the factual allegations.

Deposition: Sworn testimony taken outside of court during the discovery phase, where witnesses answer questions under oath in the presence of a court reporter.

Direct Evidence: Evidence that directly proves discriminatory intent, such as explicit statements showing bias based on protected characteristics.

Discovery: Pre-trial process where parties exchange information, documents, and testimony relevant to the case.

Disparate Impact: A form of discrimination where a facially neutral employment practice disproportionately affects members of a protected class and cannot be justified by business necessity.

Disparate Treatment: Intentional discrimination where an individual is treated less favorably because of their membership in a protected class.

E

EEOC (Equal Employment Opportunity Commission): The federal agency responsible for enforcing workplace anti-discrimination laws, including Title VII, ADA, and ADEA.

ESI (Electronically Stored Information): Digital data including emails, text messages, social media posts, databases, and other electronic records that may be relevant to employment litigation.

Emotional Distress Damages: Compensation for psychological harm resulting from workplace misconduct.

Exempt Employee: An employee who is not entitled to overtime pay under the Fair Labor Standards Act, typically because they meet specific salary and duties tests for executive, administrative, or professional positions.

F

FEHA (Fair Employment and Housing Act): California's comprehensive anti-discrimination law that provides broader protections than federal law and applies to employers with five or more employees.

FLSA (Fair Labor Standards Act): Federal law governing minimum wage, overtime, and child labor standards.

FMLA (Family and Medical Leave Act)
Federal law providing eligible employees with up to 12 weeks of unpaid, job-protected leave for specified family and medical reasons.

Front Pay: Monetary compensation for future lost earnings awarded when reinstatement is not feasible, calculated from the judgment date forward.

G

Good Faith and Fair Dealing: An implied covenant in employment contracts (recognized in California but not New York) that prevents employers from terminating employees in bad faith to avoid paying benefits or for other improper purposes.

H

Harassment: Unwelcome conduct based on a protected characteristic that creates a hostile work environment or involves quid pro quo demands.

Hostile Work Environment: A form of harassment where unwelcome conduct based on protected characteristics is sufficiently severe or pervasive to alter the conditions of employment and create an abusive working environment.

I

Independent Contractor: A worker who is not an employee and therefore not entitled to most employment law protections, classified based on factors including degree of control, method of payment, and nature of the work relationship.

Intentional Infliction of Emotional Distress (IIED): A tort claim requiring proof that the defendant's conduct was extreme, outrageous, intentional or reckless, and caused severe emotional distress.

Injunctive Relief: Court order requiring party to take or refrain from specific action.

Interactive Process: The required good-faith dialogue between employer and employee to identify and implement reasonable accommodations for disabilities under the ADA and state disability laws.

J

JNOV (Judgment Notwithstanding the Verdict): A post-trial motion requesting the court to overturn a jury verdict on the grounds that no reasonable jury could have reached that conclusion based on the evidence.

Jurisdiction: Court's authority to hear and decide particular type of case.

Just Cause: A standard requiring employers to have a legitimate, work-related reason for disciplinary action or termination, typically found in union contracts or employment agreements.

L

Labor Code: California statutes governing wage and hour laws, workplace safety, and employee rights.

Liquidated Damages: Pre-determined damages specified in statute or contract, such as the doubling of unpaid wages under the Fair Labor Standards Act for willful violations.

Litigation Hold: Legal obligation to preserve potentially relevant documents and evidence.

Lodestar Method: The standard approach for calculating attorney's fees by multiplying reasonable hours worked by a reasonable hourly rate, potentially adjusted by a multiplier in exceptional cases.

M

McDonnell Douglas Test: The three-step burden-shifting framework used in employment discrimination cases to analyze claims when direct evidence of discrimination is not available.

Mediation: A voluntary, confidential dispute resolution process where a neutral third party helps the parties negotiate a settlement.

Mitigation of Damages: The legal principle requiring plaintiffs to take reasonable steps to minimize their losses, such as seeking comparable employment after wrongful termination.

N

Non-Compete Agreement: A contract restricting an employee's ability to work for competitors or start competing businesses for a specified period after leaving employment (generally unenforceable in California).

Non-Disparagement Clause: A provision in settlement agreements where parties agree not to make negative statements about each other, subject to recent legislative restrictions in discrimination cases.

NYCHRL (New York City Human Rights Law): New York City's anti-discrimination ordinance, which provides broader protections and lower burdens of proof than state and federal laws.

NYHRL (New York Human Rights Law): New York State's primary anti-discrimination statute, covering employers with as few as one employee for certain claims.

NYLL (New York Labor Law): New York statutes governing wage and hour protections.

P

PAGA (Private Attorneys General Act): California law allowing employees to sue employers for Labor Code violations on behalf of the state and other employees, with penalties payable to the state and affected workers.

Pattern or Practice: Evidence of systemic discrimination affecting multiple employees, which can support class actions and result in broader remedial measures.

Pretext: Evidence showing that an employer's stated legitimate reason for an adverse employment action is false and that the real reason was discriminatory.

Prima Facie Case: The minimum evidence required to establish a claim that, if unrebutted, would be sufficient to prove the case.

Protected Activity: Actions by employees that are legally protected from retaliation, such as filing discrimination complaints, reporting violations, or participating in investigations.

Protected Class/Characteristic: Categories of individuals protected by anti-discrimination laws, including race, color, religion, sex, national origin, age, disability, and others.

Punitive Damages: Additional monetary awards designed to punish defendants for particularly egregious conduct and deter similar behavior, subject to constitutional and statutory limitations.

Q

Quid Pro Quo Harassment: Sexual harassment where submission to unwelcome sexual conduct is made a condition of employment benefits or where rejection results in adverse employment action.

Qualified Individual with a Disability: Under the ADA, a person with a disability who can perform the essential functions of a job position with or without reasonable accommodation.

R

Reasonable Accommodation: Modifications to work environments, schedules, or job duties that enable qualified individuals with disabilities to perform essential job functions without imposing undue hardship on the employer.

Reinstatement: A remedy requiring the employer to restore the employee to their former position or a substantially similar position.

Remittitur: A court's reduction of a jury's damage award when it is deemed excessive, often giving the plaintiff the choice to accept the reduced amount or undergo a new trial.

Retaliation: Adverse action taken against an employee for engaging in protected activity, such as filing complaints, reporting violations, or opposing discriminatory practices.

Right-to-Sue Letter: A document issued by the EEOC or state agency indicating that the complainant may proceed with a lawsuit in court, typically required before filing certain discrimination claims.

S

Settlement Agreement: A contract resolving employment disputes, typically involving monetary payment and release of claims, subject to various enforceability requirements.

Sexual Harassment: Unwelcome sexual advances, requests for sexual favors, and other verbal or physical conduct of a sexual nature that affects employment decisions or creates a hostile work environment.

Spoliation: Destruction or alteration of evidence, potentially resulting in court sanctions.

Statute of Limitations: The time limit within which a legal claim must be filed, varying by jurisdiction and type of claim (e.g., 180-300 days for EEOC charges, 1-4 years for court filing).

Summary Judgment: A court ruling that there are no genuine disputes of material fact and that one party is entitled to judgment as a matter of law, potentially disposing of the case without trial.

T

Title VII: The federal Civil Rights Act of 1964 prohibiting employment discrimination based on race, color, religion, sex, or national origin by employers with 15 or more employees.

Tort: Civil wrong (other than breach of contract) for which law provides remedy.

Tortious Interference: A claim that a third party intentionally and improperly interfered with existing or prospective employment relationships.

U

Undue Hardship: The defense available to employers for refusing to provide reasonable accommodations when such accommodations would impose significant difficulty or expense relative to the employer's resources.

Unlawful Termination: Also known as wrongful termination, refers to firing an employee for illegal reasons, such as discrimination, retaliation, or violation of public policy.

V

Venue: Geographic location where lawsuit should be filed and tried.

Vicarious Liability: Legal responsibility imposed on employers for the discriminatory or harassing acts of their employees, particularly supervisors, under certain circumstances.

Voir Dire: The jury selection process where potential jurors are questioned to determine their qualifications, biases, and suitability to serve on the jury.

W

Wage and Hour Laws: Federal and state statutes governing minimum wage, overtime pay, meal and rest breaks, and other compensation-related requirements.

Whistleblower: An employee who reports illegal, unethical, or unsafe practices within their organization to authorities or management, protected from retaliation by various federal and state laws.

Willful Violation: Under wage and hour laws, a violation committed with knowledge that the conduct was prohibited or with reckless disregard for the requirements, often resulting in enhanced penalties.

Workers' Compensation: A system of insurance providing medical benefits and wage replacement to employees injured in the course of employment, which may limit other legal remedies against employers.

Wrongful Termination: Termination of employment that violates federal or state anti-discrimination laws, public policy, or contractual provisions, distinguished from lawful at-will termination.

About the Author

Ngozi E. Bolin, Esq. brings over three decades of extensive litigation experience to this comprehensive guide on employment law. With a distinguished career spanning multiple jurisdictions, Ms. Bolin offers readers the benefit of her deep legal knowledge and practical courtroom wisdom in workplace disputes and employment litigation.

Educated under the British Commonwealth system and having studied at the Harvard Extension School, Ms. Bolin possesses a uniquely broad legal perspective that enriches her understanding of employment law across different legal traditions. Her international credentials began with her admission as a Barrister & Solicitor of the Supreme Court of Nigeria in 1989. She subsequently moved to the United States, gaining admission to the New York State Bar in 1991, the United States Court of Appeals for the Second Circuit, and the California State Bar in 2013.

Throughout her career as a skilled trial attorney, Ms. Bolin has dedicated herself to making legal knowledge accessible and affordable through unbundled services that help both legal practitioners and individuals understand and assert their workplace rights. Her expertise encompasses a remarkable range of employment law matters, including individual and class action discrimination cases, harassment claims, wrongful termination, wage and hour violations, retaliation cases, disability accommodation disputes, family and medical leave issues, employment contract negotiations, and workplace safety matters.

Ms. Bolin has successfully negotiated countless employment law settlements throughout her career, demonstrating her practical approach to achieving favorable outcomes for clients in workplace disputes. She brings to this book her philosophy that a strategic settlement often surpasses a lengthy court battle, offering readers honest assessments about when to fight in court and when to explore alternative solutions that better serve the client's interests.

Her legal acumen is evidenced by her work on several notable cases, including *Louis Capital Markets, LP v. Refco Group Ltd., LLC, et al.*, 9 Misc.3d 283, 801 N.Y.S.2d 490, N.Y.Co. (2005), which addressed complex issues of corporate espionage, unfair business practices, and employees' fiduciary duties; *Giordano v. Thomson, et al.*, 438 F. Supp.2d 35, E.D.N.Y. (2005); 2005 WL 4147932; 2006 WL 1882917; and *Davis v. Commercial Bank of New York*, 275 F.Supp.2d 418, S.D.N.Y. (2003), a case involving unwritten ERISA Plans and unjust enrichment.

Ms. Bolin's practice has encompassed employment matters across various industries, from financial services and healthcare to technology and manufacturing. This broad industry experience allows her to understand the unique employment law challenges faced by different sectors and to provide practical guidance that accounts for industry-specific considerations.

As an advocate for workplace justice, Ms. Bolin has represented both employees seeking to vindicate their rights and employers working to maintain compliant and fair workplaces. This dual perspective enriches her understanding of employment law strategy and enables her to provide balanced, practical guidance for navigating the complexities of workplace legal issues.

This guide represents the culmination of Ms. Bolin's extensive experience in employment law practice in both New York and California courts, offering readers an authoritative resource for navigating the complexities of workplace legal issues in these two pivotal jurisdictions. Her commitment to making employment law accessible and understandable shines through in every chapter, providing both legal practitioners and their clients with the tools needed to achieve successful outcomes in workplace disputes.

Made in United States
Orlando, FL
04 November 2026

90204505R00321